The Yahoo! Style Guide

The Yahoo! Style Guide

The Ultimate Sourcebook for Writing, Editing, and Creating Content for the Digital World

Chris Barr and the Senior Editors of Yahoo!

MACMILLAN

First published 2010 by St Martin's Press

First published in Great Britain in 2010 by Macmillan
an imprint of Pan Macmillan, a division of Macmillan Publishers
Pan Macmillan, 20 New Wharf Road, London N1 9RR
Basingstoke and Oxford
Associated companies throughout the world
www.panmacmillan.com

ISBN 978-0-230-74960-3

A CIP catalogue record for this book is available from
the British Library.

Book design by Charles Kreloff

Printed in the UK by Butler, Tanner and Dennis Ltd

Visit **www.panmacmillan.com** to read more about all our books
and to buy them. You will also find features, author interviews and
news of any author events, and you can sign up for e-newsletters
so that you're always first to hear about our new releases.

Contents

Section II: Speak to Your Entire Audience

Section III: Write UI Text, Email, and Mobile-Friendly Content

Section IV: Manage the Mechanics

Section V: Clean Up Your Copy

Section VI: Resources

Preface

Yahoo! began in 1994 as a hobby—a way for Stanford University PhD candidates Jerry Yang and David Filo to keep track of their personal interests on the Internet. The two were so excited by the power of this new medium that they wanted to help others tap into its potential, too. They continued to build their lists of favorite website links, and when those lists became long and unwieldy, they broke them into categories, then into subcategories—and the concept behind Yahoo! was born. A substantial, loyal audience grew quickly throughout the Internet community.

I joined Yahoo! in 1995, just as this hobby was becoming a company, to further Yahoo!'s goal of matching people and content. We developed a system of classification and a set of principles to describe what people would find on websites, and created categories that we hoped would be intuitively understandable to people searching for specific information. The myriad, minute choices we made in aggregating and organizing a vast array of content revealed an editorial point of view.

The mere act of aggregation is creation, and it was in building our website directory that the Yahoo! voice was born. Economy of language has been a cornerstone of the Yahoo! voice and a core tenet from our early days. Online audiences expect far more information, in much less space, in far less time, than ever before. Attention spans are short, and every pixel counts.

To inspire trust in this new medium, we began to develop editorial standards and practices, and we're happy to share with you what we've learned about writing and editing for the Web. Elevating content creation to the level of craft benefits everyone on the Web, and clear communication and high editorial standards are important no matter where or why you write.

Today Yahoo! is one of the most visited Internet destinations in the world, and our focus remains on connecting people to their passions—matching the right content to the right person at the right time. As much as ever, we are passionate about helping others realize the potential of the Web to enrich their lives and their communities.

We hope this guide helps you make the most of your online pursuits.

Srinija Srinivasan
Yahoo! Editor in Chief
Sunnyvale, California

Introduction

WWW may be an acronym for *World Wide Web,* but no one could fault you for thinking that it stands for *wild, wild West*: The Web has grown faster than rules and standards can keep pace. For writers and editors, this rapid growth has meant having to rely on style guides that were developed for print publishing, and cobbling together their own site guidelines as they went along.

That certainly was the case at Yahoo!. Yet Yahoo! has been creating content—and discovering what works best on the Web—for more than 15 years. Now we're sharing what we've learned.

The seeds of *The Yahoo! Style Guide* were planted with Yahoo!'s first style sheet, an in-house reference on how to create content for the website. We added style choices, new words, and writing tips as our network expanded and as writers, editors, marketers, programmers, and product managers raised new questions.

Today our guide is a beacon for all Yahoo! content creators, whether they are bloggers, editors, video producers, reporters, technical writers, marketing professionals, user-experience designers, or documentation specialists. This essential resource helps us get our content right. Now—polished and expanded for its public debut—it can help you, too.

But why, you may be wondering, have we chosen to put all this information about writing for the Web into a book? We've done it because people still like to get their information in a variety of ways, including print—even though digital media has become central to the way the world communicates. Naturally, this book has a companion website with resources, updates, and even more information.

The challenges of communicating online

Communicating clearly and concisely is a challenge even for seasoned writers and editors. The English language boasts a rich vocabulary and often-confusing rules that sometimes trip us up rather than help us refine and clarify our thoughts. On the page or on the screen, we can't use vocal tones or facial expressions to give clues about meaning. Except for the occasional smiley face ☺, we rely mainly on text.

Of course, Web publishing integrates text, audio, video, and images—in one medium. People can blog, tweet, converse, email, play games, write comments, join groups, buy and sell, and even edit each other's contributions. The Web offers a wealth of communication possibilities, but those possibilities also mean more challenges for editors, who must navigate HTML, publishing tools, and myriad page elements beyond basic copy.

So how can you determine the best way to deliver your message on the Web? How can you learn to write for websites and email with clarity and precision, and in a way that engages and holds people's interest? The answers are in this guide.

In this book, you'll discover the essentials of online writing and editing, including:

- **How to write clear, concise text.** Write headlines, navigation text, and paragraphs that engage the reader.
- **How to develop a distinctive voice.** Discover the unique personality that will set your site apart, and write copy that expresses it.
- **How to ensure readability.** Write for every reader, whether your words appear on a computer monitor or a mobile device or a laptop half a world away.
- **How to gauge and ensure accessibility.** Understand the guidelines for making your site and its content more usable for the millions of Web users with disabilities.
- **How to write for global comprehension.** Write and edit English for an international audience, and you'll make your site more comprehensible for all readers.
- **How to handle basic coding.** Explore what's behind a webpage and get comfortable editing copy that's marked up with HTML.
- **How to support search engine optimization through writing.** Choose the right words and use them strategically to raise your page ranking with search engines and to bring more people to your site.
- **What to watch out for to minimize legal risks.** Learn the basics of U.S. Internet law, including copyright and trademarks.

Your go-to guide for writing effective Internet content

Whether people access the Internet through desktops, laptops, or mobile devices, through RSS readers or email, they consume Web content at a different pace and for different reasons than they do books, magazines, or newspapers. People want their online information quickly, and they don't want to jump hurdles to find it.

They also want to be able to trust that information. The Web may lend itself to informality and individuality, but factual errors, grammatical errors, misspellings, and other mistakes detract from the credibility of websites and, ultimately, brands. You can avoid these pitfalls by consistently applying the best practices of Web writing and editing.

In *The Yahoo! Style Guide,* you'll learn both the broad principles of addressing an online audience and the specifics of effective writing and editing for the Web.

A look at what's inside

We've arranged the chapters of *The Yahoo! Style Guide* to take you from the most basic Web issues to more technical concerns, but the order you read them in is up to you. The guide includes some chapters that you'll want to read from start to finish, and others that you'll leaf through as a reference.

The book is divided into six sections:

1. How to write and edit for an online audience
2. How to develop content that speaks to all the visitors to your site in an accessible and comprehensible way
3. How to create text for a particular medium, be it website, email, or mobile device
4. How to get the mechanics right: punctuation, capitalization, numbers, and more
5. How to streamline and clean up your copy
6. Resources: a word list as well as primers on basic webpage coding, search engine optimization, and U.S. Internet law

Most chapters also include:

- "Before" and "after" examples that show how to fix problem copy
- Explanations that demystify confusing terms and concepts (look for this graphic:)
- Sidebars that deepen your understanding of elements of Web style
- Tips that include shortcuts and professional secrets
- Exercises or extended examples that give you a chance to see a chapter's ideas in practice

On the book's companion website at http://styleguide.yahoo.com, you'll find:

- Helpful resources
- Updates and other information from Yahoo! editors

The Yahoo! Style Guide distills Yahoo!'s 15-plus years of Internet editorial expertise. Just as it has helped us, so it can help you create world-class Web content that brings people to your site and keeps them reading.

Tell us what you think. Contact us at Ask_Edit@yahoo.com.

Chris Barr
Yahoo! Senior Editorial Director
Sunnyvale, California

Write for an Online Audience

Chapter 1
Write for the Web

In this chapter

- **Shape your text for online reading.** People read computer screens differently than they do printed materials.
- **Get to the point.** Put the most important information up-front, where readers can find it fast.
- **Make text easy to scan.** Organize your content to help people scan for key words and phrases.
- **Write for the world.** The Web is available around the globe. Will your text be understood in Hong Kong? New Delhi? Rome?
- **Help people navigate.** It's the designer's job to create a website that's easy to use—and it's the writer's job to make sure that the words support that goal.

Anyone can publish on the Web, but not everyone is publishing material that's ideal for online reading. Enter *The Yahoo! Style Guide,* your guide to writing and editing for the Web.

People have different expectations when they read online text—most notably, they expect instant gratification, the ability to find what they want on a webpage fast. So as a content creator, you must consider your online readers: how much text they can digest, how they scan the screen, how easily they can find and navigate your site, whether they're viewing your content on a large monitor or a tiny phone screen. You can meet their needs and expectations—and secure an audience for your site—by providing clear, organized, easy-to-understand content that works well on a variety of devices, not to mention on the Web itself.

This chapter provides an overview of the basic principles of successful Web writing; the chapters that follow will cover these principles in more depth.

Shape your text for online reading

Text that works best on the Web is text that gets to the point fast and that makes it easy for readers to pick out key information. Here's why.

Online reading is an experience that's different from reading text in print. A big part of that difference is physical: For most people, online reading takes longer—or feels as though it does.

Eye-tracking: Where do readers look first?

To catch a site visitor's eye, it helps to know where that eye is likely to look. Eye-tracking studies give us the most likely locations.

Eye-tracking technology unobtrusively follows a reader's eye movements as the person views a page. The equipment records on a "gaze map" where the person's eyes roam and where they stop to read. Several gaze maps are then plotted on a "heat map" that highlights the areas where readers looked the most.

Yahoo! eye-tracking studies reveal **a general pattern to the way people browse webpages**:

- People scan the main sections of a page to determine what it's about and whether they want to stay longer.

- They make decisions about the page in as little as three seconds.

- If they decide to stay, they pay the most attention to the content in the top part of the screen.

When people do decide to read a page, their eyes sweep horizontally from left to right, often focusing on a roughly **triangular area in the upper-left corner** of a webpage, or the upper-left corner of the webpage's main block of content. But this pattern varies depending on a page's layout and purpose. For example, a person's eyes will move differently over a photo-heavy slideshow, a text-heavy blog, or a page with a two- or three-column layout.

This black-and-white rendering of a heat map indicates where visitors' eyes traveled on a webpage. Here, white space and lighter areas indicate the areas that visitors' eyes spent the most time on. The X's indicate mouse clicks. (Map generated by Eyetools software; original map generated in full color)

This Yahoo! Finance guide loads important words like "savings" and "budget" in the upper-left corner of the content area. It also includes a numbered list of topics above the fold (that is, in the top part of the screen that the site visitor sees before scrolling down) so that people can see right away what the guide covers.

A computer screen displays text at a lower resolution, with less detail and sharpness than a printed page, so letters are fuzzier. And many people feel that their eyes tire faster reading text on a screen (especially a smaller screen) than reading type on paper.

Most online readers scan first. According to computer usability expert Jakob Nielsen, "People rarely read Web pages word by word; instead, they scan the page, picking out individual words and sentences."[1] Eye-tracking studies, which examine where people's eyes roam on a webpage, reveal these basic truths about site visitors:

- They scan to see whether the content is relevant.
- They are more likely to scan the top of the page than the bottom.
- They look at headings, boldfaced terms, and images.

Scanning requires less brainpower than reading. **Concise sentences that convey their point quickly are more likely to grab visitors** than long, complex sentences and are more likely to entice people to explore further.

TIP Look at your page as if you're visiting it for the first time, or enlist a friend who's never seen it before. Where does your eye go first as you try to determine the gist of the page? This is the area that should contain the most important words, headlines, links, and other content. Loading relevant words and images in that area helps people quickly determine whether your page has the information they need. Often this part of the page is the triangular area in the upper-left corner. See "Eye-tracking: Where do readers look first?" on page 4.

Get to the point

Readers assess webpages in an instant. **Your content has a few seconds—three or less!—to encourage people to read more**, to take action, or to navigate to another of your pages. Impatient readers will click the **Back** button in a hurry or will stop skimming and go to a search box.

To get to the point fast and keep people on your site, follow these **three guidelines for effective online writing**:

1. Keep it short.

- Use short words, short sentences, short paragraphs, bulleted lists, and short pages.
- Slim down copy from print sources (a company brochure, for example) to suit the online format.

Example

Before

Architronixx, founded by an architect, Jay Pogue, an engineer, Barry Beasley, and a sound engineer, Mari DeHart, was a totally new concept in 1981, when it was founded. The idea—a firm that merged architecture, structural engineering, and acoustics—was brand-new. Today, Architronixx is still the leader in the field it pioneered almost three decades ago, and our buildings have garnered praise from national and international authorities...

After

In 1981, Architronixx invented a new concept: buildings that combine innovative architecture, intelligent engineering, and acoustic design. Today, Architronixx is still the leader in the field it pioneered almost three decades ago.

Learn more about how our designs work.

Walk through our award-winning buildings.

Read about our founders.

---

2. Front-load your content.

- In general, put the most important content in the upper-left area of the screen. Put other important pieces of information at the top of the page.
- Decide what's most important to communicate, and emphasize it with prominent headings, boldface type, and other visual cues.
- Put the most important information at the beginning of headlines, paragraphs, and sentences. Don't spend time leading up to your point.
- Place the most important words at the beginning of page titles, headlines, subheadings, and links. The most important words are typically your *keywords,* which are the words and phrases people may use in search engines when trying to locate your type of content. For information on keyword selection and placement, see Chapter 17, "Optimize Your Site for Search Engines."
- Place important but supplemental or tangential material in a secondary position on the page.

TIP   If your content is unavoidably lengthy or complex, consider putting a summary or a bulleted list of topics that the page covers at the top of the page.

3. Keep it simple.

- Include only one or two ideas per short paragraph.
- Choose common words over more difficult ones. Even if more technical or sophisticated language is appropriate for your site, your readers will appreciate simpler language in the areas where their eyes are scanning to determine what a page is about.

T I P Write for a lower reading-comprehension level than you expect many of your readers to have, and you'll make all your readers happy. To learn how to assess readability, see "Test your copy's readability" on page 10.

- Delete fluff. Direct, objective text—not promotional copy—is more helpful to the site visitor, and readers perceive it as more trustworthy. For more about this topic, see "Get to the good stuff" on page 293.

Example

Before

Not only can you indulge in relaxing spa treatments at this newly renovated hotel, but so can your dog. The Paws-and-Relax Resort offers complete individual and customized service for people and their canine companions, focusing on deep-tissue massage and acupuncture. No other spa packages in the city offer this decadent, pet-friendly deal.

After

The newly renovated Paws-and-Relax Resort offers relaxing customized spa treatments for you and your dog.

Pamper yourself and your pet with deep-tissue massage and acupuncture.

No other spa package in the city offers this decadent, pet-friendly deal.

Short, simple, and front-loaded: These qualities are Web-writing essentials, whether you're crafting text for an email or a webpage, whether readers are viewing your copy on a mobile device or a desktop computer. As we delve into different types of content, we'll mention these principles again and again.

Make text easy to scan

Help people scan for important information by breaking up text into digestible, interesting chunks.

- **Meaningful headlines and subheadings** break up a page of text by visually grouping related chunks of information. Avoid overly cute or clever headlines that may confuse or alienate visitors. Just say what the section is about. For help with writing compelling headings for the Web, see Chapter 4, "Construct Clear, Compelling Copy." Well-written headings also help search engine optimization (SEO). For details, see Chapter 17.
- **Bulleted lists** (like this one) help readers spot important points. "Lists" on page 65 gives guidelines for creating effective, well-formed lists.

Example

Before

Everyone loves a picnic, which makes this deluxe picnic basket set the perfect gift. You'll find it's fully loaded with plates, glasses, flatware, and napkins for four, plus a bread knife, a cutting board, salt and pepper shakers, and a corkscrew. It even comes with a fleece blanket for the family to sit on. Buy it now for only $49.99.

After

This deluxe picnic basket set makes the perfect gift. It's fully loaded with:

- Plates, glasses, flatware, and napkins for four
- Bread knife and cutting board
- Salt and pepper shakers
- Corkscrew
- Fleece blanket

Buy it now — $49.99

- **Tables** organize and make sense of information and add a graphic element to a page.
- **Short paragraphs**, with one or just a few related sentences, leave white space on a page and draw attention to key ideas. See "Paragraphs" on page 64.
- **Bold text** catches the reader's attention. But be careful not to overuse this effect: Too much bold text is hard to read and obscures the essential information.
- **Pull quotes**—particularly important or engaging snippets of your text set off in an eye-catching way—can be used as graphic elements that also underscore key points. But beware of fancy for-

matting: In one study by Nielsen Norman Group, people ignored a key area of a website because the words were in large red text and resembled promotional copy.[2]

TIP These principles also apply to publishing online versions of printed documents such as brochures, press releases, newsletters, and manuals. Cut, restructure, and rewrite the content as necessary so that people can grasp the core message quickly and easily.

For more detailed information on writing headings, sentences, and paragraphs that work well on the Web, see Chapter 4.

Write for the world

Even though you are writing for a specific audience (see Chapter 2, "Identify Your Audience," and Chapter 3, "Define Your Voice"), your actual audience may have a variety of characteristics you haven't considered. For example, they may have disabilities that affect how they access and navigate your site; they may also be older or younger than you realize, more or less proficient in reading comprehension, and more or less knowledgeable in the subject matter of your site.

Keep in mind, too, that your site may be viewed in Antarctica or Zambia—virtually anywhere in the world. Your readers may not speak English as their first language. Even native English speakers may be American, Australian, British, Canadian, or another nationality.

The Web is a global, multicultural environment, so **write to appeal to the widest possible audience**:

- **Keep words and sentences short and simple** unless your site specifically targets a sophisticated audience that expects complexity.
- **Use gender-neutral terms whenever possible** (for example, *firefighter* instead of *fireman* or *humankind* instead of *mankind*).
- **Avoid location-specific references.** Writing *our country* and *foreign country* and sometimes even *us* and *we* automatically alienates readers who are not in the same country or interest community as you.
- **Avoid culture-specific slang or puns.** For example, baseball metaphors may not be understood outside the United States.

Example

Before

The swimwear will be promoted in May by our country's best-known swimmer. The style has already gained popularity in a number of foreign markets.

After

The swimwear will be promoted in May by Australia's best-known swimmer. The style has already gained popularity in many countries.

For more instruction on how to make your language accessible and inclusive, see Chapter 5, "Be Inclusive, Write for the World."

Test your copy's readability

Your readers may include kids, people who don't speak English as their first language, and busy people who need to decide quickly whether a site is relevant. All of them appreciate a clear, straightforward voice based on simple words and sentence structures. That doesn't mean you need to talk down to your audience; on the contrary, you're respecting your readers by not wasting their time.

Readability statistics count characters, words, sentences, and paragraphs and tell you the reading level of your writing. Testing readability is easy. Microsoft Word, for example, can show you how your copy scores on the Flesch Reading Ease test and the Flesch-Kincaid Grade Level test.

The **Flesch Reading Ease test** checks syllables per word and words per sentence. The test rates text on a 100-point scale: The higher the score, the more understandable the copy. Aim for a score of 60 or higher.

The **Flesch-Kincaid Grade Level test** scores text according to U.S. grade-school levels. For most websites, a sixth- to eighth-grade reading level is appropriate for readers who scan. If your audience is younger or less proficient in English, you may want to target a sixth-grade level or lower.

To test your copy in Microsoft Office Word 2007 for Windows:

1. Make sure that your copy of the software is set up to show readability statistics:

   - Click the **Microsoft Office** button, then **Word Options**.
   - Click **Proofing**.
   - Under **When correcting spelling and grammar in Word**, check the **Check grammar with spelling** and **Show readability statistics** checkboxes.

2. Check the Flesch Reading Ease score and the Flesch-Kincaid Grade Level score:

    ■   Highlight your copy. (If you are checking an entire document, you do not need to highlight the text.)
    ■   Click the **Review** tab. In the **Proofing** menu, click **Spelling and Grammar**.
    ■   Click **No** (you do not need to check the rest of the document).
    ■   In the pop-up **Readability Statistics** window, note the scores under **Readability**.

Readability Statistics	
Counts	
Words	1099
Characters	5006
Paragraphs	30
Sentences	61
Averages	
Sentences per Paragraph	0.0
Words per Sentence	11.4
Characters per Word	4.1
Readability	
Passive Sentences	4%
Flesch Reading Ease	77.8
Flesch-Kincaid Grade Level	4.9

OK

Readability statistics displayed in Microsoft Word

To test your document in Microsoft Office Word 2008 for the Mac:

1. Set up your software to show readability statistics:

    ■   From the **Word** menu in the menu bar, choose **Preferences**.
    ■   Under **Authoring and Proofing Tools**, click **Spelling and Grammar**.
    ■   Check the **Check grammar with spelling** and **Show readability statistics** checkboxes.

2. Check the Flesch Reading Ease score and the Flesch-Kincaid Grade Level score:

    ■   Highlight your copy. (If you are checking an entire document, you do not need to highlight the text.)
    ■   From the **Tools** menu, choose **Spelling and Grammar**.
    ■   After the spelling and grammar check, click **No** (you do not need to check the rest of the document).
    ■   In the pop-up **Readability Statistics** window, note the scores under **Readability**.

If you are using another version of Microsoft Word, your menu choices may be different.

Alternatively, you can check the grade level of your text according to the **Fry Readability Formula**:

1. Choose a 100-word sample of text (you may want to try three different samples to get an average).
2. Count the number of syllables in the 100 words.
3. Count the number of sentences.
4. Look at a Fry Readability graph (widely available on the Web). Find the number of syllables in your sample along the horizontal line (*x*-axis) and the number of sentences along the vertical line (*y*-axis). Where those lines intersect, you'll see a grade level on the graph.

Help people navigate

Your site's content includes more than articles and marketing copy: Links, menus, and other site elements are part of the content mix, too. The clearer and more consistent the writing, the easier the site will be to use—and usability is key to keeping people on your site.

Usability refers to how easily site visitors can interact with a site and use it to achieve their goals. **A site is more usable when it is easy to navigate, meets visitors' needs and expectations, and provides a satisfying experience.**

Usability depends a lot on a site's design and underlying technology, but writers and editors can contribute to (or, if they're not careful, diminish) a site's usability.

The following guidelines represent some **usability best practices** and a few tips for implementing them:

Make sure that every page orients people to your site and has its own clear navigation. Not every visitor will start on your homepage.

- Provide direction. On every page, make it clear where people are on your site and what they can do next.
- Keep visitors engaged. Give them a "call to action": something to do or somewhere to go next on your site. Number pages that appear in a sequence (a multipage article, for instance) to indicate where in the sequence a person has landed (for example, page 3 of 12).

Write clear links.

- Label links and buttons so that people know how to print, email, rate a story, comment, and so on.
- Use descriptive language in *link text* (text that appears underlined or colored to show that it's clickable) to communicate what will happen when people click it.

Example

Before
Enter the contest for a chance to win! *(The link goes to a page with information about the grand prize, not to a contest entry page. This will frustrate readers who expect to enter right away.)*

After
You could win your dream home. *(The link goes to a page with information about the grand prize, as readers will expect.)*
or

<u>Enter the contest</u> for a chance to win! *(The link goes to a contest entry page, just as it suggests.)*

T I P   The instruction "Click here to . . ." is wordy and sounds dated. Action steps—like "Learn more" or "Buy now"—are a better choice.

- When appropriate, confirm people's actions with messages like "Your bid has been submitted" or "Thank you for your payment."

Label everything.

- Add captions to images, and label the images with alternative text. Alternative text, or *alt text,* is inserted into the HTML code. Over a slow connection, this text will appear in the image's space before the image loads; it will also enable vision-impaired people using screen readers to hear a description of the image. For best practices regarding alt text, see "Alt text and image captions" on page 132.
- Use keyword-rich phrases in titles and captions for videos. The captions enable deaf users to understand the audio portion of your video; the keywords help search engines find it. For more on optimizing video for online searches, see "Images and video" on page 412.
- Label advertisements and advertorials as such so that you don't mislead readers.
- Identify any content provided by site users (for example, message board posts, user reviews, or comments following a story).
- Give proper attribution to content provided by third parties.

For specific guidelines on writing user-interface text and other copy that orients people on your site, see Chapter 7, "Write Clear User-Interface Text."

Ideas in Practice

Example: Rewrite for Web readers

The passage below for the homepage of a fictional business, The-Blog-Hog, is full of fluff. Read our solution following it to see how we would make this content work for the Web.

Before

Welcome to The-Blog-Hog.com. Why do we call ourselves that? Because we help you root out problems with your content and start hogging site traffic. Are you too busy to publish as often as you should? Are you losing your users because you can't be bothered responding to comments? Are your posts so boring that you couldn't get readers to swallow them if you wrapped those stories in bacon? Well, we'll help you put some lipstick on that pig, take it to market, make your users squeal like it's Christmas morning, and turn your meek little piglet of a blog into a rip-roaring razorback.

The-Blog-Hog offers professional ghostwriting and coaching services to bloggers. Every blogger needs help with his site sometimes. We've helped large corporate sites like Smoot-Hawley World Imports, medium-sized blogs like fashionista review Belle in a Handbasket, and even one-person advice blogs. And we can help you, no matter whether your blog is personal or professional, big or small, and whatever the subject. We can help you grow your audience, improve your site's content, and track metrics for the site's performance, including unique users, geotargeting, session duration, and pathway analysis.

We can coach you in powering up your prose—or we can just write the blogs for you. We can help you set a writing strategy and then execute it, including figuring out the right voice for your audience, the optimal frequency and length of posts, subjects that will engage your readers, and angles on those topics that will make readers want to return again and again.

We can also help you improve the features and functionality of your blog to make it more usable. For example: adding photos and videos, links, tags, a blogroll, TrackBack links, an archive, feeds, and much, much more.

Of course, your blog is nothing without an audience; you need to build your community and converse with it. Don't resort to playing sock puppet and commenting on your own posts! We'll teach you how to get readers to go hog-wild posting comments, how to filter and moderate comments, how to respond, and more. We can also help you get the word out and promote your blog.

Finally, we can help you measure your blog's performance so you know whether you're knocking it out of the park. Either we can create customized reports for you, or we can show you how to use tools to get the metrics that matter to you.

After

What is The-Blog-Hog?

The-Blog-Hog offers professional ghostwriting and coaching services to bloggers. Whatever the size and subject of your site, we can help you **write better blogs**, **build your community**, and **measure your blog's performance**.

How The-Blog-Hog can improve your blog

The-Blog-Hog can train you to be a better blogger, or we can root out problems with your content and do the work for you. Our services include help for:

Blog writing. Establish a voice that will engage your readers.

Functionality. Improve your blog's features and usability.

Community. Learn how to converse with your community and increase your audience.

Measuring performance. Track your site's performance with tools or our customized reports.

Find out more **about us**.

Read about our clients and their **success stories**.

Solution notes

Our sample copy's central problems were length, redundancy, and a failure to get to the point immediately. It's supposed to be text for a homepage, so a visitor would probably want to know: What does The-Blog-Hog do? Are its services right for me? These two questions should be addressed prominently at the top of the page.

Instead of calling out The-Blog-Hog's benefits, the first two paragraphs wasted space on puns, an explanation of the company's name, a description of clients, and jargon about measuring performance that may be esoteric for some readers. Most of that text could be relegated to secondary pages with titles like "About Us" and "Success Stories." Similarly, the last four paragraphs listed many examples that could be moved to subpages about each service.

Our edit chops down the copy to homepage essentials: a brief introduction to the company's services, with links to more information. We put the most important information up-front; called out the company name and other keywords in headings and links; and stripped self-serving copy, unnecessary words, and culture- and gender-specific phrases. The original copy was 407 words; our edited copy is 124 words.

Chapter 2
Identify Your Audience

In this chapter

- **Do your research.** Find out who your site visitors are and what they need.
- **Create an audience profile.** Use your research data to develop a well-defined model user to represent your target audience.
- **Check out the competition.** Analyze how similar websites are serving their audiences and figure out how you can make your site stand out.

Using the right voice to speak to your audience is crucial. First, however, you must be able to answer this question: **Who *is* the audience for your website?** (Hint: "Everyone" is not the correct answer.)

People visit websites to find specific information or to perform a task as quickly as possible. If a site doesn't deliver what they want, the way they want it, they'll leave faster than you can say "gone." That's why it's critical to **understand the people who are visiting your site, what they want, what they need, and how they pursue their goals online**.

If you ask these questions *before* you launch, you and your team can shape your site and its content to accommodate your potential audience's point of view. If your site is already online, you may think that you know your audience well, but remember that the Web changes fast. Take time periodically to make sure that you are still addressing your audience's ever-evolving needs.

T I P If your audience, like Yahoo!'s, includes a broad spectrum of people, **target the core audience you can serve best**.

Do your research

Identifying an audience is like making a sketch of someone. You add eye color, nose shape, hairstyle . . . and eventually the face appears.

Don't worry about getting the full picture all at once. Start with the questions you can answer definitively, then do your homework to fill in the most important missing information. You'll be surprised at how soon you have drawn a real person: **a profile of your target user**.

To get the most complete picture, **seek both quantitative and qualitative information**.

- Quantitative data—such as visitor demographics and the average amount of time a visitor spends on a page—tells you who your users are and what tasks they're performing on your site.

- Qualitative information—such as reader comments or answers from surveys and focus groups—tells you why people visit and what they want, need, and expect. Qualitative research is especially useful when you don't have an existing website and want to define your potential audience.

T I P   Sources for these types of data can include server logs, tools that measure webpage traffic, customer-service feedback, and information from your organization's marketing department. Methods for collecting additional data include onsite polls, user surveys, focus groups, interviews, and eye-tracking studies. See our online Resources page at http://styleguide.yahoo.com for tools and services.

Ask quantitative questions

Measurable data will give you a solid foundation for understanding your audience. If your site has a marketing department, those colleagues may be able to furnish you with their audience research, which will help you refine your own list of questions. Demographics and site traffic are often fruitful areas of inquiry, but investigate any audience information that seems relevant.

Demographic information—age, gender, profession, and so forth—can help you visualize your audience. It may even reveal that your core audience isn't who you thought it was. For instance, you might adjust your content if you discover that your visitors are younger than you expected, that a third of them speak Spanish, or that many are self-employed.

Questions about demographics might include:

- What are your visitors' ages?
- Are they students, retirees, business owners, or part- or full-time employees? If they are employed, what are their jobs, and are those jobs related to your site's subject?
- How many of your visitors are female? How many are male?
- How much money do they make? What do they spend their discretionary income on?
- How much do they spend annually online?
- Where do your visitors live? What are their ZIP or postal codes? What percentages are in the same city as you? The same region? The same country?

- What is their first language? Which languages do they speak and in what percentages?
- What are their education levels?
- What are their races and ethnicities?
- Do members of your audience have disabilities that affect how they access your site? (See Chapter 6, "Make Your Site Accessible to Everyone.")
- Do they have political or religious views that may influence how they perceive your site?
- Are there any other cultural factors that might affect how they perceive and use your site?

T I P A survey is an efficient way to gather demographic data. You can also get such data from Yahoo! Web Analytics (http://web.analytics.yahoo.com) or a for-pay audience measurement service—or, if your site requires registration, from registration data. See our online Resources page at http://styleguide.yahoo.com for audience measurement tools.

Traffic patterns and other sources of quantitative data are also useful. You might want to find answers to questions like these:

- How much time do people spend on your site? Do they get in and out as quickly as possible, or do they linger and interact?
- Which pages get the most traffic?
- Which links are clicked the most?

T I P Tools such as Yahoo! Web Analytics and Google Analytics provide quantitative data about your site's users, what paths they took through your pages, how long they spent on the site, what words they searched on, and so forth.

Ask qualitative questions

Why do people visit your site, and are they satisfied with their experience?

You can deduce some of your visitors' objectives by using audience measurement tools and by reading comments and customer feedback. For more complete information, you can conduct interviews, surveys, or user testing.

Questions like the following will help guide an investigation of qualitative information.

- What is your audience's main reason for visiting your site? Possible answers may include:

to read	to look for a job
to buy products	to learn something
to search	to download or upload files
to be entertained	to read stories
to play games	to watch videos or view photos
to do research	to post an advertisement
to blog	to give feedback
to communicate with others	to see what's new or upcoming
to network (for example, to meet new people, to get a date)	to share content such as photos, videos, or documents
to complete a task (for instance, to back up a hard disk)	to find information about you or your company
to get service or support	to ask for advice

- How well does the site answer your audience's content needs?
- What do your visitors find most valuable? Least valuable?
- Can people easily find what they want? If not, why not?
- What would people add to make the experience better?
- Why did people choose this site? How does it benefit them?
- Would visitors recommend this site to a friend? Why or why not?

Create an audience profile

When you've collected as much visitor information as you can, write an audience profile. Start by summarizing the strongest responses you've collected: questions that had a clear majority result (for example, perhaps 90 percent of your audience indicated that Web-based email was their top online activity).

Examples

Average age range: 35–45

60 percent of users are female

72 percent are employed part- or full-time

53 percent use the Internet primarily at work
Top Internet uses: Web-based email, photo sharing, online shopping

Develop a model user

Marketers, website designers, and writers sometimes create a character to illustrate who their core audience is. This model user is based on real data and represents the majority (or a significant portion) of the audience. Some people even add a photo or an illustration to help them visualize their model user.

A model user helps you focus. When you're writing an article, designing a site, or creating a marketing campaign, it's simpler to concentrate on what will please one person than it is to try to account for everyone's preferences.

The character sketch of your model user can include whatever information you judge most important. For example:

- Name (Make one up that suits what you know about the character's attributes. This is the only element that should be invented; everything else should be based on data.)
- Age
- Gender
- Education level
- Family information
- Personal information (What are the user's hobbies and interests?)
- Work information
- Technology (How is the user accessing the Web?)
- Requirements for assistive technologies, such as screen-reading software for vision-impaired users
- Web savvy
- Expectations of your site (What does the user want to do? Why did the user choose your site?)
- Business or personal goals
- Quotes collected from sources like open-answer survey questions, customer-service feedback, or interviews—particularly quotes that add personality to the profile

Once you have determined the characteristics, **write a profile of your model user**.

Example

Name: Jane

Age: 42

Gender: Female

Education: College graduate

Family information: One child; parents live far away

Work information: City government administrator

Technology/Web savvy: Jane accesses the Web on an iMac through a wireless DSL connection. "I use the Web a fair amount, but I'm not a technical person, and I don't quite understand all that I'm doing."

Goals/Web uses: Jane first got online to chat. Now she spends time emailing, searching, and checking personal finances. She searches for entertainment like movies, music, and travel. She also likes to check the news several times a day, whenever she can: "Since 9/11, I'm a news junkie."

Jane passes information to her family and friends about safety issues, such as the latest information about earthquake preparedness or car-theft scams. She does most of her communication online by email.

Jane also spends time sharing photos: She recently uploaded pictures of her son's soccer game and told her parents, who live thousands of miles away, that the photos were available online.

Jane likes to do research before going on vacation so that she can plan the best trip and get good deals. For her family reunion, she sent emails to family members to coordinate their travel plans, including the URLs of some sites plus brief site descriptions.

Your write-up can be a concise list of characteristics or a fuller narrative, whichever level of detail will serve your purpose of writing effectively for your visitors. **Use the profile as a benchmark when you craft content** (see Chapter 3, "Define Your Voice"). Ask yourself: How can I best write my message for "Jane" (or "Miguel," or "Wanda")? Be sure to share the profile with others who write for the site.

T I P   A single model user is ideal for keeping your message focused, but some sites—particularly larger ones with a broad, varied audience—can benefit from two or three model users.

Check out the competition

The best resource for understanding your audience is the audience itself. But it doesn't hurt to look at how your peers or competitors are catering to their audiences. Analyzing the competition's approach is **particularly useful if you're launching a new site and don't have an audience to evaluate yet**.

Decide how intensively you want to research the competition. You can simply click through the sites and take notes about what you think works and what doesn't, or you can conduct user testing with people who use your site or the competition's.

Use this information to **think about how your site can distinguish itself**. Are your competitors pursuing the same target audience, or different segments? (What might your competitors' model users look like?) What will make your site stand out to visitors and make them want to return? Can you offer something no other site does? Determine what your competitive advantages are, or could be, and play up those benefits when planning your content.

Researching your competition should be for discovery and comparison only. The decisions you make for your site cannot be based solely or even primarily on what a competitor does. After all, you don't know how your competitor made its choices or whether those choices have been successful. **Base your decisions on data that indicates what is right for your site.**

Another way to view your audience: Advertiser metrics

Understanding your site's current and potential advertisers and their interests may help you as you develop a picture of your audience. For instance, a large advertiser of men's sporting goods may target active men between the ages of 17 and 34. You may find it useful to segment your audience according to the metrics used by this advertiser, such as age group, gender, and participation in sports activities, in addition to income level, marital status, and so on.

Ideas in Practice

Exercise: Analyze an audience

Determining your website's target audience, developing a model user, and creating a site that meets your audience's needs can take some practice. One way to practice is by doing audience analysis in reverse: Start with a site that's already developed and see if you can figure out who its audience is.

In this exercise, study a familiar site to determine its audience and to evaluate how (and how well) that site is addressing its visitors. Then apply what you learn to filling out the portrait of your own target audience.

Follow these steps to identify an audience:

1. **Pick a favorite site and look for clues about its target audience.** Examine a site you're familiar with—either one that you use on a regular basis or a competitor's site. Be sure to check the site's About Us or company information page and any FAQs. The "Audience indicators" column in the following chart will give you ideas about what kind of information to look for, and we've filled in some sample results in the middle column to show what you might find. (For more examples of audience characteristics, see the lists of questions under "Ask quantitative questions" on page 18 and "Ask qualitative questions" on page 19.)

2. **Use this sample chart (or one like it) to record your findings**, but don't expect that you'll uncover information for every indicator. For instance, you may not be able to tell whether the site is directed toward men or women, or how comfortable the target audience is with technology. Add rows to the bottom of the chart for any other audience indicators.

Name and/or URL of the site you're studying: _____

Audience indicators	Examples	Answers for the site you're studying
Site type	News, sports, shopping, social, dating, travel, blog, photo sharing, entertainment.	
Types of content on the site	FAQS, blogs, articles, audio, video, photos, user-contributed, interactive.	

Audience indicators	Examples	Answers for the site you're studying
Age groups and other cohorts the site appeals to	Children, teens, students, adults 18–29, adults 30–39, adults 40–49, adults 50–59, adults 60–69, adults 70 and older, parents with young children.	
Gender the site appeals to	Male, female, both.	
Marital status the site is directed toward	Single, in a relationship, separated or divorced, married, any.	
Education level the site is directed toward	Grade school, high school, some college, college, graduate school.	
Audience's comfort level with technology and the Web	New to computers, moderately comfortable, very comfortable, tech savvy.	
Interests the site speaks to	Games, sports, politics, entertainment, movies, religion, music, fashion, careers, hobbies, health, travel, cars, pets.	
Tasks the site helps people complete	Read, research, socialize, upload, download, comment, blog, share, view, play games, search, rate, learn, pay bills, email, chat, shop.	
User comments, quotes, forums, and feedback that indicate audience characteristics and preferences	(Input from site users can also give you clues about education level, comfort with technology, etc.)	

3. **Create a model-user profile.** Using the characteristics you've listed, develop a model user for the site you chose for this exercise. You can use the elements under "Develop a model user" on page 21. Add as much detail as you feel is necessary, including examples and quotes where appropriate. This sample chart includes a few characteristics to focus on.

Model-User Profile

Model-user name:	
Age:	
Gender:	
Education level:	
Marital status:	
Occupation:	
Interests:	
Business or personal goals:	1. _____
	2. _____
	3. _____

4. **Ask yourself:** Is the site you've just reviewed serving this model user as well as possible? How could it do a better job?

Chapter 3
Define Your Voice

In this chapter

- **Give your site a personality.** A strong, unique voice distinguishes your site from others.
- **Consider the context.** Draw on brand identity, your site's purpose, and audience expectations to shape your voice.
- **Develop your site's unique voice.** Create a voice chart that will keep your content consistent no matter who creates it.
- **Translate voice into words.** Use vocabulary, grammar, and even the organization of your paragraphs to express your voice.

Your *voice*—whether you are a writer or an artist—expresses your unique style: in words, on the screen, in a video, in a song, or in a photo. On the Web, voice is the way your site expresses its distinctive personality and point of view.

This chapter will guide you in **developing a voice for your site that works for Web readers generally and your readers specifically**.

Give your site a personality

A website's voice should be apparent in all its elements. This includes graphics, images, layout, typefaces, colors—and, of course, words, whether those words make up FAQs, marketing messages, articles, or the site name itself.

Example

The Yahoo! name is a good example of how voice is expressed through words and design. One of the meanings of *Yahoo!* is the acronym's spelled-out phrase: "Yet Another Hierarchical Officious Oracle," which suggests that the company founders had a sense of humor about their work. But you don't have to know the acronym's meaning or even the site to get an impression of the company. The name alone—*Yahoo!,* with that essential exclamation point—sounds friendly and approachable, both qualities of the brand.

YAHOO!®

The logo's playful, unaligned typeface and purple color reinforce the energy and whimsy of the voice graphically and convey another Yahoo! core value: fun. You can practically hear *Yahoo!* being shouted.

Finding the right voice is essential to connecting with your audience. Voice contributes to a good user experience by giving your pages a consistent "sound," which enhances readability. An effective voice makes people feel at home on your site through content that speaks their language, literally and metaphorically. And it communicates what your site and your brand are about.

A compelling voice also gives you a **competitive advantage**. People visit certain sites simply because they find the content friendlier or more entertaining, interesting, or credible than another site's coverage of the same subjects.

Example

Look at the sports coverage of two newspaper sites from the same city—say, the *New York Times* (www.nytimes.com) and the *Daily News* (www.nydailynews.com). Both write about local teams such as the Yankees and the Jets, but the way they write their stories is significantly different. Compare the headlines, subheadings, and body copy to see how each publication expresses its voice.

Consider the context

To give your site a personality, first identify the context: your brand identity, your site's purpose, and your audience's expectations. Consider all of these as you begin to define the characteristics of your voice.

Your brand

Your site's voice communicates the essence of your brand. If your company is a venerable financial services institution, for instance, your content should use words that convey trustworthiness, confidence, dependability, continuity, and credibility. Your copy (and the accompanying graphics) shouldn't seem offhand or whimsical.

Before

At Pinstripe Financial Services, we take a pretty conservative approach to banking your Benjamins, but that doesn't stop us from finding ways to multiply your money. Plus, we've got tips that'll mean more money for you, less money for the Tax Man. <u>Give us a try</u> today—your first consultation's on us!

After

At Pinstripe Financial Services, we take a traditional approach to preserving your wealth, balancing your need to conserve assets with your need to increase them. Our advisers can also counsel you on tax strategies. <u>Contact us</u> today for your free consultation.

Your site's purpose

Your site's voice should always reinforce the site's purpose. For instance, if the main purpose is to sell, then your content—whether it's a blog, a product description, or a FAQ—should be phrased in a way that helps the reader make a decision or execute a transaction. If the purpose is to provide guidance on a complicated topic—technology or green living, for example—then your voice should be informative and straightforward.

One purpose of the Yahoo! Green site is to show people how they can make small changes that will add up to a big, positive impact on the environment. This Green Picks blog entry[3] imparts an idea that can support visitors' efforts to embrace an Earth-friendly lifestyle. The format is informal and Web-appropriate, and the voice is approachable, encouraging, informed, and sympathetic.

Go meatless just one day a week

By Trystan L. Bass
Posted Tue Apr 21, 2009 11:43am PDT

More from **Green Picks** blog

Related topics: Health, Food and Drink, Veggies

Most Americans love a burger (or bacon), but we also know there can be too much of a good thing. Studies continually point out that eating a lot of meat leads to heart disease and cancer. Plus, worldwide livestock farming creates 18% of all greenhouse gas emissions -- that's a little bit more than the world's transportation emissions. But it's pretty easy to improve our health and the planet's and still enjoy our food.

33 votes

buzz up

3 diggs

digg it

The Johns Hopkins School of Public Health suggests we go meatless on Mondays. Just one day a week without meat can reduce your consumption of saturated fat by 15% and reduce your chances of heart disease. Scientists estimate that if every American lowered meat consumption by just 20%, it would lower greenhouse gasses as much as if everyone in the country switched to driving Toyota Priuses (and think how much cheaper and easier eating less meat is!).

T I P   Before you embark on developing your voice, make sure that you know the purpose of both your brand and your site. Your company's mission statement is a good place to start.

Your audience

You know who your readers are and what they expect from your content, your site, and your brand. Make sure your site's voice speaks specifically and directly to them, in their own language.

Example

This Yahoo! Music blog appeals to an audience of music lovers. The voice of the blog is knowledgeable, irreverent, rock 'n' roll.[4]

> ### Reality Flashback: Lady Gaga On 'SYTYCD'
> Posted Sun Mar 15, 2009 5:07pm PDT by Lyndsey Parker in Reality Rocks
>
> Last year, I praised a "So You Think You Can Dance" results-show performance by a then relatively unknown pop diva named Lady Gaga. I was going positively gaga for this albino-wigged, Krystle Carrington-shoulder-padded, Jane Fonda-leotarded, lightning-bolt-faced, LCD-spectacled show-woman, and I predicted big things for her.

Example

This Yahoo! Sports blog speaks to its target audience: sports fans. The voice is knowledgeable but also familiar—that of a friend who's making a casual observation.[5]

> ### Morning Drive: Golf's youth movement gets even younger
> By Jay Busbee
>
> This will make some of you feel insanely old. On September 17, 1991, Guns N' Roses released "Use Your Illusion." (A week later, Nirvana would release "Nevermind" and instantly render GN'R irrelevant, but that's another story.) On that same day, a child was born. Well, lots of children, obviously, but only one of them is going to be playing in the 2009 British Open.
>
> Ryo Ishikawa, all of 17 years old, has qualified to play in next month's British Open at Turnberry courtesy of a three-shot victory in the Yomiuri Classic this past weekend.

Same voice, different platform

So far, we've been talking about your voice on the Web. But your voice must be recognizable on any platform and in any format, whether the content is in a cell phone browser, an email newsletter, or an automated customer response. (For more on writing for email and newsletters, see Chapter 8. For tips on writing for mobile readers, see Chapter 9.)

Examples

Here, the same voice is translated for three different messages and platforms. The site sells pet products to pet-obsessed owners, and the voice is petcentric, cute, sassy, and fun.

Blog entry on website
Fish calm hyperactive dog
When we met Jumper, he had his nose pressed hard against a tank full of brightly colored tropical fish. Nose prints decorated the glass like polka dots, testifying to his devotion. His mom, Bobbie Jones, says nothing calms down her yellow Lab like staring at a tank full of his scaly pals. "Jumper gets to run around outside all day," she explained, "but that doesn't keep him from going crazy in the house." On cue, Jumper leaped on her lap and began licking her face. "When we got the fish tank," she laughed, "that did the trick. He's in love."

We'd have to agree. He was back at the tank, eye to eye with a tiny pink and blue tetra.

Cell phone/RSS reader
Fish calm hyperactive dog
How can a few fishy friends keep an overactive Lab quiet for more than 15 minutes? Read on to find out.

Email
We're sorry we dropped the yarn ball on your March 22 order, but we're glad you let us know. We've already reshipped your Kitten-Mittens along with a free gift coupon you can use anytime to order treats for you or your pet--it's on us. Fetch us up on the Web anytime, or give us a whistle at 1-866-XXX-XXXX to tell us how we're doing.

Develop your site's unique voice

You've considered your brand, your site's purpose, and your audience. Your next step is to start sketching a description of a voice that fits all three. Consider which qualities you want your voice to convey.

Choose voice characteristics

Just as you might describe a friend as quirky, funny, and intelligent, you can also identify the unique qualities of your site's voice. The following table lists some voice characteristics. **Choose at least four or five descriptors**—culling from this list and brainstorming your own adjectives—that can sum up your site's intended voice. Jot down the adjectives; you'll use them later to create a voice chart.

authoritative	friendly	quirky
brash	fun	respectful
caring	humorous	romantic
cheerful	informative	serious
conservative	irreverent	smart
conversational	matter-of-fact	sympathetic
dry	nostalgic	trendy
edgy	passionate	trustworthy
enthusiastic	playful	unapologetic
formal	professional	upbeat
frank	provocative	worldly

Identify enough characteristics to describe your voice fully and make it distinct. If you're drawing a blank on adjectives, go back to your audience research (see Chapter 2, "Identify Your Audience") and list the characteristics your site visitors would want. Fill in any gaps between their expectations and the voice you're developing.

> **Example**
>
> Let's say your site is a parenting network for your metropolitan area. Your audience research indicates that people want positive, straightforward, respectful treatment of topics such as local children's activities, parenting advice, and local school information.
>
> Voice characteristics you've listed for your site include "playful" and "irreverent." Consider: Will these characteristics clash with audience expectations? Playfulness may not be too far out-of-bounds, but irreverence can come across as the opposite of respectfulness and may not be appreciated if parents in your metropolitan area have indicated that they are conservative about childrearing.

Make your adjectives specific. Many Web publishers characterize their voice as "casual," but there can be significant differences between the casual voice of a personal blog, a celebrity-gossip site, and a women's health resource. Similarly, most news sites want to sound up-to-the-minute and authoritative, but the creators of an individual news site will want to consider how their voice should differ from the competition's.

Level of formality

Will your readers expect your site to be intimate and chatty, professional and formal, or something in between? The Web lends itself to informality and a conversational voice, but make sure that you have the right level of familiarity for your audience and for the subject matter.

Think about your readers: They may accept less-formal grammar, such as contractions and use of the first person (*I* and *we*). But will they accept swearing, depictions of violence, sexual references, and the like? Do such expressions fit your brand?

Tone

Tone is the attitude your site's voice conveys. For example, a trendy, smart voice can have a tone that is ironic, snarky, enthusiastic, or earnest.

Consider which tone is appropriate for your audience and your subject matter. Will people understand irony, appreciate humor, expect the text to sound optimistic? Like your voice, **your tone should match readers' expectations; it should also be appropriate for the message**.

> **Example**
>
> **Before**
> Two weeks before her murder, the woman reported her husband's behavior to police. Twice she visited the precinct to seek help, only to be turned away both times. Nice job, officers—or should we say twice as nice? *(Sarcastic, critical tone inappropriate for straightforward news site)*
>
> **After**
> Two weeks before her murder, the woman reported her husband's behavior to police. Twice she visited the precinct to seek help, only to be turned away. No doubt many in the department are questioning those decisions tonight.

 ## Voice vs. tone

Voice expresses your site's basic personality—authoritative, trendy, practical, and so on. *Tone* expresses the mood or feeling of the voice—friendly, angry, annoyed, excited. So a site with a consistent voice might communicate in different tones, depending on the topic at hand.

Create your own voice chart

Now that you've chosen some descriptors and thought about the right tone and level of formality for your site, you can plot those points on a voice chart. Use the chart to make sure that your writing is always on track with your unique voice and not wandering off in another direction.

Map out your voice with a three-column grid: List your adjectives in the left column, describe those qualities more fully in the middle, and then translate each characteristic into practical writing tips. (For more guidance, see "Exercise: Chart your voice characteristics" on page 43.)

Example

This **sample voice chart** is for the fictional site BFF (Beauty, Fashion, Fitness), which targets teenage girls who are looking for tips on beauty and health and who want to see how their fashion icons are styling themselves.

Voice characteristic	Description	Writing tips
Trendy	Fresh, buzzy, and in the know.	Be a trendsetter: Feel free to use slang and to invent the occasional word. Use the present tense. Update the homepage at least hourly for breaking news, daily for features on health and fashion trends. If it's hot and trendy, girls should find it first on BFF.
Fun	Playful, feisty, and funny, but never catty or having fun at someone else's expense.	Be lively and colorful. Keep it positive and age-appropriate: 13 and up.
Enthusiastic	Upbeat, empowered, and as excited about our subjects as our readers are.	Be enthusiastic but not giddy or over-the-top. Exclamation points are OK once in a while—use them sparingly.
Accessible	Friendly, open, stress-free. BFF should sound like a cool big sister or a savvy best friend—smart and knowledgeable but not intimidating.	Be casual and conversational. Keep your stories short and simple and the language at about an eighth-grade level. But don't dumb down or be condescending.

Voice characteristic	Description	Writing tips
Inclusive	Everybody's welcome.	Assume that readers are teens and female. You can say "we" in that sense: "We all crave a new dress for summer." But don't assume that readers share the same race, religion, sexual orientation, or abilities. Also, most of our audience is in the U.S., but 20% is in Canada—don't exclude those girls. (Avoid statements like "We all wish we were old enough to vote in the presidential election this fall.")

Share your voice chart with other writers, bloggers, and editors who contribute to your site. Your content may vary somewhat in voice from section to section or from writer to writer, but generally contributors should orient their copy to your site's voice.

Voice variation

Various areas of your site or different stories on your site may require slight variations in voice. For example, an investors' report will likely sound more buttoned-down than a blog post, and you might address your Japanese clients more formally than your U.S. customers.

Sites that have more than one purpose can feature variations on the core voice while remaining true to the overall brand. For example, a TV studio with children's, daytime, and Spanish-language divisions may have sites or pages that speak differently to each audience.

Yahoo!, for instance, is a large network with many sites and audiences. The Yahoo! brand voice aims to be human, current, innovative, simple, friendly, credible, trustworthy, fun, smart, and daring. Individual sites within the Yahoo! network may emphasize certain qualities over others.

Examples

Each of these three Yahoo! sites employs a different aspect of the Yahoo! voice in its coverage of the 2009 inaugural celebrations for President Barack Obama.

Shine, a lifestyle site for women, looks at Michelle Obama's inaugural gown in an approach that's warm and respectful but also dishy and fun.[6]

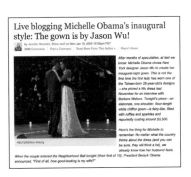

The Yahoo! News blog naturally takes a more serious and comprehensive approach to inauguration coverage, including its story about the gown. The voice in this post, "Obama Inauguration: Hits and Misses," sounds both expert and casual, which is appropriate for Yahoo! and for blogs.[7]

Finally, the mission of Yahoo!'s Buzz Log editors is to capture the Zeitgeist—what's fresh, up-to-the-minute, and being searched for right now. The Buzz Log's stories about the inauguration, including this one about searches related to inaugural ball gowns,[8] are informed and fresh and provide the links that visitors want.

Miss: Clinton confirmation

Several members of Obama's Cabinet and high-level appointees were confirmed in the Senate after Obama's swearing-in. One person who will be hanging back: Hillary Clinton. AP reports that Sen. John Cornyn of Texas is blocking her confirmation:

Cornyn's spokesperson says the senator has concerns about foreign donations to Bill Clinton's foundation:

> "Senator Cornyn is a strong proponent of complete transparency and has fought for as much throughout his time in office. He is keeping all of his options on the table."

His objection could delay Clinton's confirmation by a day or two, but barring any extraordinary circumstances, she is widely expected to win approval from the Democrat-controlled Senate.

Hit: First fashion

No, not Barack. We're talking about the Obama women: First lady Michelle Obama wowed the crowds in a sparkly yellow-gold sheath dress with a matching coat by Isabel Toledo. Always the practical shopper, she topped off her outfit with olive-green gloves from J.Crew and green shoes. First daughters Malia, 10, and Sasha, 7, strutted their fashion feet in colorful pink and blue coats, also from J.Crew.

Addressing the Inaugural Dresses
by Vera H-C Chan
Jan 20, 2009

Now that Americans have had the inaugural address, it is time for a peek at the inaugural dresses.

The search for what to wear to the inaugural balls has taken women (and men) to high-end designers, boutiques, consignment shops, and personal closets.

Web-wise, the site DressRegistry.com received a lot of buzz for its empathetic and tech-wise approach to avoiding the gaffe of duplicate dresses, and allowed gawkers an advance peek.

What may be out of style: lavishness (or garishness, depending on one's take). Given the current economic and political climes, the 10 official balls themselves have, according to USA Today, been "toned down from past inaugurations." (And some non-official gatherings have had to slash ticket prices or be nixed altogether.)

Accordingly, some people will follow suit in secondhand ensembles, although fresh designer duds will also make the rounds. Here's a look at what celebrants have thrown together for the 2009 inauguration, and the behind-the-scenes fashion dramas leading up to this day:

• **WWMW (What Would Michelle Wear)?** Glamour called chain store White House Black Market the "inaugural dress HQ" when **Michelle Obama** wore a $148 cotton dress on "The View" last summer. The first lady did don another chain-store buy for the swearing-in ceremony (J.Crew gloves), but she opted for designer Isabel Toledo's yellow dress and coat for the rest of the outfit. Ideas of what her evening attire should be launched a thousand sketches, but the field may have narrowed to Narciso Rodriguez.

Translate voice into words

Now that you have your voice chart, you're ready to write. Your vocabulary, grammatical choices, and even the organization and rhythm of your paragraphs will all express your voice.

Vocabulary

Simple words are helpful to less proficient readers and to those who quickly scan your webpage. For the Web (and for other platforms, such as cell phones), use words that are short, common, and unlikely to be misread. (To gauge your text's difficulty, see "Test your copy's readability" on page 10.)

Example

Before

We entertained the notion of holding biweekly meetings at which committee members would introduce and review issues related to the rooftop gardens; however, the idea was ultimately discarded.

After

We considered holding meetings every two weeks to discuss the rooftop gardens. In the end, we decided that meetings were not the answer.

Choose words that suit your voice. For example, if your voice is conservative and authoritative, stay away from slang. If "cutting edge" is one of your voice characteristics, feel free to choose words that have not yet graced a dictionary's pages and even to coin new words as your content requires.

Example

Before

Miss G. has apparently separated from her husband of only three months, according to multiple inside sources. The star's representative denied the report. *(Unadventurous choice of words for a trendy celebrity-gossip site)*

After

The inside line is that Miss G. has split with her hubs of only three months. The star's rep denied the report.

Sentence structure

Children first learn basic sentences structured as subject-verb *(The dog chews)* and subject-verb-object *(The dog chews shoes)* because these are short and easy to understand. Although varying the sentence structure makes for more interesting reading, the simple **subject-verb-object is often the best option online**. This structure puts the most important information—the actor (subject) and the action (verb)—right up-front, which works for visitors at many levels of English comprehension and for those who quickly scan content.

The degree of formality also influences sentence style. Informal sites can include sentence fragments (which lack subject, verb, or both) and sentences that begin with a conjunction (such as *and* or *but*). Complete sentences express a more formal attitude.

More formal

The film's score seemed as if it had been developed for a different movie. It evoked a mood and even a culture totally unrelated to what was on the screen. However, the bad score wasn't the film's biggest problem. *(All full sentences)*

Less formal

The film's score seemed like it belonged in a different movie. Totally unrelated moodwise—and even culturewise. But that wasn't the worst of it. *(Sentence, sentence fragment, sentence starting with the conjunction "but")*

For more information on sentence structure, see Chapter 4, "Construct Clear, Compelling Copy."

Organization

Well-organized webpages help people navigate your site: **Short pages with compact paragraphs and lists are ideal**, and simple, concise **headings help people find what they're looking for**. Break subjects into bites that the visitor can understand right away.

This advice goes for most sites, regardless of voice. But you can also **organize your content in a way that expresses your voice**, as in these examples for the fictional business Left Coast Inn.

Before

A trip to this seaside town wouldn't be quite as nice without a stay at our top accommodation pick. The Left Coast Inn has only a few rooms but serves them all well, and also cooks up amazing breakfasts with home-baked goodies and local organic eggs and milk. Available to guests most of the time—though not on rainy days, of course—are a hot tub in a quaint garden setting and a small reading library that includes books on local lore, history, and ecology. Plus, you're only a short drive or a healthy hike to the beach. Dogs are allowed in some rooms for a fee.

Speaking of the beach, that's where our favorite restaurant is, too. Don't miss the Seawall Café, one block up from the state beach. It serves just soups, salads, and sandwiches, but everything is fresh, the coffee is good, and the people are friendly.

After *(Organization for a warm, friendly vacation site)*
A trip to this seaside town wouldn't be complete without a stay at our top choice for accommodations.

The Left Coast Inn has only a few rooms but serves them all well. Dogs are allowed in some rooms for a fee. And you're only a short drive or a healthy hike to the **beach**.

The owner-chef cooks up amazing **breakfasts** with home-baked goodies and local organic eggs and milk.

A **hot tub** in a quaint garden setting is available to guests most of the time— though not on rainy days, of course. On those days, try the small **reading library** that includes books on local lore, history, and ecology.

Don't miss our favorite local restaurant, the **Seawall Café**, located one block up from the **state beach**. It serves just soups, salads, and sandwiches, but everything is fresh, the coffee is good, and the people are friendly.

After *(Organization for a practical, bare-bones travel tips site)*
Accommodations
The Left Coast Inn is our top pick for this seaside town. It has only a few rooms, so book early. At the inn you'll enjoy:

- Amazing breakfasts with home-baked goodies and local organic eggs and milk
- A hot tub in a quaint garden setting
- A small reading library with books on local lore, history, and ecology
- A good location: You're only a short drive or a healthy hike to the beach

Dogs are allowed in some rooms for a fee.

Eats
The Seawall Café, one block up from the state beach, serves just soups, salads, and sandwiches, but everything is fresh, the coffee is good, and the people are friendly.

Choose the organization and flow that works for your target audience and subject matter.

Punctuation

Rules about punctuating abound (see Chapter 10, "Punctuate Proficiently"), but there's room in the rules to let your voice speak. For instance, a gossip site may use ellipses (. . .) for dramatic effect. A less trendy site, such as a bank's, may consider dashes too casual and avoid them.

In general, **keep punctuation simple**: Uncluttered and easy-to-read sentences are best. If you find yourself using comma after comma after comma, try making two (or even three) shorter sentences out of that long one. Avoid the overuse of exclamation points or emoticons: Your words should be so clear and strong that they don't require extra emphasis.

Example

Before

Oh, no, not again! Miss G. brought her pup to the awards ceremony! But her fluffy accessory outshone her ensemble. :-P

After

Aww, Miss G. brought her puppy to the awards. Her pet: cute. Her dress: hideous.

T I P While you're watching your exclamation points, watch out for an overuse of "loud" formatting, too. Using too much boldface or italic and employing many different font sizes and colors in an attempt to emphasize areas or catch the site visitor's eye can backfire: People may find your site too distracting and hard to read; they may also mistake your content for ads and move on.

Jargon

Avoid unnecessary jargon, or specialized or technical terms. Some of your visitors won't understand what you're saying. Even those who do may have to slow down to get your exact meaning—and Web readers don't like to slow down.

Example

Let's say you describe your Internet access service like this: "Our broadband service has the fastest pipeline this side of Oahu. Sign up today, and you'll shoot the YouTube at record speeds!"

Your readers might not understand that *pipeline* and *shoot the tube* are surfing references—wave surfing, not Web surfing—and might miss that *pipeline* is a metaphor for the wire or fiber that carries communication signals. You don't want your audience thinking that you're selling a series of tubes.

If a technical term is appropriate to your subject (as in the following example), you can include the term with a brief explanation.

Example

Before

At age 2, your child likely participated in parallel play with other children instead of interacting with them. You can expect a change in this behavior around age 3, when children begin to notice and take an interest in their peers.

After

At age 2, your child probably played alongside other children but did not interact with them—an activity called parallel play. You can expect a change in this behavior around age 3, when children begin to notice and take an interest in playing with their peers.

Voice snapshot: Yahoo! Green

Environmentalism can be a harsh subject. The icebergs are melting, chemicals in everything could kill us, and the only way to make a real, lasting change is to live off-grid in a yurt eating raw food . . . right?

Wrong. The mission of Yahoo! Green is to show a broad, mainstream audience how anyone can make small changes that will add up to create a big, positive impact on our environment. Our site is friendly and approachable, not dogmatic or preachy, and our message is encouraging: "You can do this."

We want more people to understand how important environmental issues are, so we take time to explain confusing topics.

For example, *greenwashing* is a trendy term among eco-insiders that generally refers to organizations diverting attention away from their practices that harm the environment by drawing attention to their practices that are supposedly pro-environment. But the people in our audience may be just learning about the topic. That's why our site breaks down the jargon into straightforward language that doesn't talk down to them and suggests simple actions they can take to implement change in everyday life.

—*Trystan L. Bass, senior editor and Yahoo! Green contributor*

Naturally, there are times when only insider terminology will do—for example, when you're serving a particular type of customer, or when simplifying or substituting words leads to inaccuracy. In these cases, make sure that you're using the words correctly and consistently and that you explain them quickly in the text. Read "Junk the jargon" on page 308 for tips on when jargon may be appropriate and for ways to identify and eliminate it when it's not.

Culture-specific references

When it comes to informal language, it's critical to know your readers. By default—but especially if you have a large, varied readership—**your language should have mass appeal**. Be careful with slang, clichés, and other references that are specific to one group, region, or culture. For instance, readers outside the United States (and even some U.S. residents) might not understand a baseball-derived reference like "batting a thousand."

Example

Before
The start-up has some great software but has put a big goose egg on the board as far as profits go. If the owners want to get out of the bush leagues and make it to the big IPO show, they'll have to show investors that they know how to grow the business. *("Goose egg," "bush leagues," and "big show" are all baseball slang, and "IPO," a term that the audience might or might not understand, refers to "initial public offering," when a private company begins to sell stock to the public.)*

After
The start-up has some great software but isn't profitable yet. If the owners want the company to become publicly traded, they'll have to show investors that they know how to build the business.

On the other hand, if you're purposely targeting a narrow segment, such references might be appropriate and appealing. A site for fans of the local high school basketball team, for instance, might feel cozier if it included basketball slang, local cheers, player nicknames, and so on.

For more information on using language accessible to a worldwide audience, see Chapter 5, "Be Inclusive, Write for the World."

Wordplay

Techniques such as metaphor, simile, alliteration, rhyme, and repetition can be an elegant way to make a point, to grab attention, to make your message memorable, and to help readers see something in a new way. However, be certain that your readers will understand an expression so that you're enhancing, not obscuring, the meaning.

Example

Before
The governor's new proposal was about as well-received as a foie gras concession at a PETA rally. *(Obscure reference: Will readers understand it?)*

After
The governor's new proposal was about as well-received as beef stew at a vegetarian potluck.

Whatever rhetorical device you choose, use it to reinforce your message, not to be cute or to show off.

Ideas in Practice

Exercise: Chart your voice characteristics

Have you ever visited a website where the user comments were more interesting than the content? That site probably lacked a distinct voice. Every FAQ and Contact Us page doesn't need to be a work of art, but every page should speak with the site's voice.

In this exercise, you'll create a voice chart: a detailed description of how your site should sound. When you've finished describing your voice characteristics, spread the word. Give each of your site's content creators a copy, and ask them to use it. This chart will help writers see when they're straying from the site's voice and can be especially helpful for new writers who may not be familiar with your site.

To create your chart:

1. Fill in your site name, a few key audience attributes (see Chapter 2), and brand attributes (if you have a marketing department that has outlined them).

2. List at least 5 one-word adjectives that describe your site's core qualities. You may need more

adjectives to define your voice thoroughly, but choose fewer than 10 total. (See "Choose voice characteristics" on page 31 for suggestions.) Enter each adjective under "Voice characteristic" in the chart.

3. Put your chosen adjectives in context—write a fuller description of what each word means with respect to your site and its style.

4. Get specific in the Do's and Don'ts columns about techniques and strategies (see "Translate voice into words" on page 36). Include sample phrases and sentences that illuminate your point. For the don'ts, it may help to think about elements of your competition's style that you *don't* want to emulate.

Voice chart

Site name:

Audience attributes:

Brand attributes:

Voice characteristic	Description	WRITING TIPS AND EXAMPLES	
		Do's	Don'ts

Sample voice chart

Site name: Yahoo! Green

Audience attributes: Mainstream, educated, slightly techie, curious about green issues but may be new to the subject

Brand attributes: Friendly, trustworthy, fun, smart, inclusive, passionate, informed, balanced, straightforward, respectful

Voice characteristic	Description	WRITING TIPS AND EXAMPLES	
		Do's	Don'ts
Positive	Yahoo! Green wants to empower users and to emphasize "you can do this." We're not defeatist or alarmist. Being green isn't a chore; it's an active, fun lifestyle choice.	Adopt a positive, can-do tone. Show readers how being green benefits their health and budget as well as the planet. Example: *Line-drying your clothes saves money on your electricity bill and conserves energy.*	Don't focus on bad news, on chastising environmental offenders, or on "the sky is falling" scare tactics. If you present a problem, follow it up with possible solutions. Example: Use a headline like *How Your Toilet Paper Can Save the Planet,* not *Why Your Toilet Paper Is Killing the Planet.*
Active	Yahoo! Green is about learning but also about *doing.* We offer practical advice that readers can act on easily.	Topics and language should be active. Write hands-on how-to stories, and choose active verbs and other lively words that encourage readers to take action. Explain results. Example: *Driving just 10 miles per hour slower can reduce fuel consumption by 20 percent.*	Don't take the attitude "This is somebody else's problem." Remind readers why the problem matters to them and how they can act. Don't end a story without telling readers what they can do next.
Accessible	Yahoo! Green is friendly and approachable. We're talking to everyone, not just to environmental insiders. We advocate equally for the green cause *and* for our audience: We want readers to understand how greener living makes their daily lives better.	Use a conversational, inviting voice. Favor clarity over cleverness. Remember that the audience is broad: Be inclusive and keep the language PG-13. Assume that readers are smart and engaged but may be newcomers to green subjects. Stay close to home: Focus on simple, everyday things that anyone can do. Explain any terms that are becoming more widely used. Make sure readers understand them in context. For example, *greenwashing* and *hypermiling* need definitions on first use.	Don't assume that readers have a lot of background knowledge about a topic. For example, instead of saying *carbon sequestration,* say *burying carbon dioxide underground* if it's necessary to discuss the topic. Don't get too technical. Users may not know or care a lot about public utilities, chemistry, and the scientific details. However, consumer technologies like cars and computers usually have broad appeal.

Voice characteristic	Description	WRITING TIPS AND EXAMPLES	
		Do's	Don'ts
Knowledgeable	We know what we're talking about, and we get our facts right. We want to sound like the reader's friend who's in the know.	Offer clarity. Explain issues that can be confusing or contentious, like climate change. Give readers an overview. Put problems in context. Ask the questions readers want answered. Example: *Paper or plastic bags?* Use selective statistics (but don't overdo it). Example: *Recycling 1 million cell phones can reduce greenhouse gas emissions equal to taking 1,368 cars off the road for a year.*	Don't be wishy-washy. Explore different points of view but present your own informed opinion. Don't be preachy or dogmatic, and don't talk down to readers. For example, don't say *There's no excuse for not recycling every bit of waste you produce, every day.* Instead, say *It's a challenge to recycle every bit of waste we produce every day, but remember: Every time you recycle or reuse, you contribute to the health of the planet.*
Informal	Our voice, like our message, is straightforward and simple.	Adopt a casual and friendly but respectful tone. Use the second person (*you, your*) and write as if you're speaking to somebody one-on-one. Use everyday vocabulary. Contractions are OK.	Don't get fancy; keep your writing style simple. The topics are hard enough to understand without making the wording difficult, too. Use *green* and *eco* compounds sparingly—ditto *green* as a verb.

Ideas in Practice

Example: Give copy a voice makeover

The following article could be found on all sorts of sites: lifestyle, environmental, crafts, frugal living, and so on. It has some useful ideas—but it might put you to sleep before you get to them. It's not easy to scan, either, and the first paragraph meanders before it gets to the point.

Read the article and then our makeover of it to see how we would revamp the voice—here, we chose the voice we outlined for our fictional BFF site on page 34. We rewrote the introduction to focus on fashion, one of the BFF (Beauty, Fashion, Fitness) pillars, created subheadings and bullet points to help readers scan the page, and edited the story to make the voice more appealing to BFF readers.

Before

How to recycle your wardrobe

You buy clothes made from sustainable materials, such as organic cotton grown without pesticides and colored with nontoxic dyes. You wash your clothes with phosphate-free detergent and hang them out to dry in the sun. You're taking care of your clothes while taking care of the environment, but are you doing everything you can to green your wardrobe? Are you consuming new clothes when you could be conserving your old ones and saving some money, too? Consider the following ways you can keep your pledge to reduce, reuse, and recycle.

Reduce: Don't buy new garments unless you absolutely need them, and don't toss things that can be mended. Almost anyone can sew on a button or restitch a seam, and learning how to hem pants is easy. Your local dry cleaner or tailor can help with tougher repairs, like alterations or sweater and suit reweaving. Spending just a few dollars can keep your favorite clothes out of the trash can.

Reuse: If you just don't like the look of your clothes anymore, consider remaking them. Dye them a new color; decorate them with fabric paint, brooches, beads, and other add-ons; cut off sleeves, collars, or pant cuffs; take the pieces apart and make new outfits. You can find all sorts of ideas online. And salvage the leftover fabric—you can use it to patch your jeans, wrap presents, or dust the furniture; and craft-y types can use the scraps for doll clothes, quilts, and other projects.

Recycle: When you really need a new item of clothing, shop secondhand. You can find interesting things at shops that range from thrift stores to designer consignment boutiques, and of course you can shop online, too. Bring a bag of clothes you're not wearing anymore to trade in. You'll save money and closet space. If you don't like what's in the shops, organize your own swap meet and trade clothes with friends.

After

Re-fashionista! Get a new look the green way

Anyone can buy decent clothes off the rack, but real fashionistas know how to make any old thing look stylish and fresh again. Plus, while you're turning friends green with envy at your fashion sense, you're greening your wardrobe, saving tragic outfits from the trash heap, and saving money, too.

You've heard about "reduce, reuse, recycle"—well, here's how to repair, re-flair, and re-share your clothes.

Repair: Therapy for your threads

We'd all like to buy a new outfit every week. But let's face it: Even if you had the money, would you have the closet space? Think mending, not spending. Dig through your closet to find clothes that can go back in rotation after a little TLC.

- Learn how to sew on buttons, restitch a seam, and hem pants and skirts.
- Take tougher repairs and alterations to your neighborhood dry cleaner or tailor. Some can even reweave holes in sweaters.

Re-flair: Outcast makeover

Like the first guy you dated, that dress seemed great once upon a time, and now it's all wrong. Don't dump it—get creative. Look online for lots more makeover ideas.

- Dye the piece or decorate it with fabric paint, brooches, beads—you name it.
- Chop off the sleeves, change the neckline, raise the hem or make it asymmetrical, take the pieces apart and make something new.
- Save the scraps. You can find 101 uses for these: Patch your jeans, wrap presents, and get crafty with other projects.

Re-share: Clothes-swap till you drop

Mirror, mirror on the wall, what's the fairest trade of all? Clothes swap! Before you spend a fortune at the mall, consider adopting vintage clothes that could use a good home.

- Shop at secondhand-clothing stores. They don't all smell like mothballs. Look for designer consignment boutiques, used-clothing shops in happening neighborhoods, and online auctions.
- Cash in. Trade in old clothes—you'll save money and make space in the closet.
- Throw a swap party. Invite your fierce friends to bring their castoff clothes, shoes, and accessories, and everyone can trade for funky—and free!—new outfits.

BFF says: Remember to take care of the environment when you take care of your wardrobe. Wash your clothes with phosphate-free detergent and hang them out to dry in the sun. And when you must buy new clothes, look for sustainable materials, such as organic cotton grown without pesticides and colored with nontoxic dyes.

Chapter 4
Construct Clear, Compelling Copy

In this chapter

- **Headings.** Create headlines and subheadings that distill content, make stories easy to scan, and break up text into readable chunks.
- **Sentences.** Write strong, concise, informative sentences that compel people to keep reading.
- **Paragraphs.** Keep them short, simple, and on one topic.
- **Lists.** Simplify complicated steps, organize ideas for your readers, and add welcome white space to a page.

Clear, compelling writing makes online content easy to scan and understand. It grabs a reader's interest and doesn't let go.

Enticing, well-written headlines can reach out from searches and mobile devices to pull people into your site; ho-hum headlines send them away. Would you rather read a story headlined "Link found between dinosaurs and barnyard birds" or "How *T. rex* turned into a chicken"?

Once the headline invites people in, it's up to your content to keep them reading. For example, would you be likely to stick with this story?

Our intrepid restaurant reviewer, known affectionately as Barney, found the food at Marta's latest bistro, newly renovated on the north side of town, to be, as he put it, "Bland beyond belief."

Or would you prefer this one?

"Bland beyond belief."
That's how our intrepid reviewer Barney sums up the food at Marta's latest bistro, new on the north side.

Headlines and strong content work together to create compelling Web copy. **Master the basic building blocks that make content work**—headings, sentences, paragraphs, and lists—and readers will return for more.

Headings

Headings—which include headlines and subheadings—**perform several important functions**: They give readers a glimpse of your content, they organize that content into readable chunks, and they tell a story that makes it possible to grasp the gist of the content quickly.

- **Headlines** are the top-level headings that precede the main text. They're coded **<h1>** in HTML (see "Anatomy of a webpage" on page 372). Depending on your publishing tool, a headline may also serve as your page's **<title>** tag, which becomes the linked heading in search results (for examples, see "Page titles" on page 409). And the headline may be the only snippet of text that people see in an RSS feed or in a mobile phone browser.
- **Subheadings** are the lower-level headings that organize text into chunks. They're coded **<h2>**, **<h3>**, and so on in HTML.

Organize your webpage with headings

Headings are your basic page-organizing tool. The headline gives readers a glimpse of the whole story (*Hansel and Gretel foil witch, escape*), and the subheadings lead readers through the content by helping them understand what's in each small section (*Witch captures children, Hansel tricks witch, Gretel saves brother, Children arrive home*).

T I P   Does your content pass the "heading test"? Scan an article reading only the headings. If you can understand the flow and substance of the story, your content passed the test. If something seems confusing, you may need to rewrite the headings or even reorder some paragraphs.

Help readers distinguish different heading levels:

- **Arrange headings in decreasing levels of importance**—headline (**<h1>**), second-level heading (**<h2>**), third-level heading (**<h3>**)—much as you would in an outline.
- **Distinguish each heading level visually.** Headings are generally displayed in boldface so that they stand out from the text. The headline is generally the largest font, the second-level heading is smaller, and so on.

See how these heading levels look on a webpage in "Headings and lists 101" on page 51.

Headings and lists 101

A **headline** is the line at the top of an article. It may appear elsewhere—for example, as a link in a list of headlines. Generally, the headline is marked in HTML with an **<h1>** tag.

Subheadings break up the text of an article visually or thematically. They add both interest and white space to a page and guide readers through your content. In HTML, subheadings are typically marked with **<h2>** and **<h3>** tags.

We use the word *headings* when referring to both headlines and subheadings. Both humans and search engines scan headings to learn what a page is about and to decide whether it's relevant.

Programmers tend to refer to **<h1>**- and **<h2>**-type HTML tags as *header tags* (for more on HTML tags, see Chapter 16, "Get Familiar With Basic Webpage Coding"). And the word *header* also refers to a repeating section at the top of a page or document—the opposite of *footer*.

Bulleted and numbered lists pull out or order important points. They can also give readers variety and a visual rest by breaking up a block of text.

The example at right from the U.S. National Eye Institute shows many of these elements: The headline states the topic. The second-level headings use title-style capitalization and also appear as contents in a bulleted list. The third-level headings are all capitalized in sentence case (see "Capitalization" on page 239).

Glaucoma ——— [Headline]

This information was developed by the National Eye Institute to help patients and their families search for general information about glaucoma. An eye care professional who has examined the patient's eyes and is familiar with his or her medical history is the best person to answer specific questions.

Table of Contents

> Glaucoma Defined
> Causes and the Risk Factors
> Symptoms and Detection ——— [Bulleted list]
> Treatment
> Current Research
> More Information

Glaucoma Defined ——— [Second-level heading]

What is glaucoma? ——— [Third-level heading]

Glaucoma is a group of diseases that can damage the eye's optic nerve and result in vision loss and blindness. Glaucoma occurs when the normal fluid pressure inside the eyes slowly rises. However, with early treatment, you can often protect your eyes against serious vision loss.

What is the optic nerve? ——— [Third-level heading]

The optic nerve is a bundle of more than 1 million nerve fibers. It connects the retina to the brain. (See diagram below.) The retina is the light-sensitive tissue at the back of the eye. A healthy optic nerve is necessary for good vision.

Credit: National Eye Institute, National Institutes of Health

T I P   If you find that you need to use more than three levels of headings to organize your copy, stop! This is a red flag that your copy may be overly complex and may need to be pared down.

Write strong headlines

Successful headlines tell the gist of the story in a few powerful words. Headlines that don't engage the reader are not successful. Inaccurate or misleading headlines are worse: Sensationalized ones may bring curious readers to your site but will soon drive them away and harm your site's credibility.

To write an effective headline, you must read and understand the story and compress the most important information into a few meaningful words. That's a tall order for a short bit of copy, but it's a skill anyone writing or editing for the Web should try to master.

TIP Most of the rules related to headline writing apply to all headings. Subheadings, however, are less likely to be clickable links, and they don't typically appear in other locations, such as search results, the way headlines do.

Follow these steps for **effective headline writing**:

1. Review the content thoroughly

Read the story, watch the video, click through the slideshow. Before you start writing, make sure you thoroughly understand the content so that you can give it an accurate headline.

2. Identify the content's tone

Is the content serious or lighthearted, professional or confessional, matter-of-fact or over-the-top? Give your headline a tone that suits the content. For example, if you're writing a serious story about a natural disaster, the headline should not be frivolous. The tone should also be appropriate for your audience and true to your site's identity, standards, and voice. (See "Voice vs. tone" on page 33.)

3. Determine the point of the content

Why are you publishing this content? Why will your readers be interested in it? Figuring out the larger significance of a story, its unique angle, or what makes it different from similar webpages will help you write a headline that speaks to your audience. Consider the following examples focusing on a fictional product.

Examples

Griblak's "CoolBlue" face moisturizer poses health risks (*An article targeting health professionals highlights medical findings about a questionable product.*)

Griblak's "CoolBlue" moisturizer: Get out of my face! (*A report and warning on the same product, for a breezy teen beauty blog, aims at preventing the product's use.*)

You should be able to find the story's point in the first paragraph. If you can't, edit your page to put the most important point at the beginning (see "Paragraphs" on page 64).

4. Consider where the headline will appear

Is the headline for the homepage, for a category or section page, or for an article? Will the headline turn up in RSS feeds, on mobile devices, in search results? Make sure your copy will work wherever it appears. Some tips:

- **Story-level headlines** are important to readers and search engines, and they show up in newsreaders and other content aggregators as well. Focus on search keywords for SEO purposes (see Chapter 17, "Optimize Your Site for Search Engines"). If you have to choose between being clever and being clear, choose clarity.
- **Section-level headlines** should appeal to engaged readers who are interested in that section's topic, helping them scan stories to find what they want. The headlines should balance keywords with enough intrigue to inspire clicks.
- **Homepage headlines** are often promotional: They sell content to casual readers. Again, favor clarity over cleverness, and employ search keywords to draw readers to your site.
- **Mobile headlines** should be as brief as possible, focusing on keywords and linking to the website for more information. (See Chapter 9, "Streamline Text for Mobile Devices.")

 Keywords: The words or phrases people may type into search engines when trying to locate your type of content.

5. List five or six keywords that should be in the headline

If you have done keyword research for your page (see "Charting keywords with a keyword research tool" on page 399), you already know the words to target. Otherwise, ask yourself which words *you* would use in a search to find this story. Proper nouns—the names of people, places, and things—are good. Avoid abbreviations, because people tend to spell out words in searches. Then use those five or six keywords in a short sentence, which you will later trim to headline length.

Example

Your keywords
Fab-U-Loz Chocolate, baby boomers, heart attack prevention, longevity

Draft sentence

Study finds Fab-U-Loz Chocolate prevents heart attacks in baby boomers.

If you're stuck, try pulling something out of the first paragraph of the story. But don't cheat by repeating a sentence verbatim for the headline. Readers don't want to see the same verbiage twice, and search engines won't like the repetition either.

TIP When you have a draft of your headline, enter the phrase into a search box and compare the results:

- Is your wording more compelling than your competition's?
- Has anyone else used identical wording? If so, you probably want to change yours— you'd be competing directly, and the other story has already built up some search momentum.
- Look at the top results: Which keywords do they have in common? You probably want to use those, too.
- Is there a keyword or a story angle that the top results *aren't* using? Take advantage of it.

6. Use a verb that's strong, active, fresh, and accurate

Subject-verb-object (*Hercules slays Hydra!*) is often the best structure for a headline, because it puts the actor (subject) and the action (verb) first. **Every word has to pull its weight in a headline**, and a dynamic verb can do a lot of heavy lifting. Assuming both are accurate, which headline would you be more likely to click: "Peace talks end" or "Peace talks collapse"? Seek verbs that are:

- **Strong.** Use short, staccato, urgent, muscular verbs in your draft headline. The strongest have just one or two syllables, with stress on the second syllable to propel the rhythm forward. Examples: *duck, win, hail, free, extol, sing, lash, reject, rout, stomp, shellac, seize, switch, destroy, save, urge, revive.*

Example

Before (weak)

Greeks gain entry to Troy, win

After (strong)

Greeks seize Troy

■ **Active.** Use the active rather than the passive voice, and the present tense unless past tense is necessary. Active verbs put the actor first and sound livelier than passive verbs, which can sound static or abstract. (See "When to use the passive voice" below.)

Example

Before (passive)
Hare beaten by tortoise in footrace

After (active)
Tortoise beats hare in footrace

■ **Fresh.** Choose a verb that hasn't been overused (for pointers, see "Invigorate your prose" on page 57). Check a thesaurus when you need a shorter or more interesting verb, but be careful to choose a synonym that means exactly what you want to say. Synonyms can have slightly different connotations. For example, one word-processing program suggests *airy* as a synonym for *fresh*, but *airy* wouldn't make sense as the bold heading of this bullet item.

When to use the passive voice

Sometimes the passive voice is preferable, even advisable—as when the actor is relatively unimportant or unknown. Consider which words (especially names or other nouns) people would use when searching for the story.

Examples

Before
Grand jury indicts Mayor Smith for fraud

After
Mayor Smith indicted for fraud *(The actor—the grand jury, as readers will learn in the story—is not important here; the person indicted is. A person would probably search on "Mayor Smith" and "fraud" rather than "grand jury.")*

Before
Mugger attacks off-duty cop outside police station

After
Off-duty cop mugged outside police station *(The actor—the mugger—is unknown; the act—a cop got mugged—is more interesting and more likely to be searched on.)*

- **Accurate.** Make sure your strong, active, fresh verbs represent the story accurately. Consider: The headline "Stocks crash" conveys a different idea than "Stocks fall" does. Remember: Your headline may surface in a feed on its own, with no accompanying story or image to give it context. Could someone misunderstand it?

7. Be concise, be specific

Refine your draft headline to make it brief, to the point, and more informative. Put the two most important words first, where they're most likely to be read.

Example

Before

Gold medal goes to Jones *(The gold medal is important, but it's not the real point of the story.)*

After

Jones wins gold medal *(Even if this headline is shortened for space, the first two words will tell the story.)*

8. Edit and proofread your headline

When you have a headline that's complete, compact, and compelling, walk away from it for a few minutes—and then edit and proofread it one more time (see Chapter 15, "Proofread and Test Before You Publish"). Ask:

- Does the headline summarize the content accurately?
- Are the voice and tone appropriate?
- Are the most important pieces of information—the actor and the action—first?
- Is the sentence structure simple and easy to understand at a glance?
- Do strong, intriguing words compel a reader to keep reading?
- Is there any ambiguity?
- Have you checked the grammar, punctuation, style, and spelling, especially the spelling of names and keywords?

TIP Your headline might end up in an RSS feed or an aggregator the instant it's published. Make sure that there are no embarrassing typos or other errors *before* you push the content live.

Invigorate your prose

Headings are like poetry: Every word must serve a purpose, and every word must work. That means using only strong, powerful, fresh words. Cut and replace weak verbs, words that take up space without adding meaning, clichés (see "Cut the clichés" on page 305), and "headlinese"—*nab, rap, mull, heist, flap,* and *hike*—words that you see only in headlines or hear in old gangster movies.

Examples

Before
Bank heist nets tot millions

After
6-year-old robs bank, steals millions *(The hackneyed, headlinese words "heist" and "tot" are replaced with clear, meaningful words.)*

Before
What, me worry? Economy, say experts, is as sound as a dollar

After
Experts call economy "sound," urge trust *(Clichés—"What, me worry?" and "sound as a dollar"—are inaccurate and take up valuable space, especially at the beginning of a heading. Use strong words and accurate quotes.)*

Establish heading styles

Your headings express your site's voice, both in the words you use and in the way you style them.

Design may dictate how many characters you can allot to headings. Beyond this, however, you will likely have some decisions to make. Should you capitalize headings as you would a sentence, or as a title? Should you use full sentences or fragments? The heading style you choose is important, and so is sticking with it consistently throughout the entire site.

T I P If your site comprises many sites and properties, as the Yahoo! network does, it may be difficult to ensure a consistent heading style throughout. Instead, make heading styles consistent within each site.

Consider the following when deciding on a heading style.

Capitalization

The three main styles of capitalization used in headings are **sentence case** (*Governor signs the Virginia school tax bill*), **title case** (*Governor Signs the Virginia School Tax Bill*), and **all uppercase** (*GOVERNOR SIGNS THE VIRGINIA SCHOOL TAX BILL*), which you should reserve for headings in plain-text emails. Whichever style you choose, be sure to use it consistently across your site. See "Capitalization" on page 239 for more information on applying capitalization styles.

Punctuation

Headings don't generally include periods or other ending punctuation. If you want to include question marks and exclamation points, be stingy with them.

- Question marks can be effective if the content answers the headline's question. Generally, though, a direct statement is better.
- Exclamation points usually mark an attempt to add excitement that should be conveyed by strong words instead.

Examples

Are polar bears in decline? *(For an article about a study finding that, yes, the polar bear population is in decline)*

Scientists debate fate of polar bear population *(For an article about a summit called to debate this issue)*

Example

Before
Dolphin helps diver find sunken treasure!

After
Dolphin leads diver to sunken treasure

Parallel structure

Are all your subheadings sentence fragments (one word or short phrases), or are they complete sentences? Used consistently, either choice is fine. But—unless there's a very good reason for including it—one long sentence among several fragment subheadings will stand out, and not in a good way. Grammatically and aesthetically it can look sloppy.

- Headings of the same level should be consistent, but they need not match other levels. For example, you may decide that second-level subheadings will all be imperative sentences and third-level subheadings will all be questions.
- Try to start most subheadings with the same part of speech, such as a verb or a noun. This will make them easier to scan.

Examples

Before

Holiday Gift Gadgets for Everyone *(Headline)*

Point the way with GPS *(Subheading that starts with a verb)*

Accessorize a mobile device *(Subheading that starts with a verb)*

Compact cameras with big features *(Subheading that starts with a noun that could be misread as a verb—especially when it follows other subheadings starting with verbs)*

After

Holiday Gift Gadgets for Everyone *(Headline)*

GPS devices for finding the way *(Subheading that starts with a noun)*

Accessories for mobile devices *(Subheading that starts with a noun)*

Compact cameras with big features *(Subheading that starts with a noun)*

TIP Sometimes it makes sense to break a rule. If you have to force the headings into unnatural language to make them parallel, don't. (For more on parallel structure, see "Parallelism: Matching, balancing, making sense" on page 341.)

Sentences

Headline writing is good practice for sentence writing. Good sentences are concise and well-formed, using logical word order and solid grammar. They are easy for all readers to digest quickly, even people with limited literacy or fluency in English. (For pointers on writing for an international audience or for translation, see Chapter 5, "Be Inclusive, Write for the World.")

These **guidelines for clear writing** cover the basics.

Make sentences easy to scan

Readers who scan websites for interesting content do not want to plow through a lot of words. One practical way to keep sentences short is to consider the number of words you're using: Aim for sentences with no more than 25. Many word processors can show you how many words you have in a sentence. You also aid scanning when you:

- **Express one main point per sentence.** More ideas mean more complex sentences. Don't get sidetracked.

Example

Before
More than 3,000 residents fled the raging fire, which has burned 10 square miles, while the governor promised to send more firefighters immediately.

After
More than 3,000 residents fled the raging fire, which has burned 10 square miles. The governor promised to send more firefighters immediately.

- **Front-load your sentences.** Put the most important information at the beginning of the sentence, where scanning readers are likely to see it. Using simple subject-verb-object sentence structure can help: This format automatically puts the actor (subject) and the action (verb) first. In particular, use this structure for your most visible text, the first sentence in a paragraph.

Example

Before
Riding on her 10-year-old Welsh pony, Pinky, for the first time this year, Gloria Nguyen won the preteen barrel race. *(This sentence is technically subject-verb-object, but it starts with a long phrase.)*

After
Gloria Nguyen won the preteen barrel race in her first ride of the year on Pinky, her 10-year-old Welsh pony. *(The subject, verb, and object start the sentence.)*

T I P For easy reading and scanning, we advise using short, active sentences with subject-verb-object construction and front-loaded information, especially in important places like headlines, lists, and the first lines of paragraphs. However, when every sentence has the same structure and rhythm, even writing that's about a fascinating subject can start to drag. *Gloria Nguyen won the preteen barrel race in her first ride of the year on Pinky, her 10-year-old Welsh pony* is a great way to begin a paragraph. But you may want to "back in" to the next sentence with an opening phrase, just to mix it up a bit: *More than a one-trick pony, Pinky later won his own Best Horse in Show trophy.* Variety is key to a good reading experience.

- **Maintain order.** If you list a series of items and then explain each item, explain the items in the order in which you listed them.

Example

Before

Our firm offers you two types of accounts: the Basic Account and the Plus Account. The Plus Account includes access to premium services in addition to basic services. The Basic Account includes access to our full line of basic services for safeguarding and increasing your wealth. *(Basic Account is introduced first, but Plus Account is explained first.)*

After

Our firm offers you two types of accounts: the Basic Account and the Plus Account. The Basic Account includes access to our full line of basic services for safeguarding and increasing your wealth. The Plus Account includes access to premium services in addition to basic services. *(Order of introduction and order of explanation are the same.)*

- **Keep "if" before "then."** State the condition (*if*) first, followed by the consequence (*then*). This order gives readers the topic of the sentence right away, which helps their comprehension as they continue reading and allows them to save time by skipping ahead to the next sentence if they aren't interested.

Example

Before

Click the **Edit** link if your email address is incorrect.

After

If your email address is incorrect, click the **Edit** link. *(Put the condition, which starts with "if," first. Note that "then" can often be omitted.)*

Make sentences easy to understand

You can make sentences easy to understand by using simple words and basic word forms and avoiding complex word order:

- **Use basic verb forms** as much as possible: infinitives, imperatives, and the simple present, simple past, and future tenses:
  - ◆ Infinitive (the *to* form of the verb): *To open the document, click the icon.*
  - ◆ Imperative (a command or request form of the verb): *First open the document.*
  - ◆ Simple present: *First you open the document.*
  - ◆ Simple past: *First you opened the document.*
  - ◆ Future: *First you will open the document.*
- **Use active verbs.** The active voice makes stronger statements than the passive voice and may be easier for nonnative English speakers to understand. For information on when the passive voice is appropriate in a sentence, and for tips on strengthening your verbs, see Chapter 13, "Shorten and Strengthen Sentences."
- **Keep subject and verb close together.** When the noun (or pronoun) and verb are separated by a lot of other words, readers have to hunt for the words that belong together. This can be especially confusing if the extra words include other verbs. This structure slows comprehension of your message.

Example

Before

Good writers, no matter how much they like to interrupt themselves with a verbal diversion, imagine a magnet between subject and verb.

After
Good writers imagine a magnet between subject and verb, no matter how much they like to interrupt themselves with a verbal diversion.

■ **Avoid splitting verbs.** Try not to separate parts of infinitives (such as *to walk*) or phrasal verbs that include an adverb (such as *switch off* or *log on*). This makes readers hunt for words that belong together. However, *do* split a verb if doing so sounds more natural or makes a point: *The company plans to more than triple its workforce in Asia.* See "Old 'rules' that no longer apply" on page 348.

Examples

Before
She likes to slowly walk along the seashore.

After
She likes to walk slowly along the seashore.

Before
Don't switch the power off before you shut the computer down.

After
Don't switch off the power before you shut down the computer.

■ **Stay positive.** Positively constructed sentences tend to be more effective (and easier to understand) than the same information stated negatively. Positive sentences also make your site's voice sound friendly.

Example

Before
Don't forget to pick up your children by 5 p.m. Unfortunately, our school cannot be responsible for their safety after the holiday carnival has ended. *("Don't forget," "Unfortunately," and "cannot" are all negative wordings that can make readers feel scolded; "cannot be responsible" negates your credibility.)*

After

Please remember to pick up your children by 5 p.m., when the holiday carnival ends. **School facilities will close at 5 p.m.** As always, we will monitor the children's activities during the event. *("Please remember" is a pleasant reminder; the important information is bolded. The final sentence underscores your credibility.)*

- **Avoid multiple negatives.** Sometimes negatives (such as *no, not, nothing, no one*) are unavoidable. But sentences with more than one negative word can be difficult to understand. Rewrite such sentences to keep them positive. (One exception: sentences with *neither* and *nor*. For information on constructing sentences with *neither . . . nor* and other correlatives, see "Parallelism: Matching, balancing, making sense" on page 341.)

Example

Before

You may not activate Parental Controls if no member account is created.

After

Before you can activate Parental Controls, you must set up a member account for each person.

Paragraphs

Paragraphs, like sentences, should be concise, especially since you have only a few seconds to capture a reader's attention. Short paragraphs are easy to scan and understand. Follow these basic guidelines:

- Build every paragraph on **one** idea or topic.
- **Front-load** the essential point. Put the most important information—a topic sentence or a conclusion—first. In journalism and online, if readers aren't hooked by the first few words in a paragraph, they probably won't read further.
- Keep paragraphs **short**—two or three sentences is often enough.

Example

Before

Creating a financial portfolio is fast, easy, and free. You can create and maintain as many portfolios as you like with a single account. If you don't yet have an account, you will need to register for one before you can create a portfolio (registration is free and also allows you to take advantage of our many other products and services). We currently offer several different ways to track your portfolio (select a link to learn more):

(Too many ideas in one paragraph)

After

Creating a financial portfolio is fast, easy, and free. With a single account, you can create and maintain as many portfolios as you like.

If you don't have an account, you must register for one before you can create a portfolio. Registration is free and allows you to take advantage of our many other products and services.

We offer several ways to track your portfolio. <u>Learn more now</u>.

(Each idea gets a separate short paragraph)

Lists

Sometimes the most effective way to present information is in a list. Lists can draw a reader's attention, make text easier to scan and read, add white space to a page, shorten copy, relate items, and show a sequence or the level of importance.

A list may be numbered, bulleted, or embedded in a sentence. Each type of list has its proper use.

Using numbered lists

Use a numbered list when the sequence or numbering of the list items is important, as with the steps in a procedure or a top 10 list.

Example

To create an eruption:
1. Stack four Mentos candies next to a plastic bottle of carbonated soda.
2. Open the bottle of soda.
3. Drop in the candies.
4. Stand back.

T I P Brief items may work better as a numbered or lettered list embedded in the sentence. For example: *The story "The Truth About Harold's Brain" was disqualified from the contest finals because (a) we could not confirm that this story told the truth, (b) we could not confirm Harold's identity, and (c) we could not locate the author.*

Using bulleted lists

Bulleted lists work best for related items when the sequence is not important. Ideally, each item in a bulleted list carries the same weight and importance; for example, all items could be movie titles or features of a new product. If possible, each item should also be approximately the same length.

Try to use parallel construction for items in a bulleted list. Each should start with the same part of speech—noun, verb, and so forth.

Example

Muriel instructed the wedding DJ not to play any of these songs:
- "Brick House"
- "Celebration"
- "Macarena"
- "The Chicken Dance"

Muriel's partner noted that Muriel needed to:
- Lighten up already
- Realize that she was not the only person getting married

Example

Our weekend "staycation" involved:
- Going out for breakfast, lunch, *and* dinner
- Splurging on spa treatments
- Seeing a midnight movie at FilmWorld
- Sleeping until noon

Introducing lists

Most lists need a heading or a sentence of introduction to let the reader know why the list is important. Introduce a numbered or bulleted list with **a sentence fragment or a sentence ending in a colon**.

Examples

For lunch we had:
- A tuna sandwich
- A bag of chips
- An oatmeal cookie

You should see what Inna made us for lunch:
- A portobello mushroom sandwich
- French fries
- A chocolate-chip cookie

_____

If you introduce the list with a sentence fragment, make sure that each list item can complete the sentence logically.

Example

Before

Your cover letter should include:
- A description of your current responsibilities
- Your job search

(Your cover letter can include reasons for your job search or information about your job search, but not the search itself.)

After

Your cover letter should include:
- A description of your current responsibilities
- Reasons for your job search

_____

Styling list items consistently

Follow these guidelines for **capitalizing and punctuating** the items in a numbered or bulleted list:

- **If one or more of the list items is a complete sentence:** Capitalize the first word of every list item and use ending punctuation after each item. A list item is considered a complete sentence if, removed from the context of the list, it could stand on its own as a sentence. This may include an item that completes the list's introductory line, if the item reads like a full sentence on its own (see the following example).
- **If all the list items are sentence fragments:** Don't use any ending punctuation—even if the items complete a sentence fragment that introduces the list. The first word of each list item can be either uppercase or lowercase. Capitalize every item the same way in every list in the document or on the site.

Examples

All complete sentences
To reach the hotel from the airport, you can:
- Reserve the hotel shuttle.
- Hire a taxi.
- Ride an airport shuttle.
- Ride a public bus.

(Although each list item completes the fragment "you can," each could also be considered a complete sentence if removed from the context of this list.)

One complete sentence (see last item), requiring all items to have periods
Hotel policy states:
- No pets.
- No smoking.
- No late checkouts. Checkout time is 11 a.m.

All sentence fragments, capitalized
Guests can reach the hotel from the airport using any of the following:
- The hotel shuttle
- A taxi
- An airport shuttle
- A public bus

All sentence fragments, lowercased

Guests can reach the hotel from the airport using any of the following:

- the hotel shuttle
- a taxi
- an airport shuttle
- a public bus

TIP   If some items in your list are sentences and some are sentence fragments, you may have a nonparallel list. (See "Parallelism: Matching, balancing, making sense" on page 341.)

Lists within lists?

Avoid embedding a list within a list—a complicated list can be hard to follow. If you must embed a list within a list, use a different bullet style for the embedded list.

Examples

Bulleted lists

Guests can reach the hotel from the airport using any of the following:

- The hotel shuttle
- A taxi
- An airport shuttle
- A public bus:
    - No. 4 "Springtown"
    - No. 16 "Balboa Express"
    - No. 1 "Kent Street"

Mixed lists

You voted, we listened. Your favorites, in order, were:

1. Candy
    - Dark chocolate
    - Milk chocolate
    - Gummi worms
2. Cake
    - Cupcakes of any kind
    - Red velvet cake
    - Yellow cake

Ideas in Practice

Example: Hook readers with head-turning headlines

In print, headlines aim to grab readers' attention—sometimes by being witty rather than by summarizing the story. Subheadings, if any, are there to break up the text visually or thematically. On the Web, headlines and subheadings perform those functions and more: They're the most important text on the page for readers and search engines. Because headlines may be read out of context, without accompanying photos and sometimes without the rest of the story, they must be literal and loaded with search keywords.

In the sample blog below, read *only* the headline and subheadings. Do you know what the story is about? If not, the headings haven't done their job. Read our solution to see how we would turn these headings into head turners.

Before

Say It Ain't So, Joe

Can a mom-and-pop coffee shop survive a recession? The Bean Scene community has been obsessed with that question lately, as you independent coffee retailers (and your fans) wonder how you can stay afloat when large companies are sinking.

The bad news
There's no such thing as a recession-proof business. Customers are feeling the economic crunch, and while they first eliminate big expenses like cars and vacations, they also cut back on little luxuries and conveniences like movie tickets, restaurant meals, and specialty coffee.

More bad news
Shops must be smart to survive even when the economy is healthy. According to the U.S. Small Business Administration, just 44 percent of small businesses survive for four years, and only 31 percent see a seventh anniversary.

The good news
Lots of small businesses do survive, even thrive, during a recession. The secret of success is no secret at all: Do what good businesses always do; namely, listen to your customers, focus on strategies that work, and quickly eliminate strategies that don't. Shops that are responsive and creative should do well in any economy.

Get in the Espresso Lane

In our readers' poll, 82 percent of you were "very sure" or "pretty sure" that your coffee shop would make it through the next year, which is great news. Here are some of the tips you shared for keeping the customers coming in:

- Offer a rush-hour "express lane" for people buying regular coffee, and discount the price so that it competes with home brews.
- Promote specials at nonpeak hours: Try Macchiato Mondays, Afternoon Tea.
- Give discounts to students or local businesses.
- Offer loyalty cards (buy 10, get 1 free).
- Cater: Make sure local businesses know that you can provide refreshments for their meetings.
- Provide customers with a home office away from home—with Wi-Fi, printers, and the like.
- Attract lunchtime crowds by adding sandwiches or soup to the menu.
- Sell coffeemakers, grinders, and beans for customers who like your products but want to save money by making coffee at home.

After

Coffee Shops Battle Recession

Can a mom-and-pop coffee shop survive a recession? The Bean Scene community has been obsessed with that question lately, as you independent coffee retailers (and your fans) wonder how you can stay afloat when large companies are sinking.

Cash-strapped consumers kick coffee

The bad news: There's no such thing as a recession-proof business. Customers are feeling the economic crunch, and while they first eliminate big expenses like cars and vacations, they also cut back on little luxuries and conveniences like movie tickets, restaurant meals, and specialty coffee.

Small businesses struggle in all economies

Shops must be smart to survive even when the economy is healthy. According to the U.S. Small Business Administration, just 44 percent of small businesses survive for four years, and only 31 percent see a seventh anniversary.

You can prosper during an economic downturn

The good news: Lots of small businesses do survive, even thrive, during a recession. The secret of success is no secret at all: Do what good businesses always do;

namely, listen to your customers, focus on strategies that work, and quickly eliminate strategies that don't. Shops that are responsive and creative should do well in any economy.

8 ways to keep your coffee shop in the black

In our readers' poll, 82 percent of you were "very sure" or "pretty sure" that your coffee shop would make it through the next year, which is great news. Here are some of the tips you shared for keeping the customers coming in:

1. Offer a rush-hour "express lane" for people buying regular coffee, and discount the price so that it competes with home brews.
2. Promote specials at nonpeak hours: Try Macchiato Mondays, Afternoon Tea.
3. Give discounts to students or local businesses.
4. Offer loyalty cards (buy 10, get 1 free).
5. Cater: Make sure local businesses know that you can provide refreshments for their meetings.
6. Provide customers with a home office away from home—with Wi-Fi, printers, and the like.
7. Attract lunchtime crowds by adding sandwiches or soup to the menu.
8. Sell coffeemakers, grinders, and beans for customers who like your products but want to save money by making coffee at home.

Solution notes

Our sample blog had a multitude of headline problems, from inconsistent capitalization to bad puns, which are neither informative nor consistent with the serious tone of the blog. (Would you want someone joking if you were worried about your business going under?) Most important, though, the headings didn't summarize the blog. If the headline "Say It Ain't So, Joe" popped up as a link in your news feed, you'd have no idea what the story was about and perhaps wouldn't click to find out.

People interested in a blog like this would likely look for words such as *coffee, recession, small business,* or variations on *economy,* so those are the keywords we put in our revised headings.

Speak to Your Entire Audience

Chapter 5

Be Inclusive, Write for the World

In this chapter

- **Banish bias.** Use language that's friendly, fair, and credible to everyone.
- **Write gender-neutral copy.** Choose words that naturally include both men and women.
- **Write for an international audience.** Write clearly constructed sentences using simple words to help readers grasp your meaning.

"Are you talking to *me*?"

That's a question your site's visitors are asking as they decide whether to read further or find another website. If they feel confused, excluded, or offended by your content, they won't be back.

Although your first priority is to serve your target audience (see Chapter 2, "Identify Your Audience"), your site should welcome everyone. And "everyone" is likely to be a diverse bunch. After all, the three letters that begin most Web addresses—*www*—stand for *World Wide Web*.

To assume that your readers are all men, or all American, or all in their 20s, for example—even if your target audience *is* young men living in the U.S.—is a mistake. On the Web, you are often writing for a diverse audience, even an international one. Bias-free writing that is easy for every reader to understand will help you communicate with the world.

Banish bias

A basic principle of medical practice, "First, do no harm," might well be rephrased for content writers as "First, do not assume"—that is, **do not assume that you know who's reading your website**. Your audience is not homogeneous; its members almost certainly vary in age, race, gender, physical abilities, nationality, culture, sexual orientation, and so on.

Biased language, no matter how mild, excludes members of your audience and can even lead to inaccuracies that damage your credibility. For example, using the pronoun *he* in reference to judges is both factually wrong and liable to offend some of your readers (not to mention some present and former justices of the U.S. Supreme Court).

Some **guiding principles for avoiding bias**:

- **Determine whether a group-specific reference is relevant.** If a person's age, race, or gender is not relevant to the story, don't mention it. If you're writing about the first woman admitted to Harvard Medical School, gender is relevant; but if you're writing about a local surgeon who has won a prestigious grant, her gender probably isn't the point of the story (winning the grant) and doesn't need to be specially mentioned.

- **Be exact.** Do you say *Chinese* when you mean *Chinese American*? *African American* when you're talking about black people around the world? *Girls* when you're referring to adult women? *Retirees* when *senior citizens* or *people 65 and older* would be more precise? (Some people retire in their 40s, and the "official" retirement age may vary by country.) Use exact words and the terms favored by the group.

- **Beware of false generalizations.** If you find yourself implying that *all* members of a group behave the same way—as in "Women are lousy drivers"—stop. Similarly, speaking for "everyone" or using broad terms like *normal* makes readers wonder, "Everyone but *me*? Normal compared to *what*?" *Normal* is not the opposite of *disabled, adopted, single-parent, gay, poor, minority,* or other words that may describe an individual.

- **Use *us* and *them* cautiously.** If you use pronouns like *we* or *us* to signal solidarity with your readers, make sure that they share your traits or opinions. You probably should not say, "We all love a good pinot," for example, unless you're writing for a site aimed at wine aficionados. Likewise, using *they* or *them* to mean "other people" or "people not like us" may show bias.

- **Don't make the characteristic the person.** Referring to a group by a characteristic, as in *the deaf,* can sound as though you're limiting them to that one characteristic. It's fine to say *women* or *Cuban Americans,* but you're often better off making a trait an adjective rather than a noun: *deaf people* rather than *the deaf, black people* rather than *blacks, elderly people* rather than *the elderly,* and so on.

- **Watch out for bias inherent in slang and other figures of speech.** Common expressions often have roots in biased or dated thinking. For instance, the expression *what a gyp,* meaning *what a rip-off,* was likely derived from a prejudice against Gypsies (or the Romany people, as most prefer to be called) and a belief that they were thieves. Similarly, it might seem innocuous to say "You can't teach an old dog new tricks" or "This is not your grandma's website," but consider how older readers will respond to those phrases. Not only are clichés like these likely to be offensive, but they are also a sign of stale writing that needs refreshing.

- **Don't overcompensate.** Trying to be too solicitous can also undermine your credibility. Don't overcorrect by using made-up words like *waitron* or co-opting an in-group's slang or usage—no matter how well-meaning you are or how hip you want to appear. Stick to standard terminology and aim for neutrality.

T I P Record your site's language policies in your style guide or word list (see Chapter 19, "Keep a Word List"), whether you're establishing general principles of bias-free writing, instructing writers to favor one term over another, or barring certain words and phrases.

Write gender-neutral copy

Often a person's gender is not relevant to the story you're telling. And calling attention to gender can seem sexist: There's no need to describe the flier of a downed plane as a *female pilot,* and there's no reason to describe Queen Victoria as a *mother of nine* in a discussion of the Boer Wars. (Gender-neutral text makes translation easier, too. See "Write for an international audience" on page 80.)

Avoiding gender bias can be tricky, because it's sometimes built right into familiar words (like *actress* or *fireman*). In the not-so-distant past, students were taught to use masculine words generically, as in "Man is a product of his environment." Nowadays such usage seems dated and biased—not to mention incorrect, as 50 percent of "man" is womankind.

Fortunately, it's possible to use gender-neutral language without resorting to *he or she, he/she, s/he,* and other clumsy constructions.

When to avoid gender-specific pronouns

Here's a good rule of thumb: **Be specific.** Use *he, his,* and *him* when talking about men and boys, and *she, her,* and *hers* when talking about women and girls. But **avoid using masculine or feminine pronouns generically**, as in "Every doctor must complete his residency" or "Every doctor must complete her residency."

Some writers avoid those pronouns by using *he or she, his or her*: "Every doctor must complete his or her residency" (awkward). Others solve the problem by using the nonspecific *their,* as in "Every doctor must complete their residency"—a grammatically controversial usage that could provoke criticism. Such phrasing is not usually necessary.

Instead, use one of these **strategies for eliminating gender-specific pronouns**:[9]

- **Use the imperative.** The command form of a verb lets you use the second person (*you* and *your*) rather than the third person (*he* and *his* or *she* and *her*).

> **Example**

Before
A caller should enter his passcode to join the meeting.

After

Enter your passcode to join the meeting.

■ **Make nouns and pronouns plural.**

> **Example**

Before

Each job applicant should email his or her resumé to human resources.
Each job applicant should email their resumé to human resources.

After

Job applicants should email their resumés to human resources.

■ **Repeat the noun, especially if it helps clarify meaning.**

> **Example**

Before

A cooking student should respect the chef and keep his knives sharp. *(It's unclear whether "his" refers to the student or to the chef, and whether either is male.)*

After

A cooking student should respect the chef and keep the chef's knives sharp.

■ **Eliminate the pronoun.**

> **Example**

Before

When you're instant-messaging a friend, send them a graphic to show them how you feel.

After

When you're instant-messaging a friend, send a graphic to show how you feel.

■ **Substitute *a* or *the* for the pronoun.**

Example

Before

You may know the person who sent the attachment, but that doesn't guarantee that his or her file is virus-free.

After

You may know the person who sent the attachment, but that doesn't guarantee that the file is virus-free.

■ **Use the passive voice when the actor is unimportant.**

Example

Before

I called the cable company, but they haven't activated the service yet.

After

I called the cable company, but the service hasn't been activated yet.

■ **Rewrite the sentence.**

Example

Before

Select another member as your Music Mentor, and the songs that he/she rates high will be added to your playlist.

After

Songs rated high by the member you select as your Music Mentor will be added to your playlist.

Replace gender-specific words

Most gendered nouns in English are related to professions. Usually, these terms can be replaced by neutral ones. **Replace feminine or masculine nouns with nouns that work for everyone**—change a word like *stewardess* or *steward* to another, such as *flight attendant*. Try the following substitutions:[10]

Do not use	Use
actress	actor
businessman	businessperson (or be specific: stockbroker, shopkeeper, store owner, executive, etc.)
chairman	chair, chairperson
craftsman	craftsperson, artisan
fireman	firefighter
layman	layperson
mailman, postman	mail carrier, letter carrier (for people who deliver the mail); postal worker, postal employee (for any post office employee)
man (a person)	person, individual, human, people
to man (verb)	to operate, to staff
mankind	humanity, people, the human race, humankind
manmade	synthetic, manufactured, artificial, constructed, handmade, fabricated, handcrafted, machine-made
manpower	workforce, staff, personnel, workers, employees, labor, labor force
policeman	police officer
salesman, saleswoman, saleslady	salesperson, sales representative, sales clerk
spokesman	spokesperson, representative
stewardess, steward	flight attendant
waitress	server, waitperson

Write for an international audience

Because the Web is a worldwide medium, your site visitors probably come from more than one country and more than one culture. Collectively, they probably speak several languages. It's a good practice to **make the text on your site clear to as many people as possible**.

Clear language helps everyone

Writing for worldwide readability may **extend your global reach**. The online U.S. population is more than 163 million people.[11] Sounds impressive, but those millions represent just a small percentage of the total Internet audience. Globally, more than *1 billion* people are surfing the Web—and it's a safe bet that English is not the first language for most of them.

In the U.S., most people speak English and many are native speakers; nonetheless, English **reading comprehension may still be an issue**. According to the U.S. Department of Education, 43 percent of Americans have low (basic or below-basic) literacy skills.[12]

T I P Are you optimizing your site for a U.S. audience? Don't assume that all Americans speak English. People in the U.S. are a diverse lot who speak more than 300 languages.[13] Although 80 percent of U.S. households speak only English at home,[14] that percentage varies widely by region. In Texas, for example, 66 percent of people speak only English at home;[15] in California, the number is closer to 50 percent.[16] If you don't take these factors into account, you may unknowingly exclude potential readers or customers.

Writing for a worldwide Web audience makes your text more understandable to everyone—including your core readership. It also makes a translator's job easier, if you offer your content in multiple languages. (For more information on translation and website localization, see "Standardize, internationalize, or localize?" on page 82.)

Making your content understandable to people with varying reading skills doesn't mean dumbing it down or losing your unique voice. Be literal, simple, and clear, and use your best judgment about what will sound natural to your audience. For example, some of the techniques in this section may lengthen your sentences or make them sound slightly repetitive to a native speaker of English. Know your audience, and consider their needs.

To encourage global readability, start with the basic principles of good writing for the Web (see Chapter 1, "Write for the Web," and Chapter 4, "Construct Clear, Compelling Copy") and **follow these five best practices**:

1. Keep the sentence structure simple (subject-verb-object).
2. Include "signposts": words that help readers see how the parts of a sentence relate.
3. Eliminate ambiguity.
4. Avoid uncommon words and nonliteral usages (such as slang or irony).
5. Rewrite text that doesn't translate literally.

T I P   How easy is it to translate your text? For a quick idea of how well you've applied the principles in this chapter, test some of your copy in a free online translator like Yahoo!'s Babel Fish (http://babelfish.yahoo.com). Try translating a block of text or a full page into a chosen language. Do the results make sense? If not, check your copy again, paying particular attention to word order and choice, sentence structure, and spelling.

Standardize, internationalize, or localize?

If your site attracts a national or international readership (or you suspect that it might), think about the experience you're giving that diverse group. Consider revamping your site; or, if you're just starting out, build it with that group in mind.

You have three basic choices: to standardize, to internationalize, or to localize your site.

Standardization is the one-size-fits-all strategy: a single language and the same content for both domestic and international readers. This approach can work just fine for a narrow audience, such as the one for a neighborhood clothing boutique.

A standardized site may also offer minimal international content, such as a page for every country where the company does business. For example, the site of a Viennese opera house might offer program descriptions in multiple languages but ticketing only in German. Generally, this type of "standardization-plus" doesn't provide the best user experience, because text usually drives the user experience.

Internationalization involves developing a website or a piece of content in such a way that it can be localized later. The internationalized site itself might not offer content optimized for more than one audience, but the text is designed to be easy to translate and understand, with simple syntax, clear wording, and little or no slang or culture-specific references. For instance, a global news service might want to internationalize its stories so that news sites worldwide can grab copy from the wire and translate it quickly into their local languages.

Localization means adapting a site or its content for a particular language, region, or group. Research shows that most users prefer sites in their local language, so localization offers a better user experience: The site adapts to readers rather than the other way around.

The degree of localization can vary significantly. All localized sites feature text in the local language, which may be copy that was translated from a parent site or a partner. The content, coding, and design may go beyond translation to customization: The site may convert date formats and currency, use a layout and images that will appeal to that culture, and create original content for the local audience. Highly localized sites address a specific audience, so elements like slang and cultural references (see "Culture-specific references" on page 42) might be acceptable and even desirable.

What should you do? If your site has a limited regional readership, standardize. If not, internationalize your site, starting with the writing techniques in this chapter. If you want to go all out—and you have the money, the team, and the time to do it right—localize. Localization is a labor-intensive process that requires a complete strategy: You'll probably need to involve other groups at your company (such as marketing and design), to hire translators and Web developers, and to recruit local experts and content creators.

Keep sentence structure simple

If you are familiar with a language other than English, you already know that word order varies: Some languages put the subject after the verb (*barks the dog*), the verb at the end of the sentence (*the dog at the squirrel barks*), or adjectives after the noun (*the dog noisy*).

People who speak and read some English are prepared for basic English word order, even if it's different from what they're used to. But more complex sentences can be confusing and can slow such readers (as well as native English speakers) considerably. Help all readers find value in your site by keeping sentences short and simple.

Follow these **guidelines to construct clear sentences** (for more details on these basic guidelines, see "Sentences" on page 59):

- **Limit the number of words per sentence.** Brevity is especially important when you're giving directions or instructions, or when the copy is dense with numbers or technical information.
- **Use subject-verb-object sentence structure.** Subject-verb-object is one of the most common word orders worldwide, the basic syntax for English, Romance languages such as French, and more.[17] It will be familiar to many readers.
- **Keep verbs simple and active.** Often the hardest part of a language to learn, verbs have many tenses, many persons, irregular conjugations, and so on. Help your readers by using the simplest form that makes sense and is grammatically correct.
- **Avoid double negatives.** A hearty *no* is useful, particularly when you're warning users not to do something. But double or multiple negatives slow down readers; it's better to keep the expression positive or to use just one negative. The reader wants to know what to do, not what *not* to do. (See? That was hard to read.)
- **Word questions positively whenever possible.** Negative questions—such as "*Don't* you think durian is the most delicious fruit on the planet?"—can be confusing. In the United States, a *yes* response means "Yes, I think that durians are delicious." But in some other countries, a *yes* means "Yes, I do *not* think that durians are delicious; in fact, they smell like a soiled diaper full of decomposing onions."

Signpost your sentences for an international audience

Native English speakers often omit words that help explain how the parts of a sentence relate to each other. For example, they might say, "Most sentences include subject, verb, and object" rather than "Most sentences include *a* subject, *a* verb, and *an* object." Omitting such words reduces repetition and makes the sentence shorter and more natural sounding—as we suggest throughout this book. But such cropping also makes the sentence less precise. And when you know that your site will be speaking to an international audience—for instance, if it is an online course that will be translated into Spanish, or a business website with global clients—precision is essential. It helps nonnative English speakers navigate your content, and it helps translators (human and electronic) stay true to your meaning.

Plant some "signposts" along the road: words and punctuation that can be especially helpful for less proficient readers.

Follow these guidelines to **write simpler sentences for an international audience**:

Signpost: Repeat words as necessary to clarify meaning

Native English speakers tend to leave out some small words in casual writing as unnecessary for understanding. And most of the time, this is fine. But just because you know what you're talking about doesn't mean that others will.

- **Repeat a verb that belongs with more than one subject or that has more than one object** so that readers don't have to fill in the blank.

> **Example**
>
> **Before**
> New members visiting for the first time and any guests must check in at the registration desk to receive an annual or day pass.
>
> **After**
> New members visiting for the first time must check in at the registration desk to receive an annual pass. Guests must check in to receive a day pass.

- **Repeat helper verbs that belong with multiple verbs.** (Use your judgment: This technique may result in sentences that sound repetitive to native English speakers. Follow this guideline when your audience includes many whose first language is not English, when your copy will be localized or translated, or when you need to clarify long or confusing sentences.)

> **Example**

Before

If equipped with the DishWash 2.0 plug-in, the Housekeeper 3000 robot can hand-wash your fine china, crystal, and other valuables and place dishwasher-safe items in the washer.

After

If equipped with the DishWash 2.0 plug-in, the Housekeeper 3000 robot can hand-wash your fine china, crystal, and other valuables and can place dishwasher-safe items in the washer.

■ **Repeat subjects and verbs as necessary** to make it absolutely clear who's acting.

> **Example**

Before

Jorge likes fishing trips but not John. *(Because there's only one verb, "not" seems to go with "likes": Jorge likes fishing trips but does not like John.)*

After

Jorge likes fishing trips, but John doesn't. *(Repeat at least part of the verb to clarify.)*
or
Jorge likes fishing trips, but John doesn't like them. *(Repeat the verb and the object if a significant portion of your audience may need the extra help.)*

■ **In a series, repeat markers** such as *to* with each infinitive verb, and possessives, especially if a lot of words separate the elements in the series.

> **Examples**

Before

They changed their wedding vows to "I promise to love and honor you, care for you in sickness and in health, order pizza on Fridays, let you sleep late on Saturdays, and hire a housekeeper so that we never argue about laundry on Sundays."

After

They changed their wedding vows to "I promise to love and honor you, to care for you in sickness and in health, to order pizza on Fridays, to let you sleep late on Saturdays, and to hire a housekeeper so that we never argue about laundry on Sundays."

Before

The latest model of the company's voting machine records the users' rates of error and votes. *(A machine that records error rates is fine, but only people should vote.)*

After

The latest model of the company's voting machine records the users' rates of error and the users' votes. *(Repeat the possessive "users'" to prevent misreading.)*

Better

The latest model of the company's voting machine records the users' rates of error and also records the users' votes. *(Repeat the verb as well as the possessive for additional clarity.)*

Signpost: Retain words like *then, a, the, to,* and *that*

Particularly in long sentences and series, keeping these little words aids understanding.

- Include both halves of word pairs such as *both-and, either-or, neither-nor,* and even *if-then.* (These are called correlative conjunctions.) Many native English speakers leave out the word *then* in *if-then* constructions, but in long sentences or when the readers aren't native English speakers, *then* can be helpful. For more information on other correlative conjunctions, including *both-and* and *either-or,* see "Common grammatical mistakes" on page 331.

Example

Before

If you give the baby applesauce but don't wear an apron that covers you from head to toe, you'll end up wearing the applesauce.

After

If you give the baby applesauce but don't wear an apron that covers you from head to toe, then you'll end up wearing the applesauce.

■ Include an article (*a, an,* or *the*) for every noun in a series. Some sentences will be clear enough without repeated articles, but if there's any room for confusion, use an article with each noun.

Example

Before
When I make gazpacho, I always dice a tomato, half a cucumber, yellow onion, and red pepper.

After
When I make gazpacho, I always dice a tomato, a half a cucumber, a yellow onion, and a red pepper.

_____

■ Include *that* after these verbs: *assume, be sure, ensure, indicate, make sure, mean, require, specify, suppose,* and *verify.*[18] *That* signals to the reader that a separate subject and verb follow. Also, repeat *that* if the verb applies to multiple clauses.

Examples

Before
Make sure all the images on your webpage have alternative text.

After
Make sure that all the images on your webpage have alternative text. *("That" helps readers see that a separate subject and verb follow: "all the images . . . have.")*

Before
If you care about searchability, specify that all the images have alternative text and all the videos have a keyword-rich description.

After
If you care about searchability, specify that all the images have alternative text and that all the videos have a keyword-rich description.

_____

■ Include *that* with restrictive (essential) clauses that modify a noun. For example, in the sentence "I looked at a lot of cars, but the one that I want is a blue hybrid," "that I want" is a clause describing the noun. *Restrictive* means that the clause is essential to the meaning of the sentence. You can't remove a restrictive clause—in the preceding example, cutting "that I want" would leave you with "I looked at a lot of cars, but the one is a blue hybrid," which doesn't make sense.

Writers sometimes omit *that* from restrictive clauses, but doing so removes a marker that helps many readers untangle nouns and verbs and comprehend the sentence. (For more information on essential and nonessential clauses, see "that, which" on page 325.)

Example

Before

Muriel wants to take a vacation in Buenos Aires, but the hotel she likes is fully booked, and the tango school her dance teacher recommends closes in August for the ski season.

After

Muriel wants to take a vacation in Buenos Aires, but the hotel that she likes is fully booked, and the tango school that her dance teacher recommends closes in August for the ski season.

Signpost: Stay away from unclear referents

Pronouns that don't clearly stand for any noun in particular—called unclear referents—can lead to confusion.

- Avoid using *this, that, these,* or *those* as standalone pronouns. If you do, readers have to backtrack to see what the pronoun refers to, and they may not be able to tell. Try to pair these words with a noun.

Example

Before

The skateboarders never walk down the stairs; they like to skate past people on the ramp or slide down the railing. This can lead to skinned knees and broken bones. *(What causes the injuries: falling off the railing? running into people on the ramp? both?)*

After

The skateboarders never walk down the stairs; they like to skate past people on the ramp or slide down the railing. These activities can lead to skateboarders getting skinned knees and broken bones. *("These activities" clarifies that the writer is referring to skating on both ramp and railing, and the second half clarifies that only the skateboarders are likely to be injured.)*

■   Beware the genderless pronoun. *They* and *them* and *it* are English pronouns with no gender, but some languages don't have gender-neutral pronouns. In French and Italian, for example, pronouns, like nouns, are almost always masculine or feminine. The result: Words like *it* and *they* have a high potential for confusion and can cause difficulties for translators. For example, if Italian translators cannot tell whether *it* refers to *knife* (masculine) or *fork* (feminine) in a sentence, they can't tell whether to translate *it* as *lo* (a masculine pronoun) or *la* (a feminine one). So don't use genderless pronouns unless it's absolutely clear which nouns they're related to.

Example

Before

Press and hold the red button for 10 seconds to shut down the machine. After 30 seconds, press the On button next to the display, but watch it carefully during start-up in case any error codes appear. *(Does "it" refer to the machine? the On button? the display?)*

After

Press and hold the red button for 10 seconds to shut down the machine. After 30 seconds, press the On button next to the display. Watch the display carefully during start-up in case any error codes appear.

Signpost: Punctuate clearly

The more careful and consistent you are with standard English punctuation, the more likely that readers will understand a sentence's structure. Commas and hyphens in particular can help clarify. Follow our guidelines for using commas and hyphens (see Chapter 10, "Punctuate Proficiently"), but when the guidelines leave room either to use or to omit a comma or a hyphen, retain the mark for added clarity.

Be alert to ambiguity

English is an elastic language—you can make a single statement in a dozen different ways by varying the word order and using synonyms. But that very flexibility and variety can challenge your readers, and a misplaced word can lead to misunderstanding.

Avoid *-ing* words

Words ending in *ing* can confuse readers, because they serve multiple grammatical roles.

- Gerunds (nouns formed from verbs): *Voting is a right.*
- Adjectives: *The U.S. House of Representatives includes 435 voting members, plus nonvoting delegates from territories and the District of Columbia.*
- Parts of verbs: *Americans are voting in record numbers.*
- Parts of nouns: *Voting machines aren't as reliable as old-fashioned paper ballots.*
- Parts of phrases modifying nouns: *People voting absentee must submit their ballots by June 1.*

Not all languages have equivalents to *-ing* words. If you must use one, make sure that the word's meaning is clear.

Example

Before

Formatting Menus *(Is this heading using "formatting" as an adjective, describing a type of menu, or is it using "formatting" as a verb, explaining how you can format menus?)*

After

How to Format Menus

Avoid ambiguous words and usages

Sometimes a word can seem ambiguous because it has multiple meanings. For instance, *once, right,* and *since* are notoriously confusing, even for native English speakers. For ways to prevent misreading caused by these words, see "Words that may confuse readers" on page 329.

In his book *The Global English Style Guide,* John R. Kohl notes some other words and constructions that can cause confusion:[19]

- ***Require* + infinitive.** Readers should have no trouble understanding the meaning of *require,* but they may have more difficulty telling who or what *require* applies to. Be cautious when using *require* with an infinitive (the *to* form of a verb).

Example

Before

Three sailors are required to cook for the crew. *(Does that mean that the job requires three people or that three sailors must report to the kitchen while the rest of the sailors complete other assignments?)*

After

The job of cooking for the crew requires three sailors.

or

Three sailors must cook for the crew; all other sailors should clean the decks.

- *Appear* **+ infinitive.** Use caution with *appear,* which can mean either *become visible* or *seem.* Make sure that readers can identify which meaning you intend.

Example

Before

The dialog box appears to offer suggestions for rescuing the file. *(Is the dialog box popping up to offer suggestions? Or is the dialog-box message poorly written, and the writer is guessing that it's offering file-rescue tips?)*

After

The dialog box appears and offers suggestions for rescuing the file.

or

The dialog box seems to offer suggestions for rescuing the file.

- *Has* **or** *have* **+ past participle.** Kohl notes that this combination can also be confusing. Past participles can be part of a past tense, such as *roasted* in *I have roasted the chicken*. But past participles can also modify nouns, as in *I have a roasted chicken in the refrigerator*. So, when readers encounter *has* or *have* with a past participle, they may not be able to tell immediately whether the participle is part of the verb or is describing the noun.

Example

Before

My email application has deleted messages in the inbox.

After

My email application keeps deleted messages in the inbox.

or

My email application deleted messages from the inbox.

Eliminate the uncommon

Simple sentence structure and carefully placed words will help all readers navigate your text. But if you know (or suspect) that your audience includes less proficient readers, be vigilant in cutting words and usages that your readers may not understand or may have to slow down to decipher.

Eliminate uncommon words

Common words are more understandable than uncommon words, so the latter should generally be avoided. For a broad general audience, follow these guidelines:

- **Spell out shortened words** such as *app* (application), *con* (contra, confidence game, convict), *specs* (specifications or spectacles), *stats* (statistics), *vet* (veteran or veterinarian), *dupe* (duplicate or victim of deception), and *rep* (representative, reputation, repertory, or repetition). Some readers may not know these shortened forms, or they may mistake one definition for another. Use the whole word.
- **Avoid slang and idioms** unless you are certain that most or all of your audience is a highly specific group. Slang is culture-specific, region-specific, and sometimes group-specific. Australian slang is different from American slang, Londoners and Liverpudlians don't use the same idioms, and interest groups such as video gamers and baseball fans have their own unique vocabularies. And one word can have many meanings. For example, *cracker* can refer to malicious hackers, to early settlers of Florida, to white people (as an insult), to firecrackers, or to snacks.
- **Avoid professional and technical jargon**, including buzzwords specific to your company. If a technical term is really the only accurate or appropriate word, define the term right where you use it, instead of sending your reader to a glossary. For tips on getting rid of jargon, see "Junk the jargon" on page 308.
- **Avoid clichés** such as *think outside the box* or *pay through the nose.* Well-worn phrases are annoying to people who have read them countless times, and they often don't make literal sense, which renders them incomprehensible for nonnative English speakers and inconvenient for translators. See "Cut the clichés" on page 305.
- **Avoid neologisms**—new, made-up words and phrases. These can confuse or annoy readers, and, of course, they aren't easily translated. Check the most recent edition of your dictionary—if the word's not there, it may be too new to use.
- **Spell out acronyms** unless they're widely recognized (like *USA*). For details, see "Acronyms and other abbreviations" on page 234.
- **Avoid uncommon foreign words.** Some non-English words, such as *vice versa, in vitro,* and *hors d'oeuvre,* are common enough to include in your writing. Check the dictionary if you're not sure. But generally, simple English words—*appetizer* instead of *hors d'oeuvre,* for example—are a better choice. If you must use a less common non-English phrase, translate it where it appears or describe it in context.

- **Avoid unnecessary abbreviations.** An abbreviation such as *Wi-Fi* may be better known than its full-length spelling (*wireless fidelity*). However, abbreviations that seem common to you may be foreign to your readers. Substitute English words for Latin abbreviations like *i.e.* (*that is*) and *e.g.* (*for example*); spell out unnecessary abbreviations such as *n/a* (*not applicable*) and *aka* (*also known as*); and be cautious with measurements—if readers use the metric system, *lb.* and *in.* might confuse them.

- **Avoid unnecessary variations.** Synonyms enrich the language, but introducing less common words only for the sake of variety may challenge your reader. Furthermore, you may use the wrong word: Many synonyms are not exact matches; words have different connotations and nuances. Be especially careful and consistent with keywords (you want to repeat those) and with any terms you're using in help text or in the user interface. Make a list of terms that your site uses regularly (see Chapter 19), and see Chapter 7, "Write Clear User-Interface Text," for information on writing navigational copy.

Example

Before

Our <u>weekly newsletter</u> keeps you up-to-date on what's happening at the track. The bulletin contains track stats and results, our picks for upcoming races, and insider anecdotes. <u>Subscribe</u> today. *(Are the newsletter and the bulletin the same thing? If not, which one will the **Subscribe** link go to?)*

After

Our <u>weekly newsletter</u> keeps you up-to-date on what's happening at the track. <u>Subscribe</u> today to start receiving track statistics and results, our picks for upcoming races, and insider anecdotes.

T I P   Dictionaries and search engines are indispensable tools for editors. Consult the dictionary to make certain that you're using the correct word in the correct way, with the correct spelling (and not, for example, using *lite* instead of *light*). Use a search engine to help you make an informed decision about standardized phrasing, such as whether more people search on *cell phone* or *mobile phone*.

Eliminate uncommon usages

You want readers to understand your meaning immediately. The simplest way is to eliminate obscure, nonstandard, or variant usages that may baffle them.

- **Don't try to convert one part of speech to another.** Resist the urge to turn nouns into verbs, adjectives into nouns, and so on. For instance, *mouse* in the sense of *computer mouse* is recognized by dictionaries as a noun but not as a verb. Instead of saying *mouse over the link,* say *roll your cursor over the link*. Similarly, don't say *I GIF'd the photo* or *you have to PIN your new credit card.*

- **Avoid nonstandard and indirect verb usages.** Writers occasionally slip into colloquial speech. Avoid nonstandard verbs, such as *goes* or *I'm like* instead of *says* (*And then she goes, "I'm not cleaning my room tonight"* or *When I saw John I was like, "Dude! You've changed!"*) and *gets* instead of the passive *is* (*Autosave ensures that your file automatically gets saved*). Also, avoid indirect or unnecessarily complex constructions such as the *have* clause here: *Sign the contract and have it faxed to the lawyers.* Simpler and easier to understand is *Sign the contract and fax it to the lawyers.* Keep your verbs as active and direct as possible.

Example

Before
Set up Remote status, and your work email gets forwarded to your home email account.

After
Set up Remote status, and your work email is forwarded to your home email account.

Better
Set up Remote status to forward your work email to your home email account.

- **Use contractions cautiously.** Readers should know common contractions like *it's* and *she's,* and some may even understand an irregular contraction like *let's* (*let us*). But negative contractions—even simple ones like *can't* and *don't*—can be easily misread by people who are scanning quickly. You may want to spell these out for the sake of clarity if the information is especially important (for example, *Do not click **Buy** before you complete the form*). Also, avoid slangy, outdated, or less usual contractions such as *ain't, that'll, could've, shan't, 'tis,* and the unwieldy *shouldn't've.*

Rewrite text that doesn't translate easily

Simplifying words and sentence structures will go a long way toward making your content more reader friendly. But don't neglect the details: Subtle differences in culture or convention can render your copy less accessible to a worldwide audience. Be aware of these potential problem areas and rewrite as necessary.

Cultural and local conventions

Even though the Web is a worldwide medium, cultural conventions differ greatly by region, religion, age, and other demographics. Know your audience and what kind of experience it wants.

- **Formality.** Web content tends to be informal and conversational, but some groups and cultures may be offended by what they consider overly familiar language (for instance, *Hey, you guys!*). Study your target audience (see Chapter 2) to gauge the level of formality it expects.
- **Appropriateness.** Does your audience consider some topics, like sex or politics, off-limits? Will your readers accept suggestive language or graphic violence?
- **Cultural references.** If you say *It's hardly a white wedding, Keep it PG-13, I won't accept a room on the unlucky 13th floor,* or *That's just not cricket,* then you're making culture-specific references. Readers may miss your exact nuance or even the entire meaning. Only the U.S. assigns the movie rating PG-13, for example, and many East Asians consider 4 unlucky, not 13. And although many societies have adopted Western-style white wedding dresses, in some cultures white is a funeral color; what's more, not everyone will understand *white* as an allusion to virginity—they may think it's a racial connotation. Be careful with any reference to local customs, local history, sports, holidays, seasons (wintertime north of the equator is summertime south of the equator), and the like.
- **Local references.** Avoid using highly local terms unless you're sure that 90 percent of your audience is from the same city or region. For instance, referring to the *South Side* is fine if your audience lives in Chicago, Illinois, but anyone else may wonder, "The south side of what?" If you must use the reference, briefly explain it in context.

Numbers

Be careful with numbers and units of measurement. What you consider "standard" may not be. Consult Chapter 12, "Apply a Consistent Style for Numbers," for a complete guide to number style.

- **Measurements.** Most of the world uses the metric system. Even English units vary in some respects—for instance, a pint, a quart, and a gallon are different amounts in the U.S. and the U.K. For precision, many cooks and bakers worldwide use recipes that list ingredients by weight in grams or by volume in milliliters rather than in cups or tablespoons. Consider whether you should list amounts in both systems.
- **Abbreviating units of measurement.** Spell out abbreviations. Notations such as *20 mi., 5 oz.,* or *6'3"* won't mean much to a person who uses the metric system. Check your units, too: Something that seems standard, such as *MB* for *megabytes,* may not be—*MB* won't be understood in France, where the term is *mega octets,* abbreviated *Mo.* See "Units of measure" on page 273.
- **Currency.** Several countries (including Australia, Canada, Barbados, Liberia, and Singapore)

use a "dollar," but each dollar has a different value. Be careful with generic currency references such as *cent* or *pound;* know when your audience may not understand a phrase (*That store used to be a five-and-dime*); and, when necessary, indicate which currency you're talking about (such as *US$5*). See "Money and currency" on page 279.

■ **Date and time formats.** Unlike the U.S., most countries refer to dates in a day-month format (*9 March*) rather than a month-day format (*March 9*). It's safer to spell out dates (March 9, 2012) in running text than it is to use a slash format: *3/9/2012* could be taken for either March 9, 2012, or September 3, 2012. (See "Dates" on page 266.) If you must use a format with slashes or hyphens, as on a registration form, make sure to label the fields clearly.

■ **Phone numbers.** Does your format for phone numbers use hyphens, spaces, or parentheses? Do you need to include international calling codes on your contact pages? (For tips on formatting phone numbers, see "Phone numbers" on page 282.)

■ **Address formats.** Different countries use different address formats. Readers in India, for example, may not understand a reference to ZIP codes, and pull-down menus from which people choose their state would be useless to someone outside the U.S. Consider your audience.

As funny as a heart attack: Use rhetorical speech with care

"Be literal, be simple, and be clear" is the core principle of writing for a broad audience. Rhetorical speech is the opposite. Rhetorical techniques require a sophisticated understanding of the language, so they're not ideal for less proficient readers or for people who are scanning a page. Avoid the following techniques, or be very careful about how you execute them:

■ **Humor, including puns, wordplay, and irony.** Humor is not universal, irony may be misperceived, and wordplay can be obscure. You don't want to risk offending anyone. Unless you're positive that readers will get the joke, use humor sparingly and appropriately.

■ **Metaphor, simile, hyperbole (exaggeration), and other figures of speech.** Comparing one thing to another can illuminate meaning—when the reader has time to mentally process the analogy. Otherwise, a figure of speech introduces an extra concept that can be perplexing. Although it may be entertaining to say *After we revise the requirements, the programmers will go back to the engineering cave to see if they can make fire,* it's better to be literal: *After we revise the requirements, the programmers will rewrite the code to see if they can make it meet those requirements.*

Punctuation and capitalization

Conventions for punctuation and capitalization vary internationally. If you decide to adopt a different style from what this book recommends (see Chapters 10 and 11 for complete information on punctuation and capitalization), document your variations in a style guide or word list (see Chapter 19).

- **Capitalization.** The capitalization of words and acronyms varies from country to country. For instance, Americans capitalize both *AIDS* and *HIV,* but British publications use *Aids* and *HIV*. In the U.S. many writers capitalize each word in *Frequently Asked Questions* (FAQ), but in France *FAQ* stands for *Foire aux questions,* with only the first word capitalized. Consider the capitalization style your readers will expect for acronyms, headlines, and the like, and be consistent. For general capitalization rules, see Chapter 11, "Abbreviate, Capitalize, and Treat Titles Consistently," and for tips on treating elements such as buttons and links, see Chapter 7, "Write Clear User-Interface Text."
- **Quotation marks.** For rules about quotation marks, see page 224. Be aware, though, that American English and British English rules differ and that some countries use different marks, such as «», to set off quotations.
- **Symbols.** Icons, symbols, and special typographical characters can carry different meanings from culture to culture. Check whether your site visitors will see the same thing you do. For instance, some countries use a check mark (✔) to indicate *yes,* but Japan and Korea use an open circle (O), and in the U.S. a check mark can indicate both yes (on a ballot, for example) and no (on a graded examination). Also, watch your Net-speak: Not everyone will understand that *br@* is read as *brat* or that *b&width* means *bandwidth.*

Ideas in Practice

Example: Welcome the world

The passage that follows is website text for a fictional golf course called Red Grouse Greens. Until recently, Red Grouse Greens was private and for men only; now it has been bought by an international company and accepts both male and female players. Eventually, this copy will be translated into multiple languages for the parent company's website, to help attract tourists from around the world. Read our solution to see how we would edit the text to make it more inclusive for its global audience and more easily translatable.

Before

Red Grouse Greens

Men who love golf come from all around the country to Red Grouse Greens for first-class golfing. Our 18-hole links, designed by award-winning architect Rob McGuffin, offer stunning views of the Carolina coast and are located less than 15 miles from the Myrtle Beach International Airport. You'll enjoy the superior service that has kept Red Grouse Greens on the Top 100 Clubs list from Back Nine magazine for the past 10 years.

Come for a day trip (make a reservation for a tee time) or join us for a longer golf vacation. Our all-inclusive packages start at $900 per person for three days during high season (5/1 to 9/10) and feature airport transfers, a stay in our luxury villas, four-star low-country cuisine, lessons with our pros, full access to the clubhouse and pool, complimentary golf cart rental, and all green fees and taxes.

Club rules

To ensure a safer and more enjoyable experience for all, please observe the following rules:

1. Red Grouse Greens adheres to the USGA's rules of play.

2. Tee times not confirmed at least 24 hours in advance may not be honored.

3. Caddies cannot be booked by phone in advance; however, you can request a favorite when you turn up for your tee time at the clubhouse. If your caddie gives you the excellent service we expect he will, please feel free to give him a gratuity.

4. You can rent a cart at the clubhouse. To do so, drivers must be at least 18 years old and possess a valid driver's license, which they must present to rent a cart. You shouldn't drive carts within 30 ft. of the greens unless you have a special disability permit — the handicapped can get a permit at the clubhouse.

5. Players proceeding to the next hole should first repair any divots, cleat marks, or other damage to the course.

6. Golfers are expected to wear proper attire: full-length pants (no jeans or sweats) or Bermuda shorts, and shirts with collars (no T-shirts). No hats in the clubhouse.

7. Cell phones are banned except in villas. These can be used everywhere by physicians, if they set them to silent mode.

8. There is no smoking at the clubhouse or course.

For more information, contact us by email at info@redgrousegreens.com or by phone at (800) XXX-XXXX.

After

Red Grouse Greens

Myrtle Beach, South Carolina, USA (map and directions)

Golf lovers from around the world come to Red Grouse Greens for first-class golfing. Designed by award-winning architect Rob McGuffin, our 18-hole oceanside course offers stunning views of the South Carolina coast and is less than 15 miles (24 kilometers) from Myrtle Beach International Airport. Our superior service has kept Red Grouse Greens on Back Nine magazine's Top 100 Clubs list for the past 10 years.

Reserve a tee time for a single day, or join us for a longer golf vacation. Our vacation packages start at US$900 per person for three days during the high season (May 1 to September 10). All package prices include:

- Transportation between the airport and the club

- Lodging in our luxury villas, which have full kitchens, laundry machines, and more

- Meals at our four-star restaurant, which specializes in South Carolina's "low country" cooking, with lots of fresh local seafood (menu)

- Golf lessons with our professional instructors

- Golf cart rental

- All green fees (the cost of playing the course) and taxes

Club rules

To ensure a safe and enjoyable experience for everyone:

1. Follow the U.S. Golf Association's (USGA's) rules of golf.

2. Confirm your tee time at least 24 hours before you play, or you may lose your reservation.

3. Please don't call the clubhouse to reserve a caddie. But you may request your favorite caddie when you arrive for your tee time. We expect our caddies to provide excellent service. If they do, please feel free to tip them. Typically, golfers tip caddies 50 percent of the caddie fee.

4. You can rent a golf cart at the clubhouse. Cart drivers must be at least 18 years old and must show a valid driver's license (any U.S. or international license, or an international driving permit). Keep carts at least 30 feet (9 meters) away from the greens. Golfers with disabilities can get a permit from the clubhouse to drive closer to the greens.

5. Replace any grass torn up by your golf clubs or your shoe spikes, and repair any other course damage before you proceed to the next hole.

6. Wear proper attire on the course and in the clubhouse: full-length pants (no jeans or sweatpants) or knee-length shorts or skirts, and collared shirts (such as a golf or a polo shirt—no T-shirts). Don't wear hats in the clubhouse.

7. Don't bring your mobile phone onto the course or into the clubhouse. We allow phones only in the villas. Doctors may bring phones anywhere but must turn off the sound.

8. Don't smoke in the clubhouse or on the course.

For more information, email Red Grouse Greens at info@redgrousegreens.com or phone us for free at +1-800-XXX-XXXX.

Solution notes

Red Grouse Greens is now part of an international company, so it needs to speak to an international audience. For starters, the original copy didn't tell readers where exactly the course was, so we added a line under the top heading to show city, state, and country, as well as a link to a map and directions.

Because site visitors are probably golfers, they may understand golfing terms such as *links, tee time,* and *green fees*—but it wouldn't hurt for the copy's editor to consult a translator or a colleague in another country. We kept some of the golf jargon, because people might include those terms in searches.

International readers likely wouldn't know what *low-country cuisine* is—nor would many U.S. residents—so that kind of local terminology should be more fully described or should link to more information. *Airport transfer, villa,* and *all-inclusive* are words that someone in the travel business might use, but the terms may mean different things to different people. They should be reworded or, if they are common search terms, retained but explained. Subtle potential problems include words and phrases such as *gratuity* and *set to silent mode.* We chose to replace those two with *tip* and *turn off the sound,* words that are more common and more likely to be understood immediately.

We changed the wording of the club rules to make them imperative do's and don'ts, which simplifies the sentence structure and eliminates some potentially confusing negatives. Throughout the text, we made several little changes: We eliminated bias, used more common words, offered alternative measurements, clarified date and currency formats, added more information (such as tipping standards), and so on. Though the edited text is somewhat longer than the original, it is more understandable and informative.

Chapter 6

Make Your Site Accessible to Everyone

In this chapter

- **Provide access for millions more visitors.** People with disabilities are a significant portion of your potential audience.
- **Learn how people with disabilities use the Web.** Make sure that your site's design takes accessibility tools into account.
- **Gauge your site's accessibility.** Key questions to ask about your content and design.

Millions of people have some sort of disability, and many of them use the Internet to communicate, to research, to shop, to do business. So making your website accessible to as many people as possible makes sense—and it takes just a little thought and planning to accomplish.

Although website accessibility is mostly the site designer's job, writers and editors can contribute in many ways. The first step is to realize that *disabled individuals are in your audience right now.* Think about how they will experience your site.

Provide access for millions more visitors

People who are blind, deaf, both blind and deaf, or limited in their mobility can and do use the Web every day. But because many websites are not built to be *accessible*—that is, to be used by as wide a range of people as possible—the online experience for these individuals is often frustrating. Think, then, how popular a website can become when it does take accessibility into account. It has the potential to reach millions more visitors.

People with disabilities often use the computer with the help of specialized hardware and software. For example, a blind person can use screen-reading software to hear what is on a webpage. But the availability of such software doesn't mean that people with disabilities can experience any webpage they encounter. To ensure that they can experience *your* content, you'll need to **optimize your site so that it can be accessed by the tools that disabled people use**.

And there's a bonus: When you design a site with disabled people in mind, your content will generally be more usable for nondisabled people, too. Consider the curb-cut in a sidewalk. It was originally put there for people using wheelchairs, but all kinds of people find it convenient: kids on skateboards, parents pushing strollers, people pushing shopping carts, bicyclists—the list goes on. A sidewalk with a curb-cut is more usable by more people than a sidewalk without one. That's the essential goodness of accessibility.

Facts about disability

Just how many disabled individuals are we talking about?

Estimates vary, depending on who's counting and how they define disability. These figures, however, get pretty close:

Disabled individuals, U.S.	55 million[20]
Disabled individuals, global	650 million[21]
Aggregate annual income of disabled individuals, U.S.	$1 trillion[22]
Aggregate annual income of disabled individuals, global	A lot. (As far as we know, a reliable estimate doesn't exist. If you find one, tell us: Ask_Edit@yahoo.com.)

Big numbers, certainly. But there's one more number worth remembering when you're developing an accessible site or product: 2.7. On average (as first reported in an unpublished study conducted at Boston's Suffolk University in the early 1980s), for each individual with a disability, there are 2.7 people who care passionately about that person—perhaps a family member, a professional caregiver, or a next-door neighbor.

These people make a difference: When something good happens to the disabled person, the 2.7 applaud loudly and let it be widely known. And when something not so good happens—say, a website is found to be inaccessible—the blazingly fast word-of-mouth criticism begins.

You want to have those 2.7 people on your side.

If you multiply 2.7 by the estimated number of disabled people in the United States, you get 148.5 million people; add the 55 million disabled individuals themselves, and you'll see that **some 200 million people may in some way be affected by the issue of accessibility**—and that's just in the United States. Clearly, the number of people you can influence by designing an accessible site is nothing short of huge.

In the United States and around the world, these numbers get bigger every day. Wars, malnutrition, poor prenatal care, medical advances that help people survive once life-threatening injuries, a large and aging baby-boomer population—there are lots of reasons for the continuing increase in the number of individuals with disabilities, and lots of reasons why accessibility is not an option but a necessity.

 ## What are the "right" words to use when talking to or about disabled individuals?

This is a common question, and the answer has more to do with dignity than design, and more to do with comfort than correctness. And it's a question with more than one answer. Just as there is no homogeneous group of disabled individuals, so there is no one opinion on which words are "correct."

For example, some people consider these terms politically correct. To others, though, they may be condescending:

- *Handi-capable*
- *DisABLED*
- *Handi-kids*
- *Physically challenged*

What about *handicapped*? According to the *Oxford English Dictionary*,[23] it is "a word of obscure history," most likely related to the practice of imposing a limitation on the superior participant in a game to equalize the participants' chances of winning. But many people find the term offensive, believing that it is related or at least similar to the phrase *cap in hand*, which refers to a humble, even submissive, manner. For this reason, it is wise to avoid the term.

Referring to the heterogeneous group of individuals with disabilities as "the disabled" denies the individuality of members of that group. *Disabled* is an adjective—don't "adjectify" disabled people by using it as a noun.

In our opinion, the words *disabled* (when used as an adjective: *disabled people, disabled individuals*) and *disability* (*people with disabilities, individuals with disabilities*) are best. Of course, others hold different opinions, and hold them tenaciously.

Finally, keep in mind that the word *normal* could be offensive. If you refer to nondisabled individuals as "normal," consider what you imply about disabled individuals. *Your* norm should be to avoid that usage.

Learn how people with disabilities use the Web

How does a blind person use a computer? How does a person who is paralyzed from the neck down move a cursor on a screen or click icons and links? How does a deaf-blind person interact with a website? They do so with accessibility tools.

Accessibility tools

There are just as many ways to use a computer as there are computer users—or at least it seems so when you start to learn about accessibility. To better understand accessibility tools, you can search the Internet for videos demonstrating the technologies. Better yet, visit your local university and talk to students and faculty members with disabilities.

Some examples of what you might find:

- **Someone who is totally blind uses software called a screen reader.** This can be installed on any computer that runs Windows, Linux, or Mac OS. A screen reader provides spoken feedback when the person performs an action, such as opening the browser window by pressing the Enter key, navigating through a webpage using the Tab key, navigating through menus using the arrow keys, opening an email message, or simply typing. (For reasons that should be obvious, blind people don't use a mouse.)

- **A person with limited vision often relies on screen-magnification software.** These solutions can simply increase the size of the text, images, and mouse pointer. Or they can provide more sophisticated enhancements, such as tools that enable the user to change color and contrast, and even to view content through a virtual magnifying glass that can be dragged around the screen with a mouse. Some screen-magnification programs come with an option that gives people spoken information about the items they are pointing at.

- **A person with a physical disability that makes typing on a regular keyboard too difficult uses an onscreen keyboard instead.** People who can't move their hands can navigate with head motions rather than with a mouse. An onscreen keyboard can be controlled with a single switch, a head mouse, a head stick, or another accessory that requires little pressure or a minimum number of key presses. Some onscreen keyboards automatically scan through the keys, allowing people to enter their choices by pressing a switch. Other onscreen keyboards offer a "dwell" feature: People move their heads to control the cursor, and enter the text or click links by dwelling on the key of their choice.

- **A deaf-blind person interacts with a computer by using a refreshable Braille display.** The display is usually controlled by a screen reader. Some modern Braille displays come with a built-in keyboard that allows people to type text, click items on the screen, and read the content of webpages, spreadsheets, text documents, and so forth.

TIP Most operating systems—such as Apple's Mac OS, Microsoft's Windows XP and Windows Vista, and the GNOME desktop on Linux—include different combinations of the software tools we've mentioned. These tools may not always be on a par with their commercial counterparts, but they can provide a strong first step toward accessibility.

Design that prevents access

A website that is not designed to accommodate accessibility tools presents significant roadblocks to site visitors with disabilities—and they're not likely to remain visitors for long.

Your goal, then, should be to **ensure that your site can be experienced by people using computer accessibility tools**. This means following guidelines for accessible design, which we'll touch on in the next section. It also means being aware of frustrating experiences like these:

- A blind person, after carefully crafting her comment on a blog entry, cannot submit it because she can't read the misshapen letter-number combination preceded by instructions such as "Please enter the characters you see in the box below." Called *CAPTCHAs* in computing jargon, these letter-number combinations are intended—in the awkward words of too many sites—to "prove that you are human" and not a computer pretending to be a person. (Incidentally, many sighted people have problems reading these, too.)
- A deaf person cannot understand a video that everyone is raving about, because it provides no closed captions.
- A person who has limited motor skills but uses a keyboard to navigate cannot reach the content on the homepage of a website because it takes so long to tab through all the menus. (A **Skip to content** link would take him directly through the menus, allowing him to enjoy the site.)

Consider the many ways people access your site, and make sure that the site is designed so that anyone can use it.

Gauge your site's accessibility

We don't have space in this chapter to address the widely varying challenges that disabled people face while using computers. (For more about Web accessibility, see our online Resources page at http://styleguide.yahoo.com.) But Yahoo!'s hundreds of millions of monthly users include a huge number of disabled adults and kids from around the world, and these individuals have taught us—and remind us all the time—what matters most to them. They are our real-world experts. If you are in a position to create accessible products, you'd be smart to include similar experts to assist you.

Accessibility: Is it the law?

Legislation is playing an increasingly important role in the story of Web accessibility around the world. Many countries are developing their own guidelines and policies, so what may be judged to be an accessible website in one country may not be judged to be so in another. Figuring out which laws apply to your site, if any, can therefore be confusing, but worldwide standards are slowly emerging. For a summary of different countries' accessibility policies, visit:

http://www.w3.org/WAI/Policy
http://en.wikipedia.org/wiki/Accessibility

We can't advise you on how to ensure that your site is legally accessible. But be aware that designing an accessible website may be a requirement rather than an option in certain situations. For example, a company in the United States that receives funds from a federal agency must be in compliance with the accessibility standards described in Section 508 of the Rehabilitation Act of 1973 (see http://www.section508.gov/index.cfm?FuseAction=Content&ID=3).

So, in addition to all the reasons that we've described for making your site accessible to individuals with disabilities, keep in mind that legislation in this area is becoming increasingly noteworthy worldwide.

10 questions for testing accessibility

If you're involved in the design of a website, you have the greatest opportunity to make sure that your site is usable by everyone. But writers and editors can improve a site's accessibility, too. Some of the following guidelines, such as always including alternative text with images, are typically the responsibility of content creators. And writers and editors often contribute to a site's design or redesign, which presents an opportunity to ask questions that lead site designers and stakeholders to consider accessibility. (For five specific ways in which writers and editors can contribute, see "Top 5 steps that writers can take to make their content accessible" on page 112.)

Of course, making a website accessible can be daunting, especially if you start thinking about it late in the process. What to do? Where to begin?

The following short list of accessibility questions based on our experience at Yahoo! can help. These questions don't address every possible consideration, because accessibility issues can be complex. But **if you can answer yes to these questions, your project will be usable by most individuals with disabilities**.

Audience

1. Did the people who built your site consider individuals with disabilities when they designed it?

    A "yes" answer means that you are already halfway to making your site accessible. All too often, Web developers forget that people with disabilities may want to use the site, so accessibility features are never even proposed.

2. Did people with disabilities help or advise during the design and testing process?

    Include children and adults with disabilities in your design and evaluation sessions. Not all disabled individuals are knowledgeable about website design, but they are certainly experts on their own experiences and will point out the parts of your site that they can't use. It's likely that they will identify design problems that you would not have discovered any other way.

Usability

3. Is your site easy to use without a mouse (in other words, with only a keyboard)?

    For many people with disabilities, the mouse is either inaccessible or inconvenient. (Try using a mouse, for example, with your eyes closed or with one finger.) For them, a site is accessible only if it can be navigated with nothing but a keyboard. So make sure that you can navigate your site easily just by using combinations of the Tab key, arrow keys, and shortcut keys. It's easy to test this: Just put your mouse in a desk drawer and see how far you get.

4. Do all the actionable elements on your site (input fields, buttons, radio buttons, checkboxes, and so forth) have text labels associated with them?

    People who can't see your site layout need an alternative way to orient themselves—for instance, to determine whether their onscreen cursor is filling in a checkbox or sitting in a search box waiting for them to type. These elements must be clearly labeled, with the label coded to be associated with the field, so that a screen reader will be able to identify the element. Otherwise, the site will be confusing at best, totally unusable at worst.

    It's easy to check whether input fields and other actionable elements on your site have useful labels. For example, does an address-entry box in which people type their city have the word *City* next to it? If so, great—but you're not done yet. Is the label actually associated with the field? To check, click once on the word *City*. If the label has been properly associated with the **City** field, your cursor will show up in that field.

Example

Input fields with labels:

3. In case you forget your ID or password...

Alternate Email	
Security Question	- Select One - ▼
Your Answer	

Use 4 characters or more — not case sensitive.

The third field, labeled "Your Answer," is associated with the label if the cursor appears in the input field when the user clicks "Your Answer."

---

5.   If your site uses CAPTCHA image verification, does it provide an alternative solution for visually impaired and deaf-blind users?

Example

Type the code shown [   ]

sAc dBH

Try a new code

CAPTCHA image verification

These misshapen characters are actually *pictures* of letters and numbers. They cannot be read aloud by a screen reader, which can read only text, not images. So, because blind people can't hear that text, they can't reproduce it to move on to the next step.

Alternatives to this kind of test can be provided to those who rely on screen readers:

- You can let the person respond by email.
- Misshapen characters can be replaced with questions that only humans can understand. Examples include simple logic puzzles such as:
  Forty-two, Monday, 19, green, lamp: The color is _____.
  Left is to right as up is to _____.
- The person can be asked to type letters and numbers that are spoken.

Visual and sound elements

6.   Do all your site's images have alternative text?

Alternative text, or *alt text*—a description of a graphic that enables a blind person to "see" the accompanying picture on a website—may be the simplest of all accessibility features to implement. Yet many people forget to include alt text with images. For best practices regarding alternative text, see "Alt text and image captions" on page 132.

Alt text is also an important part of optimizing a site for search engines. See "Images and video" on page 412 to learn how alt text can be used to improve your site's rank with search engines.

7.   If your site has video content, do you provide closed captions for people who have hearing impairments?

Deaf viewers are unable to hear the audio portion of any video on your site. Without closed captions, they will miss important information. To understand how frustrating this can be, simply mute the sound on your own computer while browsing a site that has video.

Closed captions are useful not only for accessibility but also for making the video content of your site searchable. If search engines can find the text stored in your closed-caption files, then exponentially more Web users are likely to find your videos. (To learn more about search engine optimization, or SEO, see Chapter 17, "Optimize Your Site for Search Engines.")

Transcripts of videos can be useful for SEO as well, and they are a nice bonus if you want to provide them—but don't consider them a replacement for closed captions.

8.   If your site relies on color or visual effects to convey information, does it provide an alternative for colorblind people and people with limited vision?

Avoid communicating with site visitors through visual cues exclusively. Instructions such as "Click the green button to begin" or "Fields marked in bold are required" may be meaningless to an individual who is colorblind or who has impaired vision. If your design does, in fact, require a green start button, be sure to provide a text equivalent so that people who can't see that color can understand which button is the start button.

9.   If your site relies on spatial directions, do you offer alternatives for blind people and people with limited vision?

It makes little sense to direct a blind user to click the link located "to the right." Where, exactly, is that? Phrase your instructions so that they don't rely exclusively on the geography of your page layout. For example, you can say instead, "Use the links in the navigation bar."

10. Is the text on your site readable for everyone?

What looks good and readable to you may be just the opposite for some people. For example, dark-blue links on a light-blue background do not provide adequate contrast for some. And not everyone can read 12-point type, let alone 10-point.

So how do you create a site that meets the needs of disabled individuals but conforms to your aesthetic vision and conveys your brand identity? By enabling your visitors to modify elements of your design. For instance, let people choose:

- Foreground and background colors
- Type size
- Link color

T I P If you're using an application or a service to deliver your content rather than developing a site from scratch, these 10 questions for testing accessibility are still important to ask. For example, to create a blog, you might use an application like Blogger, LiveJournal, or WordPress. When you're deciding which to use, examine the features of each application or service (view a demo if one is available), and ask whether it already incorporates accessibility features.

Top 5 steps that writers can take to make their content accessible

1. Make sure that all images have useful alt text. See "Alt text and image captions" on page 132.
2. Provide closed captions and transcripts to go along with videos.
3. Eliminate instructions and other communications that can't be understood if the reader can't see the page.
4. Get rid of instructions and communications that rely on color to convey meaning.
5. Check that any site or service you use to publish content incorporates accessibility features.

The best argument for accessibility: It's good for business

Imagine a store that sells all kinds of attractive and popular products. Now imagine that the items are placed on the top shelves, far out of reach for all but the tallest customers. You could argue that such a strategy puts the store owner in the sales-prevention business. **Who's going to buy what they can't see?**

Now imagine that the products have been placed so that they are easily accessible. Everything's where it ought to be. But someone forgot to build a door.

Silly examples, sure: What kind of business would keep its products and services out of the reach of its customers? What kind of business would prevent customers from even entering the store?

If your website is inaccessible to customers with disabilities, these silly examples might describe your site.

Among the many reasons for building accessibility into a website, the reason that perhaps needs to be emphasized most for businesses is this: **Individuals with disabilities are customers.** They have products they want to buy, services they want to use, and content they want to experience. **And they have money to spend** on products and services.

But before they can be your customers, they must be able to enter your website and view your wares. (Your competition, by the way, may already have figured this out. Accessibility is fast becoming more the rule than the exception.)

Individuals with disabilities can and do use the Internet to communicate, to research, to browse, to buy. And you can easily make them your customers. All you need to do is make your site accessible.

Ideas in Practice

Checklist: Is your site accessible?

Are you turning customers and readers away from your site? You might be, if you haven't considered whether your site can be experienced by people with disabilities.

The following list includes basic questions about your site that will help you begin to understand whether it can be accessed by disabled individuals. A "no" answer means you may have some work to do to make your site usable by everyone in your potential audience.

See "10 questions for testing accessibility" on page 108 for guidance related to each question.

Question	Yes	No
Audience		
Did the people who built your site consider individuals with disabilities when they designed it?		
Were people with disabilities included in the site design and testing process?		
Usability		
Is your site easy to use without a mouse (in other words, with only a keyboard)?		
Do all the actionable elements on your site (such as input fields, buttons, radio buttons, checkboxes, and so forth) have text labels associated with them?		
If your site uses CAPTCHA image verification (those hard-to-read letter-number combinations that you're asked to type to prove that you are a person rather than a computer), does it provide an alternative for visually impaired and deaf-blind users?		
Visual and sound elements		
Do all your site's images have alternative text?		
If your site has video content, do you provide closed captions for users with hearing impairments?		
If your site relies on color or visual effects to convey information, does it provide an alternative for colorblind people and people with limited vision?		
If your site relies on spatial directions, do you offer alternatives for blind people and people with limited vision?		
Is the text on your site readable for everyone?		

Write UI Text, Email, and Mobile-Friendly Content

Chapter 7

Write Clear User-Interface Text

In this chapter

- **User-interface text basics.** Look at your site from the user's point of view.
- **Page titles.** Remember to write these crucial pieces of copy.
- **Text links.** Use wording that's more strategic than "click here."
- **Buttons and other UI elements.** These guide visitors through your site—make sure that the wording is clear.
- **Alt text and image captions.** Describe the images on your page (not everyone can see what you see).
- **Feedback messages and error messages.** Write these in simple, everyday language, not "engineerese."
- **Help and FAQs.** Make it easy for people to get answers to questions and to understand how to use your site.
- **User-instruction mechanics.** Find out how to refer to buttons and keyboard keys in text, whether to choose *click* or *click on,* and more.

Can first-time visitors find their way around your site easily and locate what they're looking for? Before you say yes, put yourself in front of *their* keyboards.

Your site's usability depends on the design and features of your user interface (UI), but it also depends on the quality of your *user-interface text:* the copy that orients people on your site and helps them move around it. Clickable headings, links, and buttons; feedback and error messages; and user-assistance text like FAQs and help pages—they can provide site visitors with a great experience or can frustrate and confuse them.

This chapter presents some **best practices for creating the copy that helps people move around your site with ease**.

Usability: How easily site visitors can interact with a site and use it to achieve their goals. Many websites engage in usability testing to ensure the best experience for their users.

User-interface text basics

User-interface snippets like the text of buttons, forms, and FAQs are some of the most influential and (ideally) helpful pieces of copy on a site, and they should get as much of an editor's attention as any other text.

Think about it: How often have you abandoned a registration form, a checkout procedure, or a site because you couldn't navigate, couldn't understand the process, or couldn't find help? If you've ever done so, you're not alone: Studies show that more than half of those who start shopping online give up before paying.[24] Customers cite many reasons for bailing out, including bugaboos that writers and editors can help improve: annoying registration forms, procedures with too many steps, a lack of customer support or help information, an inability to determine user names and passwords, and so on.

Keep these **general guidelines** in mind as you and your team develop your site and write UI text:

- **Use consistent terminology.** For instance, don't call a feature a "Shopping Cart" on one page, a "Cart" on another page, and a "Shopping Basket" on a third. Choose one term, note it in your word list (see page 433), and use it everywhere. In addition to eliminating confusion, consistent terminology helps people stay oriented on your site or in a process, such as a registration or checkout procedure.

- **Create written "signposts" to guide visitors around your site.** These can be in the form of a text-link "breadcrumb trail" (for example, <u>Recipes</u> > <u>European</u> > <u>Italian</u> > <u>Pasta Fagioli</u>) at the top of the page, <u>Next</u> and <u>Previous</u> links at the bottom and top of long articles, a navigation bar that highlights the section that a person is in, and so on.

T I P   Create a consistent page-to-page experience. Place repeating page navigation (often called persistent navigation) in a consistent location throughout your site. For example, if a **Help** link appears in the top-right corner of your homepage, it should appear in the top-right corner of subsequent pages.

- **Anticipate questions and needs.** And respond to them by placing the right piece of text where the reader needs it. For instance, if a file on your site requires specific software to open it (such as Adobe Acrobat or Flash), place a link to download the software near the file. Similarly, place explanations related to the use of personal information (such as your site's privacy policy) close to any request for personal information.

Read on for specific guidance on the different types of UI text you'll find on most sites.

Page titles

The page title is the band of text you see at the top of your browser window. **The page title, or <title> tag, is one of the most important pieces of copy on your site.** It tells site visitors what they can expect to find on the page, and for people with a slow Internet connection, it's often the first text they see.

The title of this page is "News, Blogs, and Tools for Living Green | Yahoo! Green." The text is entered into the HTML code making up the page, inside the <title> element, which looks something like this: <title> News, Blogs, and Tools for Living Green | Yahoo! Green</title>. (To see how the <title> tag and other HTML elements make up a webpage, see "Anatomy of a webpage" on page 372.)

The page title will appear in many places, such as:

■ The title bar of most browser windows

■ The label of a browser tab

■ A list of search results, as the link text

News, Blogs, and Tools for Living **Green I Yahoo! Green**
News, blogs, and tools for living **green**. Environmental tips to save money, stop pollution, and help fight global warming.
green.yahoo.com - 166k - Cached

- A **Favorites** or **Bookmarks** menu (consider how the title will look in a long list of bookmarks)

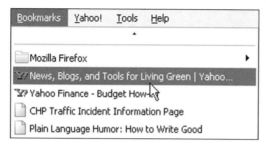

- A browser's **Back** and **Forward** menus and **History** panel

- The Windows taskbar

- The program-switching Alt+Tab interface on a PC

Because it can appear in so many places, the page title is a key component in building an informative user experience. The page title also carries weight with search engines—and it's often ignored or forgotten by site creators. Take this snippet of text seriously.

T I P Web designers call the page title "required text" because the HTML **<title>** tag must be included to form a webpage. But computers won't know whether you have written text in the tag or not. So, even if you forget to write the page title, some sort of default text will appear. That's why it's possible (and not uncommon) to see webpages with nothing but hyphens or placeholder text in this essential area of the page. When you review your pages online, begin by checking the page title.

Check out my website, Untitled Page

A surprising number of people fail to include any **<title>** tag text at all when creating their web-pages. To see how many, go to any search engine and enter **untitled document**, **untitled page**, or even **type title here**. You'll get hundreds of thousands, millions, or even tens of millions of results. Don't let your page be one of them!

Follow these **page-title guidelines**:

- **Make the first 65 characters count.** Most search engines index the first 65 characters, which can become the linked headings on search-results pages. Put the most descriptive words about your webpage first in the title, and don't waste a single character.

Example

Before
YouMe – The Most Fabulous Website in the World for Inside Information About You and Me

After
YouMe - Inside Information About You and Me

- **Use the words that people will most likely type into search engines** when they're seeking content like yours. If your product or company name is well-known and will probably be part of people's search queries, use the name in homepage and other top-level page titles. But if people are more likely to search on words other than your product or service name, make those words prominent in your page titles. You may even want them to precede your site or company name. See Chapter 17, "Optimize Your Site for Search Engines," to learn more about choosing and using search keywords.

Before

Me-Yow! Inc.

After

Me-Yow! Hats for Cats and Other Cat Apparel *(People are searching on "Me-Yow!" but also on "cat apparel.")*

- **Give each page a title that reflects its specific content and purpose.** Don't just paste the same title onto every page. Deep-level page titles, such as product detail pages, should communicate distinct, descriptive content and use words that people may search on.

- **Use consistent syntax** (such as *site name - section title - page name*) for titles on pages of the same level.

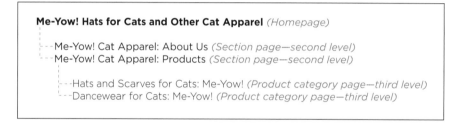

- **Orient the user in multipage processes,** such as the checkout process on a retail site. Use the page title to communicate location as well as progress within the process.

Checkout - Enter Shipping Information - Step 1 of 4 - Me-Yow!

Checkout - Enter Payment Information - Step 2 of 4 - Me-Yow!

Checkout - Review and Submit Your Order - Step 3 of 4 - Me-Yow!

Checkout - Order Confirmation - Step 4 of 4 - Me-Yow!

T I P   Some special characters, including the em dash, may not always display correctly in the page-title area. That's why it's standard in page titles to separate phrases with a colon or a hyphen. For more on special characters, see "Special characters" on page 386.

Text links

Text links are clickable pieces of copy that enable people to jump to another place on the page or to another page on your site ("internal links"), or to another site ("external links"). They can be embedded within the body of text <u>like this</u> or they can stand alone, as in a **Next** link in a page's bottom-right corner, leading the reader to the next page of a continuing article. Sometimes headings are clickable links. (For guidelines on writing and styling effective headings, see "Headings" on page 50.)

Writing link text

Good usability depends heavily on site visitors being able to understand where they are and where they can go. Effective link text helps them get oriented and stay oriented. Follow these **guidelines for wording links**:

- Write short, descriptive text about where the link leads ("Next page," not "To go to the next page, click here"). Text that describes what's on the next page is even better: "The president's 101st day" or "How Internet phone calls work."
- When possible, use the same words in your link text that the reader will see as a heading on the resulting page. For example, if the page you're linking to is called "Our Company," phrase the link "Our Company," not "About Us."
- To optimize your page for search engines, **use search keywords**—words and phrases your audience is likely to type into search boxes—in your link text when possible. See Chapter 17 for details.
- Avoid using generic calls to action like "click here" and "go here" in link text. Phrases like "click here" do not describe where the link goes, use up valuable space and reader time, and waste an opportunity to improve your site's chances with search engines through the strategic use of keywords in link text. Finally, "click here" sounds dated: People have been using the Web long enough to understand that they are meant to click a link.

Examples

Before
<u>Click here</u> to configure your dream car for pickup at a showroom near you.

After
<u>Configure your dream car</u> for pickup at a showroom near you.

Before
View our shipping rates <u>here</u>. Read our returns policy <u>here</u>.

After

View our <u>shipping rates</u>. Read our <u>returns policy</u>.

T I P   If links are similar to each other and appear close together—for example, in a series or a bulleted list—be consistent by linking similar phrases or similar parts of speech. For instance, if you link all the words in "<u>Read our returns policy</u>" on one line, be sure to link all the words in "<u>View our shipping rates</u>" on another. Or shorten both links to "Read our <u>returns policy</u>" and "View our <u>shipping rates</u>."

- In general, avoid using "More…" (or other text ending in ellipsis points) as a link, because it doesn't tell people where the link will take them or what action they should take. Active, descriptive link text is best.

Example

Before

<u>Videos of the week</u>
A sleeping cat falls off a window ledge. A dozen monkeys dance. This week's wedding disaster. <u>More</u>...

After

<u>Videos of the week</u>
A sleeping cat falls off a window ledge. A dozen monkeys dance. This week's wedding disaster. <u>More funny videos</u>.

Exception: "More…" can be effective in certain situations—for example, at the end of a list of product links on a retail site. In such a case, the site visitor can easily grasp that "More…" means more of the types of products listed. However, if you have the space, "More" plus a keyword or two can better your site's chances with search engines (see Chapter 17).

Example

Camping gear:
    <u>Backpacks</u>
    <u>Camp kitchen</u>
    <u>Lighting</u>

> Sleeping bags
> Tents
> More...
Snow gear:
> Clothing
> Shoes
> Skis
> Sleds
> More...
("More..." on its own may be adequate at the end of clearly categorized lists such as these.)

Example

Camping gear:
> Backpacks
> Camp kitchen
> Lighting
> Sleeping bags
> Tents
> More camping gear...
Snow gear:
> Clothing
> Shoes
> Skis
> Sleds
> More snow gear...
("More" plus a keyword such as "snow gear" is better if you have the room—it's clearer, and it may help with search engine optimization.)

■ Don't include the URL as link text, unless you want the reader to become familiar with the URL.

Before

Check out Yahoo! Finance at http://finance.yahoo.com/.

After

Check out Yahoo! Finance. *(No need to include the complete URL)*

Before

Shop for punk baby clothes and more at Bootleg Bäby.

After

Shop for punk baby clothes and more at Bootleg Bäby. Find us at bootlegbaby.com. *(To help people learn the URL)*

Use consistent terminology for your calls to action

Use *call-to-action* verbs when instructing visitors to *select* a menu item, *check* a box, or *enter* text. Choose a good verb for each situation and stick with it throughout your site. For example, Yahoo! uses *check* and *uncheck* with checkboxes, *select* and *deselect* with radio buttons. Consistent terminology helps visitors—especially those who are less comfortable with English—feel comfortable navigating your site.

Consider using one of the verbs from these sets as your standard call to action. Be sure to document your choice in your word list (see page 433).

customize, personalize, or *individualize*
edit, change, or *modify*
create or *compose*
sign in, log in, or *log on*
register, sign up, or *subscribe*
sign out, log out, or *log off*
check, select, or *choose*
uncheck or *deselect*
type or *enter*
post or *publish*
email or *mail*
IM, instant-message, or *message*
open or *expand*
close or *collapse*

Choosing a style for link text

Capitalize and punctuate link text consistently throughout your site. (If your site is a network of smaller sites, as Yahoo! is, be consistent within each individual site.)

Consider the following **guidelines for link text**:

■ Use **sentence case** for the text (see "Capitalization" on page 239 for the rules governing sentence case). If the link falls in the middle of a sentence, <u>like this</u>, lowercase it just as you would any other common word or phrase in the middle of a sentence.

Exception: Many sites use title case for persistent navigation links such as <u>About Us</u>, <u>Contact Us</u>, <u>Copyright</u>, and others that appear on all pages of a site. (These links typically correspond to the title of a top-level page or section—for example, the **About Us** link corresponds to a page titled "About Us.") Title case is also common for each link in a breadcrumb trail (<u>Home</u> > <u>Computers</u> > <u>Computer Peripherals</u> > <u>Printers</u>).

■ In general, add a period to a link if it's a complete sentence. Add a question mark or an exclamation point if one is needed to convey tone or meaning (for both sentences and sentence fragments).

■ But **don't link ending punctuation**, such as periods and question marks.

Examples

Welcome to Me-Yow!. <u>Send us feedback</u>.
<u>A picture of Bigfoot</u>?
Where are <u>my orders</u>? Where is my <u>shopping cart</u>?
Help us improve our site: <u>Participate in a user survey</u>.
Read our <u>August newsletter</u>.
<u>Learn more</u>.
<u>About Us</u> | <u>Contact</u> | <u>Copyright Information</u> | <u>Privacy Policy</u> | <u>Subscribe</u> *(Persistent navigation)*
<u>Books</u> > <u>Shopping and Services</u> > <u>Booksellers</u> > <u>How-To</u> *(Breadcrumb trail)*

■ Don't include a period at the end of a simple one- or two-word link that is not in running text and is not a complete sentence.

```
Showing comments 1-5 of 161    Next >>
```

For information on how to refer to a link in running text (for example, "Click the **About Us** link") and whether to use *click* or *click on* in such an instruction, see "User-instruction mechanics" on page 144.

Buttons and other UI elements

People may also interact with buttons, radio buttons, and checkboxes to use your site. These too need consistently stated, helpful text.

Input fields (for instance, a search box or a box where you type in your email address to subscribe to a newsletter) are also UI elements. The copy preceding the input field, often called the input field label—for example, the words *Enter your password* next to a box where people must type in their password—is another kind of UI text.

Search Now

Button

Check the box next to a topic to get summaries of articles emailed to you.

☐ All topics

☐ Buying a fuel-efficient car

☐ Commuting

☐ Finding a green job

Checkboxes with introductory text

Select your service type:

○ Cable

○ Satellite

○ Antenna

Radio buttons

Search for questions: [   ] Search

Input field with label

Writing text for buttons and other UI elements

Buttons and other elements that enable people to input information or otherwise interact with your site are sometimes collectively called user prompts. Follow these **guidelines** when creating text for them:

■ Keep the text active and to the point.

■ Use a verb that communicates the action you want the person to carry out, such as *search, move, submit, check, sign in, join, sign out, create.* Avoid using verbs that end in *ing.*

Be specific: *Delete* or *remove*? *Create* or *add*?

For a good user experience, favor words that express the precise action of a user prompt. The words *delete, remove, create,* and *add* can be problematic, but it's relatively easy to choose the right one.

When choosing between *delete* and *remove*:

■ Use **delete** when the action will permanently delete an item. For example, use it when referring to deleting an address from a user's account (*delete address*) or deleting an account (*delete account*).

■ Use **remove** when the action will take an item away from its current position or location but won't delete it permanently. The item will still be available in another location. For example, *remove item from shopping cart.*

When choosing between *create* and *add*:

■ Use **create** when the action will produce a new item. For example, *create account* or *create new project.*

■ Use **add** when the action will add an item to a list or to a group of existing objects. For example, *add task to list* or *add item to shopping cart.*

Styling text for buttons and other UI elements

Sometimes text is written directly on a button (for example, *OK* or *Search*); sometimes text is next to a checkbox or other similar UI element (for example, *Remove from cart*). When creating text, the **basic rule is to stay consistent**: Capitalize and punctuate buttons and other UI elements consistently throughout your site. (See "Capitalization" on page 239 for styles of capitalization.)

For information on how to refer to buttons and other elements in running text (for instance, how to visually distinguish a button name in a sentence), see "User-instruction mechanics" on page 144.

Consider these **guidelines for UI text**:

- **Button text:** Title case; no ending punctuation except in the rare situation where a question mark is called for.

- **Checkbox text:** Sentence case; ending punctuation only if it's a complete sentence.

When sending messages: ☑ Save a copy of the message in the Sent folder.
☐ Automatically add new recipients to my contacts.

- **Radio button text:** Sentence case; ending punctuation only if it's a complete sentence.

What's the problem you are experiencing?
◉ I forgot my password.
○ My password doesn't work.
○ I forgot my Yahoo! ID.
○ My account may have been compromised.

- **Input field labels:** For the most cohesive look and feel across the site, aim for consistent placement, capitalization, and punctuation of all input field labels.

  - ◆ If the labels tend to be short (two words, for instance), either title case or sentence case is acceptable, and either no ending punctuation or a colon is acceptable. Labels are usually placed above the input fields or to the left of them.
  - ◆ If you need to precede an input field with a longer phrase or a complete sentence, favor sentence case—it's easier on the eyes. Use ending punctuation if it's a complete sentence, or use a colon. For example, *Why are you reporting this story?* and *I am reporting this story because:* are two possible labels for an input field in a form for reporting abuse.

My Name	First Name	Last Name
Gender	- Select One - ▾	
Birthday	- Select Month - ▾	Day	Year

Title case, no ending punctuation

Type comments here.

Sentence case, ending punctuation for complete sentence

Yahoo! ID:

(Ex.: free2rhyme@yahoo.com)

Password:

Title case, colon

Choose your city:

[▾] [Go]

Sentence case, colon

- **Instructions and other text preceding a form:** Sentence case is common; use ending punctuation only for complete sentences. If the text is very short (three words at most), you can probably consider it a title and use title case, which is acceptable as long as all similar text uses the same style of capitalization.

Please enter your shipping information below.

Name	First Name	Last Name
Address Line 1		
Address Line 2		
City		

Sentence case, ending punctuation for complete sentence

Shipping Information

Name	First Name	Last Name
Address Line 1		
Address Line 2		
City		

Title case, no ending punctuation

Alt text and image captions

Some people won't be able to see the images on your site—for example, people who use a text-only browser (such as those on some mobile devices), or people who are blind and use a screen reader. It's therefore important to **add alt-text descriptions to images** and, when possible, to provide image captions.

Writing and styling alt text

Alt text is the description that you type into an image's **alt** HTML attribute, in the HTML code for the page. If an image doesn't load, its alt-text description appears in its place. Blind people who use the Tab key and a screen reader instead of a mouse to access your site will hear the alt text spoken by the computer.

Example

When the image appears

What the "green collar" economy means for you

By Lori Bongiorno   Posted Thu Jan 29, 2009 6:21pm PST for greenpicks   138 Comments

Learn which industries will benefit from the new economic stimulus plan and what old skills can be repurposed into eco-friendly jobs. Read full post »

When the image doesn't appear

What the "green collar" economy means for you

By Lori Bongiorno   Posted Thu Jan 29, 2009 6:21pm PST for greenpicks   138 Comments

Construction workers, iStockPhoto

Learn which industries will benefit from the new economic stimulus plan and what old skills can be repurposed into eco-friendly jobs. Read full post »

T I P   Alt text also helps search engines find images when people limit their search to images. To learn how to optimize images and alt text for search engines, see Chapter 17.

Always consider your audience when writing alt text. Will the description be useful to people viewing it on mobile devices? To people hearing it spoken by a screen reader? Some **best practices for styling alt text follow**.

- Write alt text that is specific to each image.
- Limit alt text to a phrase or one short sentence.
- Make the alt text meaningful and functional in the context of the page rather than merely descriptive. For instance, if you have a picture of a pen next to your email link, "Send us an email" is more meaningful alt text for the image than "Picture of a pen."

Examples

For a picture of the Golden Gate Bridge with all its lights off for Earth Hour, accompanying a story about Earth Hour:

Before
Alt text: "0014-ggsf.jpg"

After
Alt text: "Golden Gate Bridge goes dark for Earth Hour."

For a picture of a dog scratching at fleas, accompanying a story about plant-based pest-control products:

Before
Alt text: "Dog"

After
Alt text: "Dog scratching at fleas"

TIP If an image is merely decorative and does not contribute to the page's text or have a function associated with it (for example, it is not clickable), many authorities recommend leaving the **alt** attribute empty so that a person using a screen reader will not have to spend time listening to the screen reader say things like "Decorative curlicues." (To learn more about alt text and other ways to make sure that people with disabilities can experience your site, see Chapter 6, "Make Your Site Accessible to Everyone.")

- Use sentence-style capitalization for alt text. (For capitalization styles, see "Capitalization" on page 239.)
- Use ending punctuation for complete sentences.

Image captions

An image caption gives readers more **information about the image** itself or about the story it illustrates. Captions read by a screen reader are also helpful to people who can't see images.

It's still wise to write alt text for an image even if the image has a caption—for search engines, it's desirable to have the extra text associated with the image. But avoid using the exact same wording for both alt text and caption.

Example

Alt text
Orsini-Jones kicks winning goal.

Caption
Giuliana Orsini-Jones, in her final game, kicks the ball straight through the goalie's legs to score the winning point and claim the Gold Cup for the Brisbane–West Nile youth soccer team.

Feedback messages and error messages

Never leave site visitors in the dark when they've made an input error, when they need to wait, or when they've encountered some sort of problem. Immediately let them know what's happening and what to do next.

Helpful feedback messages

Use feedback messages to orient visitors to their location on your site or to acknowledge their actions. For example, after people submit a question, they might see a page saying, "We're processing your request—this may take a few minutes." Or after customers have purchased something, they might receive feedback saying, "Thank you for your order. Please print your invoice."

For these kinds of feedback messages:

- Clearly confirm the user-initiated actions.
- Provide information in a consistent, straightforward manner.
- Be courteous. If people may need to wait, tell them.

User-friendly (not user-frightening) error messages

The most important type of feedback—and often the most overlooked from an editorial perspective—is the error message. A well-written error message can create a trust-building safety net for your website's applications.

Error messages are an integral part of the user experience. Yet many sites, to their detriment, treat them as an afterthought, using wording that seems to have been created solely for engineers. Such messages often leave site visitors frustrated about what just happened and confused about what to do next.

Example

!

Error 678!

Error messages: Getting technical

Typically written by site designers or software engineers, error messages—like any other text—need editing to make them as clear and as tight as possible. But to ensure an accurate, effective error message, you must first know two basic facts:

1. **The reason for the error.** For instance, was it a customer error, such as inputting a faulty promotional code? Or was it a system error, such as a communication problem between internal systems? The reason for the error should determine how the message is crafted. Should the customer *try again* or *try again later*? There is a big difference.

2. **The action a visitor can take to correct the error and move on.** Your objective is to move visitors quickly from the glitch back to their task. These examples give the visitor information about how to correct and move on: *Please check the code and re-enter it* or *Sorry, this offer code is no longer valid. Please enter a valid code* or *If the problem persists, please contact Customer Service.*

You can usually obtain these two facts from the product manager, a site engineer, or another teammate who knows the technicalities of error conditions.

To **make your error messages user-friendly**:

- **Be specific.** Help the person understand what went wrong.

Example

Before
Invalid data

After
Enter a day from 1 to 31.

- **Be constructive and positive.** When an error is caused by something the user has done, don't chastise or place blame. Instead, tell people what they need to do to set things right.

Example

Before
You entered a ZIP code of the wrong length.

After
Please enter a 5-digit ZIP code.

- **Be helpful.** If the error involves filling out a required field, have the form remain filled in as much as possible with the information the user provided. Draw attention to the missing field or fields by using markers such as exclamation points, asterisks, or the word *Attention* before any missing field. Explain what such markers mean—for example, with an instruction like "Fields marked with an asterisk (*) are required." You can use red text in addition to these methods, but don't rely solely on people being able to see the color—some of your site's visitors may be color-blind; others may be blind (see Chapter 6).
- **Avoid technical jargon.** In all your UI text, but especially in error messages, write so that the average person with little or no technical background can understand what's going on.

Example

Before
Are you sure you want to navigate away from this form?

After
Are you sure you want to close this window?

- **Be courteous.** Consider the reaction of the site visitor suddenly faced with your error message. Use polite language, and employ a friendly tone if it's appropriate for your site. One way to achieve a friendly tone is to use the second person—*you* and *your*. But don't use these pronouns if the result could be interpreted as suggesting blame.

Example

Before
Sign-up rejected. You did not enter a password of the required length.

After
Please enter a password that is at least 8 characters.

■ **Use the appropriate capitalization.** Messages in sentence case are easier to read than those in title case or in all uppercase. (See "Capitalization" on page 239 for the rules governing sentence case.) Use all uppercase letters only for brief one- or two-word alerts such as "warning" or "time-sensitive."

Example

WARNING: Previous version detected. Delete all previous versions of this program before installing the new one.

Example

Before
Email Address Not Found, Please Try Again

After
Email address not found. Please try again.

Better
We can't find this email address. Please check the address and try again.

Help and FAQs

Online help and FAQs (lists of frequently asked questions) are part of *user-assistance text,* which also includes tutorials, wizards, manuals, and more. Entire books (and technical writing courses) exist to teach people how to write user-assistance material; what follow are some basic guidelines for common types of website help.

All user-assistance text is driven by the same issue: People are seeking help with some aspect of your site. They may be confused or annoyed. Give them the information they need with concise, direct writing that gets right to the point.

The basics

Follow these **general principles when writing user-assistance text**:

- Use simple, friendly, straightforward language.

Example

Before
The first thing that you will need to do is to create an account for sharing your photos.

After
First, create an account for sharing your photos.

_____

- Avoid jargon, hype, and marketing-speak.
- Be consistent in your presentation, terminology, typography, and voice. For example:
    - If you use boldface to visually distinguish button names (see "Strategies for making the names of UI elements stand out in text" on page 146), bold the names in all sections of your help topics.
    - Use consistent terms for UI elements. Don't call a radio button a radio button in one place and then call it a circle somewhere else.
- Use *simply* and *just* sparingly in instructions. Overusing them can sound condescending.

Example

Before
To view an image, simply click **View**. To return to your original page, just click **View** again.

After
To view an image, click **View**. Click **View** again to return to your original page.

_____

- When linking to another page, use words, not URLs, for the link.

Example

Before

For more information, go to http://www.bootlegbaby.com/FAQ/.

After

For more information, read our FAQ.

■ Break up long passages of text into easy-to-read chunks. See "Paragraphs" on page 64.

FAQs

A website's FAQ typically includes questions that the site owner anticipates being asked or that site visitors actually do ask regularly.

Use these basic **guidelines to develop questions**:

■ **Write questions as if the user were asking them.** People will be looking for the problem as *they* see it, not the solution you know to be the case.

♦ Avoid using technical language and jargon unless it's necessary for the reader to recognize the technical term.

Example

Before

How can I troubleshoot the lower filter midcycle when Code 6 indicates substandard operation of the unit?

After

What does "Code 6" mean?

♦ Avoid writing questions that the user would not ask and that are clearly designed to deliver specific information (particularly self-serving or marketing information).

Example

Is the Housekeeper 3000 robot an excellent value when compared to the cost of a housecleaning service over time?

- **Write all questions in the same person.** That is, write questions all in first person (*How do I close my account?*) or all in second person (*How do you close an account?*).
- **If a question has a "yes" or "no" answer, state that first and then explain the answer.**

Will the Housekeeper 3000 robot wash windows?

Yes. It will wash windows once a season. To activate the seasonal window-washing function, refer to the Master Code list for the Wash Windows code.

Task-based help

Task-based help **explains how to do something specific**. Your explanation may be fairly simple, or it may require a series of instructional steps. As you write your instructions, visualize yourself performing the task. When you've finished writing, try following your own instructions to the letter—or better yet, enlist someone else to try them. Any gaps, confusing passages, or annoying repetitions should become apparent right away.

Organizing task-based help

You can organize task-based help in two basic ways: (1) through a simple **list** of commonly performed tasks like *Edit my account information* and *Contact the site administrator* or (2) through a series of **questions** about performing a specific procedure. These questions can be from your FAQ (*How can I donate artwork to your archive?*), or they can focus on how to get the most out of your services (*I can't upload photos by clicking **Upload**. What should I do?*).

In general, follow these **basic organizational guidelines**:

- Avoid beginning each question in a series with the same word or words. Doing so forces the reader to plow through several words to get to the unique part of the question.

Example

Before
How do I change my billing information?
How do I change my shipping information?
How do I track my order?
How do I cancel my order?

After

How do I...

Change my billing information?

Change my shipping information?

Track my order?

Cancel my order?

■   Make sure that each item in the list completes the question.

Example

Before

How do I...

How do I place an order? *(Doesn't complete "How do I . . . ")*

Pay by check?

Can I track my order? *(Doesn't complete "How do I . . . ")*

After

How do I...

Place an order?

Pay by check?

Track my order?

Explaining how to do something

The explanation part of task-based help is often written as a series of steps. Follow these basic **guidelines for explaining a procedure**:

■   If you need to include an introduction to a procedure, start with an infinitive (the *to* form of a verb). This will get your reader to the point quickly.

Example

Before

You can change the default appearance of your database by following these steps:

After

To change the default appearance of your database:

■ Break explanations of more than two actions into numbered steps. This makes the procedure easy to read and simple to follow.

TIP Create numbered lists using HTML or whatever code is appropriate for your publishing tool. Don't use manually entered numbers and indention. See Chapter 16, "Get Familiar With Basic Webpage Coding," for help with coding common HTML elements such as lists.

Example

Before
You can select which celebrities you'd like to receive news about by first clicking the Celebrity News button on the Profile Setup page. In the window that pops up, choose the names of the celebrities you'd like to receive news about. If you don't see the name of the celebrity you are interested in, enter his or her name in the text box at the bottom of the page. Click Finish.

After
To select the celebrities you'd like to receive news about:
1.   On the Profile Setup page, click **Celebrity News**.
2.   In the pop-up window that appears, choose the names of the celebrities you'd like to receive news about. If you don't see the name of the celebrity you are interested in, enter the person's name in the text box at the bottom of the page.
3.   Click **Finish**.

■ Avoid creating a list with a single numbered step. Instead, incorporate the step into the introductory text.

Example

Before
To install the software:
1.   Click on the downloaded file and follow the prompts.

After
To install the software, click on the downloaded file and follow the prompts.

■   To ease reading and scanning, indent all wrapping lines of the numbered or bulleted text so that they left-align with each other and not with the numbers or bullets. See Chapter 16 for the HTML coding for such a list.

Example

Before

To set up your horoscope profile and start receiving information:
Step 1: Enter your name and birth information. You will need your birth date, the exact time of your birth, and the city and country in which you were born.
Step 2: Enter the email address to which you would like your detailed horoscope sent. State whether you would like a one-time detailed horoscope, a daily horoscope based on your sun sign, or both.
Step 3: Enter your billing data.

After

To set up your horoscope profile and start receiving information:
1.   Enter your name and birth information. You will need your birth date, the exact time of your birth, and the city and country in which you were born.
2.   Enter the email address to which you would like your detailed horoscope sent. State whether you would like a one-time detailed horoscope, a daily horoscope based on your sun sign, or both.
3.   Enter your billing data.

For more information on creating and formatting lists, see "Lists" on page 65.

T I P   In help text, a picture is much better than a thousand words. Include images whenever possible.

User-instruction mechanics

When explaining how to do something (for example, how to move around a site or a software program), you often need to refer to buttons or checkboxes, or to keys on the keyboard. Clarity and consistency are important.

Referring to users

When referring to site visitors, members, consumers, subscribers, viewers, or other people visiting your site, follow these guidelines:

- In general, address people directly by using the second person (*you, your,* and *yours*).

Example

Before
Users may choose a password between 8 and 15 characters in length.

After
You may choose a password between 8 and 15 characters in length.

Better
Choose a password between 8 and 15 characters in length. *("You" is understood.)*

- Although this book sometimes employs the word *users* to refer to site visitors, be aware that *user* can sound techie or impersonal. Depending on the context, consider using something like *member, consumer, reader, subscriber, customer, person, people, participant, or visitor.*

Referring to links, buttons, and other UI elements

When referring in text to links or to the label or text of interactive elements such as buttons, radio buttons, and checkboxes:

- **Use the same wording and capitalization that people will see on the onscreen element.** Double-check that the instructions you're giving match the words and capitalization of the text exactly. For example, if a button label uses title case, use that when referring to the button. See "Capitalization" on page 239 for capitalization style rules.

Example

Change Display Order

Before
To change how your appointments are displayed, click CHANGE MY DISPLAY ORDER.

(Actual button text doesn't include "my," and capitalization is title case, not all capital letters.)

After

To change how your appointments are displayed, click **Change Display Order**.

■ **Make labels stand out visually.** To distinguish a label from the surrounding text, use bold-face for the label of the onscreen element or enclose it in quotation marks. Boldface is preferred, but be consistent in your choice. (See "Strategies for making the names of UI elements stand out in text" below.)

T I P   Whichever way you choose to make labels stand out visually in text, you may want to use the same convention for referring to text that the user must type in and to other technical elements, such as HTML tags and attributes. For example (if you use boldface to visually distinguish such elements): *Type **Calico cat** in the **alt** attribute of the **<img>** tag, then click **Save Changes***.

Strategies for making the names of UI elements stand out in text

In this book, we advocate boldface to visually distinguish labels from text in a sentence. Here's why.

Initial capital letters

Some websites rely on the use of initial capital letters to make the UI element name stand out: *Click the Start Over button.* But this style gets tricky when you're dealing with things like checkbox names, which tend to be written in sentence case: *Check the Remember my settings checkbox and click Save.*

Solutions for this problem include using initial capital letters even when the actual on-screen element does not use them *(the Remember My Settings checkbox)* or using quotation marks only for onscreen elements that don't appear in title case: *Check the "Remember my settings" checkbox and click Save.* (For information on capitalization styles, see "Capitalization" on page 239.)

Quotation marks

Another solution is to use quotation marks to distinguish all onscreen elements: *Check the "Remember my settings" checkbox and click "Save."* But if you're writing something like help text with a lot of instructions, your copy can become cluttered with quotation marks. In addition, if you use quotation marks around text that the user must input, people may think they must also type in the quotation marks. Consider which is easier to comprehend:

At the prompt, type **copy**

At the prompt, type "copy"

Bold

Many websites use boldface type to distinguish onscreen elements: *Check the* **Remember my settings** *checkbox and click* **Save**. This is our choice. Not only does it eliminate the problems noted above, but it's also easy for the eye to pick out.

Two cautions, however:

1. If you're also using boldface to highlight key words or topics or new terminology in your copy, you may end up with too much boldface—a situation that overwhelms the eye so that nothing stands out.
2. Search engines notice boldface. A lot of button and checkbox names set in boldface could diminish the value of any other text set in boldface, as far as search engines are concerned (see Chapter 17).

Referring to keyboard keys

It is usually **not necessary to visually distinguish the names of keyboard keys** from the surrounding text. If you do, bold the key names or put them in quotes. Whichever you choose, be consistent.

For keys that must be pressed simultaneously, separate the keys with a plus sign (Alt+Tab) or with a hyphen (Alt-Tab)—again, consistency is important. The plus sign is more commonly used and may be easier to read than the hyphen. It also properly indicates that the user is meant to type a combination of keys, not a sequence.

When referring to keys on the keyboard, use the following terms:

Alt	End	Pause
arrow keys	Enter	Print Screen
Backspace	Esc	Reset
Break	F8	Return (Macintosh)
Caps Lock	Home	Right Arrow
Clear	Insert	Scroll Lock
Command (Macintosh)	Left Arrow	Select
Control (Macintosh)	Num Lock	Shift
Ctrl (Windows)	Option (Macintosh)	spacebar
Del or Delete	Page Down	Tab
Down Arrow	Page Up	Up Arrow

Examples

If your text is disappearing as you type, you may have accidentally pressed the Insert key.

Press Ctrl+Alt+Del to bring up the Windows Task Manager.

In Yahoo! Messenger, get your friend's attention by pressing Ctrl+G (Command+G on the Mac). Your friend's window will shake and buzz.

Referring to keyboard and mouse actions

Use consistent language when instructing people to perform an action on the keyboard or with a mouse.

Keyboard actions

When describing a keyboard action:

■ Use *press* to describe the action someone takes on the keyboard. Don't use *hit* unless you're writing something especially casual or colloquial: *Hit Esc quick or your guys in the swamp are goners.*

■ In general, use *type* to describe entering text, although *type in* can be used to describe entering text into a text box. *Enter* is an acceptable alternative to *type,* as long as you're sure there will be no confusion with the Enter key.

Example

Before

Enter your ID and hit the Enter key. *(In general, don't use "hit" for a keyboard action.)*

After

Type your ID and press the Enter key.

Type your ID and press Enter. *(If there's no chance of confusion, omit the word "key.")*

Mouse actions

When describing the actions someone can take with a mouse:

■ **If the person can perform no other action** on the object (and the object is obviously click-able), use *click, double-click, right-click,* and so on, without the word *on.* Objects that are obviously clickable include buttons, radio buttons, links, icons, menu items, and tabs.

Example

Before

Click on the **Edit** link. *(No need for "on" if the object is a link.)*

After

Click the **Edit** link.

Click **Edit**. *(If there's no chance of confusion, omit the word "link.")*

■ **If the person can perform some other action** on the object, such as opening or deleting it, use *click on, double-click on, right-click on,* etc. The object might be a photograph, a file name, a folder, or a similar object.

Example

Before

Click the photo you want to edit.

After

Click on the photo you want to edit. *(Include "on" if the object is a photo or a file.)*

- Avoid using *hover over* or *mouse over* to describe moving the cursor over something—people less familiar with computers and computer jargon may not know what you mean. Use a clearer phrase such as *hold your cursor over* or *move your cursor over*.
- Avoid using *press* or *hit* to describe the mouse action; use *click* or *click on* instead. Reserve the use of *press* for keystrokes.

Example

Before

When you see the monkey appear, press the **I See the Monkey** button.

After

When you see the monkey, click **I See the Monkey**.

- Don't include the words *with your mouse* when describing an action such as clicking or scrolling. It's understood.

Example

Before

Right-click on the file with your mouse.

After

Right-click on the file.

- Remember that the screen object being manipulated is the cursor, not the mouse. Write *Put your cursor on the link and click,* not *Put your mouse on the link and click.*

Ideas in Practice

Example: Give visitors good directions

In this example, you'll see "before" and "after" versions of four webpage fragments for a fictional site where people can create music video playlists:

1. Registration form to set up an account
2. Registration confirmation page

3. Main page for creating video playlists
4. FAQ explaining playlist requirements

Imagine trying to use the website featured in the "before" images. In each, you'll see that the UI text needs editing to give the user a simple, clear, and consistent experience.

Before

Page 1: Registration form to set up an account

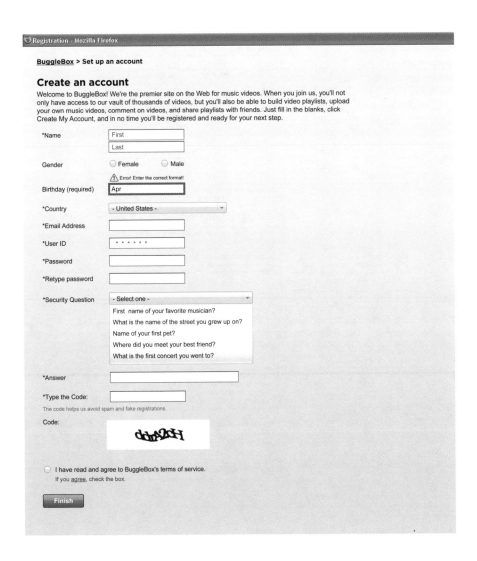

After

Page 1: Registration form to set up an account

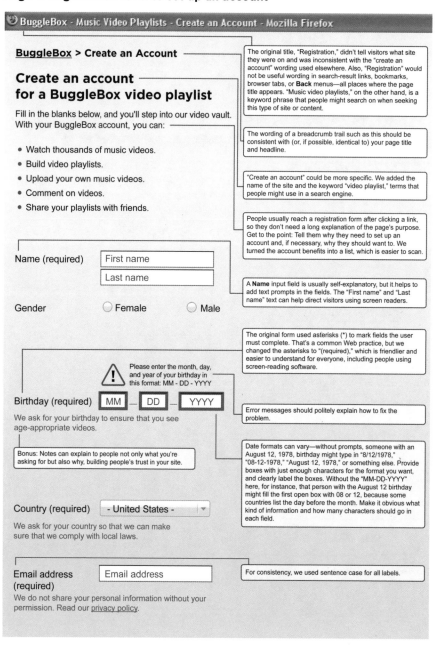

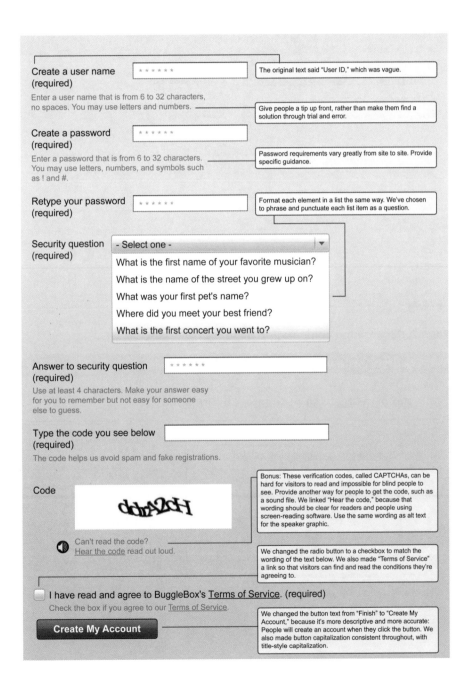

Create a user name (required)

******

The original text said "User ID," which was vague.

Enter a user name that is from 6 to 32 characters, no spaces. You may use letters and numbers.

Give people a tip up front, rather than make them find a solution through trial and error.

Create a password (required)

******

Enter a password that is from 6 to 32 characters. You may use letters, numbers, and symbols such as ! and #.

Password requirements vary greatly from site to site. Provide specific guidance.

Retype your password (required)

******

Format each element in a list the same way. We've chosen to phrase and punctuate each list item as a question.

Security question (required)

- Select one -

What is the first name of your favorite musician?

What is the name of the street you grew up on?

What was your first pet's name?

Where did you meet your best friend?

What is the first concert you went to?

Answer to security question (required)

******

Use at least 4 characters. Make your answer easy for you to remember but not easy for someone else to guess.

Type the code you see below (required)

The code helps us avoid spam and fake registrations.

Code

ddbA2cH

Bonus: These verification codes, called CAPTCHAs, can be hard for visitors to read and impossible for blind people to see. Provide another way for people to get the code, such as a sound file. We linked "Hear the code," because that wording should be clear for readers and people using screen-reading software. Use the same wording as alt text for the speaker graphic.

Can't read the code? Hear the code read out loud.

We changed the radio button to a checkbox to match the wording of the text below. We also made "Terms of Service" a link so that visitors can find and read the conditions they're agreeing to.

☐ I have read and agree to BuggleBox's Terms of Service. (required)

Check the box if you agree to our Terms of Service.

Create My Account

We changed the button text from "Finish" to "Create My Account," because it's more descriptive and more accurate: People will create an account when they click the button. We also made button capitalization consistent throughout, with title-style capitalization.

Before

Page 2: Registration confirmation page

BuggleBox - Music Video Playlists - Thank You - Mozilla Firefox

BuggleBox > Create an account > Complete

Congratulations! You're all set, and we've sent your account details to the email address you entered. Enjoy the site!

After

Page 2: Registration confirmation page

BuggleBox - Create an Account - Account Confirmation - Mozilla Firefox

BuggleBox > Create an Account > Confirmation

Congratulations!
You have a BuggleBox account, and we've sent your account details to the email address you entered.

Now you can watch videos, create your own video playlist, or check out our homepage to see what's new.

The original page title, "BuggleBox - Music Video Playlists - Thank You," didn't match the wording on the page and didn't tell new members where they were in the account-creation process. We considered keeping "Music Video Playlists" in the page title for the sake of consistency, but the extra words would've made the title 68 characters long, and the title should be no more than 65 characters (the browser name—here, "Mozilla Firefox"—doesn't count). Also, this page does not require keywords, because it's not a page that people would find through search engines.

The original text told people to enjoy the site but didn't offer any next steps or links to go elsewhere on the site. Stranded visitors would have been forced to use the breadcrumb or to re-enter the site's URL. We added this sentence to give them avenues into the site.

A breadcrumb may not be absolutely necessary on this page, but it's best to be consistent. We changed the wording on the third phrase from "Complete" to "Confirmation" to be consistent with the page title.

Before

Page 3: Main page for creating video playlists

Untitled Page - Mozilla Firefox

Create a video playlist

To make your own video Collection, simply (1) click videos in the left column and (2) drag them to the right. Delete tracks from your playlist by clicking the X, and click Save when you're all done. Search for additional videos using the search box below the list. Click the Play button to hear a sample of the video first. Don't forget to share your playlist with friends.

Select videos

▶ Keytar, "Acid Wash"

▶ Justin Time, "Unicorn Chaser"

▶ Lay-Lo, "Assassin Avenue"

Your jukebox

Name

> Name

Description

My Videos
1. Keytar, "Acid Wash" ⊗
2.
3.
4.
5.
⊞ Show all 25

▶ The Shuffles, "Podrophenia"

> Save

▶ Beta Max, "RTFM"

> Clear The Form

▶ Red Belles, "Catch and Release"

> Play

▶ TSA, "Aluminum Cucumber"

> Share your playlist.

Now that you've created a playlist, click Play Playlist to rock out and share your playlist to let your friends enjoy the mix. Or visit the homepage to see which videos we've added today.

Having trouble creating your BuggleBox Jukebox? Visit our troubleshooting tips.

After

Page 3: Main page for creating video playlists

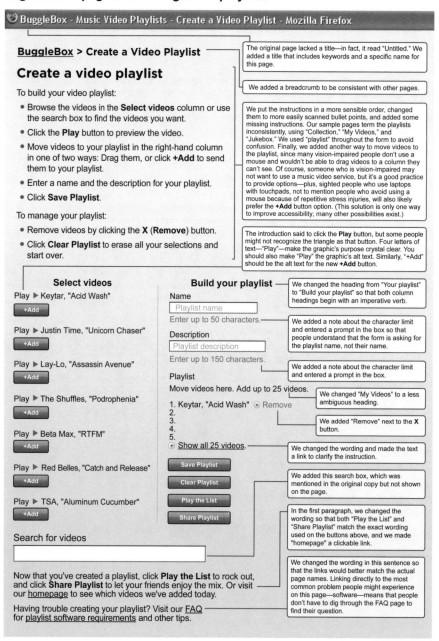

BuggleBox - Music Video Playlists - Create a Video Playlist - Mozilla Firefox

BuggleBox > Create a Video Playlist ——— The original page lacked a title—in fact, it read "Untitled." We added a title that includes keywords and a specific name for this page.

Create a video playlist

——— We added a breadcrumb to be consistent with other pages.

To build your video playlist:

- Browse the videos in the **Select videos** column or use the search box to find the videos you want.
- Click the **Play** button to preview the video.
- Move videos to your playlist in the right-hand column in one of two ways: Drag them, or click **+Add** to send them to your playlist.
- Enter a name and the description for your playlist.
- Click **Save Playlist**.

We put the instructions in a more sensible order, changed them to more easily scanned bullet points, and added some missing instructions. Our sample pages term the playlists inconsistently, using "Collection," "My Videos," and "Jukebox." We used "playlist" throughout the form to avoid confusion. Finally, we added another way to move videos to the playlist, since many vision-impaired people don't use a mouse and wouldn't be able to drag videos to a column they can't see. Of course, someone who is vision-impaired may not want to use a music video service, but it's a good practice to provide options—plus, sighted people who use laptops with touchpads, not to mention people who avoid using a mouse because of repetitive stress injuries, will also likely prefer the **+Add** button option. (This solution is only one way to improve accessibility; many other possibilities exist.)

To manage your playlist:

- Remove videos by clicking the **X (Remove)** button.
- Click **Clear Playlist** to erase all your selections and start over.

The introduction said to click the **Play** button, but some people might not recognize the triangle as that button. Four letters of text—"Play"—make the graphic's purpose crystal clear. You should also make "Play" the graphic's alt text. Similarly, "+Add" should be the alt text for the new **+Add** button.

Select videos	**Build your playlist**

We changed the heading from "Your playlist" to "Build your playlist" so that both column headings begin with an imperative verb.

Play ▶ Keytar, "Acid Wash"
[+Add]

Name
[Playlist name]
Enter up to 50 characters. ——— We added a note about the character limit and entered a prompt in the box so that people understand that the form is asking for the playlist name, not their name.

Play ▶ Justin Time, "Unicorn Chaser"
[+Add]

Description
[Playlist description]
Enter up to 150 characters. ——— We added a note about the character limit and entered a prompt in the box.

Play ▶ Lay-Lo, "Assassin Avenue"
[+Add]

Playlist
Move videos here. Add up to 25 videos. ——— We changed "My Videos" to a less ambiguous heading.

Play ▶ The Shuffles, "Podrophenia"
[+Add]

1. Keytar, "Acid Wash" ⊗ Remove
2.
3. ——— We added "Remove" next to the **X** button.
4.
5.

Play ▶ Beta Max, "RTFM"
[+Add]

⊕ Show all 25 videos. ——— We changed the wording and made the text a link to clarify the instruction.

Play ▶ Red Belles, "Catch and Release"
[+Add]

[Save Playlist]
[Clear Playlist]
[Play the List]
[Share Playlist]

We added this search box, which was mentioned in the original copy but not shown on the page.

Play ▶ TSA, "Aluminum Cucumber"
[+Add]

In the first paragraph, we changed the wording so that both "Play the List" and "Share Playlist" match the exact wording used on the buttons above, and we made "homepage" a clickable link.

Search for videos
[   ]

Now that you've created a playlist, click **Play the List** to rock out, and click **Share Playlist** to let your friends enjoy the mix. Or visit our homepage to see which videos we've added today.

We changed the wording in this sentence so that the links would better match the actual page names. Linking directly to the most common problem people might experience on this page—software—means that people don't have to dig through the FAQ page to find their question.

Having trouble creating your playlist? Visit our FAQ for playlist software requirements and other tips.

Before

Page 4: FAQ explaining playlist requirements

⚙ Untitled Page - Mozilla Firefox

BuggleBox > **FAQ** > Software

Software Requirements for Creating Playlists

To use the Playlist Manager, you need the following software and versions:
PC: Windows XP or 2000, IE 6.0, Firefox 1.5 or higher, Flash player 9 or higher
Mac: OS X, Firefox 1.5 or higher, Safari 1.2 or higher, Flash Player 8 or higher

Next

After

Page 4: FAQ explaining playlist requirements

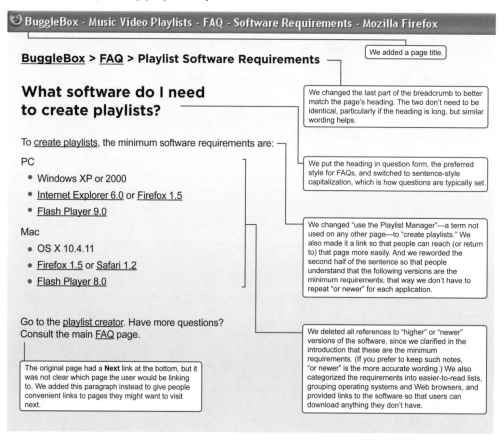

Chapter 8

Write Engaging Email and Newsletters

In this chapter

- **Use email as an outreach tool.** When is email the best way to reach your audience?
- **Build better email messages.** Increase the chances that your email will be opened, read, and responded to.
- **Create specific customer communications.** Guidelines for newsletters, promotional messages, and service announcements.

Email can be a powerful extension of your website. It can reach out to your audience with helpful updates, it can remind them how much they like your site, it can inform them about new features or products, and it can draw them back to your website to engage them more deeply. Properly designed and distributed, newsletters and other user communications can also enhance your brand and create a more personal connection with your audience.

Writing effective email involves many of the same techniques as writing website content: crafting informative headings, using short sentences, constructing strategic links, using clear and simple wording. But on a website, the audience chooses to come to the content, whereas with email the content goes out to the audience—so an email message must work doubly hard to gain attention and persuade people to click.

Beyond writing, how you distribute and manage your email has an impact on user satisfaction, not to mention on your reputation for credibility and reliable service.

Use email as an outreach tool

Many types of organizations with an online presence rely on email to communicate with their customers and members. Retail sites email order confirmations and sales promotions; political organizations send alerts about actions and requests for support; and sites of all kinds send announcements such as notices about service interruptions or outages.

No matter what kind of website you're writing for or what size your organization is, the success of your email communications will depend not only on the content but also on two less tangible concerns: how well you manage the administrative details of an email list—keeping the addresses up-to-date, testing, sending, and so on—and how well you respect recipients' wishes.

Consider your resources

Before you begin a large email campaign, consider whether your organization can handle the administrative and technical aspects of email outreach. For example:

- Can you manage a large list effectively? Which address will the replies from email recipients go to? How will you keep track of invalid email addresses? How will you handle subscriptions and requests to unsubscribe?
- Can you personalize each email by automatically filling the **To** field or other portions of the message for each recipient?

Bulking up: Email service providers

Email service providers—sometimes called email marketing service providers or email marketing providers—help organizations manage bulk email delivery. For example, if you want to send a newsletter to 100,000 subscribers, an ESP can handle that process and can maintain a list of invalid addresses to delete from your next mailing.

ESPs can also contribute valuable information and feedback about your email strategies. For example, ESPs can provide tracking data showing how many recipients opened an email, and whether one link was more successful than another in coaxing recipients to click it. They can also segment an audience based on interests or other information you provide and can help your organization send targeted messages to specific segments.

Of course, you can do a lot of this work yourself with email management software. Campaigner, Campaign Monitor, and Constant Contact are three of the better-known packages. The question is whether you have the time to do the work yourself, or whether you'd be better off outsourcing it to an ESP.

For more information about ESPs, including specific providers, go to the websites of Forrester Research (www.forrester.com), MarketingSherpa (www.marketingsherpa.com), and BuyerZone (www.buyerzone.com).

- Are you confident that your emails will appear as you intend them to in all the email clients used by your recipients?

Software tools can help with some of these objectives. But if this level of email maintenance is beyond what your organization can handle on its own, and if you can afford it, an email service provider (ESP) can take over the technical aspects for you. See "Bulking up: Email service providers" on page 160.

TIP The News & Resources section of Yahoo! Small Business includes information on email marketing: http://smallbusiness.yahoo.com.

Respect the recipient

The point of emailing the people who use your website is to draw them to your site and to strengthen your relationship with them. That's why the most effective email considers the recipient first:

- Your message should build on the **relationship** you have with your site's visitors.
- Your message should be related to the recipients' interests or activities—and **relevant** to the recipients' needs.
- Your message should **respect** the recipients' preferences. Ideally, send email only to people who "opt in," or specifically ask to receive email from you. Or, if you choose an "opt out" model, be certain that you send email only to those who haven't opted out, or asked to be removed from the mailing.

Adhere to antispam laws

To the recipient, there's a fine line between effective marketing and unwanted bulk mail, or spam. Spam is regulated in the United States under the CAN-SPAM Act, which went into effect in 2004 and was clarified in 2008. Make sure that your promotional email messages comply with CAN-SPAM regulations.

You can find general information on CAN-SPAM at http://www.ftc.gov/spam. The European Union has its own directives governing spam, and other countries and regions may have their own laws, too. For information specific to your situation, consult a lawyer who is familiar with the antispam laws of the relevant countries.

We discuss specific types of customer email, such as newsletters and promotions, later in this chapter. The following **guidelines** are effective for all customer-directed communications.

- **Consider what your recipients expect from your message.** For example, is the audience for your email narrower than the audience for your website? If so, write your email with that specific audience in mind. (See Chapter 2, "Identify Your Audience.")
- **Adapt your voice to suit the message.** For instance, the voice of a marketing email is generally different from the voice of a service announcement. In most cases, you'll want to keep the tone conversational, friendly, and helpful. (For more on establishing a voice for your site and adapting it to various situations, see Chapter 3, "Define Your Voice.")
- **Include a clear call-to-action link** from your email to your site. Guide the recipient on what to do next.

Example

*This portion of an HTML email includes several call-to-action links. The most prominent is the **Watch Demo Now** button near the top of the email.*

- **Consider the whole experience.** Create a consistent, compelling experience from your email message to the page on your site that the message links to (called the landing page). See "Promotional emails" on page 177 for tips.
- **Test, test, test.** Be sure your email message is ready to go before you send it. Proofread it carefully (see page 364 for tips). Then test its appearance (and whether it arrives at all—different ISPs and services have different spam-filtering rules) on all major email clients and services. The appearance of your message will vary across platforms. For more information, see "Testing, testing" on page 170.

Build better email messages

Many of the principles that apply to writing Web content also apply to email writing:

- **Meaningful headlines and subheadings** tell readers what your email is about.

- **Short paragraphs and sentences** hold the attention of readers.
- **Bulleted and numbered lists** break up the message visually and help readers take in information quickly.
- **Front-loaded content**—important words at the beginning of sentences, and important information and your call to action at the top of the email—gives readers what they need to see without their having to scroll.
- **Effective links** lure readers to your site.

But **email content is different from Web content** in a number of ways:

- **Customization.** You can tailor email content to specific sectors of your audience and, based on the data you collect or track, even to an individual's location.
- **Layout and image options.** Email messages come in two flavors: HTML and plain text. HTML can contain images and look just as polished as your website; plain text must be written and laid out using only the characters you might find on a typewriter. Text email is favored by recipients who don't want to wait for images to load, including many who are viewing their messages on a mobile device.
- **Outward communication.** On your site, people come to you; in email, you are reaching out to them. This allows you to target your message to recipients and to communicate the exact action you want them to take. Whatever that action is, your email should highlight it: Your call to action, be it a button or a text link, should be prominent and crystal clear. (See "The body of the message" on page 171.)
- **Formatting.** Email programs may be less likely than Web browsers to render special characters and formatting correctly. So, even if you use coded characters such as smart quotes and em dashes on your site and in an HTML email, avoid using them in a plain-text email. (For more information on special characters, see "Special characters" on page 386.)
- **The subject line.** It's critical to write a compelling and informative subject line—it's the first thing recipients see, and it's what motivates them to open the message or to ignore it. (See "The subject line" on page 167.)

To and From

The **To** field lists the people you're addressing directly; the **From** field reveals the sender. In both fields, use names that enhance the credibility and professionalism of your communication. A small-business owner, especially, should take care to send customer-directed email messages from an email address that recipients will recognize as coming from the business's website.

Example

Before

From: seller@eee-mail.net
To: Sally Shopper
Subject: Your order with Bootleg Baby

After

From: seller@bootlegbaby.com
To: Sally Shopper
Subject: Your order with Bootleg Baby

You can also set up your email so that your business name, not an email address, populates the **From** field. This option is especially helpful for readers who are scanning their inbox.

Example

Before

From: seller@bootlegbaby.com
To: Sally Shopper
Subject: Your order with Bootleg Baby

After

From: Bootleg Baby
To: Sally Shopper
Subject: Your order with Bootleg Baby

TIP People may want to reply to the emails you send them. If you have a large list of recipients, you won't want all the feedback coming to your official **From** address—especially since "feedback" can include bounce messages, those automatically generated emails that tell you that your message could not be delivered to a particular address. Email service providers (see page 160) and email management software will typically let you specify a different address for receiving replies (a Reply-To address), and yet another address for receiving bounced messages (a Return-Path address).

For a **customer communication**, you can populate the **To** field a few ways:

- With an individual name. (See "Bulking up: Email service providers" on page 160.) This is the most professional option.
- With an *email alias*—a single address that's connected to a distribution list of your recipients. This method allows you to email a group of people while protecting the privacy of each individual in the group. For example, the alias members@redgrousegreens.com could reach all the members at the Red Grouse Greens golf club. But if you use this method, it's best to set up your mailing so that a more professional-looking phrase appears in the **To** field—for example, you can have "Red Grouse Greens club members" appear instead of the address members@redgrousegreens.com.

T I P   If you do use an alias, make sure that everyone on the recipient list really needs to receive the message. Review the list periodically to see whether any names should be added or removed. (According to CAN-SPAM, a request to be removed from a promotional email must be honored within 10 business days of receiving such a request.) To create an alias, refer to the help section of your email software. In Microsoft Office Outlook, click **File** > **New** > **Distribution List**.

- With a single email address that you control and that's associated with an appropriate group name, using the **Bcc** field to hide the addresses of your recipients. For example, the Red Grouse Greens golf club could contact its members with "Red Grouse Greens club members" appearing in the **To** field, and individual addresses in the **Bcc** field.

 ## Cc and Bcc: C what?

You probably know that the **Cc** and **Bcc** fields are used for sending copies to people other than the primary recipient, but you may wonder what these abbreviations mean.

Both derive from the days of the typewriter. To make one or more copies, the typist inserted a "carbon"—a special sheet of paper coated with ink—between two sheets of typing paper. The pressure of the keys created replicas of the original document. These replicas could be filed for reference and also sent to a second recipient—in which case the typist put *Cc: John Jones* at the bottom of the document, indicating that a *carbon copy* went to John Jones. Typing *Bcc: John Jones* on John Jones's copy indicated that he was sent a *blind carbon copy*—the recipient of the original document didn't know that Jones received a copy.

Cc and Bcc

The **Cc field** is an FYI zone. For emails to business colleagues and peers, include in this field any people who need the information in the email but don't need to reply or take action.

The **Bcc field** is for emails to recipients who need the information but whose inclusion or addresses you want to keep private.

Many businesses and organizations rely on email service providers or email marketing software to distribute customer messages, so they don't often use the **Cc** and **Bcc** fields. But some small organizations (and some larger ones sending email to a small audience) use the **Bcc** field to email a group while protecting the privacy of all recipients.

Put recipients' addresses in the **Bcc** field and one of your own addresses in the **To** field, and your recipients won't see anyone else's address—they'll see only what you put in the **To** field. You can specify an appropriate group name to appear in the **To** field instead of your own address.

Example

What you send
From: counseling-group@county.org
To: oversharers-news@county.org
Cc:
Bcc: person-x@address, person-y@address, person-z@address, . . .
(The address counseling-group@county.org is associated with the name "County Counseling Group," and oversharers-news@county.org, an address owned by the sender, is associated with "Oversharers Anonymous members.")

What recipients see
From: County Counseling Group
To: Oversharers Anonymous members

T I P   If you're using the **Bcc** field to prevent others from seeing all your recipients' addresses, triple-check your work. Make sure that you don't accidentally enter names in the **Cc** field! Such mistakes can and do happen and could violate the privacy of those individuals, bringing serious consequences—legal and otherwise.

The subject line

The subject line is one of the most important components of a successful promotional message or newsletter. It can determine whether a person opens an email message or deletes it. The subject line also directs recipients to pay attention to specific articles, products, and information when they do open an email. Know your goal for a particular email and make sure that the subject line reflects it by directing the recipient, subtly or overtly, to pay attention to whatever you want to highlight.

Here are some best practices for subject lines.

Make **subject lines short** and easy to scan:

■ Keep subject-line text under 55 characters, including spaces. Front-load your most important words into the first 30 characters—they are the most visible. Some email applications cut off long subject lines; the number of allowed characters varies.

Example

Before
From: Bootleg Baby
Subject: Sunday is the first day of our sample sale--save big on little items

After
From: Bootleg Baby
Subject: Sample sale starts Sunday--save big on little items

T I P You can also keep the subject line short by using ampersands (&) and commonly understood abbreviations: *We have cars, trucks & RVs.* And because it's unnecessary to include a serial comma before an ampersand, you save a valuable character. (See "Commas" on page 204.)

■ Use consistent capitalization—sentence case or title case—from message to message. Sentence case is easier to get right: You're less likely to make a capitalization mistake. Also, many people find sentence case easier to scan. And it looks friendlier—after all, people don't usually use title case in the subject lines of email sent to peers. (See "Capitalization" on page 239.)

> **Example**
>
> **Before**
>
> Subject: Sign Up Now for Mardi Gras Events *(Title case: Initial letter of most words capitalized)*
>
> **After**
>
> Subject: Sign up now for Mardi Gras events *(Sentence case: First word and proper nouns capitalized)*

Clearly and accurately describe the content of your message. When subscribers think they've been tricked into opening a message, they may resent it—and unsubscribe. Moreover, in the U.S., CAN-SPAM law requires that the subject lines of all commercial emails accurately and directly reflect the message content. (See "Adhere to antispam laws" on page 161.) Some tips:

- When possible, develop a standard format for subject lines. For example, begin each line with standard text, then tailor the rest of the line to convey the current message's content.

> **Example**
>
> Subject: Your order with ROFL Gifts: Order confirmation
> Subject: Your order with ROFL Gifts: Items on back order
> Subject: Your order with ROFL Gifts: Shipping notification

- Write the subject line with the **From** field in mind. Recipients look at both lines to determine whether an email message is from a trusted source.

> **Example**
>
> From: Yahoo! Sports
> To: Yahoo! Sports Fans
> Subject: Sign up now for Fantasy Football

T I P Using standard wording in subject lines is useful for peer-to-peer email, too. Your workgroup might decide to use terms such as *FYI, RSVP, Alert, Action required, Today,* and so on, for the beginning of subject lines. Such code words let recipients sort and filter messages and help them figure out—before they open the email—whether they need to act right away.

■ If it's appropriate for your voice, strike a balance between being straightforward and being fun.

Example

From: Yahoo! Personals
Subject: Not all of the good ones are taken

Tell and compel. Spark interest with one or more of the following strategies:

■ Inform. Subject lines should convey something important, timely, or beneficial. They should say to the recipient: "If you don't open and read this message, you'll miss out on something of real value to you."

■ Grab the reader's attention. Your email message is competing with many others. The subject line must intrigue recipients like a well-written headline, prompting them to open the message immediately.

■ Include a compelling, specific detail. Prices and recognizable names are often effective. Used sparingly, words like *deal, sale, special, favorites, best-sellers,* and *hottest* can also be effective— although these sorts of words may also increase the chances that your message will be swept into the junk mail folder. (See "Testing, testing" on page 170.)

Example

Before
From: Trapper Sports
Subject: Sale

After
From: Trapper Sports
Subject: This week only: Sale on camping gear and more

Choose your words carefully to avoid spam filters. An email service's spam filter looks for patterns to decide whether an email message is spam or not. There is no one word or phrase that will trip a filter. Filters begin with the subject line, but they look through the entire message. Still, avoid the following filter-triggering words, formatting, and punctuation marks in subject lines:

ALL CAPS	!
$	free (especially at the start of a subject line)
win	remove
click here	credit
bad credit	your credit
your bills	best rates
low rates	buy (especially at the start of a subject line)

T I P   To avoid spam filters, encourage the recipients of your message to add you to their contacts list or to their email application's list of safe senders. For example, in Microsoft Office Outlook for Windows, people can go to **Actions** > **Junk E-mail** and select **Add Sender to Safe Senders List**. In Yahoo! Mail, people can either right-click on your email message and select **Add Sender to Contacts** or click the icon or **Add** link next to your address. You can set similar preferences in other email clients.

Testing, testing

One great advantage of email as a marketing and communication tool: You can easily measure its performance.

Testing subject lines

If you use an email service provider (see page 160) or use software to collect email response data yourself, consider drafting two different relevant subject lines for the same customer-directed message. Test both to see which one is more effective. Test Subject Line A with one sampling of recipients and Subject Line B with another, like this:

- Send the email with Subject Line A to 10 percent of the intended recipients.
- Send the email with Subject Line B to another 10 percent of recipients.
- Analyze the resulting data to determine which subject line was more effective. Ask:
  - Which subject line prompted more users to open the email?
  - Which subject line coaxed more people to click to your site?
  - How accurately did the subject line convey the topic of the message? (A subject line that does a good job of setting reader expectations may yield a lower "open rate" but encourage a higher percentage of people who open it to click to your site. Conversely, a less specific subject line might encourage lots of people to open a message, in which case you would see a high open rate—but if those people were expecting different

content, you may notice fewer clicks on links, a high rate of complaints, or even lots of people unsubscribing.)

■ Shortly after you test, send the email with the winning subject line to the remaining 80 percent of recipients.

Testing different calls to action, images, and layouts

You can also use this method to test different calls to action, different images, and different layout options for the body of the email, to see which garners the best response. For example, one option might include a call-to-action button at the top of the email and use a paragraph layout; another option might be longer but use an easy-to-scan list format and place a call-to-action button at the bottom of the email. For newsletters, you might experiment to see which story grabs more attention in the lead spot—although your scheduled window to send out the email may not be wide enough to accommodate a layout test like this. With newsletters, you might instead analyze data from one edition and integrate what you learn into the next edition.

Testing messages on different email clients

Finally, don't forget to test your email messages to ensure that they're appearing the way you intend them to, and that they arrive in the recipients' mailboxes. Test your messages on all major email clients and services—AOL, Apple Mail, Entourage, Eudora, Gmail, Microsoft Office Outlook, Thunderbird, Windows Live Hotmail, Yahoo! Mail, and others, as well as popular mobile mail programs. How the message appears will depend on the recipient's email program, and different ISPs and services have different spam-filtering rules. Such testing is another service provided by ESPs (see "Bulking up: Email service providers" on page 160). Software tools and online services can also help with this type of testing.

The body of the message

An email message is not a letter. People are more likely to scan it than they are to read it thoroughly, so write accordingly. Consider the following guidelines.

Keep it short:

■ Stick to one topic per email if possible. (Of course, a newsletter may cover subtopics related to its main topic—for example, a sports newsletter may include news about many different sports.)

■ Be even briefer in email than you are on your website—more and more people are reading email on their mobile devices.

T I P Some usability experts recommend that you cut text by 30 to 50 percent when transferring it from print to the Web. When writing an email, you might want to *start* by making a 50 percent cut of whatever it is you want to say, whether you're sending a meeting invitation or a customer newsletter.

- Avoid packing your email with too much text information and too many images. Instead, provide a link to more complete information on your website. (Following this guideline can also help you keep the file size of your email messages small, which is important because recipients might not wait for a large message—such as one with lots of large or animated images—to download.)

T I P Images in an HTML email can be a great way to attract attention, but having too many images may work against you. Many people have their preferences set to not download images automatically (this is the default setting on many email clients), and many mobile browsers don't display images, period. For those recipients, the more pictures you have in your design, the more empty space they'll see when they open the email. Be sure to have enough text in the design so that your message is conveyed even without the images. (And remember to add alt text—see page 132.) Finally, it's wise to provide a link to a plain-text version for those viewing email on mobile devices, and a link to a webpage version for people having trouble viewing images.

- If your message must be longer than one screen of body text, it is often a service to the reader to provide a summary at the top. Briefly describe what the message is about, emphasizing any action the recipient is expected to take. This helps recipients grasp the most salient points quickly. In an HTML email, items in the summary can even be linked to their corresponding sections in the body of the email.

Make it easy for people to **scan and understand**:

- Deliver on the expectations you created in the subject line—and do it early on.
- Place the most important information at the beginning of the message or highlight it visually. Place anything else of importance at the top of the message. A portion of a graphic or headline should peek "above the fold" (that is, in the area of the screen that is visible before scrolling) to intrigue readers enough to scroll for additional information.
- Give the recipient just one thing to do—for example, click one link to learn more about your new product. If you must include more links—for instance, if you're sending a newsletter with several story links you'd like the reader to click—lead with the most compelling or important one.
- Organize information in small chunks, with visual clues like separators, headings, and lists. This helps the reader to connect related pieces of data and to separate unrelated data. **For HTML**

email that doesn't have a set design, format with bullet points and white space. Use boldface to separate sections and to call out important information. Format **plain-text email** with line breaks and lines of asterisks. Use all uppercase (*READ THIS EMAIL*) sparingly, and include white space to make scanning easier. (See "HTML email vs. text email" on page 174 for more ideas.)

■ For HTML email, include alt text for images and buttons. If a recipient's email service doesn't automatically display the images, the person will at least see the alt text describing the image, instead of a blank box. (To learn more about alt text, see "Alt text and image captions" on page 132.)

T I P To include an image in an HTML email, be sure to link to the image using HTML (see "Anatomy of a webpage" on page 372 for an example). Don't paste the physical image into your message. If you paste it in, it's going to arrive as an attachment, which may cause some recipients to delete your email immediately.

Compel the reader to **take action**:

■ Visually highlight a call to action and place it near the top of the email. For promotional email, consider placing a prominent call-to-action link or button at both the top and the bottom of the email.

■ State clearly and prominently what recipients can or should do—and possibly why taking that action benefits them.

Example

In this portion of an HTML email, the headline states prominently how recipients can benefit when they search: They can find their dream home.

■ Check that email recipients can complete every action successfully. For instance, if your email is promoting a discount, test the link, check the landing page on your site, and make sure the checkout procedure registers the discount.

TIP Try the three-second test: Can you absorb the important points from your email in just three seconds? Ask friends or colleagues to take the test. Can they? If not, rewrite, reformat, and try again.

HTML email vs. text email

Email can be sent either as HTML or as plain text. Unlike HTML messages, plain-text emails don't include graphics, special characters, or hypertext links.

If you're offering a newsletter or other subscription email, it's good to offer recipients both plain-text and HTML options. If you're using an email service provider (ESP) to manage your bulk email delivery, prepare both an HTML version and a plain-text version. The ESP's software can determine which version the recipient can receive.

Follow these **guidelines for plain-text email**:

- **Group information visually.** Use lines of asterisks, hyphens, or equal signs to set off headings or sections of the message.
- **Use all capital letters** for important parts of headings and for select words that you might highlight using italics or boldface in HTML. All-uppercase text is acceptable in plain-text emails as long as you don't overdo it. (If your message seems to be shouting or is visually overwhelming, you've overdone the capitals.)
- **Include URLs instead of linked text.** Avoid writing "click here" to introduce a URL, since URLs may not be clickable in a plain-text email.

Examples

If you have any questions, please contact Customer Service at:
http://www.bootlegbaby.com/Contact/Customer.htm

Club members can take advantage of three FREE golf swing seminars.
Improve your game:
http://www.redgrousegreens.com/Promotions

TIP Arrange text emails so that you don't need to include ending punctuation after a URL. That way, people who copy the URLs and paste them into their browser's address bar won't accidentally pick up a period at the end. For more information on including URLs in text, see "Website names and addresses" on page 255.

- **Keep lines short.** A safe length for lines of text is 68 characters. Test your email by viewing it in a variety of popular email programs to check that lines are appearing as you'd like them to. (See "Testing, testing" on page 170.)

Example

A segment of a plain-text email newsletter:

```
************************************
JOB FILE
We're hiring! Two internship opportunities available for
motivated MBA students. Contact us at jobs@address.

************************************
CLASSES AND OPPORTUNITIES
Business Class members will receive spring discounts on the
following professional development opportunities.

Program: Biz. Wise.

Classes new for spring:
++ People Management 101 ++
Learn how to hire the best and bring out the best in your hires.
++ Interview Intensive ++
This one-day course will help you determine the right questions to
ask to find the right person to hire.
```

Create specific customer communications

Email is a versatile tool for contacting your customers. You can send messages ranging from a simple automated shipping notification to a content-rich newsletter. Whether your email is promotional or informational, remember to respect the recipients' preferences, and make certain that your message is relevant to their needs and interests.

Newsletters

A newsletter is a topic-specific, content-rich communication sent to subscribers on a regular basis, whether daily, weekly, every other week, or monthly. It typically features original content that's written specifically for the newsletter audience and that's timely and valuable. Newsletters are an effective way to deliver information directly to the reader, to draw people back to your site, and to establish or strengthen an ongoing relationship. But send newsletters *only* to people who have subscribed, and always offer a clear link to unsubscribe.

A well-designed, well-developed, and well-managed newsletter has the potential to keep customers engaged and to foster their loyalty. Researchers at Nielsen Norman Group, in summarizing their 2006 report "Email Newsletter Usability," noted that "newsletters can create much more of a bond between users and a company than a website can."[25] As many as 69 percent of the participants in the study said they looked forward to receiving at least one newsletter.

But how do you get subscribers to read the newsletter they've asked for? Email recipients (newsletter subscribers included) are mercilessly selective about what they'll spend their time on. Even people who have asked to receive a newsletter may not read it or even open it.

The key is setting expectations and meeting them. The more you depart from what subscribers signed up for, the more likely they are to unsubscribe. In addition to the usual best practices for writing Web content (see Chapter 1, "Write for the Web," and Chapter 4, "Construct Clear, Compelling Copy"), follow these **newsletter-specific guidelines**.

Use a **standard format**:

- **Settle on a name and a standard template for your newsletter**, and use both consistently. Doing so helps recipients recognize your newsletter instantly. Also, readers will become familiar with the layout and will appreciate being able to scan the newsletter quickly.
- **Begin the subject line with standard text** (such as the newsletter name), followed by a colon and a short description of that issue's highlights.

Examples

Subject: Sports This Week: The new tennis champion
Subject: Sports This Week: College basketball bets
Subject: Sports This Week: Which teams will play for the Cup?

Concentrate on the **subject line and headlines**:

- **Write a compelling subject line.** For subject line tips, see page 167.
- **Create brief, compelling newsletter headlines**, favoring clarity over cleverness. Typically, subscribers want to know the contents of your newsletter and whether reading it is worth their time. See "Headings" on page 50 for tips.

Meet subscriber **expectations for schedule and content**:

- **Establish a reasonable frequency** for sending your newsletter. Don't irritate people by emailing too often.
- **Communicate your schedule.** At the time they subscribe, let people know when and how often they can expect your newsletter to arrive. For example, the following text introducing the sign-up form for the Yahoo! Music newsletter includes the frequency of delivery near the subscription link.

Example

Yahoo! Music Backstage is your pass to discovering music! Sign up below and each week we'll send you the latest in music from the hottest artists: music videos, concert updates, and promotions—including exclusive presale ticket offers and ticket sweepstakes for sold-out concerts.

- **Stick to your delivery schedule.** Miss even one newsletter shipping date, and you risk not meeting subscribers' expectations. Increase the frequency, and you risk annoying subscribers. Keeping a regular schedule shows your reliability.
- **Place ads sparingly**, keeping your reader's perspective in mind. Like your message, ads should be relevant and targeted to the recipient. You may want to limit them to one per email. That's better for everyone: The recipient is not inundated with ads, and the advertiser is more likely to get a click.

Tell readers how to **subscribe and unsubscribe**:

- **Make the subscribe process easy.** Include a subscribe call to action as a button or link (or both) with text about the newsletter on your website or in your customer email.
- **Make the unsubscribe process really easy.** Obscuring the unsubscribe process can hurt your business. If recipients have a hard time unsubscribing, they may mark your email as spam to filter it out of their inboxes. If enough people do this, your newsletter may stop reaching anyone who uses that email service.

Promotional emails

As a marketing tool, email has several advantages over traditional direct marketing. Email costs far less, is kinder to the environment, reaches recipients more quickly, and can generate a fast response. It also delivers useful data: You can find out how many people opened your message, how many people clicked and where, and how many people unsubscribed.

Newsletter alternatives

A good newsletter is labor-intensive to produce. It should be written from scratch for a specific audience, not patched together with content from your website. And the information must be timely and valuable so that people will open and read issue after issue. What's more, you have to keep up the schedule you've established—writing, editing, and delivering with predictable frequency. All that can quickly become overwhelming without adequate staff.

If you or your organization cannot support a newsletter, or if such a content-rich communication isn't appropriate for your site, consider these alternatives:

- **RSS news feed.** People subscribe to feeds of headlines or of content related to certain topics. Subscribers receive headlines in one convenient, centralized location. The downside: An RSS feed is more efficient but less personal than a newsletter, and it is unlikely to build a strong relationship with recipients. And a feed in a newsreader faces even heavier competition than a newsletter in a crowded inbox. People typically choose among hundreds of headlines from various feeds, so they are even more selective.[26]

Example

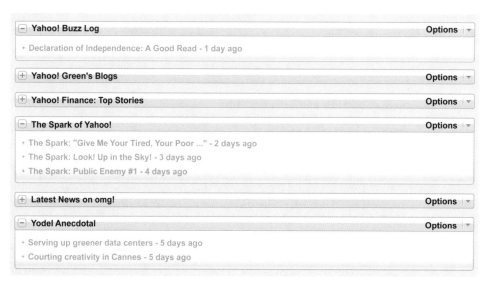

Six RSS feeds on a My Yahoo! page, three expanded to show individual headlines

- **Email alert.** People sign up to receive alerts related to topics they specify. Providers include news sites (for updates related to a specific topic), sports sites (for up-to-the-minute information on a specific sport or activity, such as when a favorite team scores), and retail sites (for notices about sales).
- **Blog.** Blogs can be a less formal way to communicate and build a relationship with site visitors. Unlike newsletters, blogs can offer community and interaction among the audience members.
- **Daily digest.** People subscribe to an automatically generated collection of the day's activity on a website. This is ideal for sites with frequent postings, such as message boards or blogs.
- **Monthly digest.** If your site features a lot of original content such as articles or blog posts, consider excerpting some of the best in a monthly digest. This type of communication can help readers who have been away from your site to re-engage and catch up on the latest news. It also gives you an opportunity to encourage them to come back to your site.

And email can be customized to the recipient. For example, email can begin with the recipient's name (*Dear Hilario,*) or feature personalized content based on the subscriber's stated location; a site for mothers-to-be can send information and offers based on the subscriber's due date; and retail sites can send targeted product offers based on a customer's previous purchases.

But there are some disadvantages to email marketing. Customers view marketing email as disposable—only a small percentage of recipients will open a promotional email. Much of it goes into the trash without being read; some, deflected by email filters, doesn't even make it to the inbox. And usability research shows that even when recipients do open an email message, they don't read it—they scan for items that interest them.

To help your promotional email compete:

- **Consider your audience.** If you're emailing new customers, focus on the high-level features and benefits that your business offers. If you are emailing current customers, encourage them to engage more often with your organization.
- **Make the message compelling.** Make it easy for recipients to get your key points fast. The goal is to engage recipients and to motivate them to click a link within the first two to three seconds. (For more tips on ways to achieve this, see "The body of the message" on page 171.)
    - ◆ **Focus on a single subject (for example, a sale) and clearly announce that subject in the first sentence.** If you provide details about your promotion, include them in your email, but assume they won't be read. Include the details on your landing page, too.
    - ◆ **Make your offer of immediate importance.** Announce a deadline and motivate the customer to act now.

Example

Before
Subject: Save 20% on photo books

After
Subject: Today only: Save 20% on photo books

TIP Consider which day is best for sending your email. For example, if your audience uses your site in the context of their business, a message sent between Tuesday and Thursday may be best for securing readers. If your content focuses on recreation or arts, consider sending your message on a Thursday or Friday, when people are planning their weekends.

- **Pay attention to the landing page**, which is the webpage where people will land when they click a link in your email. Make sure that it provides a consistent experience with the email by leveraging the keywords and imagery used in the email. But the content on the landing page should provide information beyond what is in the email.
- **Make your message instantly recognizable and make it your own.** Convey your brand identity with voice, tone, color, and images. (See Chapter 3 for more information on defining your voice.)

Service announcements

Websites send service announcements to notify people of a change to a product or service.

Example

From: YouMe Inc.
Subject: Important notice for YouMe Digest subscribers

Next month, YouMe's weekly digest will become a monthly newsletter. You are receiving this notice because you chose to subscribe to YouMe Digest. You will automatically receive the first issue of YouMe Monthly on March 1.

Learn more about <u>YouMe Monthly</u> now. *(This link takes readers to YouMe's FAQ.)*

No thanks. I want to <u>unsubscribe</u>.

When writing service announcements:

- **Clearly identify the message as a service announcement** in the subject line so that it's clear why you're contacting the recipient. For example, start the subject line with a phrase like *Important notice about*.
- **Keep the text of the message short, direct, and clear**, especially if the reader must take action. Explain the steps briefly and clearly. For tips on creating a short and compelling message, see "The body of the message" on page 171.
- **Anticipate common concerns or questions**, and direct readers to the appropriate place to express them or to find answers. If possible, include links for the reader to click to submit feedback and to find more information. Make sure the links take the reader straight to a relevant page, such as a FAQ—not to your homepage, where they'll have to figure out where to look.
- **Don't use the announcement to sell or promote** a product or service. Avoid sales pitches or marketing language.

Ideas in Practice

Example: Stick to the essentials in your email

Email is supposed to be a convenient, efficient means of communication. But at some point, we've probably all quit reading a message that rambles on and on, and dreamed of deleting our entire inbox to make a fresh start.

Don't be the email bore that readers ignore. Focus on the essential points, organize them efficiently, and write a subject line that makes your audience want to read more.

The following email newsletter is from a fictional farmer to people interested in her produce. While you'd want to retain the writer's sense of rapport with her current and potential customers, including her friendly voice, you wouldn't want to keep all the text, especially if you could direct interested readers to her website instead. Read on to see how we would rewrite and reorganize her text-only email (no HTML) for brisker browsing. (Note: This is the copy that the farmer, Josephine, sees before she sends it out.)

Before

To: subscriber1@address, subscriber2@address, subscriber3@address, subscriber4@address, subscriber5@address, subscriber6@address, subscriber7@address, subscriber8@address . . .

From: josephine@farmerinthedell.net
Cc:
Bcc:
Subject: FREE GIFT! When you subscribe to one of our CSAs in the next week

Hello, customers, and happy spring!

After months of snow and rain, it was a pleasure to see the spring sunshine come out this week and to get back to work in the fields. We've been busy planting, picking, and chasing away the baby rabbits. The bunnies are pretty cute, hopping through the fields and twitching their ears, and we're glad they approve of the veggies, but we don't want them munching up the produce meant for you.

All of you who have been asking about asparagus will be thrilled to know that this week we're boxing up bunches of gorgeous white, green, and purple asparagus. We'll have all three varieties at the farmers' market, but come early for the white, before the chefs grab it all.

Also fresh from the fields and at the market this week: green garlic, golden beets, fennel, romaine lettuce, spring onions, red chard, baby carrots, spinach, blood oranges, Fuji apples, mint, and lemon thyme.

Haven't used green garlic before? It has a milder, less biting flavor than mature garlic cloves but can be used in the same ways. Here's a quick and easy recipe:

Green-garlic soup
3-4 T. olive oil
1-2 bunches of green garlic
1/2 baguette or other crusty bread, cut into 1-inch cubes
1 c. dry white wine
1 qt. chicken stock
4 eggs
Parmesan cheese

Thinly slice the white and light-green parts of green-garlic stalks and sauté in a couple tablespoons of olive oil until the garlic is soft and golden brown. Remove the garlic to a bowl.

Add more olive oil to the pan and brown the bread cubes until they are crunchy. Set the croutons aside.

Add the wine to the pan and reduce it by half. Add 1 quart of good chicken stock and boil. Season with salt and pepper to taste.

Crack an egg into a bowl and pour it carefully into the stock. You can add up to four to the soup. Poach the eggs for a few minutes, long enough to set the white but not the yolk.

Ladle the soup into bowls, over croutons, and grate Parmesan cheese over the top.

Visit our website for more recipes.

Want to speed up your produce shopping? Sign up for our community-supported agriculture (CSA) program. Each week we'll pack a box just for you with our finest, freshest vegetables and fruit (see the list above for this week's selections), and you can pick it up either at the farmers' market or at one of our other drop-off points around town. We offer four box sizes, with prices starting at $25 per week. Check out our website for more information on our boxes and how the CSA program is good for consumers and farmers alike.

Also, if you subscribe to a CSA this week (March 14-21), we'll throw in a gift: a jar of our homemade blackberry preserves. You've never had anything so delicious on your toast or oatmeal, and a spoonful is great in marinades and salad dressings, too. For more information about this offer, go to our homepage and click the "special offer" link.

We look forward to seeing you at the market. Find us by the south entrance (map and directions on our site); we're there Wednesdays and Saturdays from 7 a.m. to 1 p.m.

Sincerely,
Josephine
Farmer in the Dell

To unsubscribe from this newsletter, go to http://www.farmerinthedell.net/unsubscribe.

After

To: josephine@farmerinthedell.net [Farmers' Market
Flavors subscribers]
From: newsletter@farmerinthedell.net [Farmer in the Dell]
Cc:
Bcc: subscriber1@address, subscriber2@address,
subscriber3@address, subscriber4@address,
subscriber5@address, subscriber6@address,
subscriber7@address, subscriber8@address . . .
Subject: Farmers' Market Flavors: Asparagus and green garlic

Hello and happy spring!
Farmer in the Dell has a great crop of spring veggies this week--
approved by the baby rabbits we've been chasing away from them.

In this issue of Farmers' Market Flavors:
*   What's fresh at the market this week
*   Recipes
*   Produce subscriptions
*   A gift for new produce-box subscribers

++

ASPARAGUS AND MORE AT THE MARKET
We're bringing bunches of gorgeous asparagus to the farmers'
market--come see our fresh-from-the-fields produce.

WHEN: Wednesday and Saturday, 7 a.m. to 1 p.m.
WHERE: Farmers' market, near the south entrance
WHAT:
*   Asparagus: green, white (limited supply--come early),
     purple
*   Green garlic
*   Golden beets
*   Fennel
*   Romaine lettuce
*   Spring onions
*   Red chard
*   Baby carrots

* Spinach
* Blood oranges
* Fuji apples
* Mint
* Lemon thyme

Map and directions to the market:
http://www.farmerinthedell.net/market

+++

RECIPES
Haven't used green garlic before? It has a milder, less
biting flavor than mature garlic cloves but can be used in
the same ways. We especially like it in:
* Green-garlic soup
* Penne with spring vegetables in green-garlic cream
  sauce
* Green-garlic and fennel bruschetta

Find these recipes and many more on our site:
http://www.farmerinthedell.net/recipes

+++

SPEEDIER SHOPPING WITH A PRODUCE SUBSCRIPTION
Speed up your produce shopping! Sign up for our
community-supported agriculture (CSA) program, and
each week we'll pack a box of produce just for you.

WHAT: A box of our finest, freshest vegetables and fruit
(four box sizes are available). See the market list above
for this week's selections.

WHEN & WHERE: Weekly. Pick up your box at the farmers'
market or at one of our drop-off points. Locations and
schedule: http://www.farmerinthedell.net/csa/locations.html

COST: $25/week and up.

FREE GIFT FOR NEW CSA SUBSCRIBERS
Sign up for our CSA this week (March 14-21) and we'll

throw in a gift: a jar of our homemade blackberry
preserves. You've never had anything so delicious on your
toast or oatmeal, and a spoonful is great in marinades and
salad dressings, too.
Sign up today for farm-fresh produce:
http://www.farmerinthedell.net/csa/specialoffer.html

++

We look forward to seeing you at the market!

Sincerely,
Josephine
Farmer in the Dell

You are receiving this email because you signed up to
receive the weekly Farmers' Market Flavors newsletter.

To unsubscribe from this newsletter, go to:
http://www.farmerinthedell.net/unsubscribe

To forward this mailing to a friend, go to:
http://www.farmerinthedell.net/forward

Farmer in the Dell is located at 42 Creek Road, Guinda, CA 95637.

Solution notes

Farmer in the Dell's original newsletter did a few things right: It contained substantial information, spoke to its audience, and seemed to be timely. But it could have benefited from less text; better organization; smarter use of the **To**, **From**, and **Subject** fields; and more links to the website.

To and Bcc: Remember that this is the copy Josephine sees before she sends it out. We changed the **To** line to Josephine's email address (josephine@farmerinthedell.net) but specified a different phrase—*Farmers' Market Flavors subscribers*—to appear instead of the address. We then included subscribers' real email addresses in the **Bcc** field. When recipients open the email, they will see *Farmers' Market Flavors subscribers* in the **To** line, and they won't see any of the addresses in the **Bcc** field. Alternatively, Josephine could create an email alias to use in the **To** field (again, with a professional-looking phrase such as *Farmers' Market Flavors subscribers* appearing instead of the bare address); the alias would redirect the newsletter to all subscribers' email addresses but prevent exposure of each individual address. If Josephine uses email management software or an email service provider to send out her newsletter, she can set up her mailing so that recipients see their own email address in the **To** line.

From: Josephine could keep her own email address (josephine@farmerinthedell.net) in this line, because the domain does include the business's name. But if she uses that same email address for personal correspondence, emailing suppliers, and so on, she may not want that inbox inundated with messages from newsletter subscribers. That's why we changed the email address in the **From** line to a different email address that Josephine or her staff can manage separately: newsletter@farmerinthedell.net. We specified *Farmer in the Dell* to appear instead of the bare address—this also reinforces the business name. (You may have noticed that in the original newsletter, Josephine didn't use the Farmer in the Dell name until the end, where readers are less likely to see it.)

Subject: The original line was 65 characters—too long, so we cut it to 51. Although the unedited subject might have been eye-catching, readers might not have seen it at all, because the word *free* could have triggered spam filters to dump the message in a junk folder. Also, the old subject line didn't tell readers that this was their regular newsletter or where the message was coming from; it focused on a promotion that was nice but not the main point of the newsletter, and it may have been confusing, if readers didn't know what a CSA was or what time period *the next week* referred to. Our revised subject line may not be the most exciting, but it is clear, establishing the name of the newsletter—Farmers' Market Flavors, which will be used in the subject line every week—and noting two products that might catch a customer's interest.

Body: The original message was text-heavy and difficult to scan. What we did:

- We chopped the introduction to one sentence. Although the original was friendly and fun, it didn't offer readers any valuable information. We kept a little of the original to preserve some of the voice, and we made sure to mention the business name right away.
- We added a quick summary describing the issue's highlights, for readers who want to skip ahead.
- We added formatting—dividing lines, capitalized headings, and white space—to make the text more scannable. Because this is a non-HTML email, we also forced line breaks so that no line exceeds 68 characters.
- We put the most important information first. Farmer in the Dell seems to do a lot of its business at the farmers' market, and the original newsletter noted that customers were asking about asparagus. So, our first subsection focuses on asparagus and other produce coming to the market.
- We broke information into chunks and trimmed the copy. The itemization of the week's produce is a perfect candidate for a bulleted list (we used spaces and asterisks, not special characters, since this is a text-only email). Similarly, the farmers' market hours and location and the CSA details are easier to find and to digest when broken out with headings. Another benefit of this

layout: It can be used week after week, giving the newsletter a consistency that will communicate professionalism. Consistent organization may also make the newsletter easier for the writer to assemble and for readers to scan.

■ We gave clear calls to action, such as asking customers to come to the market or to visit the website.

■ We added links pointing to the site. The original email had just one link, and that was for unsubscribing. Links not only drive readers to your site, but also help you cut text from the message. The green-garlic soup recipe, for example, would be much easier to read and print from the site than from an email.

Chapter 9

Streamline Text for Mobile Devices

In this chapter

- **Write for the small screen.** Brevity is best.
- **Consider how copy will look on mobile devices.** Make every word count.
- **Make SMS text brief and audience-appropriate.** Keep characters to a minimum and messages appropriate to the audience.

> Imagine
> shoehorning your
> webpage onto a
> matchbook cover.

That's what mobile devices do to your content. And more and more people are accessing Web content on the go, not to mention making use of text messaging—to communicate with friends, of course, but also to receive alerts from schools, businesses, and other organizations. So, while your primary concern is likely to be the readability of your website on a laptop screen or a monitor, you'd be smart to think about how your content appears on the matchbook-size screen of a mobile device.

Make sure that you consider how your site will appear in miniature and that you know how best to use SMS.

Write for the small screen

Screens on cell phones and mobile devices can be described as small, smaller, and smallest. A typical screen has about 13 lines. That's it. Space is at a premium, and readability is an issue.

Mobile users want to access content quickly, and without having to scroll or squint. They have no patience for pages cluttered with unnecessary words, images, or navigation elements.

The solution is clear: Write concisely. Keep mobile readers in mind when you're tempted to write long sentences on your webpage. And content specifically intended for mobile devices (or at least likely to be viewed on them)—headlines, weather, sports results, restaurant reviews—should be even more succinct than the usual webpage copy.

T I P Many websites feature modified sites for mobile users. Often the URL to the mobile website begins with *m.* or *mobile.* For instance, in place of www.yahoo.com, type **m.yahoo.com**. For AOL, type **mobile.aol.com**; for MSN, type **mobile.msn.com**.

Consider how copy will look on mobile devices

Mobile readers don't want to wait for content—and mobile networks are notoriously slower than dedicated connections. Streamlined webpages appear faster than dense, complicated ones.

Mobile users are also apt to scan instead of reading blocks of text. They tend to skim the left side of the screen looking for headings, bulleted lists, and words that jump out at them. (See "Eye-tracking: Where do readers look first?" on page 4.)

Make every word count:

- Put the most relevant and useful information at the top of the page.
- Break up text into easy-to-read chunks of related information.
- Keep sentences and paragraphs short.
- Use words with fewer syllables.
- Create narrow, bulleted lists.
- Eliminate unnecessary white space (it forces users to scroll).

T I P Some white space is beneficial. For example, replacing a paragraph with a bulleted list can open up welcome white space that helps the reader scan.

Example

Before

Our favorite restaurant of the moment is Khanh's Khafé, a charming, quiet, out-of-the-way little gem tucked into an alley in back of the newly revitalized theater district. Asian fusion pastries (like the lychee jelly dim-sum doughnuts), unusual coffee and tea drinks, and desserts (love the Spicy Cold Sundae, a Thai ice coffee gelato sundae sprinkled with tiny frozen Thai chilis). The food is yummy, the prices are great, and they're open until midnight every night. Five stars.

After
Today's pick: Khanh's Khafe, 42 Jackson Alley, Theater District
What to order: Spicy Cold Sundae, lychee jelly dim-sum donuts
Why: Charming, tasty, open till midnight
Price: $
Rating: *****

■   When writing user-interface text for a site that's intended for mobile devices, consider using abbreviations or contractions if extra characters could wrap the text to another line. This is particularly important for things like navigation links that appear on all your webpages and other text that repeats across your site. See "Space-saving abbreviations for mobile content" on page 193.

Example

Before
Updated 20 hours and 10
minutes ago

After
Updated 20 hr. 10 min. ago
or
Updated 20h 10m ago

TIP   Some mobile browsers do not support special characters such as smart quotes (" "), tiny graphic symbols (★), and accented letters (é). See "Special characters" on page 386 for more information on using special characters in online content.

Make SMS text brief and audience-appropriate

SMS—short message service—is a service provided by most cell phone carriers to send text messages to mobile devices. Targeted text messages are becoming increasingly popular as marketing tools for businesses and as a channel for information and alerts from schools, local government agencies, clubs, and other organizations.

Write alt text for images

Mobile devices use a variety of browsers to display Web content, and some of those browsers don't display images.

The solution: **Describe each image with *alt text***—meaningful, useful alternative text. Alt text enables people who are viewing your page with a text-only browser to understand your message even without the images. Such text is inserted into the HTML code. For example, if you have a picture of a volleyball player, you would place text such as *Volleyball player* into the image's alt text when the page is built. In a browser that doesn't display images, this text will appear in the image's space. To see how alt text fits into a webpage's code, see "Anatomy of a webpage" on page 372. For best practices regarding alt text, see "Alt text and image captions" on page 132.

Alt text for images is also an essential part of making websites accessible for people who may be using screen readers or other accessibility tools to visit your site. See Chapter 6, "Make Your Site Accessible to Everyone."

When you write text messages, it's important to **keep the character count to a minimum**—not only to get to the point quickly but also to keep costs down. (Many mobile phone plans charge more for messages containing more than 160 characters.)

Example

Before
Thanks for joining Birdwatchers Anonymous's rare bird mobile-alert tip line. A Blue-footed Booby has been spotted nesting in a tree on the University of California Berkeley campus for the past three days. *(Too many words, too many characters)*

After
Birdwatchers Anonymous rare-bird alert: Blue-footed Booby on Cal campus. More at bird-anon.org. *(Minimum characters and words, basic information, link to details)*

It's OK to make your informational messages informal. But **abbreviated spelling is not considered a best practice in the business and professional world**. Unless you are certain that your target audience finds informal or slang abbreviations acceptable, stick to standard spelling.

Example

Not appropriate

Bc of blzrd 2day, clsses cncld.

Appropriate

Because of today's blizzard, classes are canceled.

Space-saving abbreviations for mobile content

These short abbreviations may be necessary for a site that's designed to be or likely to be viewed on mobile devices.

Days of the week

M, Tu, W, Th, F, Sa, Su (no periods)

Example: *Hours: 9a-9p M-F, 10a-7p Sa, 10a-6p Su*

Months

Jan, Feb, Mar, Apr, May, Jun, Jul, Aug, Sep, Oct, Nov, Dec (no periods)

Example: *Grand opening: Jan 11, 2010*

Time

a.m.: a (no period, no space between number and *a*)

p.m.: p (no period, no space)

Example: *Hours: 9a-5p*

second: s (no period, no space between number and *s*)

minute: m (no period, no space)

hour: h (no period, no space)

day: d (no period, no space)

Example: *2h 30m*

Avoid the format *2:30* to indicate duration (2 hours and 30 minutes), because people may mistake it for the time of day (two-thirty).

U.S. states

Use U.S. postal abbreviations if necessary, but note that these may not be as clear to everyone as traditional abbreviations. See "Place names" on page 246.

For other abbreviations and symbols associated with numbers, see Chapter 12, "Apply a Consistent Style for Numbers."

Use SMS text wisely:

- Limit messages to 160 characters, including spaces.
- Dn't abrve8! Use short words and spell them out.
- Avoid long URLs—they can put you over the 160-character limit all on their own.

T I P   Need to provide a URL that's longer than a simple domain name? (A *domain name* is the first part of a URL, such as *yahoo.com* or *whitehouse.gov*.) Try one of these workarounds:

- Send message recipients to your homepage, and make sure there's an obvious link to the desired URL on that page.
- Use a permanent redirect. Ask your website administrator or producer to create smaller URLs that will redirect visitors to the desired URL. Several online redirection services can also create shorter URLs that redirect visitors. Two caveats: (1) Because these services mask the actual URL, they may be blocked by email or message services. (2) Redirects can have a negative impact on search engine optimization (SEO). For more on how links contribute to SEO, see Chapter 17, "Optimize Your Site for Search Engines."

Manage the Mechanics

Chapter 10

Punctuate Proficiently

In this chapter

- **Apostrophes.** You'll need them for contractions and possessives.
- **Colons.** To capitalize after them or not: That is the question.
- **Commas.** Little marks, lots of meaning.
- **Dashes.** Em dash—or en dash? When to use which.
- **Ellipsis points.** When to use three dots . . . and when to use four.
- **Exclamation points.** Use these sparingly!
- **Hyphens.** Help with decision making about these teeny-tiny marks.
- **Periods.** They're not just for ending sentences.
- **Question marks.** Think you know everything about these marks?
- **Quotation marks.** Their many uses, plus the answer to your question, "Do they go inside or outside other punctuation?"
- **Semicolons.** They're not like commas; they're not like colons either.

Modern writing tends to be lightly punctuated. Compare a page from a Victorian novel with a recent newspaper article or blog post, and you'll see far fewer semicolons and commas in the contemporary piece, not to mention shorter sentences overall.

Nevertheless, punctuation still plays an important role in reading comprehension. Those little marks help readers absorb the meaning, the rhythm, and sometimes the mood of a sentence.

Something as simple as a little comma can make a big change in meaning.

Example

Before
Ralph the cat lived with a widower, barely managing on his pension. *(Checks are made out to Ralph the cat.)*

After

Ralph the cat lived with a widower barely managing on his pension. *(Checks are made out to the widower.)*

What you want is punctuation equilibrium: just enough marks to make a sentence comprehensible at a glance.

On the Web, punctuation also brings up issues beyond the basic usage rules you may have learned in school. Some punctuation marks have "special character" versions—"smart" quotation marks instead of straight ones, for instance—and these characters may not always show up correctly in online content.

This chapter contains guidance on using punctuation in your Web writing, including the main usage rules for the most frequently occurring punctuation characters, listed in alphabetical order.

Apostrophes (')

The apostrophe has two main functions: to indicate the omission of letters or numerals and to form a possessive. It is occasionally, but rarely, used to make a plural.

Indicating omitted letters or numerals

Apostrophes can signal the omission of one or more letters in a word, or one or more digits in a number.

The most common use is in **forming contractions of verbs** (*I'm, it's, they're*). Common contractions sound friendlier and less formal than the spelled-out verb and are generally preferable as long as they don't confuse the reader.

Two caveats:

- Spelling out a verb phrase (like *cannot, do not,* and *must not*) can be useful: *Do not* can add emphasis to warning messages, for example. And *cannot, does not,* and other negative forms can be clearer and appear more formal and authoritative than their contractions.
- Less common contractions such as *would've* and *that'd* may be less immediately understandable, especially for readers who aren't native English speakers. (For more on writing for an international audience, see Chapter 5, "Be Inclusive, Write for the World.")

Apostrophes stand in for omitted letters in representations of **dialect and speech** so that the text more closely resembles common pronunciations. A word of warning, though: Few writers outside of Mark Twain can pull this off successfully. Most readers find text that's written in dialect annoying.

Examples

Knowing when to hold 'em and when to fold 'em, poker upped the ante with its World Series.

This flick will be rockin' and reelin' in theaters next month.

Apostrophes can also indicate **omitted numerals**. When you cite a decade of years, use an apostrophe to indicate the omitted century. Be sure to use an apostrophe (') and not a single opening quotation mark ('). (See "Decades and centuries" on page 268.)

Example

The first baby boomers were born in the late '40s.

Forming possessives

With a few exceptions, form possessives like this:

- For most **singular nouns**, add an apostrophe and an *s* (*'s*) to the end of the word.
- For **plural nouns that don't already end in *s***, add an apostrophe and an *s* (*'s*) to the end of the word.
- For **plural nouns that already end in *s***, just add an apostrophe.

Example

Singular nouns

the cyclist's urine test
the campus's science
  building
George Lucas's latest film
Mr. Phipps's new house
Jesus's words
Moses's mother
Degas's paintings
Arkansas's legislature
the witness's testimony
the box's contents

**Plural nouns that
don't end in *s***

children's activities
alumni's contributions

**Plural nouns that
already end in *s***

the players' scores
the Phippses' new house
the witnesses' statements
the boxes' contents

Exceptions to the general rules:

- For **names that end with an *eez* sound**, use an apostrophe alone to form the possessive.

Examples

Ramses' wife

Hercules' muscles

According to Jones's review, the computer's graphics card is its Achilles' heel.

- For **singular proper nouns that are formed from a plural word** (such as *United Nations*), use an apostrophe alone to form the possessive: *United Nations'*. (But use an apostrophe and an *s* to form the possessive of their abbreviations: *U.N.'s.*)

Examples

the New York Dolls' back catalog

the United States' foreign policy

General Motors' CEO

the U.S.'s foreign policy

GM's CEO

- Don't use an apostrophe when forming any **possessive pronoun**, including *its, yours, hers, ours,* and *theirs.* (For an explanation of the difference between commonly confused possessives and contractions—like *its* and *it's*—see "Words that may confuse writers" on page 318.)

 ## What if there's one noun and two possessors?

It depends on whether the possessive shows shared ownership.

Ike and Tina's songs rock.

Ike and Tina created the songs together, so put an apostrophe and an *s* in the word nearest the noun.

Or are there really two possessors and two possessions?

Ike's and Tina's shoes were worn out after the tour.

Obviously they couldn't wear the same shoes; at least one pair belongs to each individual. So both owners need an apostrophe and an *s*.

Advanced apostrophes: The genitive

Adding an apostrophe to a noun makes that noun look like a possessive. But *children's choir, war's casualties, Alzheimer's disease,* and similar constructions are genitives. The term *genitive* comes from a Latin word that denotes generating, or begetting. It is also related to the word *genus*, and like a genus, it is used to classify another noun.

Unlike a typical possessive, the genitive doesn't indicate ownership; it indicates some other relationship between the first and second noun.

A genitive can indicate:

- The source, as in *the buyer's counteroffer*
- The agent, as in *the fielder's error*
- The object of an action, as in *the child's rescue*
- The purpose, as in *ladies' lingerie*
- A type, as in *a doctor's appointment*
- Length, as in *two weeks' vacation*

Careful writers use an apostrophe in such cases: *teachers' union* rather than *teachers union.*

The genitive has two quirks: First, you can use it without the primary noun, as in *We are going to the doctor's.*

Second, you can use it after *of* to indicate possession. *A dream of Jeannie* (not the genitive) is different from *a dream of Jeannie's.* In this case, the genitive noun (here, *Jeannie*) must be a living thing or a person, and the word before *of* (*dream*) must constitute only a part of the whole (all of Jeannie's dreams). Thus, you'd write a *friend of Bill's*—because Bill has many friends—and not *a friend of Bill,* the same as you'd write *a friend of his* and not *a friend of him.*

Forming plurals

Usually, **plurals should not have an apostrophe**, even if they are abbreviations or numbers. *ATMs, Drs.,* and *1990s* are all correct. (See "Acronyms and other abbreviations" on page 234.)

Exception: Use an apostrophe in the plurals of letters and words if those plurals would be confusing without it. (Single letters in particular can look confusing without the apostrophe.)

Examples

Samara walked me through the do's and don'ts of project management.

Do it now—no ifs, ands, or buts.

Enough with the thank-yous!

I'm rooting for the Oakland A's baseball team this year. *("A's" without the apostrophe could look like the word "as.")*

I got straight B's on my report card this semester. *("B's" without the apostrophe could look like the abbreviation for a potentially offensive word.)*

Dot your i's and cross your t's.

The three R's

Colons (:)

A versatile mark of punctuation, the colon is most often used to introduce:

- A table, an illustration, or a list (like this one)
- An element (or a series of elements) that amplifies or illustrates the information preceding it
- A long quotation
- An important statement or words that the writer wants to emphasize
- The second part of a heading or title

Examples

Two things are certain: death and taxes. *(Emphasizes words)*

We knew that the cave was full of bats: It had that smell, that warm mammal smell, with just a hint of guano. *(Introduces an element that amplifies how we knew)*

The company president stated: "There will be no layoffs for the foreseeable future. We have enough cash reserves to see us through many months. I look forward to building an even stronger company with our talented team." *(Introduces a long quotation)*

I'd better not have to tell you people again: Don't block the fire exit with your product samples. *(Emphasizes an important statement)*

I just finished reading "The Lives of a Cell: Notes of a Biology Watcher," by Lewis Thomas *(Sets off title from subtitle)*

In a sentence, **capitalize the first word after the colon** if what follows the colon could function alone as a complete sentence. Use a single space following the colon.

Example

This is it: the chance we've been waiting for!
This is it: We'll never have to work again!

Place colons **outside quotation marks**.

Example

I feel sad when I hear the ending to "The Road Not Taken": "And that has made all the difference."

Don't use a colon after a verb when introducing a list in running text.

Example

Before
He decided he would: go to school, get married, and have two children.

After
He decided he would go to school, get married, and have two children.

But do **use a colon when introducing a bulleted or numbered list**. (For more on creating parallel lists and punctuating them consistently, see "Lists" on page 65.)

Example

He decided he would:
- Go to school.
- Get married.
- Have two children.

Commas (,)

The comma serves two main purposes: First and most important, **it separates elements**, such as items in a series.

Second, just as an apostrophe indicates missing letters, so a comma **indicates a missing word or words**: *The bread was fresh; the salad, crisp; the terrine, divine.*

Separating items in a series

"To my parents, Ayn Rand and God."

That classic example—purportedly from a book's actual dedication page—shows the confusion that can ensue when a comma is omitted before *and*. Including the comma before *and* (called a serial comma) clears up the ambiguity.

Follow these rules when writing a series of items:

■ In a **series** consisting of three or more elements, separate the elements with commas. When a conjunction (like *and* or *or*) joins the last two elements in a series, include a comma before the conjunction.

> **Examples**
>
> Confirm your name, birth date, and gender.
> You may buy our gizmos online, in a store, or by mail.

T I P A series can consist of nouns (*apples, oranges, and pears*), verbs (*sing, dance, and act*), phrases (*where to go, what to do, and when to do it*), or even clauses that have a subject and a verb each (*Mei wants to hike, Sandra wants to explore the caves, and everyone wants to see the waterfall*).

■ When using an ampersand in place of *and* in a series (acceptable only in company names and when space is severely limited), do not insert a comma before it. The combination of **comma and ampersand** creates visual clutter.

Example

Before
He went to Dewey, Cheatem, & Howe for financial advice.

After
He went to Dewey, Cheatem & Howe for financial advice.

■ Use a comma to **separate a series of adjectives** equal in rank. (Here, the comma represents the missing word *and*.)
Exception: Do not insert a comma after a "superposed" adjective, one that modifies the whole noun phrase following it. (A *noun phrase* is one or more words functioning as a single noun. A noun phrase can be quite long; for example, *aluminum fishing boat* and *handmade white linen tablecloth* can be considered noun phrases.)

Examples

He was a happy, well-adjusted boy.
Other than the cold, hard rolls and the dry, flavorless salmon, Marco enjoyed his meal.
He put brand-new snow tires on the car.
His shiny aluminum fishing boat stood out among the rusty old trawlers.
I bought an expensive handmade white linen tablecloth.
She lives in a red brick, green-gabled Edwardian-era manse.

TIP If you have a string of adjectives and can't decide whether they need to be separated by commas, try this trick: See how the sentence sounds with *and* inserted between the adjectives. If inserting *and* would result in an unnatural-sounding phrase, you are probably looking at superposed adjectives that don't need commas. Consider the phrase *five beautiful antique wooden totem poles*. Because you would not normally insert *and* between any two of those adjectives, no comma in that phrase is desirable. (In contrast, you might very well write *a happy and well-adjusted boy*.) Another clue is that you cannot switch the order of the adjectives in a series of superposed adjectives without violating English idiom: *Five antique wooden beautiful totem poles*, for example, sounds quite odd. In the original phrase, each adjective, from *five* onward, is attached to the rest of the chain and should not be separated from it by a comma.

Separating a nonessential modifier from a noun

Use a comma, or a pair of commas if needed, to indicate that a word, phrase, or clause is not essential to the meaning of the noun it modifies.

Example

Beethoven composed only one opera, *Fidelio,* which he revised several times.

A modifying word or series of words set off by commas signals the reader that it can be removed without changing the sentence's meaning. If commas are incorrectly inserted, they can lead to a wrong or improbable conclusion.

Examples

Before

I went with my friend, Sally, to see the latest Coen brothers film. *(Sadly, I have only one friend; her name is Sally.)*

After

I went with my friend Sally to see the latest Coen brothers film. *(I have many friends; the one I'm talking about is Sally.)*

Before

Editors, who earn six figures, are well-respected. *(All editors earn six figures and are well-respected to boot.)*

After

Editors who earn six figures are well-respected. *(Those editors who earn six figures are well-respected; the others might not be.)*

For additional information about using commas to set off nonessential clauses, see "that, which" on page 325.

Setting off introductory elements

A comma customarily sets off introductory words, phrases, and clauses. Of course, some exceptions apply.

In general, **use a comma after an introductory phrase that is four or more words long**.

Examples

In 1492 Columbus sailed the ocean blue.

At the library you can find a book about him.

After paying the rent, she has just enough money to buy food.

To express her true nature, the chicken crossed the road.

After great pain and months of physical therapy, Joe could walk again.

Exceptions:

■ A comma is generally advisable when a sentence starts with a transitional word or phrase (an adverbial conjunction) such as *however* (but not *but*), *nevertheless, well, yes, no, meanwhile, furthermore, still, also, hence, consequently, therefore, moreover, fortunately, unfortunately, finally, what's more, in fact,* and *after all.*

Examples

Well, this is a fine kettle of fish!

No, I don't want to eat any more pie.

Furthermore, I've decided to give up sweets entirely.

However, I'll take that piece of cheese off your hands.

But don't give me any crackers!

■ Use a comma with a shorter introductory phrase if the lack of a comma could lead to a temporary misreading.

Example

Before

After eating the baby started to burp noisily.

After

After eating, the baby started to burp noisily.

■ Use a comma to set off an introductory dependent clause. This is a clause that cannot stand alone because it begins with a subordinating conjunction such as *after, before, because, even if, given, how, if, then, unless,* or *while.* (Remember that a clause has both a subject and a verb.)

> **Examples**
>
> If it bleeds, it leads.
> Because I could not stop for Seth, he kindly stopped for me.

Although introductory elements often require commas, the same elements may not need to be set off by commas at the end of a sentence. However, listen to the rhythm of the sentence. If you pause at the beginning of the element, then set it off with a comma. If you do not pause, do not insert a comma.

> **Examples**
>
> It leads if it bleeds.
> The chicken crossed the road to express her true nature.
> Joe could walk again, after great pain and months of physical therapy.
> Joe could walk again only after great pain and months of physical therapy.

Setting off parenthetical elements

To set off a parenthetical element—whether a word, a phrase, or a clause—use a pair of commas when you intend only a slight interruption. Otherwise use a pair of em dashes or parentheses.

> **Examples**
>
> The chicken, regrettably, crossed the road.
> The rooster was, to say the least, quite saddened.
> The pig, I heard, was also unhappy.
> The cat—which hated the chicken's slow-witted squawking—looked forward to sampling the truck-spatchcocked bird.

Setting off direct address

Use a comma to set off a name, a title, or another word or phrase when addressing someone.

Examples

Dear customer,

Friends, Romans, countrymen, lend me your ears.

Madam President, I move to adjourn.

Separating independent clauses

The coordinating conjunctions *for, and, nor, but, or, yet,* and *so* can link two independent clauses (clauses that can stand alone as sentences).

T I P Use the acronym FANBOYS to help you remember these conjunctions.

Follow these rules when punctuating sentences with these conjunctions:

■ Use a comma before the conjunction.

Examples

Roscoe dropped the saliva-covered ball at her feet, but he was then distracted by a squirrel.

Hidden zones appear at level 12, and a brightly lit fountain then sprays the screen with gems.

■ Don't use a comma to separate independent clauses if they are not joined by a conjunction—that's called a comma splice. Instead, use a semicolon, add a conjunction, or if necessary, rewrite the sentence.

Example

Before

Most of us are just out of college, we can't afford a whole corporate wardrobe.
(Comma splice)

After

Most of us are just out of college; we can't afford a whole corporate wardrobe. *(Semicolon)*

Most of us are just out of college, so we can't afford a whole corporate wardrobe. *(Conjunction)*

T I P   You may be able to use a comma if it denotes a slight pause between short and closely related independent clauses: *Don't ask, don't tell. I came, I saw, I conquered.*

■ Don't use a comma before every conjunction in a sentence. Often a conjunction joins two verb phrases that share a subject. In such a case, either delete the comma or insert a second subject.

Example

Before
The chicken crossed the road, but soon regretted her decision. *(One subject: "chicken." Two verbs: "crossed" and "regretted." The verb phrase "soon regretted her decision" does not have its own subject.)*

After
The chicken crossed the road but soon regretted her decision. *(Comma deleted.)*
The chicken crossed the road, but she soon regretted her decision. *("She" inserted so that the verb phrase "soon regretted her decision" now has its own subject.)*

■ Sometimes, however, a comma helps the reader understand a complex sentence.

Example

The chicken strutted across the road thinking that she cut quite a fashionable figure, and considered herself the most favored creature of the barnyard.

Introducing quotations

Follow these **guidelines for punctuating a quotation** with commas:

■ Use a comma to introduce a complete one-sentence quote.

> **Example**
>
> The young man said, "I'm here to watch the next Triple Crown winner."

──────────────

■ Don't use a comma before an indirect or partial quote.

> **Example**
>
> The young man said he was there "to watch the next Triple Crown winner."

──────────────

■ Use a comma at the end of a quote that is followed by an attribution such as "he said."

> **Example**
>
> "I'm here to watch the next Triple Crown winner," the young man said.

──────────────

■ Don't use a comma at the end of a quote that is followed by an attribution if the quoted statement ends with a question mark or an exclamation point.

> **Example**
>
> "Why are you here?" the reporter asked the young man.

──────────────

Separating parts of place names

In running text, use a comma to set off parts of an address or a place name.

> **Examples**
>
> The spy met her controller in the basement of 100 Lexington Ave., Columbus, Ohio, on the first Monday of each month.

The company opened a branch in Edmonton, Alberta.
I would like to visit my uncle in Kolkata, India, one day.

TIP If you work for a Web publication using British English, you may find that British style allows for the use of *in* instead of a comma to separate place names: *James Joyce was born in Rathgar in County Dublin* instead of *James Joyce was born in Rathgar, County Dublin.*

Separating parts of dates

Set off the year with commas when it follows the month and date. Set off the month and date when they follow the day of the week.

Examples

Both Thomas Jefferson and John Adams died on July 4, 1826, the 50th anniversary of the signing of the Declaration of Independence.
He was born on Monday, December 31, just in time to give his parents a tax break.

Do not insert a comma between the month and the year if no date is included.

Example

He was born in December 2009.

TIP British style for dates including month, day, and year calls for a comma after the year only: *On 23 April 1616, Shakespeare died* instead of *On April 23, 1616, Shakespeare died.*

Separating parts of numbers

Use commas for numbers greater than 999 expressed in numerals: *30,000 pounds.* For more examples and some exceptions to this rule, see "The basics" on page 261.

Dashes (- and —)

Dashes generally come in two sizes: the en dash and the em dash.

En dash

An en dash (–) is longer than a hyphen but shorter than an em dash.

Use the en dash to:

- Mean *to, up to and including,* or *through* in a range of numbers, dates, game scores, pages, and so on. (For more examples of this, see "Numbers in a range" on page 280.)
- Construct a compound adjective that includes a proper noun of more than one word. (*New York, Queen Elizabeth, Lake Baikal,* and *World War II* are all multiword proper nouns.)

Examples

Abraham Lincoln (1809–1865) was president during the American Civil War (1861–1865). *(En dashes meaning "up to and including" in date ranges)*

Jim was interested in the pre–Civil War era. *(En dash connecting two-word proper noun "Civil War" with prefix "pre-")*

On the Web, **the en dash needs to be coded**—and even then it may not appear correctly in text-only emails and RSS news feeds—so many people choose to use a hyphen instead. (For information on coding an en dash, see "Special characters" on page 386.)

Em dash

Use an em dash (—), or "dash," to:

- Indicate a break in a sentence.
- Set off a parenthetical element that explains or amplifies.
- Separate a noun or a series of nouns from a clause summarizing them.
- Denote an open range, such a date range with no ending date. (For more examples of this, see "Numbers in a range" on page 280.)

Examples

Hey, is that asteroid about to hit— *(Break)*

Georgina decided to obey her father—not that she had a choice in the matter. *(Amplification)*

The Three Stooges—Larry, Moe, and Curly—sat down to dinner. *(Explanatory phrase)*

Fried grasshoppers, steamed water bugs, grilled spiders, various broiled larvae—all provide delicious, protein-rich snacks. *(Summarizing clause)*

Mick Jagger (1943—), Brian Jones (1942–1969), and Keith Richards (1943—) were among the band's original members.

A space before and after an em dash is optional as long as the use is consistent within a site or other set of webpages. For Web copy, we prefer a space on either side of an em dash. However, do not use a space on one side of a dash without using a space on the other (unless you are indicating a break in a sentence).

T I P Putting spaces around dashes can mean better line breaks: Some software treats "text—text" as one continuous word and will not break it at the dash. (This can be problematic if you are writing something like "supercalifragilisticexpialidocious—even though . . .") But an em dash with no space on either side takes up less room than its spaced-out alternative, so some people prefer it despite the line-break issue. (Headlines, for example, often look better without a space on either side of the dash.)

Not all software renders the em dash, a special character, correctly. If you use it, use the code appropriate for your content management system (see "Special characters" on page 386) and make sure it will look OK on a browser page, in a browser title bar, in an RSS feed, in a text message, or anywhere else your copy might appear. **In plain-text emails** or other communications where the em dash is unavailable, **use two hyphens** (--), with or without surrounding spaces. Be consistent in your use of spaces.

Ellipsis points (. . .)

Ellipsis points (three periods in a row) usually indicate the **omission of one or more words in quoted matter**. In print publications, ellipsis points are typically set with a space between each of the periods (. . .). But online, adding a space between each dot can lead to bad line breaks, with, for example, one dot at the end of one line and two dots at the beginning of the next. To create ellipses in Web copy, choose one of the following methods—just use it consistently:

- Insert a special character if one is supported by your content management system (see "Special characters" on page 386). But make sure the character will show up correctly anywhere your copy might appear.
- Use nonbreaking spaces in between the periods (for example, . . .). Nonbreaking spaces are special characters that must be coded in as well.
- Type three periods in a row, with no spaces in between. This is the easiest solution.

No matter which method you use, add a space before and after the ellipses. If the ellipses follow a complete sentence, end that sentence with a period, insert a space, then the ellipsis points, then another space.

Examples

The U.S. Bill of Rights states that "Congress shall make no law ... abridging the freedom of speech, or of the press."

In his "I Have a Dream" speech, the Reverend Martin Luther King Jr. declared: "Now is the time to make real the promises of democracy. ... Now is the time to lift our nation from the quicksands of racial injustice to the solid rock of brotherhood."

Ellipsis points can also indicate a **pause in speaking or an incomplete or trailing thought** by either the writer or the speaker. (A dash can also serve this function.) When an ellipsis falls at the end of a sentence and indicates an incomplete or trailing thought, do not insert a space before the ellipsis points. Doing so could result in a bad line break, with the ellipsis points appearing on the next line by themselves.

Examples

You know what they say: If you can't take the heat...
<u>Backpacks</u>, <u>sleeping bags</u>, <u>tents</u>, <u>hiking boots</u>, <u>more</u>...

Do not use ellipsis points to introduce a list, a table, or an illustration.

TIP Avoid including a word processor's symbol for ellipsis points on your webpage. This symbol may appear incorrectly, depending on your content-publishing software and the platform on which the text appears. See "Special characters" on page 386.

Exclamation points (!)

Follow these rules for using exclamation points:

- Use them sparingly for **emphatic expression**. When overused, the exclamation point loses its impact.

Before
She couldn't believe her eyes!

After
She couldn't believe her eyes.

- Use the exclamation point for interjections (*"Dude!"*) or commands (*"Duck!"*) or to express surprise or urgency (*"The house is on fire!"*).
- If the exclamation point ends a **quotation**, don't use a comma or a period after the exclamation point.

Hyphens (-)

Use a **hyphen** (-) to form compounds of two or more words and to separate some prefixes and suffixes from root words.

Forming compound modifiers

A *compound modifier* is two or more words that function as a unit. For compound modifiers that come before a noun, use hyphens to join the parts of the compound so that readers understand your intent. Consider the difference, for example, between *red and green ties* and *red-and-green ties*.

When faced with a compound modifier, follow these rules:

- **Use a hyphen or hyphens for compound adjectives preceding a noun.** (For more on compound adjectives that include a number, see "The basics" on page 261.)
Exception: Don't use a hyphen for compounds including *more, less, most,* or *least* unless the compound could be misread.

Examples

The email campaign had a better-than-average response.

Take advantage of the 30-day free trial.

The more logical solution is to begin at the beginning.

Her debut single was the most downloaded song of 2009.

Researchers then eliminated less productive plants to favor those with a high yield.

■ Use a **suspended hyphen (a hyphen followed by a space)** when the second element of the first compound modifier is omitted. The second element of the second compound modifier must appear before the noun. (This assumes there are only two compound modifiers).

Examples

We heard pro- and anti-IMF speeches.

Both the French- and Chinese-speaking participants had excellent interpreters.

Any class is going to have both under- and overachieving students.

■ **Don't use a hyphen or hyphens if a compound modifier follows a noun,** unless the modifier comes after a form of the verb *to be* (like *is, are, was, were*).

Exceptions: Certain compound modifiers don't need hyphenation even after a form of the verb *to be*. These include:

◆ Adjective + infinitive: *easy to use, harder to learn, ready to eat*
   Note: The infinitive is the *to* form of a verb.

◆ Adjective + prepositional phrase: *fresh from the field, hot off the grill*

◆ Adjective + *than* or *as* comparison: *better than average, bland as oatmeal*

◆ Adverb + past participle + preposition: *often referred to, much talked about*

 Past participle: A form of a verb, usually ending in *ed* or *en*, that can serve as an adjective or as part of a verb phrase. Examples: *damaged, constructed, sunken, written, grown, understood, struck.*

Examples

The well-behaved dog won first prize.
He was well-behaved.
Positive reinforcement made him well behaved.

Sign up now for our trouble-free service.
The service is trouble-free.

It's an easy-to-use tool.
The tool is easy to use. *(Adjective + infinitive exception)*

Sample our fresh-from-the-field produce.
Our produce is fresh from the field. *(Adjective + prepositional phrase exception)*

Her redder-than-red face betrayed her embarrassment.
Her face was redder than red. *(Adjective + "than" exception)*

This is an often-referred-to section.
This section is often referred to. *(Adverb + past participle + preposition exception)*

■ Don't use a hyphen following the adverb *very* and adverbs ending in *ly*. *Very* or an *-ly* adverb clearly modifies the following adjective, so no hyphen is needed to avoid confusion. (But note that not all *-ly* words in compound modifiers are adverbs. You can tell when an *-ly* word is not an adverb because the word following the *-ly* word cannot stand alone without changing the meaning.)

Examples

a very exciting product
a completely new production *(You can have a "new production.")*
a scholarly-looking girl *(You cannot have a "looking girl.")*

When a compound modifier contains punctuation or is too long to string together with hyphens, use quotation marks—for examples, see "Quotation marks" on page 224.

For information about capitalizing compound modifiers, see "Hyphenated compounds in title case" on page 241.

T I P What about hyphenating multiword nouns, such as *spell-checker*? If your dictionary doesn't list the phrase, and if you think a hyphen might help, then do include it. Readers can then tell which words are modifiers and which words are being modified—helpful especially for readers whose first language is not English.

Joining prefixes and suffixes

Because dictionaries take different approaches to spelling and hyphenation, you and your organization should rely on **one primary dictionary** to determine which words require hyphenation. A number of Web publications use Dictionary.com, choosing the entries provided by the *Random House Dictionary* or the *American Heritage Dictionary of the English Language*. Some use Merriam-Webster Online (www.merriam-webster.com), which is based on *Merriam-Webster's Collegiate Dictionary*. Others use YourDictionary.com, which provides entries from *Webster's New World College Dictionary*.

Decide whether to apply blanket rules for all prefixes and suffixes or whether to apply your rules only if a word is not listed in your dictionary. (Either decision is fine; just be consistent. Record your decision in your style guide and include any exceptions in your word list—see Chapter 19, "Keep a Word List.")

For **prefixes**, you may want to follow these guidelines:

■ Generally, close up prefixes with root words: *antiviral, transcontinental*.
   Exceptions:
   ◆ Hyphenate to avoid a doubled vowel (for example, two *o*'s together).
   ◆ Insert a hyphen after *co-* when it designates a shared occupation or status.
   ◆ Insert a hyphen after *e-* when it stands for *electronic* (exception: *email*).
   ◆ Insert a hyphen if the root word is capitalized.
   ◆ Insert a hyphen before a numeral.
   ◆ Hyphenate doubled prefixes.

Examples

preproduction
postproduction
superhuman
nonnative
semi-invalid *(Hyphen to separate doubled vowel)*
co-author *(Hyphen for "co-" indicating shared occupation)*
e-commerce *(Hyphen for "e-" when it stands for "electronic")*
email *(Exception: No hyphen in "email")*

pan-Asian *(Hyphen to separate capitalized root word)*
mid-20th century *(Hyphen to separate numeral)*
re-reunification *(Hyphen to separate doubled prefix)*

- Make sure that the prefix is attached to all parts of the phrase it applies to.

Example

anti-child-pornography law *(Not "anti-child pornography law")*

The guidelines for **suffixes** are simpler:

- Insert a hyphen to avoid a doubled consonant.
- Insert a hyphen to avoid a hard-to-read result.
- Insert a hyphen after a capitalized noun.

Examples

flowerlike, daffodil-like, hippopotamus-like, Renoir-like
nationwide, pew-wide, university-wide, Seattle-wide

Avoiding ambiguity

Use a hyphen when omitting it might lead to a misreading.

Examples

Before
I resent that message.

After
I re-sent that message. *(Perhaps I resent the message as well, but I am keeping my feelings to myself.)*

Before
They then heard more unbelievable stories. *(Are the stories more unbelievable than the ones previously told, or are there simply more of them?)*

After

They then heard more-unbelievable stories. *(The stories are more unbelievable.)*

Better

They then heard stories more unbelievable than the last.

T I P   If you can't decide whether a term should be open (*fan site*), closed (*fansite*), or hyphenated (*fan-site*)—and your dictionary can't help you—consider this: On the Web, hyphenated or closed-up nouns and adjectives are more helpful than open compounds, because readers who scan can see immediately that the words go together.

Periods (.)

Use a period to **end a declarative sentence**, an imperative sentence, or an indirect question. A period sometimes ends a courtesy question (a politely phrased request) or a rhetorical question (one that is asked for effect and that does not require an answer). For more information about courtesy questions and rhetorical questions, see "Question marks" on page 223.

Examples

I would like to stay. *(Declarative sentence)*
Let's stay. *(Mildly imperative sentence)*
Get a plate and sit down. *(Imperative sentence)*
She asked if we would like to stay for dinner. *(Indirect question)*

Use a period (or other ending punctuation) at the end of any **link** that is a **complete sentence**, including very short imperative sentences. But don't link the period.

Examples

Invite a friend today.
Check your results.

In HTML:
<a href="URL goes here">Invite a friend today</a>.
<a href="URL goes here">Check your results</a>.

If links are **sentence fragments**, do not use a period at the end. Use no punctuation for short items. Use ellipsis points (. . .), sparingly, if the list item is too long to include in its entirety.

Examples

Before

movie trailer, showtimes, cast information. *(Unnecessary period)*
More information. *(Unnecessary period)*

After

movie trailer, showtimes, cast information, reviews
More information...

If an **abbreviation** that includes a period (such as *U.S.* or *U.K.*) **ends a sentence**, don't include a second period.

Example

Offices are open daily throughout the U.S. *(Only one period needed to end a sentence)*

When using periods after two or more **initials in a person's name**, don't include a space between the first and second initial. When referring to a person solely by initials, do not include periods.

Example

The historian compared the presidencies of George H.W. Bush and JFK.

Question marks (?)

Use a question mark for a **direct question**.

Examples

Who wrote the book of love?
Would you like to try it?

_____

Don't use a question mark for **indirect questions**.

Examples

I wonder who wrote the book of love.
She didn't answer him; he wondered why.

_____

Many **rhetorical questions** (those asked for effect and not requiring any answer) do require a question mark. But use an exclamation point instead when the question is really an exclamation, and use a period when the question is really a suggestion or a polite request (one where a "no" answer is not anticipated).

Examples

Rhetorical questions with question marks
Can you believe it? I just bought that car, and it's already scratched.
What kind of a man are you?

Exclamations, requests, and suggestions formed as questions
Boy, do I!
How can you possibly think that!
Would everyone please rise for the national anthem.
Why don't you stop asking me questions already.
Why don't you take a long walk off a short pier.

_____

When an attribution (such as *he said, I wondered,* or *they asked*) ends a sentence, put the question mark at the end of the question, not at the end of the sentence.

Examples

Before

Who wrote the book of love, I wondered?

After

Who wrote the book of love? I wondered.

Before

"Do you know the way to San Jose," asked Judith?

After

"Do you know the way to San Jose?" asked Judith.

Quotation marks (" ")

Use quotation marks for:

- Identifying direct quotations
- Defining words
- Referring to words and letters
- Expressing irony
- Setting off long modifiers
- Setting off the titles of some works

Identifying direct quotations

When **quoting** a person, a text, or another source **directly**, use these guidelines:

- Use quotation marks to surround the **exact words** of a speaker or writer.

Examples

"There are very few people," he said, "who understand the logic."
The writer said that his works are "total fictions."

■ To indicate **quotes within quotes**, use single quotation marks. (Note: British style may differ—see "Separated by a common language" on page 229.)

> **Example**
>
> "I remember my first conversation with him," Gonzales said. "He never came in and said, 'I want my job back.'"

When to [*sic*] 'em

When you're directly quoting someone, or when you're citing the title of a work, you should retain the creator's spelling, style, and formatting (such as capitalization or italics). For example, Yahoo! style and most dictionaries prefer *all right* to *alright,* but an editor would not change the title of the Who's movie *The Kids Are Alright*. However, in a direct quotation you can insert [*sic*] after a misspelling, an unusual style choice, or a factual error—the [*sic*] lets you remain faithful to the original text while letting the reader know that the mistake is the author's, not yours. For instance, the following quote should say *shoulders* rather than *shoulder*:

The Latin student translated Isaac Newton's quote as "standing on the shoulder [*sic*] of giants."

Note that *sic* is typically set in italic type, but the brackets are not.

Be careful about using [*sic*] too often—you can generally omit it in titles, like that of the Who movie, and in quotations you might prefer to paraphrase instead.

Defining words

When defining or introducing an unfamiliar word or phrase in online copy, put the word or phrase in quotation marks on **first reference** only. (Foreign words should be in italics if possible—see Chapter 16, "Get Familiar With Basic Webpage Coding.")

> **Example**
>
> The browser will accept a "cookie" and open a new window. A cookie is a small amount of website data that is stored on your computer.

Do not enclose a word or phrase in quotation marks when it is preceded by *so-called*.

Example

The browser accepts a so-called cookie and opens a new window.

Referring to words and letters

In Web copy, use quotation marks when referring to a word as a word or a letter as a letter—for example, *the word "tranquil," the letter "q."* Although print publications (including this one) often use italic text to set these off, a single italicized letter can be difficult to read onscreen.

Examples

A surprising number of people hate the word "moist."
The word "memento" has only one "o."

In general, leave off the quotation marks if you are referring to the plural of a word or letter: *two buts, two e's.* But if the plural of a word could cause confusion, use a workaround: *two instances of "mouse,"* for example, instead of *two mouses.*

For information on forming plurals with apostrophes (or without them), see "Apostrophes" on page 198.

Example

Before
The sentence contains two friends, one misspelled, the other spelled correctly.

After
The sentence contains two instances of "friend," one misspelled, the other spelled correctly.
or
The sentence contains "friend" in two places; in one place it's spelled incorrectly, in the other correctly.

Expressing irony

Quotation marks can also indicate irony, sarcasm, skepticism, or a nonstandard usage.

Examples

My date's car "accidentally" ran out of gas.

The editor suspected that Janet's original reporting was a little too "original," and indeed the newspaper later discovered that Janet had invented several of her quotes.

_____

Be careful about using quotation marks too often in these cases: It can be tiresome to read a lot of ironic phrasing, and the subtleties may be lost on readers who are scanning or who are not fluent in English. And **avoid using quotation marks for emphasis**. They can be misunderstood as indicating sarcasm or doubt.

Examples

Not appropriate
We serve the "world's best" coffee.

The physician's shingle read
> *Dr. John Doe*
> *"Gynecologist"*

_____

Setting off long modifiers

If a compound modifier is long or contains other punctuation that makes hyphenation unsightly, use quotation marks instead of hyphens.

Examples

The cake was good, apart from the "I can totally believe it's not butter" frosting.
The U.S. military's "don't ask, don't tell" policy was introduced in 1993.

_____

Setting off the titles of some works

Although print publications typically italicize titles of major works, italic text doesn't appear correctly in all places online, so we recommend quotation marks for titles.

In general, use **double quotation marks** for the titles of books, lectures, movies, operas, plays, podcasts, poems, songs, speeches, television programs, videos, and works of art. In some cases, such as within headlines and other display type (for example, captions and pull quotes), titles can be enclosed in **single quotation marks** to save space.

For more information, including a complete list of titles that should be in quotation marks, see "Titles of works" on page 251.

Examples

"Miami Vice" starred Don Johnson and Philip Michael Thomas.

The movie version of "Miami Vice" was released in 2006 and starred Colin Farrell and Jamie Foxx.

TV's "MacGyver" starred Richard Dean Anderson, and "Magnum, P.I." starred Tom Selleck.

'MacGyver,' 'Magnum, P.I.' movie rumors fly *(Headline with limited space)*

Punctuation and quotation marks

Follow these rules for using punctuation with quotation marks:

- In general, place **periods and commas** inside quotation marks.

Example

Kevin McKidd had starring roles in "Anna Karenina," "Rome," and "Journeyman."

- If quotation marks are used to indicate a character or a string of **characters that the user must type** exactly, put any punctuation mark outside the closing quotation mark. Alternatively, reword the instruction so that the punctuation isn't near the quotation marks, or use boldface type for the string. To read about the pros and cons of boldface vs. quotation marks for this type of text, see "Strategies for making the names of UI elements stand out in text" on page 146.

Examples

For traffic conditions, type the city name, the street name, and the word "traffic".

For traffic conditions, type the city name, the street name, and the word "traffic" in the box.

For traffic conditions, type the city name, the street name, and the word **traffic**.

■ Tuck **question marks and exclamation points** within quotation marks if they're part of the quote. Put them outside if they apply to the whole sentence.

Separated by a common language: British vs. American styles for quotation marks

One of the biggest punctuation differences between British English and American English can be found in the use of quotation marks.

In American style, commas and periods almost always go inside quotation marks:

On Sundays, Mori is glued to the TV, watching "True Blood" and "Entourage."

In British style, commas and periods go inside the quotation marks *only* if they're part of a direct quote. In addition, single quotation marks are generally preferred to double quotation marks:

On Sundays, Mori is glued to the TV, watching 'True Blood' and 'Entourage'.

(The period is not part of the TV show's title, so it goes outside the quotes.)

'I can't come on Sunday', Mori said. 'I'm, uh, I've got a date.'

(The comma following *Sunday* comes after the closing quotation mark because it is not part of the quote. But Mori ended her sentence with a period, so the period is part of the quote.)

In American style, quotation marks that are inside other quotation marks are single quotation marks:

Martin Luther King said, "That old law about 'an eye for an eye' leaves everybody blind."

British style varies in this, but many British publications prefer to have single quotes on the outside, double quotes on the inside:

Martin Luther King said, 'That old law about "an eye for an eye" leaves everybody blind.'

Examples

The coach asked, "Are you ready to win?"

What does it mean to be left "high and dry"?

For more information about punctuation and quotes, see "Introducing quotations" on page 211, "Ellipsis points" on page 214, and "Exclamation points" on page 216.

Semicolons (;)

Use a semicolon to separate related independent clauses (that is, clauses that can stand alone as separate sentences) if they are not joined by a conjunction (such as *and* or *but*).

Example

He took off work to watch the World Series; he wasn't the only one.

He took off work to watch the World Series, but he wasn't the only one.

He took off work to watch the World Series, and it was a good thing that he did.

Do you have three independent clauses with the same structure and the same verb? Separate the clauses with semicolons and replace would-be repetitions of the verb with a comma. (Remember, a comma can denote an omitted word or phrase—see "Commas" on page 204.)

Example

The Cowardly Lion lacks courage; the Tin Man, a heart; and the Scarecrow, a brain.

Place semicolons outside ending quotation marks.

Example

He said, "I'm off to watch the World Series"; he wasn't the only one.

Ideas in Practice

Exercise: Punctuate to communicate

Edit the sentences below according to the guidelines in Chapter 10. Each example contains two to six errors. Can you find them all?

 To see our solution, turn to page 479.

1. Yes Bill's CD's are alphabetically-organized; so are his vintage 80's concert T-shirts, his canned vegetables and his not so effective self-help books.

2. Why don't you explore the diverse landscapes of New Zealand, where you can see beaches, tropical forests, alpine mountains, fjords, volcanoes and caves?

3. Archimedes's study of levers led him to boast, "Give me a place to stand on and I can move the earth".

4. A typical member of Generation Y Emily learned her ABCs from Sesame Street, but learned numbers by playing with her dad's defunct cell phone.

5. To have a happy healthy spring break
   - Choose a room above the hotel's first floor which may be easy to break into
   - Travel with a buddy, especially at night
   - Drink alcohol responsibly: know your limits.

6. Students, enrolling in the MBA program, will see their tuition rise by $5000 per year.

7. Jewelers recommend spending two months salary on a diamond engagement ring. However you might save a little by buying just after Valentines Day or Christmas because sales peak before those two most popular days to propose.

8. Paris' abduction of Helen started the Greeks' 10 year siege of Troy, Odysseus' Trojan-horse ruse finally ended the war.

9. The tuberculosis strain that killed the St. Paul, Minnesota man is drug resistant, un-responsive to either first or second-line medications.

10. Europe discovered the Bahamas, when Christopher Columbus landed on one of the islands in October, 1492. Before Sidney Poitier the most famous—or infamous—resident of the Bahamas was the pirate, Blackbeard.

Chapter 11

Abbreviate, Capitalize, and Treat Titles Consistently

In this chapter

- **Acronyms and other abbreviations.** When to spell them out, how to handle their plurals.
- **Capitalization.** Learn the three main styles of capitalization.
- **Company and product names.** CamelCaps Inc., eThings, and other interesting cases.
- **Email addresses and fields.** How to capitalize them (or not), how to distinguish them (or not) in text.
- **File names, types, and extensions.** What to capitalize, what to lowercase.
- **Place names.** Directions, regions, and locations.
- **Titles of people.** Is he a president or a President?
- **Titles of works.** How (and when) to set off the titles of books, movies, songs, computer games, podcasts, and other compositions.
- **Website names and addresses.** How to refer to a site, how to include a URL.

The smallest details of your content can influence a reader's perception of your website's reliability. Consistency in capitalization and the visual treatment of words—how you use such elements as quotation marks, boldface, and italics—contributes to your content's readability and speeds comprehension. And it does one more thing that's less tangible but very important: It gives the people visiting your site the understanding that your website takes itself seriously.

This chapter is all about the details: how to treat words in the titles of persons, places, and things, and how to treat the not-quite-words prevalent in Internet content—acronyms and file names, email addresses and website URLs. We offer rules and guidelines, but some choices are up to you. Be sure to record your decisions in your word list (see page 433 for details).

Acronyms and other abbreviations

An **abbreviation** is a shortened form of a word or phrase. Depending on the abbreviation, it may be written in uppercase (*ID*), lowercase (*tsp.*), or a combination of upper- and lowercase letters (*Mrs.*). It may or may not include one or more periods.

An **acronym** is a specific type of abbreviation. Acronyms are formed from the first letter or letters of the words in a name or phrase, sometimes producing a pronounceable word (*AIDS, NATO, NASA, JAMA*), and sometimes not (*ATM, CEO*). In the United States, acronyms are usually set in all capital letters.

Sometimes an acronym will enter the language as a word with its own meaning, such as *scuba*, from *self-contained underwater breathing apparatus.*

When is an acronym an initialism?

Acronyms that are pronounced as individual letters—such as *USDA, UFO,* and *DVD*—are sometimes called initialisms. The text-message abbreviations *LOL* (laughing out loud) and *IMO* (in my opinion) are initialisms; so are business names *IBM* and *GE*. It's good to know what initialisms are because some publications give different typographical treatments to acronyms and initialisms. For instance, an acronym that is pronounced as a word may be written in small capital letters (*AIDS, NATO, NASA*), while initialisms appear in all uppercase (*ATM, CEO*), sometimes with a period after each letter (*A.T.M., C.E.O.*).

When and how to introduce abbreviations

No matter how familiar an abbreviation may seem to you, some Web visitors—particularly those from countries other than your own—may be unfamiliar with the term. Use these **guidelines for introducing acronyms and other abbreviations** in your writing:

- **If the shortened form of a word may be unfamiliar** to your readers, spell it out the first time it's used or include the abbreviation in parentheses following the spelled-out form.

Example

Many sites now support RSS. *RSS,* which stands for *Really Simple Syndication,* is a method for accessing Web content. *(Define in text on first use.)*

Many sites now support Really Simple Syndication (RSS), a method for accessing Web content. *(Spell out on first use.)*

- **If the shortened form is better-known** than its spelled-out form (for example, *ATM, USB*), use the shortened form. For guidance on individual abbreviations, see "The Yahoo! word list" on page 438.

T I P Readers should understand common acronyms like *USA, U.N.,* or even *PC,* but if there's any possibility of confusion (for example, if you're using *PC* to mean *politically correct* in a discussion of computer etiquette), spell out the term the first time you use it—and perhaps again on subsequent pages if the long form isn't too burdensome. On the Web, you can't be sure a visitor will see an acronym the first time you use it. Visitors to your site won't necessarily arrive at your homepage and won't necessarily follow a sequential path through your pages.

 ## When do abbreviations need periods?

In the United States, **abbreviations of single words usually take periods**: *govt., Jan., Fri., hr.* These include abbreviations of English units of measure: *in., ft., lb.,* and so on. Exceptions include abbreviations of metric units and those related to computers and technology: *mm, km, kHz, MB.*

Abbreviations of phrases often don't take periods: *ASEAN, EU, rpm.* Those that do take periods are abbreviations of a Latin phrase (*A.D., a.m., e.g., i.e.*) or are abbreviations that could be misread without periods (*U.S., U.N.*).

If you're trying to decide how to treat a particular abbreviation, remember: On the Web, shorter is often better—and abbreviations without periods are shorter than abbreviations with them. For this reason, it makes sense to forgo periods when an abbreviation is just as clear without them; for example, *PhD* instead of *Ph.D.* But in some cases, periods can help prevent confusion. The abbreviation *in.* may look like the preposition *in,* and *a.m.* without periods may look like the verb *am.* Remember, people read quickly on the Web. Do keep your copy as sleek and concise as possible, but don't trip people up with abbreviations that could be misread.

Choosing *a* or *an*: Listen to the sound of the word

When trying to decide whether a word takes *a* or *an*, forget the *letter* a word begins with. It's all about the *sound*:

■ If a word begins with a consonant sound, precede it with *a*: *a ball, a motherboard, a historian, a utility*.

■ If a word begins with a vowel sound, precede it with *an*: *an airplane, an hour, an utterance*.

The same rule applies to acronyms and other abbreviations. Some technology-related acronyms (like *FAQ* and *URL*) are particularly confusing, because people pronounce them both ways: Some people pronounce them as words, others as letters. Decide how your site will treat acronyms such as *FAQ* and *URL,* and note the decision in your word list (see page 433) so that you can remain consistent.

Examples

a HUD official, an HBO special
a MIRV rocket, an MP3 player
a NATO agreement, an NFL quarterback
a RAM controller, an RSS news feed
a SIDS-related death, an SEC ruling
a FAQ (pronounced "fak"), an FAQ (pronounced "eff-ay-cue")
a URL (pronounced "yoo-ar-el"), an URL (pronounced like *earl*)

For pronunciation help with common Web-related abbreviations, look for individual entries in "The Yahoo! word list" on page 438.

How to form plurals of abbreviations

To form the plural of abbreviations and acronyms, add a lowercase *s*. Don't include an apostrophe unless omitting the apostrophe could cause confusion (for example, if adding an *s* by itself forms a word). For more examples, see "Apostrophes" on page 198.

Examples

PCs
URLs
PDAs

MP3s
OSes *(Exception.)*

Drs. *(Plural of abbreviated title "Dr.")*
Sens. *(Plural of abbreviated title "Sen.")*

MBAs
PhD's *(The lowercase "h" in the middle makes this one slightly confusing without an apostrophe.)*

Oakland A's *(Single-letter abbreviations, like "A" for "Athletic" here, almost always need an apostrophe and an "s" to prevent confusion—without the apostrophe, this baseball team's name could be confused for the word "as.")*

Don't add an *s* to abbreviations of units of measurement (for example, *2 in., 5 oz., 10 lb.*). For more on these, see "Units of measure" on page 273. For other abbreviations commonly used with numbers—including abbreviated months and days of the week—see Chapter 12, "Apply a Consistent Style for Numbers."

Quick-reference guide: Common abbreviations

Academic degrees

BA	BS	MA	JD	MBA	PhD	MD	DDS	RN

Professional titles and honorifics

Dr.	Gov.	Pres.	Prof.	Rev.	Sen.

Months

Jan.	Feb.	March	April	May	June	July	Aug.	Sept.	Oct.	Nov.	Dec.

See Chapter 9 for shorter abbreviations that may be necessary for mobile content.

Days of the week

Mon.	Tue.	Wed.	Thu.	Fri.	Sat.	Sun.

See Chapter 9 for shorter abbreviations that may be necessary for mobile content.

Quick-reference guide: Common abbreviations

Time

sec.   min.   hr.   day   a.m.   p.m.

See Chapter 9 for shorter abbreviations that may be necessary for mobile content. See Chapter 12 for time zone abbreviations.

Large numbers

K (thousand)   mil (million)   bil (billion)

Units of measure: English

in.   sq. in.   cu. in.   ft.   sq. ft.   cu. ft.   yd.   sq. yd.   cu. yd.

mi.   sq. mi.   mpg   mph   oz.   fl. oz.   pt.   lb.   qt.   gal.

Units of measure: metric

nm   mm   cm   m   km   ng   mcg   mg   cg   g

kg   ml   cl   l   kl   sq m   cu m   sq km   cu km   km/h

Units of measure: computer

KB (kilobyte)   MB (megabyte)   GB (gigabyte)   TB (terabyte)

kHz (kilohertz)   MHz (megahertz)   GHz (gigahertz)   dpi (dots per inch)

Kbps (kilobits/sec.)   KBps (kilobytes/sec.) Mbps (megabits/sec.)

MBps (megabytes/sec.) Gbps (gigabits/sec.)   GBps (gigabytes/sec.)

See Chapter 12 for information on how and when to use abbreviated units with numbers.

Geographic locations

U.S.   NYC   L.A.   U.K.

See Chapter 11 for U.S. state abbreviations.

Other common abbreviations

A.D.   B.C.   C.E.   B.C.E.

e.g. (for example)   i.e. (that is)   ca. (circa)   etc. (and so on)

et al. (and others)   ex. (for example)   aka (also known as)   ext. (extension)

Capitalization

The three main styles of capitalization used online and in email are **sentence case** (*The story of my life*), **title case** (*The Story of My Life*), and **all uppercase** (*THE STORY OF MY LIFE*). All uppercase is commonly called all caps.

Whichever style of capitalization you choose for your site, perhaps the most important consideration is to **use the style correctly and consistently across the site**, to ensure a coherent, deliberate look and feel. You may even decide to use more than one style of capitalization. For instance, you could use one style for article titles, one for subheadings within articles, and one for tab labels. This decision can work beautifully as long as each type of heading is consistently capitalized in one style.

For more information on writing and choosing a style for headlines and subheadings, see "Headings" on page 50. For more information on the different types of site-navigation text, see Chapter 7, "Write Clear User-Interface Text."

Less common styles of capitalization

Other capitalization styles you may notice on the Web are (1) all lowercase (*the story of my life*) and (2) capitalizing the first letter of every word, regardless of the part of speech (*The Story Of My Life*). These styles may seem easier—no decisions to make!—but they have potential drawbacks:

- **Using all lowercase** is impractical for proper nouns (*new york city, the eiffel tower*) and for titles of site features and stories, so you may end up having to capitalize some words anyway, to ensure that they stand out in running text.
- **Capitalizing the first letter of every word** is easier than learning and applying the rules of traditional title case. But this style is not yet as well-known or as well-regarded as traditional title-style capitalization.

Sentence case

Capitalize the text as if it were a sentence:

- Capitalize the first word and all other words normally capitalized (such as proper nouns).
- If the **first word is a proper noun that begins with a lowercase letter** (like *iPhone*), try to reorder the title or sentence so that you can capitalize the name as the company usually does. If reordering is impossible, capitalize the first letter and any other letter the company usually capitalizes: *IPhone*.

Examples

Tony Award winner takes Emmy, eyes Oscar

Sales of iPod soar

IPod sales soar *(Acceptable only if "Sales of iPod soar" won't fit)*

Title case

This style has more rules than sentence case:

- **Capitalize the first and last words**, regardless of the length of the word or the part of speech.
- For the words in between, **capitalize all nouns, verbs, adjectives, adverbs, and pronouns**, regardless of the length of the word. Capitalize **prepositions of four or more letters** (like *over, from,* and *with*). And capitalize conjunctions of four or more letters (like *unless* and *than*), as well as *if* and *how* and *why*.
- **Do not capitalize:**
  - ◆ Articles (*a, an,* and *the*)
  - ◆ Prepositions of three or fewer letters (such as *of, in,* and *for*)
  - ◆ Most conjunctions of three or fewer letters (like *as, and, or,* and *but*)

T I P   Verbs (even short ones like *is, be,* and *do*) should always be capitalized. Pronouns (including *he, she, it, me,* and *you*) should also be capitalized, no matter how short. And remember to capitalize both parts of *phrasal verbs,* multiword verbs that include adverbs such as *up* and *out* (for example, *tune in* and *hold on*). Phrasal verbs don't include the infinitive *to* form of a verb (*to be, to run*)—so lowercase the word *to* in such a verb.

Examples

"Don't Fence Me In"

"Walk With Me in Moonlight"

"Turn Off the Lights, I'm Home" *("Off" is an adverb here, part of the phrasal verb "turn off.")*

"She Took the Deal off the Table" *(Here, "off" is a preposition.)*

"What If I Do, What If She Won't"

"The Least She Could Do Is Cry"

■   If the **first word is a proper noun that begins with a lowercase letter** (like *iPhone*), try to reorder the title so that you can capitalize the name as the company usually does. If reordering is impossible, capitalize the first letter and any other letter the company usually capitalizes (*IPhone*). If such a noun falls elsewhere in the title, use the company's capitalization style (*iPhone*).

Examples

Sales of iPod Soar
IPod Sales Soar *(Acceptable only if "Sales of iPod Soar" won't fit)*

Hyphenated compounds in title case

If a hyphenated compound appears in title-style capitalization, capitalize the first word, and capitalize all subsequent words in the compound except for articles (*a, an,* and *the*), prepositions of three or fewer letters (like *to* and *of*), and coordinating conjunctions (*for, and, nor, but, or, yet,* and *so*). Ask yourself: If this word weren't in a hyphenated compound, would I capitalize it? If the answer is yes, capitalize it as part of the hyphenated compound, too.

Examples

The Big Spender's Budget How-To *(Capitalize any word, even "to," at the beginning or end of a title.)*
Author of How-to Book on Bee-Keeping Prone to Anaphylaxis
Governor Slams E-Book About Her Re-Election Campaign
Consumers Prefer Eco-Friendly and Cheap Products
Two-Thirds Vote Needed to Fund Research Into Blue-Green Algae Biofuel
Profits Double on Word-of-Mouth Sales
Audiences Love His Man-About-Town Sophistication
Open Your Own eBay-Based Boutique

All uppercase

This style (commonly called all caps) calls for every letter of every word to be capitalized. In general, avoid this style. It is often difficult to read, it can unintentionally convey alarm, and some people regard it as shouting.

Avoid using all uppercase for emphasis. Instead, use boldface, italics, or a graphic design. And remember that linked text already stands out: Links tend to catch the eye of a scanning reader.

Examples

Before
DOW UP 100 AT CLOSE

After
Dow Up 100 at Close

Before
Register TODAY and receive a FREE GIFT.

After
Register **today** and receive a free gift.

___

If it is not overused, **all uppercase can be appropriate in warning messages**, where a single word set in capital letters can alert readers to a situation requiring attention (*IMPORTANT: Do not click the **Back** button*), **and in plain-text emails**, where boldface and other devices for emphasizing headings can't be used (see "HTML email vs. text email" on page 174).

Company and product names

Within reason, follow an organization's conventions for how it capitalizes and punctuates its names. Many organizations (for example, FedEx) incorporate *intercaps,* or capital letters in the middle of the name. Other organizations, Yahoo! included, incorporate punctuation characters in their names.

With brand names used in text in a noncommercial context, you may have some leeway with how faithfully you need to reproduce an organization's trademarked name (see "Trademarks" on page 424). For example, you probably don't need to write product or company names in all uppercase (unless they're acronyms, like *UPS*), or use complicated graphic symbols in a name.

T I P In some cases, you may not be able to replicate a graphic symbol used in a name, particularly in a plain-text email. Example: *WALL·E* is difficult to reproduce and is generally spelled with a hyphen, *WALL-E*. When in doubt, look at some of the organization's press releases or at its copyright page if it has one—you may find an alternative way to write the title using only standard keyboard characters.

Examples

iPod

iPod shuffle

IHOP

PayPal

Visa

MasterCard

Digg

YouTube

For company, product, and website names that use all-lowercase letters, you may find it necessary to use an initial capital letter as you would for most other proper nouns. Otherwise, the names are hard to distinguish in text. But for company names that include a capital letter somewhere (for example, *eBay* and *iPod shuffle*), follow the company's capitalization in most situations—even an internal capital letter will alert the reader that the word or phrase is a proper noun. (For information on how to capitalize names like *eBay* and *iPod* in titles and at the beginning of a sentence, see "Capitalization" on page 239.)

Abbreviations in company names

Abbreviations such as these may be included as part of a business's full name:

Abbreviation	What it stands for
Co.	company
Corp.	corporation
Inc.	incorporated
LLC	limited liability corporation
LLLP	limited liability limited partnership
LP	limited partnership
Ltd.	limited
Mfg.	manufacturing
Mfrs.	manufacturers
PLC	public limited company
Pty. Ltd.	proprietary limited

It is rarely necessary to write a business's full name—*Inc.* and the like can usually be omitted. When the context does call for a business's full name, omit the comma before these terms or their abbreviations, including *Incorporated* or *Inc.* and *Limited* or *Ltd.*

Examples

Toy Captain Pty. Ltd.
Azore Sports LLC
Bootleg Bäby Inc.

Pronouns to refer to companies

When referring to your own or another company, use the third-person singular pronouns ***it* and *its***. In the United States, a company is treated as a collective noun and requires a singular verb and a singular pronoun. Referring to a company in the plural (*they, them, their, theirs*) is chiefly a British convention.

Example

Before
The company anticipates an increase in their third-quarter spending. *(Uses a singular verb but a plural possessive)*

After (U.S. style)
The company anticipates an increase in its third-quarter spending. *(Singular verb, singular possessive "its")*

After (British style)
The company anticipate an increase in their third-quarter spending. *(Plural verb, plural possessive "their")*

When **referring to your company**, it may also be acceptable (depending on your site's voice—see Chapter 3) to use the first-person plural pronouns *we, us, our,* and *ours*. Individual bloggers may also use *I, me, my,* and *mine*.

Examples

View our tutorials.
Contact us about the Housekeeper 3000 30-day trial offer.

Email addresses and fields

Email addresses are typically written in all lowercase. But if you have an address with capital letters in the **first part of the address** (the part before the @ symbol), retain those capital letters. This part of the address is unlikely to ever be case-sensitive, but a remote potential exists for Internet service providers to enforce case-sensitive addresses.

The **second part of the address** (the part after @, the *domain name*) is not case-sensitive. It is safe to write the domain-name part in all lowercase.

Email addresses are easy to recognize with no special visual treatment—no need for quotation marks or italics.

Examples

Contact us at MemberEvents@redgrousegreens.com.

Sales: sales@bootlegbaby.com
Returns: returns@bootlegbaby.com

When referring to **email fields** such as **To**, **From**, **Cc**, and **Bcc**, use initial capital letters and the same visual treatment you would use for buttons and other interface elements (we recommend boldface—see "User-instruction mechanics" on page 144).

When using *Cc* and *Bcc* as verbs instead of field names, no special visual treatment is necessary. For more on using *Cc* and *Bcc* as verbs, see their individual entries in "The Yahoo! word list" on page 438.

Examples

Enter recipients' addresses in the **Bcc** field and your own address in the **To** field.
Please Bcc me when you send that note to Juanita.

File names, types, and extensions

When referring to file names and file types, use these guidelines:

- Write **file names** in lowercase: *setup.exe, image.jpg*. In instructions, distinguish file names from the surrounding text as you would button names—we recommend boldface. See "Buttons and other UI elements" on page 128.
- Write **file types** in all capital letters: *GIF, JPEG, DOC*.
- Write **file name extensions** (generally three letters separated from the file name by a period) using lowercase letters: *gif*. Don't include the period that separates the file name from the extension. Enclose the extension in quotation marks—because if you're referring to an extension, it's the same as referring to a word as a word (see "Referring to words and letters" on page 226).

Examples

Right-click on **setup.exe** and choose **Run as**.

You can upload GIF and JPEG files.

A JPEG file usually has a file name extension like "jpg" or "jpe"; for example, photo123.jpg.

The data is exported to a CSV (comma-separated values) file.

Place names

Avoid confusion by using the correct capitalization and punctuation for compass directions, cities, states, and regions.

Compass directions

For simple compass directions, use lowercase: *north, south, east, west, northeast, northwest, southeast, southwest, northern, southern, eastern, western*.

Examples

Clouds cover western Utah, but sun is expected in areas to the east.

We traveled north by train from Bangkok, then headed for the northwestern region around Pai.

U.S. states and districts

In general, we favor spelling out state names in running text. When abbreviations are called for, we favor traditional state abbreviations (*Ariz.*) over postal abbreviations. Here's why: (1) Some postal abbreviations are not immediately recognizable (*ME* for *Maine,* for instance), and (2) if you are using postal abbreviations and need to abbreviate a list of states, the result is a pileup of ALL CAPITAL LETTERS.

When referring to the names of U.S. states, follow these guidelines:

- When referring to the U.S. capital, use *Washington, D.C.* (note comma and periods), or *District of Columbia*. *Washington* (without *D.C.*) is acceptable if there is no chance of confusion with the state. When space is tight, *Wash. DC* is an acceptable abbreviation.
- When a state name is used alone, without a city, spell out the name of the state.
- When citing a single city and state in the middle of a sentence, spell out the state name and insert a comma before and after the state: *He lived in Chevy Chase, Maryland, for three years.* See "Separating parts of place names" on page 211.
- In a list of cities and states, use traditional state abbreviations, which are different from postal abbreviations (see the following table). Include the period. If an abbreviation consists of two parts (like *N.J.* and *W.Va.*), don't put a space after the first period. Note that some state names are never abbreviated in text.
- If space is at a premium, abbreviate the state name (whether or not it is preceded by a city) using traditional (not postal) state abbreviations. But if space is extremely tight, postal abbreviations are acceptable.
- Use postal abbreviations in addresses.

State	Abbrev.	Postal	State	Abbrev.	Postal
Alabama	Ala.	AL	Illinois	Ill.	IL
Alaska	Alaska	AK	Indiana	Ind.	IN
Arizona	Ariz.	AZ	Iowa	Iowa	IA
Arkansas	Ark.	AR	Kansas	Kan.	KS
California	Calif.	CA	Kentucky	Ky.	KY
Colorado	Colo.	CO	Louisiana	La.	LA
Connecticut	Conn.	CT	Maine	Maine	ME
Delaware	Del.	DE	Maryland	Md.	MD
Florida	Fla.	FL	Massachusetts	Mass.	MA
Georgia	Ga.	GA	Michigan	Mich.	MI
Hawaii	Hawaii	HI	Minnesota	Minn.	MN
Idaho	Idaho	ID	Mississippi	Miss.	MS

State	Abbrev.	Postal	State	Abbrev.	Postal
Missouri	Mo.	MO	Pennsylvania	Pa.	PA
Montana	Mont.	MT	Rhode Island	R.I.	RI
Nebraska	Neb.	NE	South Carolina	S.C.	SC
Nevada	Nev.	NV	South Dakota	S.D.	SD
New Hampshire	N.H.	NH	Tennessee	Tenn.	TN
New Jersey	N.J.	NJ	Texas	Texas	TX
New Mexico	N.M.	NM	Utah	Utah	UT
New York	N.Y.	NY	Vermont	Vt.	VT
North Carolina	N.C.	NC	Virginia	Va.	VA
North Dakota	N.D.	ND	Washington	Wash.	WA
Ohio	Ohio	OH	West Virginia	W.Va.	WV
Oklahoma	Okla.	OK	Wisconsin	Wis.	WI
Oregon	Ore.	OR	Wyoming	Wyo.	WY

U.S. regions

Some U.S. regions and city neighborhoods are so well-known that they have become proper nouns—complete with initial capital letters. Note, though, that if your site is likely to have an audience outside the United States, you may need to qualify these names—for example, by writing "California's San Francisco Bay Area" instead of "Bay Area."

Region	Usage
Bay Area	Generally used to refer to the San Francisco Bay Area. If there's a possibility for confusion, include the city.
Deep South	Capitalize when referring to the southeast U.S. region consisting of Alabama, Georgia, Louisiana, Mississippi, and South Carolina.
Down East	Capitalize when referring to Maine.
East	Capitalize when referring to the eastern region of the U.S.
East Coast	Capitalize when referring to the region bordering on the Atlantic Ocean.
East Side, Lower East Side, Upper East Side	Capitalize when referring to the area of Manhattan east of Fifth Avenue.

Region	Usage
Eastern Shore	Capitalize when referring to the region on the east side of the Chesapeake Bay.
Midwest, Midwesterner	Capitalize *Midwest* when referring to the region that consists of Illinois, Indiana, Iowa, Kansas, Michigan, Minnesota, Missouri, Nebraska, North Dakota, Ohio, South Dakota, and Wisconsin. Capitalize *Midwesterner* when referring to a person of this region.
New England	Capitalize when referring to the region that consists of Connecticut, Maine, Massachusetts, New Hampshire, Rhode Island, and Vermont.
North, Northern, Northerner	Capitalize *North* and *Northern* when referring to the northern part of the U.S., especially the states that fought for the Union during the U.S. Civil War. Capitalize *Northerner* when referring to a person.
Northeast	Capitalize when referring to the region that consists of Connecticut, Maine, Massachusetts, New Hampshire, New Jersey, New York, Pennsylvania, Rhode Island, and Vermont.
South Side of Chicago	Capitalize.
South, Southern, Southerner	Capitalize *South* and *Southern* when referring to the region that consists of Alabama, Arkansas, Delaware, Florida, Georgia, Kentucky, Louisiana, Maryland, Mississippi, North Carolina, Oklahoma, South Carolina, Tennessee, Texas, Virginia, and West Virginia. Capitalize *Southerner* when referring to a person.
Southern California	Capitalize when referring to the area of California or its culture.
West, Western, Westerner	Capitalize *West* and *Western* when referring to the region that consists of Alaska, Arizona, California, Colorado, Hawaii, Idaho, Montana, Nevada, New Mexico, Oregon, Utah, Washington, and Wyoming. Lowercase *western* when referring to the film, book, or music genre. Capitalize *Westerner* when referring to a person.
West Coast	Capitalize when referring to the area of the U.S. bordering on the Pacific Ocean: California, Oregon, and Washington.

High winds slammed portions of the Northeast and the South and will hit the Midwest.

She is considered a Southern conservative in spite of her Northern roots.

Of all the West Coast areas, Southern California is best known for western music.

The director John Ford filmed many of his westerns in Monument Valley.

World regions

Capitalize the following regions:

Central America	East Asia	Eastern Hemisphere
Latin America	Middle East	North America
Northern Hemisphere	South America	Southeast Asia
Southern Hemisphere	South Pacific	West Indies
Western Hemisphere		

Titles of people

Capitalize a person's title only when it's used directly before a name. This rule includes titles pertaining to government positions (like *president, senator, mayor, ambassador, chief justice*), religious positions (like *pope, cardinal, rabbi*), and other organizational positions (like *chair, treasurer, general manager*).

She was appointed ambassador to the United Nations by President Obama.

The president returned to the Oval Office to greet the pope.

Pope Benedict XVI succeeded Pope John Paul II.

The school was treated to a visit by former President Jimmy Carter.

Shan Chu was named general manager of the Chicago region.

General Manager Shan Chu began her career in the mailroom.

When the honorifics *Reverend* and *Honorable* appear before a name, they should be preceded by *the*. See "Reverend" on page 468 and "Honorable" on page 454 for more information.

Alternative style: Titles and appositives

For the sake of efficiency, Yahoo! style calls for capitalizing a person's title whenever it directly precedes the name, as in *former President Jimmy Carter*. You should be aware, however, that not all publications and websites follow this rule; instead, they make a **distinction between titles and nouns used in apposition**. You may want to do the same.

Strictly speaking, the phrase *former President Jimmy Carter* consists of a noun phrase (*former president*) in apposition with a name (*Jimmy Carter*). *Jimmy Carter* is an appositive the same way that *Sally* is an appositive in *my friend Sally.* An appositive immediately follows another noun phrase and provides information about it.

Many style guides recommend treating nouns in apposition as common nouns, whether they come before or after a name. Thus, *president* is lowercased in both *Jimmy Carter, former president of the United States* and *former president Jimmy Carter.* Some guides also lowercase occupational titles, considering them descriptive phrases rather than official titles: *general manager Shan Chu.*

More examples:
The president met with Prime Minister Taro Aso. *(Title)*
The president met with Japanese prime minister Taro Aso. *(Not a title)*
A portrait of Pope John XXIII *(Title)*
A portrait of the widely beloved pope John XXIII *(Not a title)*

Titles of works

When citing the title of a book, magazine, CD, or other composition, consider two things:

- **Visual treatment.** Some titles take quotation marks or italics (for Web copy, we recommend quotation marks); some titles don't require any special treatment.
- **Capitalization style.** Titles are often set in title case.

Visual treatment of titles of works

The visual treatment of titles—whether or not to enclose them in quotation marks (or to display them in italics, if that is your style choice)—depends on the type of work and the location of the title on the page.

Titles that don't need quotation marks or italics

The following titles require no special visual treatment.

- **Games.** These include computer games, video games, and board games.
- **Magazines.** However, titles of magazine articles should be in quotation marks.
- **Newspapers.** However, titles of newspaper articles should be in quotation marks.
- **Software.**
- **Speech names that aren't actual titles.** For example, the State of the Union address, Nixon's Checkers speech.
- **Blogs.** However, titles of individual blog posts should be in quotation marks (unless the posts are titled with dates only).
- **Names of websites.**

Examples

She downloaded two games, Trapped in Suburbia and Driver's Education III.
"The Dukes of Hazzard" garnered tepid reviews from the New York Times and Time magazine.
Kevin Sites hosted the popular blog Kevin Sites in the Hot Zone.
Her book was featured in the Parsemouth blog post "Diagramming for Fun."

Titles that do need quotation marks or italics

For all other titles of works—artworks; books; chapters, headings, and other parts of books; CDs; record albums; songs; DVDs; lectures; magazine articles; movies; newspaper articles; operas; plays; podcasts and podcast episodes; poems; speeches that the speaker has titled or that use a speech line as a title; TV and radio programs; TV and radio episodes; Web shows, series, and episodes; and Web videos—follow these guidelines:

- In most cases, **enclose titles in double quotation marks**.

Examples

Check out the "Fantastic Four" trailer.
Win tickets to "A Chorus Line."
We watched a tape of Martin Luther King Jr.'s "I Have a Dream" speech.
Millions have watched "Evolution of Dance" on YouTube.
Download the latest podcast of "This American Life."
The U.S. version of the TV show "The Office" has a series of webisodes called "Blackmail." In the "Andy" episode, we learn that the character has a tramp stamp.

■ In some cases, such as within headlines and other display type (in captions and pull quotes, for example), titles can be enclosed in **single quotation marks** or indicated with italics to save space. (But note that italic may not appear in a newsreader—see "Boldface and italics" on page 382.)

Examples

'Ben Hur' breaks box-office record
Original *Great Gatsby* manuscript found

■ When including titles in a list, determine whether they are:
   ◆ **Titles in a list of like items.** In a bulleted or numbered list made up entirely of titles, the titles don't need to be in italic or enclosed in quotation marks. (Reason: They don't need to be set off from any surrounding text.)

Examples

He listed his favorite shows as "South Park," "Law and Order," and "The Honeymooners."

He listed his favorite shows as:
—South Park
—Law and Order
—The Honeymooners

   ◆ **Titles in a list of unlike items.** When including a title in a list of unlike items, however, use double quotation marks around titles that require them.

Example

Your word-of-the-day hints are:
—"Green Acres"
—Monopoly
—avenue

Capitalization styles of titles of works

Set the following titles in title case.

Type of work	Examples
Artwork.	"Starry Night" "The Thinker"
Book, chapter, heading, or other part of a book.	"Alice's Adventures in Wonderland" "Down the Rabbit-Hole"
CD, record album, song, DVD.	"Sgt. Pepper's Lonely Hearts Club Band" "Lucy in the Sky With Diamonds" "Star Wars"
Game (including computer games, video games, and board games).	Grand Theft Auto Wonder Pets: Save the Animals Chutes and Ladders
Lecture.	"Foundations of Capitalism"
Magazine or magazine article. Lowercase the word *magazine* unless it's part of the publication's title.	New York Times Magazine Harper's magazine "10 Rules for Eating Wisely"
Movie.	"It's a Wonderful Life"
Newspaper or newspaper article. In running text, lowercase *the* in a newspaper's name even if it's part of the paper's name.	the Wall Street Journal New York Daily News "Ponzi Schemes Ensnare Young and Old"
Opera.	"The Barber of Seville"
Play.	"Cat on a Hot Tin Roof"
Podcast or podcast episode.	"The Ricky Gervais Show" Episode 1 "Getting Under Your Skin"
Poem.	"The Road Not Taken" "To a Mouse"
Software. In general, follow the manufacturer's capitalization style (unless the product name is in all capital letters but is not an acronym).	Mozilla Firefox QuarkXPress XMetaL
Speech.	the Gettysburg Address the State of the Union address "I Am an African"

Type of work	Examples
Television or radio program or individual program episode.	"60 Minutes" (TV show) "One for the Road" (TV episode) "The Naked Scientists" (radio show)
Web show or series or individual episode.	"Heroes: The Recruit" (series) "Private Mills" (episode)
Web video.	"Frozen Grand Central" "Extreme Shepherding"

T I P To refer to **parts of a work** that are not titled—for example, *page, line, column, row, step*—use lowercase and numerals. Examples: *The figures in column 3 are inaccurate. After you've completed step 1, wash your hands.* Exceptions are *chapter* and *episode,* which often function as titles: *Refer to Chapter 14. We watched Episode 2 last night.* See "The basics" on page 261.

Website names and addresses

Website names and addresses (*URLs*) don't require any special visual treatment in running text—no quotation marks or italics, for example—but URLs in particular need to be treated with care so that the reader can find the site.

Website names

Follow these guidelines for referring to the **name of a website** in copy:

- When you refer to a website by its name (like *Yahoo!*) instead of its URL (like *www.yahoo.com*), follow the site's preferred capitalization style. Don't use quotation marks around the name or italicize it.
- If a publication has a print edition and an online edition, specify which edition you're referring to only if it's necessary for accuracy or clarity.

Examples

Yahoo! Sports now includes Rivals.com.

The article appeared both in Rolling Stone magazine and on Salon.com.

Corrections have been made to it on the Rolling Stone website and on Salon.com.

Read a review of the movie in Slate.

The <u>photos</u> appear this month in Us Magazine. *(Photos are appearing in both the print and online editions; no need to specify.)*

The <u>photos</u> appear this month in Us Magazine's online edition. *(Photos are a Web exclusive.)*

It's completely true, and you can read all about it in The Onion.

T I P   In general, use *on* as the preposition when referring to a website: *Today on Salon.com. Find it on Amazon.com.* But if you refer to a website magazine or newspaper by its publication title (*Salon,* for example), it's possible to use *in* as the preposition: *Today in Salon.* Note that this applies only to publication websites (magazines or newspapers), which often use *in* when referring to themselves, even when they don't publish a print version—a vestige, perhaps, of their roots in print. Using *at* is not incorrect when referring to a website, but the usage is less common: *Find it at Amazon.com. The article is at Salon.com.*

URLs

Sometimes Internet addresses, or *URLs,* point to a website's homepage; sometimes they point to a deeper page on the site.

The URL of a homepage generally includes only the site's *domain name,* which is the first part of a URL typically ending in *.com, .org, .gov, .uk, .aus,* and so on. Domain names are not case-sensitive, which means, for example, that whether you type **WWW.YAHOO.COM** or **www.yahoo.com** or **Www.yaHOO.com** into your browser, you'll end up at Yahoo!.

Anything following the domain name and its "trailing slash" (as in *www.whitehouse.gov/*) *is* sometimes case-sensitive. So, for a website's deeper-level pages (such as *http://www.whitehouse.gov /administration/cabinet*), take care to use the site's capitalization for the URL.

When including a **domain-name URL** in copy, follow these guidelines:

- Don't include *http://* at the start of URLs that include *www* and the domain name alone.
- Don't include the trailing slash (/).

Examples

Before

http://www.whitehouse.gov/

After

www.whitehouse.gov

Before

http://finance.yahoo.com/

After

http://finance.yahoo.com

- Follow the site's convention for **capitalization**. If there's no clear convention, use all lowercase for domain-name URLs: *www.yahoo.com*.

For **URLs of deeper-level pages**:

- Include the full URL of the webpage, even the *http://*.
- Follow the site's convention for capitalization—these are often case-sensitive.
- Avoid using end punctuation, such as a period, after a link—a few people might think the period is part of the URL. And even for people who know how URLs work, it's all too easy to accidentally grab the end punctuation along with the URL when copying and pasting the URL into a browser. Instead, set off URLs with a colon and a line break, or—if you have enough room so that awkward line breaks aren't a problem—put URLs in parentheses.

Examples

See what's growing in the garden this week at:
http://www.farmerinthedell.net/blog/Garden_Notes.html

Read Farmer Josephine's Garden Notes (http://www.farmerinthedell.net/Public /blog/Garden_Notes.html) to see what's growing this week.

Check out real kids wearing our latest punk baby clothes (and upload photos of your own little aspiring model):
http://www.bootlegbaby.com/community/punk-baby-clothes-photos

TIP Some sites use "tracking tags" at the end of URLs; these help site administrators gather data about visitors' clicks on a given URL. Tracking tags often begin with a question mark and have this sort of syntax:

?word=word

If you have a very long URL and notice this syntax near the end of it, you may be able to delete the tracking tag (unless, of course, it's serving a data-gathering purpose for your own site). For example:

http://www.farmerinthedell.net/farmphotos/index.html?source=ad

may still work as:

http://www.farmerinthedell.net/farmphotos/index.html

But be sure to test the URL to make sure it still works. Question marks can appear in URLs for other reasons, too.

Don't use **quotation marks** around URLs or italicize URLs.

Example

Before

Would you like to set your homepage to 'http://www.yahoo.com/'?

After

Would you like to set your homepage to www.yahoo.com?

Breaking a URL

Generally, you should avoid having URLs wrap to a second line. Occasionally, because of space constraints, you may have no choice.

If you must break a URL, break it after punctuation in the URL. But **don't break the URL after a hyphen**—some people may think you added the hyphen to indicate the break. And don't add a hyphen to indicate the break—some people will think that the hyphen is part of the URL. If you must break at a period, a slash, or some other punctuation mark that people could mistake for the end of the URL, try to start the next line with that mark, instead of ending the first line with it.

The fava beans are almost ready! See pictures of our blossoms and beans at:

http://www.farmerinthedell.net/Public/blog/Garden_Notes /PhotosFromTheFarm/Hamilton/000239-fava-beans-April-2010.jpg

---

T I P   Before you include a URL in your copy, ask yourself whether you really need to. Do you need to promote the address itself (*Visit www.bootlegbaby.com*), or can you use linked text instead (*Visit Bootleg Bäby*)? For more information, see "Text links" on page 123. One place where you do need to include URLs is a plain-text email (see the box "HTML email vs. text email" on page 174).

Ideas in Practice

Exercise: Crop, cap, and quote correctly

In the following examples, correct the capitalization, abbreviation, and punctuation to make the sentences clearer and more consistent. Use Chapters 10 and 11 to guide you. Each example includes at least two errors.

 To see our solution, turn to page 480.

1. Alternative text is text that you enter in a HTML attribute for an image.

2. Gadfly Games has had a surprise hit with their "Sandcastle" phone game, thanks to senior designer Luke Jackson's inventive sand structures and hilarious, castle-stomping monsters.

3. Inspired by the Web video An Engineer's Guide To Cats, Demetri is recording his kittens, Petaflop and Nanobot, for a piece called a physicist's guide to feline mechanics.

4. The Zoo News podcast has just released an episode called All About Alligators.

5. To upload a photo:
   Go to the Upload Photos and Videos page: www.flickr.com/photos/upload/.
   Click the **Choose photos and videos** link to browse your hard drive.
   Select the file you want and click **Open**. You can upload jpeg's, non-animated gif's, tiff's, and bmp's.
   Click the "**Upload Photos and Videos**" button.

6. eFreebird is a new mobile-phone download for concertgoers. When you load the app., it displays a flickering lighter; requests Freebird; and shouts "more cowbell," and five other annoying concert clichés.

7. The RDA for calcium is 1,000 mg. for adults 19 to 50 years old, the amount in 30 oz (a little less than 1 qt.) of fortified orange juice, which will also provide more than the RDA's for vitamins C and D.

8. Ms Cha is Managing Editor of the southeast Asia bureau of Global News, Inc.

9. Jade is catching up on some of the novels she never read in college: "The Heart is a Lonely Hunter," "Far from the Madding Crowd," "Slaughterhouse-five," "Winesburg Ohio," "Things Fall apart," and "Play it as it Lays."

10. The candidate has a great resume, but HR questioned her judgment when she included her email address, BoozeHound@Yahoo.com, and the URL for her party-girl blog, Too Much Information, http://www.TooMuchInformation.net.

Chapter 12
Apply a Consistent Style for Numbers

In this chapter

- **The basics.** When to spell out numbers, when to use numerals, and other guidelines.
- **Ages.** Referring to people and things and their years on earth.
- **Dates.** Other than those found on a matchmaking website or a supermarket shelf.
- **Time.** About a.m., p.m., time zones, and more.
- **Fractions and decimals.** Rules for writing fractions, mixed numbers, and decimals.
- **Units of measure.** English, metric, and computer-related measurements.
- **Money and currency.** Expressing dollars and cents.
- **Numbers in a range.** Stating and punctuating them.
- **Percentages.** Just two rules to remember, although 100 percent of them may be new to you.
- **Phone numbers.** Parentheses? Spaces? Hyphens? Find a style that works.

Web style favors using numerals for most numbers: Numerals save space and attract the eye in headlines, and they're easy for the reader to pick out when scanning a page. But beyond this general recommendation, questions naturally arise: Is it 9 a.m. or 9:00 a.m.? Does your product cost six dollars, $6.00, or $6? Read on for guidelines that can help you treat numbers consistently and in a way that works for the Web.

The basics

In general, **spell out** cardinal numbers (*one, two,* and so on) and ordinal numbers (*first, second,* and so on) **below 10. Use numerals for 10 and above.**

████ **Examples**

Read reviews of more than 350 restaurants in your city.

Aunt Bea's pickles won first place at the fair.

With a premium license, install the software on three computers.

Does your building have a 13th floor?

T I P   Avoid stating ordinals with superscript letters (such as *10th*, *11th*, and so on). Ordinals with superscript formatted in a word processor may not display correctly in some places, such as email. Keep your text on the same baseline: *10th, 11th*.

If space is tight or if you need to emphasize a figure or a fact, use numerals for cardinal and ordinal numbers below 10, particularly in headlines, email subject lines, and HTML page titles.

Examples

In Pamplona, 8 Injured in 'Running of the Bulls' *(Headline)*

Subject: Presentation file 1 of 2 attached *(Email subject line)*

5th Grader Wins 1st Place in Spelling Bee *(Headline)*

Use numerals when referring to numbers that a person must input, for coordinates in tables and worksheets, and for parts of a document, such as page numbers or line references.

Examples

Type **5** and press Enter.

Select row 3, column 5 of the worksheet.

Refer to line 9 of the transcript.

If a passage contains **two or more numbers** that refer to the same category of information and one is 10 or higher, use numerals for all numbers referring to that category. When numbers are treated consistently, readers can recognize the relationship between them more easily.

Examples

The delegation included 3 women and 11 men. *(Use numerals for both.)*

He was the 9th person chosen for the 10-person team. *(Use numerals for both.)*

The most popular vote-getters included three women and nine men.

Only 3 women and 11 men attended the four-day event. *(Spell out "four" because it does not relate to the same category of items as "3" and "11" do and is thus treated according to the basic rule of spelling out numbers one through nine.)*

Express **large and very large numbers** in numerals followed by *million, billion,* and so forth. If expressing a number greater than 999 in numerals, use a comma.

Examples

5 billion people

1,200 years ago

Exception: Don't use a comma with page numbers, addresses, or years—unless it's a year with five or more digits.

Examples

Page 1026 of "War and Peace" *(Page number exception)*

27010 Industrial Blvd. *(Address exception)*

In the year 2525 *(Four-digit year exception)*

In 36,000 B.C. *(Five-digit year)*

When stating ***million* or *billion* with a numeral**, don't hyphenate, even before a noun. But do use a hyphen between the numeral and *million* or *billion* if the expression is part of a compound adjective that takes a hyphen elsewhere.

Global differences in punctuating numbers

In English-speaking North America and the United Kingdom, people use a comma in most whole numbers of four or more digits: *30,000 pounds, $1,500.* But many other countries use the International System of Units, in which thin spaces are used in numbers with five or more digits: *30 000 pounds.* Numbers with only four digits are expressed without a space: *$1500.* Furthermore, styles in the United States, the United Kingdom, and English-speaking Canada call for a decimal point: *2.5 kilos.* But in continental Europe, a comma is the decimal separator: *2,5 kilos.* Use the number style that's appropriate for your location, but be aware of the differences so that you can anticipate any confusion, particularly if your website serves a global audience.

Examples

a $6 million lawsuit
the 400-million-served mark

If space is tight (for example, in headlines, tables, diagrams, or text messages), use the following **abbreviations for large numbers**:

- *mil* (million). See "mil" on page 461.
- *bil* (billion). See "bil" on page 441.
- *K* (thousand). See "K" on page 457. But note: Among other things, *K* can stand for *thousand, kilobytes, kilobits,* and *kilograms.* Use *K* only if its meaning is clear from the context.

Examples

Painting worth $2 mil stolen from museum
Investigators look into donations over $250K

Avoid starting a sentence with a numeral. If you can't avoid it, spell out the number.

Example

Before
450 gamers participated in last night's chat.

After
Four hundred and fifty gamers participated in last night's chat.

Better
Last night, 450 gamers participated in the chat.

Exceptions:

- A year may be written in numerals at the beginning of a sentence.
- It's OK to start a headline with a numeral if space is tight or if the numeral makes the headline more eye-catching or easier to scan or understand.

Examples

1967 was the Summer of Love in San Francisco. *(Year exception in a sentence.)*
8 Diet Tips *(Headline exception.)*
Two 5-Year-Old Boys Found; One Still Missing *(Using "2" next to "5-Year-Old" would make the headline harder to read, not easier.)*

If it's necessary to spell out numbers **greater than 20**, use a hyphen to connect the first part of the word (ending in *y*) to the word following it, if any.

Examples

twenty-one
one hundred forty-three

Ages

When referring to the age of **a person or an animal**, use numerals.

When referring to the age of an **object**, spell out numbers one through nine; use numerals for 10 or more.

When making a **decade reference to a person's age** (for example, *She's in her 30s*), use numerals and an *s* without an apostrophe.

Examples

The 12-year-old boy was adopted by a couple in their 40s.
The girl was only 4 years old.
Her Siamese cat is 5 years old.
The company, which is four years old, targets 5- to 10-year-olds.
The house is 150 years old.

Dates

Each part of a date is governed by its own set of guidelines.

Days of the week

Avoid abbreviating days of the week. If abbreviations are unavoidable, use the first three letters, with a period: *Mon., Tue., Wed., Thu., Fri., Sat., Sun.*

Exception: In tables or in situations where space is very tight (for example, in content intended for viewing on mobile devices), periods may be omitted, and abbreviations may even be trimmed to *M, Tu, W, Th, F, Sa, Su.*

Months

In general, capitalize and spell out the month. The abbreviations *Jan., Feb., Aug., Sept., Oct., Nov.,* and *Dec.* may be used, with periods, when:

- The month is used with a specific date (such as *November 4* or *November 4, 2009*) and you have chosen to use an abbreviated-month style consistently throughout your website.
- Space is an issue—for example, in a headline.

Don't abbreviate months with five or fewer letters: *March, April, May, June, July.*

Examples

North Plaza news: New toy store coming February 2011. *(Month not abbreviated because month plus year is not a specific date.)*

Baby Blocks announced today its grand opening on Feb. 11, 2011. Shoppers visiting the store on Feb. 11 will receive a free pair of baby booties. *(Abbreviated-month style.)*

Baby Blocks announces grand opening on February 11, 2011. Shoppers visiting the store on February 11 will receive a free pair of baby booties. *(Nonabbreviated style.)*

Toy Store Coming Feb. 2011 *(Headline with limited space.)*

Store Grand Opening Feb. 11! *(Website ad with limited space.)*

Sale Extended to March 6! *(Don't abbreviate months with five or fewer letters.)*

Years

Years are an exception to the rule that a number should not be used to start a sentence: It's OK to start a sentence with a year.

Use the abbreviations ***A.D.*** and ***B.C.*** if the date may be unclear otherwise. Place *A.D.* before the year, *B.C.* after the year.

Some writers and scholars prefer the alternative abbreviations ***C.E.*** (common era) to *A.D.* and ***B.C.E.*** (before the common era) to *B.C.* because these are nonsecular. Place both of these abbreviations after the year.

Examples

He was born around 20 B.C. and died in A.D. 25.
Around 1500 B.C.E., people in the Indus Valley wrote the Vedic texts of Hinduism.

Ordering and punctuating dates

When writing a specific date, it's clearer to **use the name of the month** (*July, May,* and so on) rather than a numeral, because the order of the month and day varies from country to country.

Example

Sample date: December 6, 2009
In the U.S.: 12/6/09
In many other countries: 6/12/09

If it's necessary to use numerals for a full date, **separate the parts with slashes** (*2/12/10*) rather than with hyphens or other marks. The slash won't break at the end of a line as the hyphen will. Make sure that readers understand which century you're talking about: Is 2/12/10 in 2010 or in 1910?

TIP With the exception of *09* and the like to indicate a year in the first decade of the 21st century, avoid using leading zeros in dates (*06/12/08,* for example) in running text. Leading zeros can be useful in a column, however: Using the leading zero makes it easier to automatically order numeric lists, because 0 comes before 1, so 09 will come before 10. (If you ask a computer to order a numeric list without leading zeros, it will put 9 after 10.)

When stating a **month and day** (for example, *January 1*), don't use the ordinal (such as *first* or *1st*) for the day.

Exception: Proper names of holidays such as *the Fourth of July*.

Example

Before

Join us for a grand reopening on May 9th.

After

Join us for a grand reopening on May 9.

When a date consists of only a **month and year** (such as *January 2010*), don't separate the two with a comma.

When stating the **month, day, and year** in a sentence, include a comma after the day and after the year.

Examples

January 1970 was an extremely cold month. *(No comma)*

The event on April 30, 2010, saw record attendance. *(Comma needed after day and year)*

Decades and centuries

To state a decade, add an *s* without an apostrophe.

Example

The cities were reconstructed in the 1930s.

To abbreviate a decade, replace the first two digits with an apostrophe: *1990s* becomes *'90s*.

Examples

These cities were built during the '30s and '40s.

His singing career came to an end in the mid-'80s.

T I P Word processors tend to incorrectly format apostrophes that are placed after a word space. Make sure you use an apostrophe ('), which curls toward the left, and not a single opening quotation mark ('), which curls toward the right. You can also use a straight quote (') if you are avoiding special characters on your site. See "Special characters" on page 386 for instructions on coding an apostrophe.

To state a century, use numerals for the ordinal (even ordinals *1st* through *9th*) and lowercase the word *century*.

Examples

By the start of the 20th century, international fairs were becoming disorganized.

The epic poem "Beowulf" may have originated as far back as the 8th century.

Time

Use **numerals** to state all times except noon and midnight. So, instead of *12 p.m.*, write *noon;* instead of *12 a.m.*, write *midnight*. Both *12 p.m.* and *12 a.m.* may cause readers to have to stop and think—*noon* and *midnight* are instantly clear to readers who scan. To avoid redundancy, don't use the number 12 with the word *noon* or *midnight*.

Example

Before

The luncheon will start at 12 p.m.

The luncheon will start at 12 noon.

After

The luncheon will start at noon.

For on-the-hour times, you needn't include the minutes: *3 p.m.* instead of *3:00 p.m.* But do include the minutes when they're necessary for consistency within text or in a table that includes other times with minutes: *Classes start at 10:00 a.m. or 11:30 a.m.*

Use **periods** with the abbreviations *a.m.* and *p.m.* (lowercase, with a space after the number but no space between the letters): *5:15 p.m.*

Avoid the redundant *in the morning* or *in the afternoon* when including *a.m.* or *p.m.* with a time.

Examples

10:15 a.m.

8:00 to 9:30 a.m.

Abbreviate **time zones** in all capital letters, without periods. Include the time zone only if there is a possibility of ambiguity or confusion.

TIP Because they are convenient and correct all year long, we favor shortened versions of U.S. time zone abbreviations (for example, *PT* in place of either *PST* or *PDT*). Use the longer form only if it is necessary to indicate standard or daylight saving time. See "daylight saving time" on page 446.

PST (PT)	Pacific Standard Time (Pacific time)	PDT (PT)	Pacific Daylight Time (Pacific time)
MST (MT)	Mountain Standard Time (Mountain time)	MDT (MT)	Mountain Daylight Time (Mountain time)
CST (CT)	Central Standard Time (Central time)	CDT (CT)	Central Daylight Time (Central time)
EST (ET)	Eastern Standard Time (Eastern time)	EDT (ET)	Eastern Daylight Time (Eastern time)
GMT	Greenwich Mean Time	UTC	Coordinated Universal Time

To indicate a time zone for audiences outside the United States, use UTC or an offset of UTC. For example, when London is not observing "summer time," its time is UTC, and Paris time is one hour ahead of London, or UTC+1. When London is observing summer time, its time is UTC+1; when Paris is observing summer time, its time is UTC+2. But avoid using GMT or UTC unless it is necessary for clarity (for example, to state the time zone of a webcast likely to be viewed across time zones).

Examples

8 p.m. PT

Midnight ET

NYC New Year's countdown telecast: 11:30 p.m. ET (UTC-5)

NYC Earth Day concert: 5 p.m. ET (UTC-4)

GMT or UTC?

Coordinated Universal Time (abbreviated *UTC*) officially replaced Greenwich Mean Time in 1972, but outside of scientific and technology contexts, many people still use and recognize *GMT*. GMT is the mean solar time at the Royal Observatory in Greenwich, London; UTC is an international standard kept by atomic clocks around the world. *UTC* and *GMT* can be used interchangeably in nonscientific contexts, but the internationally accepted *UTC* is more appropriate for the Internet.

Fractions and decimals

Whenever possible, **use decimal notation instead of fractions on the Web**. Decimals are easier to hyphenate in a compound adjective (for example, *a 1.5-gram dose*), and they prevent the bad line breaks that can occur if you are using nonformatted fractions such as *1-1/2* (for instance, where *1-* appears at the end of a line and *1/2* begins the next line). See "Decimals" on page 272 for guidance on styling decimals.

Of course, **sometimes fractions are appropriate**: People tend to use them in recipes, for example. In contexts where fractions are commonly used and conversion to a decimal would cause confusion, stick to fractions and follow these guidelines.

Fractions

If a fraction stands alone, without a whole number (¾, for instance), spell out and hyphenate the fraction: *three-quarters*.

Exception: Use a figure if space is tight—for example, in a table.

Examples

a two-thirds majority
four-fifths of the states
one-fifth of his former income

Don't spell out a **mixed number** such as *1½*. If the number can't be written as a decimal (or if a decimal is inappropriate), use numerals for the whole number and a special character (such as ½) for the fraction, with no space between the whole number and the fraction.

T I P   Avoid special characters formatted in a word processor; they can display incorrectly in online media such as webpages or email. To learn how to code a fraction character, see "Special characters" on page 386.

If a character doesn't exist to express the fractional part (you may not be able to code less common fractions, such as *3/8*), or if coding the fraction is impractical, use numerals for the whole number, followed by a hyphen and the fractional part written as *x/y* (as in *1-1/2* or *2-3/8*).

Examples

½ cup sugar
1 ¼ teaspoons salt
a 2-3/8″ nail

Decimals

Use numerals and a period to indicate decimal amounts: *8.5, 1.25*. But don't go more than two digits past the period unless your material requires that level of detail.

In running text, it isn't necessary to include .0 or .00 with whole numbers even when they are listed alongside decimal numbers: *8.5 x 11 in.*

Exceptions:

■ Do use .00 for consistency in a series with dollar amounts. (See "Money and currency" on page 279.)
■ Do use the decimal and zero(s) to provide consistency (and to ensure that numbers line up properly) in a column—for example, within a table or spreadsheet.

For amounts less than one, include a leading zero and the decimal point: *0.5, 0.75*. (Without the zero, a person reading quickly might overlook the decimal point.)

Decimals in software version numbers

Software developers use widely divergent versioning terminology (for example, *2.01ab, 2ab, 3 rev b, 3.0 rev b*), and many larger developers consider their version numbers to be a part of their product's name—in other words, a proper noun that should be written exactly as they have written it.

If your site lists many software programs (and their version numbers), we recommend applying a loose consistency: For example, include the .0 with whole numbers whenever possible (to look as consistent as possible with the inevitable "2.0.0.2010" and the like), and follow the developer's conventions when in doubt. So:

- Include the .0 with whole version numbers: *Firefox 3.0* instead of *Firefox 3*.
  Exception: Drop the .0 in headlines, email subject lines, or where space is limited.
- Include the leading zero and the decimal point with beta software: *Program Name 0.2*. (Avoid using the word *beta*—as in *Program Name Beta 0.2*—unless it is clearly part of the product name.)

Examples

Download Pix Pickr 0.3.
The plug-in works with Mozilla Firefox 3.0 or newer.
If you're using Mozilla Firefox 2.0 or older, upgrade to Firefox 3.0.3.

Units of measure

In general, numerals work well for expressing computer-related measurements and other units of measure on the Web—numerals save space, and they tend to catch the eye of a scanning reader. But beyond this general guideline, you have a number of choices to make. For instance, you could express the dimensions of a painting as *11 by 14 inches, 11 by 14 in.,* or *11″ x 14″*. In part, your choices will be based on the kind of website you have and its features and needs.

Some best practices to govern your decisions:

- Use numerals when referring to **physical dimensions**: height, width, length, depth, weight, mass, volume, distance, type size, and so on.

Examples

He ducked to go under the 7-foot doorframe.

The fish weighed 8 pounds and was nearly 2 feet long.

We had already walked 5 miles when she noticed it was missing.

An 8-point font is hard to read.

- With **units of time** (minutes, hours, days, weeks, months, and so on), follow the regular number rule: Spell out one through nine, use numerals for 10 and above.
- **Two exceptions:**
  - ◆ If your content is scientific, statistical, or technical, use numerals with units of time.
  - ◆ Use numerals in tables or graphs and other areas with space constraints.

Examples

Do you have five minutes?

We missed the first 20 minutes.

In our control group, Mouse C1 completed the maze in 9 seconds; Mouse C2, in 7.5 seconds. *(Exception for scientific material)*

- Use a hyphen for adjectives: *a 9-foot crocodile.* But don't use a hyphen if you abbreviate the unit of measure: *a 9 ft. crocodile.*
- For **English units** of measurement (inches, feet, yards, and so forth), use either the symbol, if one exists (for example, a double straight quote for inches, a single straight quote for feet), the full word, or the abbreviation with a period (for instance, *in., ft., yd.*). Use your choice consistently throughout your site or product. For instance, you might decide to always spell out the unit in your text but to use either abbreviations or symbols in tables and other tight spaces.
- The plural and singular forms of abbreviations are the same—don't add an *s* to the end. For example, *in.* is the abbreviation for both *inch* and *inches*.

Abbreviations: English units					
inch/inches	in.	square inch/square inches	sq. in.	cubic inch/cubic inches	cu. in.
foot/feet	ft.	square foot/square feet	sq. ft.	cubic foot/cubic feet	cu. ft.
yard/yards	yd.	square yard/square yards	sq. yd.	cubic yard/cubic yards	cu. yd.

Abbreviations: English units						
mile/miles	mi.	square mile/square miles	sq. mi.	miles per hour		mph
ounce/ounces	oz.	fluid ounce/fluid ounces	fl. oz.	pint/pints		pt.
quart/quarts	qt.	gallon/gallons	gal.	miles per gallon		mpg
pound/pounds	lb.					
second/seconds	sec.	minute/minutes	min.	hour/hours		hr.

T I P Although abbreviations of single words (*in.* for *inch, sec.* for *second*) usually include a period in the U.S., it is sometimes appropriate to leave out the period—in a table, for instance, or when space is very tight and misreading isn't likely.

■ For **metric units** of measurement, use either full words (*centimeters, meters, kilometers,* and so on) or abbreviations (*cm, m, km*) consistently. Don't use periods with metric abbreviations, and don't add an *s* to form plurals: *1 mm, 35 mm.*

Abbreviations: Metric units			
nanometer	nm	square meter	sq m or m^2
millimeter	mm	cubic meter	cu m or m^3
centimeter	cm	square kilometer	sq km or km^2
meter	m	cubic kilometer	cu km or km^3
kilometer	km	kilometers per hour	km/h
nanogram	ng	milliliter	ml
microgram	mcg	centiliter	cl
milligram	mg	liter	l
centigram	cg	kiloliter	kl
gram	g	kilogram	kg

Real prime marks

Inch (″) and foot (′) symbols are formed with double straight quotes (called double prime marks) and single straight quotes (called prime marks), respectively. Straight marks may be vertical or may appear at a slant (′)—either orientation is OK. But make sure your word processor does not insert "smart" (curly) quotes ("") or apostrophes ('). People who care about this sort of thing will notice if you use an apostrophe instead of a prime mark and may consider it a mark against your credibility.

T I P Superscript formatted in a word processor may not display correctly in some places, like email. To be safe, you'd have to code each instance of superscript. Save yourself the trouble and avoid superscript on the Web: Use *sq km* instead of *km²,* for instance. Or see "Special characters" on page 386 for instructions on coding superscript font.

■ If you're **using a symbol** to express a unit of measure, don't put a space between the numeral and the symbol: *a 9′ crocodile.* Similarly, don't put a space between numerals with different units of measure: *a 9′6″ crocodile.*

Examples

Sam Long, the 7-foot-3-inch center, carried the flag for the Smithtown team.
Sam Long, the 7 ft. 3 in. center, carried the flag for the Smithtown team.
Sam Long, the 7′3″ center, carried the flag for the Smithtown team.

■ When describing **two or more dimensions of an object** such as a photograph or a poster, follow these guidelines:
 ◆ If using **symbols**: Repeat the symbol for each figure. Separate the dimensions with an *x*. A space before and after the *x* is optional—as long as you're consistent.

T I P Consider that *not* using a space will save room and prevent the possibility of the dimensions breaking midstring at the end of a line. But the loss of white space between the characters will make the dimensions a little harder to read.

Examples

Order 4″ x 6″ or 8″ x 10″ prints.
Order 4″x6″ or 8″x10″ prints.

 ◆ If using **full words or abbreviations**: Do not repeat the word or abbreviation for each figure unless different units appear. Separate the dimensions with an *x* or the word *by.*

Examples

She rented a 10 x 12 ft. room.
She rented a 10 ft. 6 in. x 12 ft. 10 in. room.

◆ Don't use a hyphen with abbreviated units even if you are listing two dimensions. Do use a hyphen when you are spelling out the units.

Examples

The room had a 1.5 by 2 ft. window.
The room had a 1.5-by-2-foot window.

■ Use numerals with these other units not commonly considered units of measure:
  ◆ Digits or characters making up a code, password, or other string of characters in a technical context
  ◆ Units related to sports scores

Examples

Please enter a 5-digit ZIP code.
Enter an 8-character password.
The Australian team is ahead by 2.

For unit abbreviations you don't find listed here, see "The Yahoo! word list" on page 438.

Computer- and software-related numbers

Technical requirements for products or features often include computer- and software-related numbers that need special treatment.

Storage, memory, and processor speeds

Use the following abbreviations to describe storage and memory sizes or processor speeds.

KB (kilobyte)	kHz (kilohertz)
MB (megabyte)	MHz (megahertz)
GB (gigabyte)	GHz (gigahertz)
TB (terabyte)	

When describing storage or memory requirements:

■ Don't put a space between the number and the abbreviation for the unit.

Examples

Increase your memory from 2GB to 4GB.
System requirements include a 1.3GHz Pentium 4 processor, 512MB of memory, and 1GB of disk storage.

———————

■ Don't add an *s* after the abbreviation to form a plural.

Example

Before
You can purchase an additional 2GBs of storage.

After
You can purchase an additional 2GB of storage.

———————

■ Repeat the abbreviation in a **series**.

Example

Get a 2GB, 3GB, or 4GB external hard drive for extra storage.

———————

Other technical numbers and abbreviations

networking speeds	kilobits per second: 56Kbps megabytes per second: 400MBps megabits per second: 100Mbps gigabytes per second: 4GBps gigabits per second: 2Gbps
display-quality measurements	resolution: 1,024 x 768 dots per inch: 72 dpi
optical drive speeds (CD, DVD)	2x, 4x, 6x

T I P Consider spelling out these abbreviations the first time they are used in a particular body of text or on a webpage, because readers may be unfamiliar with them. People often confuse **bits** and **bytes** and their abbreviations.

Examples

Download files at speeds starting at 600 kilobits per second (Kbps). Upload files at speeds starting at 500Kbps.

Experience a 600Kbps connection.

Watch the slideshow on a monitor set at 1,024 x 768 pixels.

Photos submitted for the contest must be at least 300 dpi.

The DVD-RW drive boasts write, rewrite, and read speeds of 16x, 8x, and 16x, respectively.

Money and currency

For prices of a dollar or more, use numerals and the $ symbol: *a $6 coffee.*

It isn't necessary to include the decimal and two zeros for whole dollar amounts appearing in a sentence, a headline, or an email subject line. But do include the zeros if:

- They make sense in the context (for example, in a spreadsheet or another accounting context, in a price list, or in a shopping cart).
- They provide consistency within a series, table, or list (for example, *Chai lattes cost $2.75 for a small, $3.00 for a medium, and $3.25 for a large*).

For prices under a dollar, use the word *cents* with the numeral: *89 cents.* Don't include the dollar sign and the leading zero (for example, *$0.89*) unless:

- They make sense in the context (for example, in a price list or a shopping cart).
- They provide consistency within a series, table, or list (for example, *We spent only $4.99 on the centerpiece: The candles cost $0.25 each, the persimmons $3.74*).

Use a comma in dollar amounts over $999, but be aware of **global differences in punctuating numbers** (see page 263).

> ### Examples
>
> He didn't flinch at the price of the wine: $1,000 a bottle.
> Handmade llama-hair scarves for $65 *(Email subject line)*
> Thank you for your order. Your credit card will be charged $65.00. *(Checkout page)*
> Today Only: Llama-Hair Pencil Case for 99 Cents *(Headline)*
> Llama-hair pencil case (brown): $0.99 *(Shopping cart)*

Avoid using slashes as an abbreviation for *per* with money amounts, except in subject lines and other places where space is at a premium.

> ### Examples
>
> Web hosting packages start at $35 per month. *(Running text)*
> Web hosting from $35/month *(Small website ad)*

If it's necessary to specify the type of dollar, use the format **US$000**, **CAN$000**, **AUS$000**, or **NZ$000** (without a space). Note: This is the only instance where *United States* is abbreviated without periods. For euros, insert the code for the symbol, without a space (for example, *€150*), or write **EUR000**. (See "Special characters" on page 386.)

> ### Examples
>
> Membership requires an annual fee of US$299.
> Seven-day resort stay with spa package and all meals: EUR1,200.

Numbers in a range

In ranges of numbers, such as time periods or page ranges, the numbers can be separated by a hyphen or an en dash (choose one or the other and use it consistently) or by the word *to*. For more information about en dashes, see "Dashes" on page 213.

T I P   To use an en dash on your site, you must insert the code for it wherever you want it to appear. This is why many people preparing Web content choose to forgo en dashes and opt for hyphens instead. To learn how to code an en dash, see "Special characters" on page 386.

Guidelines for en dashes and hyphens:

- Use an **en dash (or a hyphen) without a space** on either side for a range of numbers: *8–10 people* (en dash), *8-10 people* (hyphen).
- If you precede the range with the word *from,* don't use an en dash or a hyphen to separate the numbers—use the word *to* instead: *from 8 to 10 people.*

Examples

Join us at the Open House July 6–7. Hours: 10 a.m.–5 p.m. *(En dashes)*
Join us at the Open House July 6-7. Hours: 10 a.m.-5 p.m. *(Hyphens)*
This offer is valid from July 1 to July 31, 2010. *(Use "to" with "from")*

_____

- Use an en dash (or a hyphen) for scores or votes as well. The en dash in the following constructions stands for *to* just as it does in a range.

Examples

Greece takes the title in a 2–1 upset over Spain. *(En dash)*
Greece takes the title in a 2-1 upset over Spain. *(Hyphen)*
Yeas outnumber nays 10–6. *(En dash)*
Yeas outnumber nays 10-6. *(Hyphen)*

_____

For an **open range of numbers**, such as a date range with no ending date, use an em dash (also simply called a dash). For an em dash, you can use two hyphens (no coding necessary) or code an em dash character. To learn how to code an em dash, see "Special characters" on page 386.

Examples

Barack Obama (1961—) was elected the 44th president of the United States. *(Formatted em dash)*

Barack Obama (1961--) was elected the 44th president of the United States. *(Double-hyphen dash)*

_____

Percentages

Use numerals with percentages.

Use either the word *percent* or the percent sign (%) in text—as long as you're consistent. Consider that the percent sign saves space, and if a passage contains two or more percentages, the percent sign is easier to spot, making it easier to compare the numbers.

Examples

Workers are demanding a 5 percent raise.
In 2008, 71 percent of U.S. electricity production still came from fossil fuel.
In 2008, 71% of U.S. electricity production still came from fossil fuel. Nuclear energy accounted for 21% and hydro for 6%, with 2% coming from other sources.

Phone numbers

Format U.S. phone numbers like this: *XXX-XXX-XXXX*. Include the area code but not the *1* before it that some people may have to dial.

Format phone numbers that require extensions like this: *XXX-XXX-XXXX ext. XX*.

Examples

415-555-XXXX
800-XXX-XXXX
707-555-XXXX ext. 29

International considerations

The primary audience for phone numbers listed on your site will most likely be people in your own country. However, the ubiquity of the Internet means that it may be wise to anticipate callers from countries other than your own. If your phone number is likely to be called by site visitors in another country, consider separate instructions; for example, "For calls originating outside the United States, dial . . ."

For international phone numbers, precede the number with a plus sign (+) and your country code, with no space in between. The plus sign indicates that callers must dial their international access code first. For example, a U.S.-based website could precede its number with the plus sign (+) and the U.S. country code (1).

Some formatting tips:

■ Separate the country and city codes with a hyphen.

Examples

+1-415-555-XXXX *(San Francisco number likely to be called from another country: plus sign, country code, area code, 7-digit local number)*

+81-3-XXXX-XXXX *(Tokyo number likely to be called from another country: plus sign, country code, area/city code, 8-digit local number)*

■ For non-U.S. phone numbers that don't contain hyphens or at least spaces to indicate where you can put hyphens, follow the local convention for styling the local part of the phone number. For instance, in some countries it is customary to close up numbers. If so, use that style. Don't try to guess where you should insert a hyphen.

Examples

+62-21-XXXXXXX *(Jakarta, Indonesia, phone number)*
+39-041-XXXXXXX *(Venice, Italy, phone number)*

Ideas in Practice

Exercise: Navigate the numbers

Edit the numbers in the following sentences to reflect the guidelines outlined in this chapter.

 To see our solution, turn to page 481.

1. The World Wide Web was born on December 25 1990 when Tim Berners-Lee sent the first communication between Web client and server.

2. Off-season rates apply, except during spring break, Mar. 7—21.

3. With wild mushrooms priced at $25.00/pound in some markets, it might be cheaper to rent a truffle pig for an hour.

4. The state's "first dog" is used to crowds—she was the 9th puppy in a litter of ten.

5. More than 6000 languages are spoken worldwide, though some linguists estimate that 7 1/2% are nearly extinct, and many more—about 50 percent total—are endangered because no children speak them.

6. Bouquets often feature an odd number of stems, such as five or fifteen, but be aware that in the language of flowers, three red roses can mean "I love you."

7. 600 peaceful protesters for civil rights were attacked by state troopers in the March 7th, 1965 march to Montgomery, Alabama.

8. Brazil led Venezuela 1 to nothing at the half but ended up losing by two points.

9. In 1996 a notebook with a 133-MHz processor, a 1.3 GB hard drive, and a 28.8K modem cost about 3K; in 2009 the same money will buy a loaded laptop with a 2.5-GHz processor, a 320GBs hard drive, and built-in wireless.

10. Hadrian's Wall was begun in 122 AD and was staffed by Roman soldiers until the legions pulled out of Britain in the early fifth century.

11. The help desk is open from 9 am-5 pm. When it's closed, call (800) XXX-XXXX for assistance.

12. The 6' 2" (1.88 ms) George Washington was grander in stature than the average male colonist in the 1700's, who was 5'9". Still, the colonists were two inches taller than the English.

Clean Up Your Copy

Chapter 13

Shorten and Strengthen Sentences

In this chapter

- **Clear out deadwood.** You can shorten nearly everything you write.
- **Start strong, stay strong.** Avoid weak openings for sentences, and keep the verbs strong.
- **Replace superfluous phrases.** Recognize the expressions that add length and little else to most writing.
- **Cut the clichés.** Your writing will be fresher—not to mention easier to translate.
- **Junk the jargon.** Send those buzzwords to the scrap heap.

Short, strong sentences are the essence of good Web content. As we noted in Chapter 1, research shows that most people don't read; they scan. Streamlined text helps your site's visitors find what they're looking for—fast.

Clear, simple text is also easier to understand. About 43 percent of U.S. adults have low (basic or below-basic) literacy skills,[27] and many of your visitors may not use English as their first language. And all readers prefer concise, direct writing. Which of these signs is more effective for a reader in a hurry?

Sentences can certainly be longer than a one-word sign, but they should be just as clear and direct. Most of the time, that means fewer words per sentence. Chapter 4 covered the basics of writing sentences that work well on the Web. This chapter is about refining your text: It contains **strategies for cutting unneeded words to let the meaning of your message shine**.

Clear out deadwood

Deadwood refers to a word or phrase that can be omitted without a loss in meaning. **Removing it shortens and clarifies your copy.** Once you recognize deadwood, it's easy to eliminate.

Look for:

■ Words or phrases that add unneeded bulk to a sentence and weaken its message (~~quite~~ right, ~~very~~ unique)

■ Common phrases that are bloated with redundant or highfalutin words (~~added~~ bonus, ~~currently~~ unavailable)

■ Unimportant words at the beginning of a sentence that push the most important information farther from the start (~~As a matter of fact, in the same way~~)

It's usually good to cut such words and phrases, but be aware that what is "deadwood" may depend on the context. In some cases you may want to retain words or phrases to emphasize a point, to maintain a certain voice, or to optimize your site for pickup by search engines.

Remove one-word deadwood

Some common words appear in sentences only because people are used to hearing them—they aren't essential to the sentence. You can usually cut the following words without losing meaning:

actively	easily	quite
actual, actually	existing	rather
already	extremely	really
always	fairly	several
any	much	simply
appropriate, appropriately	particular	suitable
associated	predefined	totally
automatic, automatically	previously	very
currently	quickly	

Examples

Before

To review previously deleted items, click the **View Deleted** button.

After

To review deleted items, click the **View Deleted** button.

Before

Always make sure that you enter the right address and that it is spelled correctly.

After

Make sure that you enter the right address and that it is spelled correctly.

Remove deadwood phrases

Unnecessary phrases at the beginning of a sentence push the meaningful information to the middle of the sentence—farther than a scanning reader is likely to reach.

Consider these **guidelines for cutting deadwood phrases**:

- Avoid constructions like *if you want to, if you wish to, if you need to, if you would like to, in order to,* and *if you're looking for.* Use the infinitive (the *to* form of a verb) or rewrite the sentence.

Examples

Before

If you'd like to block explicit content for every search, go to <u>Preferences</u>.

After

To block explicit content for every search, go to <u>Preferences</u>.

Before

If you need more information, <u>contact us</u>.

After

For more information, <u>contact us</u>.

- Replace *you can* with the infinitive and adjust the sentence as necessary.

Example

Before

You can change your avatar by clicking the **Customize** button.

After

To change your avatar, click the **Customize** button.

- Replace *you can choose to, you can decide to,* and similar constructions with a direct verb.

Example

Before

You can choose to search for airlines, hotels, or car rental chains.

After

You can search for airlines, hotels, or car rental chains.

Better

Search for airlines, hotels, or car rental chains.

- Replace expressions containing *you will need to* or *you need to* with *you must* or the imperative (the command form of the verb).

Example

Before

The first thing that you will need to do is choose a product category.

After

First, choose a product category.

- Delete *of the* in constructions like *any of the, some of the, one of the, each of the, many of the, most of the, a few of the,* and *several of the.* Delete *of* in *all of the* and *half of the.*

Examples

Before

All of the services listed here are available to our members.

After

All the services listed here are available to our members.

Before

Each of the addresses you enter is saved in your account.

After

Each address you enter is saved in your account.

■ Delete *make* in constructions like *make a copy, make a change, make a purchase, make use of, make an adjustment, make a decision,* and *make a correction* and adjust the sentence as necessary.

Examples

Before

Make a copy of the document to save it for your records.

After

Copy the document to save it for your records.

Before

To make corrections to your order, contact our sales department.

After

To correct your order, contact our sales department.

For a list of phrases that can usually be replaced with a shorter option, see "Replace superfluous phrases" on page 296.

Cut length—not clarity

Some small words that seem unnecessary to native English speakers may be cues that aid comprehension for people less fluent in English. If your audience is likely to include nonnative speakers, follow these guidelines to retain **cues that add clarity**:

■ Keep the word *that,* especially when it introduces a clause.

Example

Before

Put the car in park to make sure the wheels don't roll on an incline and the Autodrive function doesn't restart automatically.

After

Put the car in park to make sure that the wheels don't roll on an incline and that the Autodrive function doesn't restart automatically.

- Repeat helping verbs such as *can, could, may, must, might, should, would,* and *will.*

Example

Before

Items you wish to return must be packaged in their original packaging and shipped to the following address.

After

Items you wish to return must be packaged in their original packaging and must be shipped to the following address.

- Keep the word *then* in *if-then* constructions when a sentence is very long or complex. (Or, better: Rewrite the sentence so that it's shorter.)

Example

Before

If your calendar order has not arrived by December 1 and you have not already been contacted by your representative about delays, go to your My Account page and click the **Track Orders** button.

After

If your calendar order has not arrived by December 1 and you have not already been contacted by your representative about delays, then go to your My Account page and click the **Track Orders** button.

For more writing strategies that add clarity for nonnative English speakers, see Chapter 5, "Be Inclusive, Write for the World."

Get to the good stuff

Most readers aren't interested in how or why a service or feature was developed. Give them the information they came to find, and spare them the details about what you did, how you did it, how hard it was to accomplish. **Eliminate unnecessary information**, self-serving expressions, and the backstory, and get to key points quickly and efficiently. (Add a link to your company's history for people who are interested.)

Examples

Before

Way back in 2002, when our founder was enjoying her thriving dog-walking business, she suddenly realized what a great idea it would be to offer emergency dog sitting to busy professionals who discovered at the last minute that they needed to leave town on business. We created our <u>Dog Sitter Direct</u> option to meet the needs of busy professionals and others who may require these emergency services.

After

Our <u>Dog Sitter Direct</u> option meets the needs of busy professionals and others who may require emergency and last-minute services.

Before

Click **Create Account** to create your account—or select **Guest Account**, an option that was developed so that shoppers who do not want to create an account today can still purchase products.

After

Click **Create Account** to create your account—or select **Guest Account** to purchase products today without creating an account.

Start strong, stay strong

Begin your sentences with strong subjects and verbs. Tell the reader who is acting and what the actor is doing. Leading with strong subjects and verbs puts the most important words at the beginning of the sentence and condenses your text.

Avoid *there is, there are,* and *it is*

There is, there are, and *it is* push the subject away from the beginning of the sentence and add length. Rewriting the sentence to eliminate these weak openings often means you can use a stronger verb.

Examples

Before
There is a **Help** link at the top of the page. Click it.

After
Click the **Help** link at the top of the page.

Before
There is no charge for the service.

After
The service is free.

Replace weak verbs

Weak verbs dilute the strength of your message. Prune indirect verbs like *allow, enable, can, and let,* which also make a sentence longer. Substitute active, direct verbs.

Example

Before
You can save your shopping cart by clicking the **Save** button.

After
Save your shopping cart by clicking the **Save** button.
or
To save your shopping cart, click the **Save** button.

Replacing a weak verb often means rewriting the sentence.

Example

Before
This feature lets you change your settings during a call.

After
Use this feature to change your settings during a call.
or
Change your settings during a call with this feature.

Stay active

Front-load your sentences with the most important information, which is usually the actor (the subject) and what the actor is doing (the verb). The active voice achieves this best.

- *Active-voice* verbs indicate that the sentence's subject is performing an action: *Anil rolls the ball. The kitten pounced on the paper clip.*
- *Passive-voice* verbs indicate that someone or something is being acted upon: *The ball is rolled by Anil. The paper clip was pounced on by the kitten.*

The passive voice tends to make sentences longer, harder to grasp, and weaker, because the most important information—the actor and the action—is not leading the sentence.

Example

Passive voice
Movie times can be checked on his mobile phone.

Active voice
He can check movie times on his mobile phone.

The passive voice can confuse readers and cause them to lose interest in your message. The active voice clearly identifies the agent performing the action.

Example

Before

The main loggia can be accessed either by ascending the grand staircase or by using the elevator opposite the ticketing area.

After

Visitors can access the main loggia either by ascending the grand staircase or by using the elevator opposite the ticketing area. *(The subject is "visitors.")*

Better

Access the main loggia by ascending the grand staircase or by using the elevator opposite the ticketing area. *(The subject, "you," is understood.)*

However, the **passive voice is acceptable and may even be preferable in some circumstances**. It's OK to use the passive voice when the actor is implied, relatively unimportant, or unknown, or when you prefer to be indefinite.

Examples

Our products are manufactured in the United States and Brazil.
New Orleans was hit by a hurricane.
The mayor was mugged by an unknown assailant.
The superhero was unmasked at last.

TIP   Microsoft Word's grammar checker can detect many passive sentences and let you know the number used in selected text. When you check your copy's readability, you can see what percentage of the sentences is passive. See "Test your copy's readability" on page 10.

Replace superfluous phrases

You can replace many common and redundant words and phrases with briefer, more direct, and equally familiar words. However, don't choose the shorter option if confusion could result. For example, you can usually replace the phrase *in order to* with a simple *to,* but sometimes the longer phrase is helpful to avoid ambiguity.

Example

Before

He changed his plan to go skydiving.

(Did he originally plan to go skydiving and then change his mind? Or did he change his plan so that he could go skydiving?)

After

He changed his plan in order to go skydiving.

(In this example, the usually unnecessary phrase "in order to" clarifies that he changed his plan so that he could go skydiving.)

You may also find that a redundant phrase such as *revert back* is called for when you need to emphasize a point or when you want to make sure that a reader hasn't missed a critical communication such as a warning or an error message.

Watch for the following phrases, which include extraneous words, redundancy, and pretentious vocabulary.

Instead of	Use
a few of the	a few
a large number of	many, most
a large part of	many, most
a large proportion of	many, most
a lot of	many
a number of	some, many
according to our data	we find
accordingly	therefore, so
add a new	add
added bonus	bonus
adequate number (of)	enough
advance planning	planning
advance warning	warning
afford the opportunity to	give the chance, enable, let, allow *(Consider deleting the phrase)*
after the conclusion of	after
ahead of schedule	early

Instead of	Use
all of the	all, all the
almost all	most
along the lines of	like, similar to
along with	with
any of the	any
appointed to the post of	appointed
arrive at a conclusion	conclude
as a consequence of	because (of)
as a result of	because (of)
as long as	if
as of this moment	now
as well as	and
ascertain the location of	find
assemble together	assemble
at a high rate of speed	fast
at a time when	when
at such time as	when
at the conclusion of	after
at the moment	now
at the present time	now
at the rate of	at
at this point in time	now
be a combination of	combine
be able to	can
be capable of	can
be deficient in	lack
be in a position to	can, be able
because of the fact that	because
biography of his life	biography
both of the	both
by a factor of two	two times, double, twice
by means of	by, with
by virtue of the fact that	because
change the size of	resize

Instead of	Use
circle around	circle
circular in shape	circular, round
close proximity to	close to, near
cognizant of	know
come to a conclusion (an end)	conclude, end, finish
come to an agreement	agree
complimentary gift	gift
conduct a search of	search, find
consensus of opinion	consensus, agreement
continue to remain	continue to be, remain
create a new	create
despite the fact that	although
determine the location of	find
display a list of	list
does not have	lacks
drop down to	drop to
due to the fact that	because
during the time that	while
each and every	each, every
each of the	each
each time	when
edit an existing	edit
end result	result
entirely new	new
every one of the	all, every
exactly identical	identical
exactly the same as	identical to
few of the	few
fewer in number	fewer
final completion	completion
final conclusion	conclusion
final result	result
find the location of	find, locate
for a period of	for

Instead of	Use
for the most part	mainly
for the purpose of	for, to
for the reason that	because
for this reason	thus, therefore
forward progress	progress
found to be	is
free gift	gift
give a summary of	summarize
give consideration to	consider, examine
give indication of	show, indicate, suggest
give rise to	cause
half of (the)	half, half the
happen(s) to be	am, is, are
has a tendency to	tends
has been proven to be	is
has the ability to	can
has the need to	needs to, must
has the option to	can, may
honest truth	truth
if conditions are such that	if
in all cases	always *(Consider deleting the phrase)*
in an effort to	to
in case of	if
in conjunction with	with
in connection with	about
in excess of	more than
in large measure	largely
in many cases	usually
in no case	never
in order that	to, so that
in order to	to, so
in recognition of the fact	therefore
in reference to	about, regarding
in some cases	sometimes, occasionally

Instead of	Use
in some instances	sometimes, occasionally
in spite of the fact that	although, despite, in spite of
in such a manner as to	to
in terms of	in
in the case of	for
in the course of	during
in the event that	if
in the field of	in
in the near future	soon
in the neighborhood of	near, about, nearly
in the vicinity of	near, about, nearly
in view of the fact that	because
involve the use of	use
is able to	can
is capable of	can
is contingent upon	depends on
is deficient in	lacks
is found to be	is
is in a position to	can
it appears that	apparently
it is clear that	clearly
it is essential that they (it)	they (it) must
it is evident that	evidently
it is interesting to note that	note that
it is obvious that	obviously
it is often the case that	often
it is our opinion that	we think
it is possible that	perhaps
it is possible to	you can
it should be kept in mind	keep in mind, remember
it should be noted	note
join together	join
joint cooperation	cooperation
keep track of	track

Instead of	Use
located at	at
located on	on
longer in length	longer
majority of the	most
make a backup copy of	back up
make a change	change
make a copy of	copy
make a decision	decide
make a purchase	purchase, buy
make a statement saying	say, state
make additions	add
make an adjustment in	adjust
make an approximation	estimate, approximate
make an effort	try
make an inquiry regarding	ask about, inquire about
make changes	change
make corrections	correct
make edits	edit
make modifications	modify
make use of	use
manner in which	how
many of the	many
may possibly, might possibly	may, might
more complete	complete
more or less	approximately, about, roughly
most of the	most
necessary requirement	requirement
new breakthrough	breakthrough
numerous	many
on a daily (weekly, monthly, etc.) basis	daily, weekly, monthly, etc.
on a few occasions	occasionally, sometimes
on the basis of	from, because, by
on the order of	approximately, about, roughly
on the part of	by

Instead of	Use
one of the (two of the, three of the, etc.)	one, two, three, etc.
owing to the fact that	because
past experience	experience
perform a search	search
personal opinion	opinion
postpone until later	postpone
preplan	plan
present a list of	list
present time	now
previous to	before
prior to	before
provide a description of	describe
provide a list of	list
provided in	in
provided that	if
put an end to	end, stop
quite unique	unique, unusual
reach a conclusion	conclude
rearrange the order of	rearrange, change the order of
recur again	recur
refer to	see
repeat again	repeat
return back	return
revert back	revert
run the risk (of)	risk
send an email message, send an email	email
serve the function of being	is
several of the	several
share the same	share
share with	tell, notify, inform
shorter in length	shorter
situated on	on
some of the	some
subsequent	next

Instead of	Use
subsequent to	after
succeed in (finding)	find
sufficient amount of	enough
sum total	total
surrounded on all sides	surrounded
temporary loan	loan
the majority of	most
the question as to whether	whether
total number of	number of
unable to	can't
usual habit	habit
utilize	use
will be able to	can
with reference to	about
with the exception of	except, except for
would be able to	could

Examples

Before

If you have the need for a dog sitter on an ongoing basis, check out <u>Long-Term Leash</u>.

After

If you need a dog sitter on an ongoing basis, check out <u>Long-Term Leash</u>.

Before

Make sure that your phone is capable of receiving text messages.

After

Make sure that your phone can receive text messages.

Subtract additions, too

Watch for potential redundancies with these words and phrases: *and, too, also, in addition (to), as well (as)*. Pick one per sentence—that's all you need.

Example

Before

In addition, you will also find small-business resources categorized by industry.

After

In addition, you will find small-business resources categorized by industry.
or
You will also find small-business resources categorized by industry.

Cut the clichés

Excising clichés is another way to shorten and strengthen text. Clichés rob you of a chance to say something new, eye-catching, and memorable.

A cliché is any word or phrase that has become overused and strikes the reader as stale, hackneyed, annoying, or predictable. Clichés give the impression of laziness or a lack of imagination—not what you want to convey.

Clichés can also confuse nonnative English speakers and people trying to translate your text into another language. For more on writing copy that's friendly to nonnative English speakers and translators, see Chapter 5.

T I P   If you write "think outside the box," you aren't thinking outside the box. Think about what you mean to say, and say it in your own words.

Identify clichés

You might be looking at a cliché if:

- You recognize it as you write it. (It's probably a cliché if it comes too easily to mind.)
- It repeats a sound. (Examples include alliterative clichés like *tried and true* and *helping hand* and rhyming clichés like *one-stop shop* and *meet and greet*.)
- Your readers will know how it ends. (It lets the cat out of the ___.)

It's definitely a cliché if you find it in books and websites about clichés (for example, the website Cliches: Avoid Them Like the Plague, at http://www.suspense.net/whitefish/cliche.htm) or if it's in this list:

all bets are off	clear the air	in the hot seat	push the envelope
all ears	cross the line	in the red	raise the bar
apples to oranges	deep-six	jump the gun	ring a bell
at the end of the day	do a 180	jury is still out	run circles around
at the top of one's game	dot the i's and cross the t's	knock the ball out of the park	run it up the flagpole
back against the wall	drop the ball	light as air	second wind
ball is in your court	easy as pie	laugh all the way to the bank	see the light
bare bones	fine line	low-hanging fruit	step up to the plate
bend over backward	get a life	make a long story short	take it to the next level
better late than never	get the ball rolling	mission critical	think outside the box
between a rock and a hard place	get with the program	no-brainer	under the radar
bite the bullet	give 110 percent	off-the-shelf	uphill battle
bottom line	give-and-take	on fire	wake-up call
call it a day	go head-to-head	on the same page	whole nine yards
can of worms	hit the ground running	out of the woods	win-win
caught off-guard	icing on the cake	over-the-top	*x* is the new black

And be careful about phrases that seem fresh and hip—pretty soon they won't be. Certain **catch-phrases** get picked up online and, well, quickly jump the shark. Many of these Internet memes are based on lines from movies or other ephemeral pop-culture sources.

Avoid inevitable pop-culture clichés like these:

- I kiss you
- All your base are belong to us
- I drink your milkshake
- LOLcat-speak such as "I can has cheezburger?"
- Don't tase me, bro!
- I was totally pwned
- Made of fail, made of win

New not so long ago, these are already antiques. And more important: They were never right for professional communication anyway.

Cliché vs. idiom

English is full of idioms and figures of speech that don't make much sense if taken literally. Many of these are clichés, but not all.

It's impossible to write without using some idioms, but there's reason to avoid them when you can: Phrases that don't make sense literally can be hard for nonnative speakers to grasp and tough for translators to translate. And stay away from phrases that strike your ear as clichéd—they'll likely strike your reader the same way.

Conquer clichés

So how do you conquer clichés once you've identified them? In one of five ways:

- Delete the cliché altogether.

Example

Before
Avoid clichés like the plague.

After
Avoid clichés.

- Substitute a simple, direct word. Use a thesaurus (print or electronic)—but don't trust such resources completely. Make sure that you understand the meaning and connotation of the word you intend to substitute.

Example

Before
The car is loaded with all the latest bells and whistles, including newer features that are few and far between.

After
The car is loaded with advanced features and extras, including newer features that are rarely seen.

- Be informative. Don't waste space on a cliché when you can use words that enhance meaning.

Example

Before
The car is loaded with all the latest bells and whistles, including newer features that are few and far between.

After
The car is loaded with advanced features and rarely seen extras, including collision-avoidance sensors and a self-parking system.

- Use the cliché, but in an original or humorous way.

Example

Before
Nothing says "Thanksgiving" like turkey and pumpkin pie.

After
Nothing says "Thanksgiving" like tandoori turkey and pumpkin curry.

- Give the cliché a twist.

Example

Before
I woke up feeling as sick as a dog.

After
I woke up feeling as sick as a Chihuahua full of chalupas.

Junk the jargon

Jargon is the **specialized or technical language** used by members of a certain trade or profession. Those outside the group don't understand such terms or may use them differently. For example, a *firewall* has one meaning to someone in construction, another to someone in computer network

Do you misuse these clichés?

If you must use a cliché, at least use it correctly. *Perfect storm, gild the lily,* and *beg the question* are among the most-often-misused phrases.

A **perfect storm** generally refers to a confluence of negative factors resulting in a disastrous out-come. But sometimes people try to use it for a positive situation.

Not OK: *The team won because of a perfect storm of reliable hitting, solid pitching, and unflap-pable managing.*

OK: *The bank failed because of a perfect storm of managerial incompetence, the housing market crash, and the government's refusal to bail it out.*

Likewise, **gilding the lily** refers to overdoing something in a negative way, not a positive way.

Not OK: *After such an incredible meal, the fabulous chocolate mousse was gilding the lily—it was perfect!*

OK: *After such an incredible meal, the chocolate mousse was gilding the lily—it was just too rich.*

Many people think that *to beg the question* means the same thing as *to invite the question*— enough so that you may not be criticized for using the phrase in this way. But you may want to stick to its traditional meaning: To **beg the question** is to support a conclusion by citing something that is itself in need of support.

Not recommended: *His silence on the issue just begs the question, How much did he really know at the time?* (Instead, try: *His silence on the issue just invites the question, How much did he really know at the time?*)

OK: *He claims he was silent because he had nothing to say, but that is just begging the question.*

---

security. Similarly, the word *derivative* is used in one way by stockbrokers, in another way by math-ematicians, and in still other ways by linguists and chemists.

At first glance, jargon and buzzwords can give the impression that the writer must be an expert, but **usually these words cloud rather than clarify meaning**. Web readers scan a page seeking key words and phrases, and they may find your content hard to grasp if you use obscure terminology.

Think about your audience members: Do they really need to know your jargon? Sometimes it may genuinely help the reader if you use and explain a particular term—but sometimes jargon is simply insider terminology, used by people in a particular field but not by their customers or the general public. For instance, the computer-industry jargon *RSS feed* may be useful for Internet users to learn: If people want to subscribe to a feed, they'll be able to recognize the term on websites. The jargon *cloud computing,* on the other hand, probably isn't useful: People can take advantage of cloud computing even if they don't know what it means. (For the curious: It refers to accessing software and other computer resources over the Internet. The software or other resource exists on a remote server instead of on the individual's computer.)

Train yourself to write in a jargon-free, reader-friendly voice.

Identify jargon

Here are some **clues that a word may be jargon**:

- It's not in the dictionary.
- It is in the dictionary, but you're using a secondary or specialized meaning. A word such as *application,* for instance, can mean the act of applying something (*nail polish application*), a piece of computer software (*word-processing application*), or a form (*job application*).
- It's in the dictionary, but it isn't a common term your visitors will know.
- It's a typical industry term but not a word that people type into search engines. This is easy to test: Check the word in a search engine and see how many results you get and whether those results show the use of the term by your peers or by your clients. Or, test the word in a keyword research tool (see Chapter 17, "Optimize Your Site for Search Engines"), which may also show you variations and better alternatives.
- It's an acronym. Some acronyms are mainstream enough to use without explanation, but consult your dictionary and consider what you know about your audience. Americans understand *IRS,* for example, but citizens of other countries might not. And if you refer to *CMS,* will visitors know immediately whether you're talking about a content management system, the U.S. Centers for Medicare & Medicaid Services, or the Convention on Migratory Species?

Eliminate jargon

Try these strategies for transforming jargon into **useful information**:

- **Replace the term** with a simpler word or phrase, one that is also more common or more specific. Rather than telling people to "launch the application," tell them to "open WebWidget" (or whatever the program name is). Instead of "leveraging B2B synergies," say that your company is "making the most of its business relationships"—or, better yet, give specific examples.
- **Omit or spell out acronyms.** Don't use an unnecessary acronym; either spell it out or offer more direct and substantive information. For example, rather than saying *COB* (close of busi-

ness) or *EOD* (end of day), give people a specific time, like "5 p.m. PT today." If the acronym is necessary, as with a long proper name, spell out the phrase when you first use it and put the acronym in parentheses, then use the acronym on the rest of the page.

Example

The World Wide Web Consortium (W3C) is an international organization that seeks to develop Web standards. W3C started in 1994.

TIP Remember that visitors may not land on your homepage or the first page of a story, so you may need to spell out an acronym once on every page. For more information on acronyms, see "Acronyms and other abbreviations" on page 234.

- **Explain the jargon.** If you must use a technical term or an acronym, teach your readers what it means. You may need to do more than expand the acronym, however. For instance, it's not useful to tell a new Web user to "enter the Uniform Resource Locator (URL)." It's better to explain that a URL is a Web address and then show people where they can find the URL and where they should type it. Define the jargon right there on the page so that your readers don't have to search for information. If that's not possible, describe it briefly in the text and then link to another page for a full glossary definition or explanation.
- **Give examples** or make an analogy. You can say that a podcast is like a radio program, for instance. Or, if you're describing a more complicated feature, like a photo tag, you can give examples and more detail.

Example

Identify your photos with "tags": short words or phrases such as *Halloween party, cats,* or your friends' names. Tags help you sort photos—for example, click the **Cats** link to see all your cat photos—and tags also help your friends search for specific images.

- **Include graphics.** A picture can be better than a thousand words, especially for text that gives people instructions (see Chapter 7, "Write Clear User-Interface Text"). Instead of saying "Click the program icon in your taskbar," show people exactly what you're talking about.

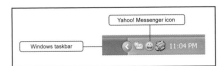

Ideas in Practice

Exercise: Clear deadwood

In the following 10 examples, how much unnecessary text can you prune? Remember this chapter's core principles:

- Keep words, sentences, and paragraphs short and simple.
- Put the actor and the action first.
- Cut any words and phrases that don't add meaning.

 To see our solution, turn to page 482.

1. To delete your existing password and select a new one, start by going to the My Preferences section.

2. If you're looking for the best deals on personal jetpacks, visit www.flyastroboy .com.

3. Before you make a decision about who'll get your vote for mayor, look at all of the candidates and their policies.

4. If you want to get fresh fruits and vegetables, you can sign up for our community-supported agriculture program to get our produce delivered to your home each week.

5. Tickets can be purchased by clicking on the shopping cart icon.

6. It is the responsibility of campers to hang food sacks between trees to avoid bears.

7. The Phone-E application allows you to make a call to your email contacts from any Web-enabled device, including your PC.

8. In addition to searching for local restaurants, you have the ability to make a reservation as well.

9. We're pleased to announce the release of our free photo widget, after six months of

development and extensive user testing. When you download the widget, you'll be able to upload photos directly from your phone to your website.

10. It is very easy to make our site your homepage. In Firefox for Windows, just go to the **Tools** menu, choose **Options,** and click the **Main** button. Replace the URL in the **Home Page** box with **http://www.yahoo.com**. Click the **OK** button to confirm your selection.

Ideas in Practice

Example: Cut the clichés

Clichés are often the first thing to skip across your synapses when you're searching for an apt phrase, so don't worry if they pop up in your first draft. But then edit that draft and root out those worn phrases.

Look at some of the vintage verbiage below (their dates of origin[28] are in parentheses), and then read on for our suggested improvements, with comments on how our edits changed the sentences.

Cliché: a drop in the bucket (1300s)
Before
The bake sale earnings have been terrific, but they're just a drop in the bucket toward our goal of sending the class to Space Camp.
After
The bake sale earnings have been terrific, but we need a lot more money to send the class to Space Camp.

Cliché: to fall between (or through) the cracks (1390)
Before
We were so busy designing the site and creating the content that registering the domain name fell through the cracks.
After
We were so busy designing the site and creating the content that we neglected to register the domain name.
(Not only does the cliché waste words, but it's also weaselly—the speaker is not acknowledging that the team messed up.)

Cliché: back to (or against) the wall (1500s)

Before

Jody is a procrastinator: She won't start writing a term paper until her back is against the wall.

After

Jody is a procrastinator: She won't start writing a term paper until the day before it's due. *(The rewrite, though about the same length, is more informative.)*

Cliché: to be over one's head (1600s)

Before

Are you in over your head with high mortgage debts? Are they ruining your credit rating? ReFiFoFumm.com can help you get a lower-interest loan.

After

Are high mortgage debts ruining your credit rating? ReFiFoFumm.com can help you get a lower-interest loan.

Cliché: to have a lot on one's plate (early 1900s)

Before

Busy working moms have a lot on their plate. For Mother's Day, what they'd really like is a few relaxing hours at the spa.

After

The perfect Mother's Day gift for busy working moms? A few relaxing hours at a spa.

Cliché: to bend over backward (ca. 1920)

Before

At Rubber Band Gymnastics, we bend over backward to help you develop your strength and flexibility.

After

At Rubber Band Gymnastics, we help you develop your strength and flexibility. *(In the original, the cliché is also a pun about what the business does, so you could leave it. But it's probably better to keep the sentence brief or to replace the cliché with more detail, such as words people might use in a search: "At Rubber Band Gymnastics, we help you develop your strength and flexibility through fun exercises on the floor, vault, balance beam, still rings, and parallel and uneven bars.")*

Cliché: to think outside the box (ca. 1975)

Before

Customers complain about our site. We need to go back to square one, think outside the box, create a paradigm shift, and make the blogosphere say "Karl's Kreative is the new black."

After

Customers complain about our site. We need to make a new one they'll love.

Cliché: low-hanging fruit (1984)

Before

Reducing your carbon footprint may seem intimidating, but you can start with some low-hanging fruit, like unplugging unused appliances.

After

Reducing your carbon emissions may seem intimidating, but you can start with some easy, low-cost tactics, like unplugging unused appliances.

(The rewrite is the same length, but it will be clearer to some readers.)

Chapter 14

Avoid Common Pitfalls in Word Choice, Grammar, and Spelling

In this chapter

- **Commonly confused words.** Word pairs and trios that you may be using incorrectly, plus words that your readers may misinterpret.
- **Frequently misspelled words.** We've all mispelled at least one of these.
- **Common grammatical mistakes.** Eight potential trouble areas and ideas for handling each.
- **Old "rules" that no longer apply.** Three rules you don't have to put up with.

Grammatical rules, correct spelling . . . do we *have* to? On the Web, new words come and go with alarming speed, casual frequently edges out formal, and sticking to rules may seem like a waste of time. But rules and forms serve an important function in writing: They create an invisible structure that helps readers understand your sentences easily, without having to stop and puzzle out the meaning.

Resources such as *The Chicago Manual of Style* can give you a solid foundation in the basic rules of grammar, punctuation, and the mechanics of style, and other books that focus on grammar go into more detail than we do here. What this chapter highlights are some common trouble spots and errors that can undermine your text's readability and even harm your website's credibility. Once you recognize these pitfalls, you can avoid them on your site.

Commonly confused words

The English vocabulary is vast and growing, and capable of conveying many subtle shades of meaning. Yet its richness can lead a writer to use a word incorrectly or to craft sentences that are easy to misinterpret.

For clear writing:

■ When you're in doubt about a word, **look it up** in your preferred dictionary and pay special attention to usage notes.
■ **Favor words with distinct meanings** over words that have multiple meanings.

Be especially vigilant about words that are known to confuse writers and readers.

Words that may confuse writers

Even the best writers can mix up words, especially *homophones*: words that sound alike even though they have different spellings and different meanings. Watch for the following homophones and other tricky words—and keep in mind that a spell-checker can't always distinguish one homophone from another.

affect, effect

Both *affect* and *effect* have several meanings. Generally, use *affect* as a verb; use *effect* when you need a noun.

> **Example**
>
> "Crouching Tiger, Hidden Dragon" had gripping fight scenes and special effects, but ultimately its love stories will affect you most.

Affect can be a noun, but only when it means the observable expression of an emotion: *Participants with a happy affect were generally more successful in the task than participants with a sad affect.* (Hint: You probably won't be using *affect* as a noun unless you're writing about psychology.) And *effect* can be a verb only when it means "to bring about," usually in the face of great obstacles: *Dismayed by his heavy work schedule, the ant hoped to effect change in the colony.*

all ready, already

All ready means "completely prepared"; *already* describes something that has occurred before a specific time.

> **Example**
>
> If you've already entered your account information, you're all ready to start.

T I P   Consider whether you need to include *all ready* or *already*. Does your sentence really need either one?

> **Example**
>
> **Before**
> If you've already entered your account information, you're all ready to start.
>
> **After**
> If you've entered your account information, you're ready to start.

all right, alright

Most grammarians say that you must never use *alright*—that it's always all wrong. Use *all right* instead.

a lot, alot

A lot is misspelled a lot. It's always two words.

a while, awhile

Awhile (one word) is an adverb that means "for a while." Use *a while* (two words) if "for a while" doesn't make sense.

> **Example**
>
> It might take me a while to learn the difference, but I'll think about it awhile to make sure that I get it.

capital, capitol

The building where a legislative assembly meets is a capitol. That is the only meaning of *capitol*. If you mean the city where the legislature meets, or if you're referring to money or other resources or to anything else, use *capital*.

Example

In the state capital, the governor spoke of raising more capital for schools before he tripped and tumbled down the capitol steps.

_____

T I P One way to remember the difference: A capit**o**l is an **o**ffice building.

compliment(ary), complement(ary)

A compliment is a form of praise; a complimentary remark is, too. And if it's free, as most praise is, it's complimentary.

A complement completes or supplements something. And two things that go well together are complementary.

Example

To thank you for your compliments concerning our cheeses, we're sending you a complimentary bottle of wine, which we hope you'll find complements the Gouda.

_____

T I P Remember that a compl**e**ment compl**e**tes or suppl**e**ments.

continuous(ly), continual(ly)

Use *continuous* for anything that is uninterrupted; use *continual* for actions that recur regularly or frequently.

Example

Continual monitoring of the servers helps to ensure continuous operation of the website.

_____

every day, everyday

Use *every day* when you mean "each and every day." Use *everyday* when you mean "ordinary."

Example

Find specialty and everyday items in our classifieds section every day.

T I P Try substituting *each day* in the sentence, and if it sounds right, use *every day*.

farther, further

In American English, *farther* refers only to measurable distance. *Further* refers to time or degree. But in British English, it's acceptable for both *farther* and *further* to refer to distance. The following example sentence uses *farther* and *further* as is customary in American English.

Example

He understood that to further his career in football, he'd have to throw the ball farther and faster.

---

fewer, less

Fewer refers to things that can be counted, such as flowers. Use *less* or *less than* for things that cannot be counted individually, such as flour.

Exception: People commonly use *less than* with time, distance, and money, even when talking about countable units like hours or dollars, because in such cases the amount of time, distance, or money is considered a single unit.

Examples

She was able to process the entries faster because there were fewer of them than before.

The grammarian was pleasantly surprised to see that the checkout sign said "10 items or fewer."

He has less muscle now than when he started running.

We were less than 20 kilometers from the shore when it happened. *(Distance exception)*

Calm down! I took less than 10 dollars from your pocket. *(Money exception)*

historic, historical

Something that is significant in history is historic; something that merely occurs in history or relates to history is historical.

> **Example**
>
> Uncle George likes to entertain us with his knowledge of little-known historical facts, but his favorite story is about the time corn prices soared to historic heights in the 1970s and he could have retired a rich man.

it's, its

It's is a contraction of *it is;* the apostrophe replaces a letter. *Its* is a possessive adjective like *his, her,* or *your,* and possessive adjectives never include an apostrophe.

> **Example**
>
> It's the first time the company has raised its prices.

T I P Try substituting *it is* in the sentence. If that sounds right, use *it's*.

lay, lie

Both words have a multitude of meanings and can be verbs or nouns. But they are most often confused when referring to putting oneself to rest (*lie*) and putting something down or placing something (*lay*). Idioms for both words abound, so check the dictionary to be sure you're using the correct word.

> **Example**
>
> Lay down your drink before you lie down for a nap.

T I P Remember that a brick**lay**er **lay**s bricks.

let's, lets

Let's is a contraction of *let us;* the apostrophe replaces a letter. *Lets* means "allows."

> **Example**
>
> Let's see if this password lets us log in.

maybe, may be

If you mean "perhaps," use *maybe;* otherwise, use the verb *may be.*

> **Example**
>
> This may be the best team ever! Maybe it has a shot at the title.

peak, peek

A peak is a pinnacle, top, or summit. A peek is a quick or furtive look.

> **Example**
>
> Take a sneak peek at how celebrities stay in peak condition.

premier, premiere

Premier can be an adjective (meaning "first," either in rank or in time) or a noun (another word for prime minister). *Premiere* means to "debut something" or refers to the debut itself.

> **Example**
>
> The company will premiere its luxury hybrid at the auto show. The much-anticipated car is expected to be the premier offering in its class, surpassing even the entry from Rolls-Royce.

principal, principle

Principal refers to a person or thing of the highest rank or importance. *Principle* refers to law or doctrine.

> ### Example
>
> The students showed the principal the 10 principles of behavior that were the principal reasons for the protest.

T I P   Many U.S. schoolchildren learn that "the princi**pal** is your **pal**." The word to use when referring to the top administrator of a school ends in *pal*. So does the word meaning "the top person or thing."

reign, rein

A monarch reigns, but you rein in a horse using its reins.

> ### Example
>
> During his reign as manager, he tried to rein in the players' salaries. When that failed, he gave the negotiators free rein.

---

rite, right

Though both words have several meanings, *rite* is generally used to mean "a ceremonial or customary act." If you don't mean that, use *right*.

> ### Example
>
> Graduation parties are an annual rite, and many seniors seem to think it's their right to have one. To them, it's a rite of passage, but I don't think they're right.

See "Words that may confuse readers" on page 330 for a caution about using *right*.

stationary, stationery

If it's not moving, it's stationary. Unless it's the paper you write on; then it's stationery. *Stationary* is an adjective; *stationery* is a noun.

> ### Example
>
> The exercise equipment manufacturer's logo—a stationary bike—appears on the corporate stationery.

T I P   A lett**er** is written
on station**er**y.

that, which

In the U.S., use *that* to introduce a *restrictive clause*—one that's essential to the meaning of the sentence: *This is the house that Jack built.* If you cut *that Jack built,* the sentence would lose its point.

Use *which* to introduce a *nonrestrictive clause*—one that can be removed from the sentence without changing the sentence's essential meaning: *This house, which Jack built, is the one I want to buy.* Here, *which Jack built* is an aside—you could remove it from the sentence without changing the key point.

Nonrestrictive clauses begin with *which* and are set off by commas—think of the commas as dotted lines marking where you can cut.

Examples

Do not respond to any message that asks for your password.
Do not respond to David's email messages, which ask for more money each time.

Example

Before
The tango school which closes during the ski season is Muriel's main reason for visiting Buenos Aires. *(The clause "which closes during the ski season" should have commas on both sides if it is nonessential. Alternatively, "which" should be changed to "that" if the clause is essential—for example, if it's necessary to distinguish this school from, say, a year-round tango school in Buenos Aires.)*

After (nonessential)
The tango school, which closes during the ski season, is Muriel's main reason for visiting Buenos Aires. *(In this sentence, "which closes during the ski season" is nonessential—there is only one tango school that the reader could think of, so it isn't necessary to distinguish it.)*

After (essential)
The tango school that closes during the ski season is Muriel's main reason for visiting Buenos Aires. *(In this sentence, "that closes during the ski season" is essential—there must be another tango school that the reader could mistake for Muriel's school of choice.)*

T I P *Garner's Modern American Usage* offers the best tip for using *that* and *which* correctly: "If you see a *which* with neither a preposition nor a comma, dash, or parenthesis before it, it should probably be a *that*." If that doesn't work, think about how the sentence sounds. If it sounds better with no pause before *that* or *which,* you probably want to use *that.*

Example

Before
We strive to provide readers with information which is accurate and up-to-date.

After
We strive to provide readers with information that is accurate and up-to-date.

Although U.S. writers use *that* for restrictive clauses (those that are essential to the meaning of the sentence), British writers frequently use *that* or *which* interchangeably. But for nonrestrictive (nonessential) clauses, British usage still requires a comma and *which.* (Note: In British usage, these are often called *defining* and *non-defining* clauses.)

then, than

If you're referring to time, or if you mean "therefore," "accordingly," or "next," use *then.* If you're making a comparison, use *than.*

Example

Download the second file (it's smaller than the first) and then open it.

---

they're, their, there

They're is a contraction of *they are. Their* is a possessive adjective like *his* or *her.* For everything else (and that's a lot), use *there.*

Example

They're filling out their forms over there.

---

who, which/that

For nonrestrictive clauses (those typically preceded by a comma), use *who* to refer to people. Use *which* to refer to an animal or a thing.

Example

> The director, who has an unmistakable style, created "The Scream," which had considerable impact.

For restrictive clauses (those not typically preceded by a comma), you can use *who* or *that* to refer to people. Some editors think that only *who* can refer to people, but in fact *that* has its place. For example, Fowler's *Dictionary of Modern English Usage* notes that *that* works well to refer to generic or unknown individuals (for example, *a man, anyone, no one*).[29]

Examples

> Directors who engage our fears often meet with box-office success.
> Who was it that said, "The only thing we have to fear is fear itself"?
> No one that I know would ever do such a thing.

Both *who* and *which* can take *whose* as the possessive form.

Example

> The director, whose style is unmistakable, created "The Scream," whose impact was considerable.

If you're struggling to choose between *who* and *whom*, see "Choosing *who* or *whom*" on page 336.

who's, whose

Who's is a contraction of *who is* or *who has*. *Whose* is the possessive form of *who* or *which*.

Example

> The customer, who's always right, remembers whose table he was sitting at that fateful night.

---

you're, your

You're is a contraction of *you are;* the apostrophe replaces a letter. *Your* is the possessive form of *you.*

Example

Receive alerts on your mobile device when you're away from your desk.

T I P   If you've written *you're,* try substituting *you are.* If it doesn't work, the word you want is *your.*

Other groups of words likely to be mistaken for each other include the following (and many others). Look these up in your dictionary if you're ever in doubt about which one to use:

accept/except	cache/cachet	foreword/forward
adapt/adopt	callus/callous	gibe/jibe
adverse/averse	canvas/canvass	hawk/hock
aid/aide	carat/caret/karat	imply/infer
allude/elude	cast/caste	leach/leech
alternate/alternative	comprise/compose/consist of/constitute	lightening/lightning
ambivalent/ambiguous	cord/chord	nauseous/nauseated
appraise/apprise	council/counsel	palate/palette/pallet
base/bass	discreet/discrete	pedal/peddle
beside/besides	elicit/illicit	precede/proceed
bloc/block	faze/phase	rack/wrack
born/borne	flack/flak	tortuous/torturous
breach/breech	forego/forgo	

For a more thorough list of commonly confused words, refer to *The Gregg Reference Manual,* pages 199–210.

T I P   If research hasn't helped you feel sure that you've chosen the correct word, select another word that conveys what you're trying to say.

Finally, be aware of some **common phrases that contain a homophone.** Writers often confuse these:

- Vocal cords (not *chords*)
- Just deserts (not *desserts*)
- To the manner (not *manor*) born (Really! It's in *Hamlet.*)
- Soft-pedal (not *peddle*)
- Free rein (not *reign*)
- Shoo-in (not *shoe-in*)
- Toe (not *tow*) the line
- A real trouper (not *trooper*)

Of course, many such phrases are clichés that you'll want to avoid anyway.

Words that may confuse readers

Certain words, such as *once, right,* and *since,* have so many meanings that they can puzzle readers. They are particularly troublesome for translators and for readers whose first language isn't English. Think carefully before using them in a sentence.

once

Once can be a noun, an adjective, an adverb, or a conjunction. Because it can be used in so many ways, it can sometimes lead readers down an incorrect path. Depending on the context, consider substituting *as soon as, one time, after, when, in the past,* or *formerly*.

Examples

Before
Press the button once you have set up your pieces on the game board. Press it twice to reset the timer.

After
Set up your pieces on the game board, then press the button one time. Press it twice to reset the timer.

Before
Once you press the button, the computer will start up.

After
When you press the button, the computer will start up.
After you press the button, the computer will start up.

Before

Once he would press any button; now he knows that some will shock him.

After

In the past he would press any button; now he knows that some will shock him.

_____

right

This word can refer to, among other things, a direction (*turn right*), a political point of view (*the right opposes that tax*), or a legal claim (*the right to free speech*); or it can mean "correct." If you mean "correct," then use *correct*. And if you mean "right" as in a direction, make sure that people know exactly where you mean.

Example

Before

After locating the right file in the right pane, drag it to the left pane.

After

After locating the correct file in the pane at right, drag the file to the pane at left.

_____

since

Since can relate to either time or causation. If you mean "because," you may want to use *because* instead—or you might reword the sentence for greater clarity.

Example

Before

Since she was 4 years old, Eleanor enjoyed dressing up in tutus and pretending to be a ballerina. *(The simple past "enjoyed" may indicate to careful readers that "Since" means "because" here, but many readers may miss that detail.)*

Since she was 4 years old, Eleanor has enjoyed dressing up in tutus and pretending to be a ballerina. *(The present perfect "has enjoyed" may indicate to careful readers that "Since" means "ever since," but again, many readers may miss that detail.)*

After

Because she was 4 years old, Eleanor enjoyed dressing up in tutus and pretending to be a ballerina.

Eleanor has enjoyed dressing up in tutus and pretending to be a ballerina ever since she was 4 years old.

Frequently misspelled words

The following words are some of the most difficult to spell—even excellent spellers have trouble with some of them.

Some words (like *minuscule*) have a variant spelling (*miniscule*). When your dictionary's main entry for a word offers multiple spellings, it's wise to choose the first one.

For even more words that are frequently misspelled, refer to *The Gregg Reference Manual,* pages 211–213.

accommodate	government	mischievous
accumulate	grammar	misspell
allotted	harass	necessary
amateur	height	noticeable
calendar	hierarchy	occurrence
cemetery	immediately	parallel
changeable	independent	pastime
collectible	indispensable	perseverance
commitment	inoculate	privilege
committee	irrelevant	publicly
conscientious	judgment	questionnaire
conscious	liaison	restaurant
definitely	license	rhythm
embarrass	maintenance	seize
existence	memento	separate
fluorescent	millennium	supersede
gauge	minuscule	withhold

Common grammatical mistakes

It's true that prose is less formal today, but you should still follow most grammatical rules. Adhering to them eases reader comprehension and increases the credibility of your website.

If you don't feel confident in this arena, take heart: You're not alone. Here are eight common trouble areas and commonsense ways to deal with them.

1. Mismatched subject and verb: We goes to school

The rule: Singular subjects should have singular verbs; plural subjects should have plural verbs: *one frog jumps, two frogs jump.*

Of course, it's not always that easy. Pronouns such as *each* and *nobody,* especially, tend to confuse everyone.

Example

Before
Each of the programmers have an extensive collection of free, software-promoting T-shirts.

After
Each of the programmers has an extensive collection of free, software-promoting T-shirts.

Use this chart to match pronouns with their correct verbs:

Pronoun	Singular or plural verb?	Example
Anybody	Singular	*Has anybody seen my pillow?*
Both	Plural	*Both of us need a nap.*
Each	Singular	*Each of us needs a nap.*
Everyone	Singular	*Everyone needs a nap.*
Few	Plural	*Few of the adults need a nap.*
Most	Plural when referring to a greater number; singular when referring to a greater part	*Most of the babies are napping.* *Most of the class is napping.*
Much	Singular	*Much has been made of circadian rhythms.*
Nobody	Singular	*Nobody naps long.*

Pronoun	Singular or plural verb?	Example
None	Plural when meaning "not any"; singular when meaning "not one"	*None of the babies are awake yet.* *None of the babies is awake yet.*
No one	Singular	*No one is awake yet.*
Somebody	Singular	*Somebody needs a nap.*
Someone	Singular	*Someone is snoring.*
Either (without *or*)	Singular	*Either is fine.*
Neither (without *nor*)	Singular	*Neither is ideal.*
Either (with *or*)	Singular or plural, depending on what follows *or*	See "Choosing the correct verb after *and, or,* or *nor*" below.
Neither (with *nor*)	Singular or plural, depending on what follows *nor*	See "Choosing the correct verb after *and, or,* or *nor*" below.

Choosing the correct verb after *and, or,* or *nor*

Many grammar books go into excruciating detail about matching subject and verb when the subject is a compound consisting of two or more elements separated by *or* or *nor*. There is only one rule for *or* and *nor*: **The verb must agree in number and person with the subject closer to it.** Believe it or not, the sentences in the following example are correct.

Examples

Either she or I am going to win the auction.
Either Mary or you are going to win the auction.
Neither she nor I am going to win the auction.
Neither Mary nor you are going to win the auction.

Because the grammatically correct verb may sound awkward, consider changing the verb or verb tense when the subjects are joined by *or* or *nor*.

Examples

Either she or I will win the auction.
Either Mary or you will win the auction.
Neither she nor I will win the auction.
Neither Mary nor you will win the auction.

For a **compound subject formed with _and_**, your verb choice depends on whether the nouns are functioning as one thing (singular verb) or as two or more things (plural verb).

Examples

Steamed mussels and French fries go surprisingly well together. _(Plural subject, plural verb.)_
Mussels and fries is the best dish on the menu. _("Mussels and fries" functions as a single unit—a dish—and so takes a singular verb.)_

Exception: When a positive subject is joined to a negative subject by _and,_ the verb agrees with the positive subject: _Compassion and not monetary riches is her main criterion for a husband._

Collective nouns

In the U.S., **collective nouns such as _team, group, band,_ and _company_ generally take singular verbs**. In the U.K., singular words that refer to groups of people usually take plural pronouns and verbs.

Examples

American English
The band fights constantly on its tour bus.
The company is announcing its third-quarter results later today.

British English
The band fight constantly on their tour bus.
The company are announcing their third-quarter results later today.

T I P   The rule to always treat _data_ and _media_ as the plurals of _datum_ and _medium_ (and to give them plural verbs: _the data are, the media are_) is becoming less stringent a "rule." In communications and technology publications, _data_ and _media_ are often treated as singular nouns: _the data is, the media is_. For more information, see these terms' individual entries in "The Yahoo! word list" on page 438.

One of the (nouns) that/who

One of the rules that often trip people up is this one. In the sentence you just read, don't mistake *One* as the subject of the verb *trip;* the subject of the verb *trip* is *that,* the pronoun standing for *rules.* (*One* is the subject of the verb *is*.)

Examples

Before
One of the rules that often trips people up is this one.

After
One of the rules that often trip people up is this one.

Before
Be one of those writers who practices good grammar.

After
Be one of those writers who practice good grammar.

---

2. Pronoun decisions: *I* or *me*? *Who* or *whom*?

Sometimes people get confused when two or more pronouns are used together. Is it *her and me, she and I,* or *her and I*? The rule is:

- Use *I, he, she, we,* or *they* for the subject or (if you're using formal English) after any conjugated form of the verb *to be*: *It was she who spoke first.* A *conjugated form* is any form other than the infinitive (*to be*) itself.
- Use *me, him, her, us,* or *them* for the object of a verb, for the object of a preposition (such as *about, of, to,* or *with*), or after the infinitive *to be*: *I've got to be me.*

It's easy to get confused. Even die-hard grammarians use a simple trick to select the correct pronouns: **Break up the sentence and try it with each pronoun individually.**

Example

She and I were surprised by her popularity. *(She was surprised and I was surprised.)*

Before

It was a surprise to she and I. *("It was a surprise to she" and "It was a surprise to I": Both sound—and are—incorrect.)*

It was a surprise to her and I. *("It was a surprise to her" is correct but "It was a surprise to I" sounds—and is—incorrect.)*

After

It was a surprise to her and me. *(It was a surprise to her and it was a surprise to me.)*

Choosing *who* or *whom*

Who and *whom* are two special pronouns that often confound writers—if they consider them at all. Use *who* as a subject and use *whom* as the object of a verb or preposition.

When faced with selecting between *who* and *whom,* don't panic. The following tips will help you figure out which one to use. And if all else fails, use *who.*

One trick for finding the correct form is to **recast the sentence in your mind, substituting *he* and *him* for *who* or *whom***. If *him* sounds correct, use *whom*. (It also helps to remember that both *him* and *whom* end in *m.*)

He is the youngest of those who finished the race. *(Substituting "he": He finished.)*

Smith, who they suspected was cheating, won the prize. *(Substituting "he": They suspected he was cheating.)*

Who shall I say is calling? *(Substituting "he": Shall I say he is calling?)*

To whom should I give the prize? *(Substituting "him": Should I give the prize to him?)*

Please give this to whoever won the prize. *(Substituting "he": He won the prize.)*

Sometimes it's better to just rewrite a sentence to avoid a potential grammatical error or a grammatically correct but awkward or formal-sounding construction. It's especially true when *who* or *whom* starts a sentence. *Who* generally sounds correct at the beginning of a sentence, but it isn't always correct.

> **Example**
>
> **Before**
>
> Whom should I give the ticket to? *(Grammatically correct but awkward-sounding)*
>
> **After**
>
> Who should receive the ticket? *(Grammatically correct and natural-sounding)*

Matching nouns and pronouns

Remember that **singular nouns take singular pronouns, and plural nouns take plural pronouns.** In the U.S., *company* is a singular noun: *The company is announcing its third-quarter results.*

When discussing an individual, use a singular pronoun: *Tell that man that he dropped his wallet.* Unfortunately, this rule can mean choosing between *he* and *she* even when the gender of the individual is unknown or unimportant, because using *they* is grammatically controversial. Try rewriting the sentence instead. (For techniques on maintaining good grammar without resorting to such awkward constructions as *he or she* and *s/he,* see "Write gender-neutral copy" on page 77.)

> **Example**
>
> **Before**
>
> When a reader sees a singular subject, they expect to see a singular pronoun.
>
> **After**
>
> When readers see a singular subject, they expect to see a singular pronoun.

Make sure that you pair nouns and pronouns clearly. For example, when you use the pronoun *it,* can you tell what *it* refers to? If not, fix the problem by repeating the noun, inserting a noun, or, if the repetition sounds too awkward, rewriting the sentence.

> **Examples**
>
> **Before**
>
> Noah swung a champagne bottle at his model ship and broke it.
>
> **After**
>
> Noah swung a champagne bottle at his model ship and broke the ship.
>
> *or*
>
> Noah swung a champagne bottle at his model ship and broke the bottle.

Better

Noah broke a champagne bottle on his model ship.

Before

She knows the names of her friends' kids, but she doesn't like them.

After

She knows the names of her friends' kids, but she doesn't like the kids.

or

She knows the names of her friends' kids, but she doesn't like their names.

Better

She knows the names of her friends' kids, but she thinks that the names are old-fashioned.

---

3. Dangling and misplaced modifiers: The funny side of grammar

A *modifier* is a word or phrase that changes or qualifies the meaning of another word or phrase. **Place modifiers as close as possible to the words they refer to.** If you don't, your sentences may say something you never intended—sometimes with unintentionally funny results.

Dangling modifiers

A *dangling modifier* is a word or phrase (often at the beginning of a sentence) that seems to modify a noun it isn't supposed to. Sometimes the dangling modifier is too far away from the noun it is supposed to modify, or the noun that it's supposed to modify isn't even in the sentence.

You can often fix a dangling modifier simply by placing the noun it is supposed to modify right after it.

Examples

Before

Using the grammar checker, grammatical errors are detected and corrected easily.
(The errors are using the grammar checker.)

After

Using the grammar checker, you can detect and correct grammatical errors easily. *(You are using the grammar checker.)*

Before

Walking by the restaurant, it would be easy to dismiss it as an '80s yuppie fern bar. *(No one in the sentence is walking.)*

After

Walking by the restaurant, you might easily dismiss it as an '80s yuppie fern bar.
or
Walking by the restaurant, a person might easily dismiss it as an '80s yuppie fern bar.

Sometimes you need to recast the sentence to associate the correct noun with the modifier.

Examples

Before

Drunk or sober, the coach wants all the players on the field right now. *(Presumably, the coach is not the person whose sobriety is questionable. The modifier "Drunk or sober" should go close to "players" instead.)*

After

The coach wants all the players—drunk or sober—on the field right now.

Before

When executed properly, the skater will complete three and a half rotations in a triple axel. *(The skater is executed.)*

After

The skater completes three and a half rotations in a properly executed triple axel. *(The axel is executed.)*

Dangling modifiers don't always fall at the beginning of a sentence—they may fall at the end. **Be careful in particular with prepositional phrases.** These can modify either nouns or verbs and may therefore puzzle readers. A *prepositional phrase* includes a preposition (such as *at, on, above, between, with, for, into, through, out, off, toward*) and an object.

Examples

Before

Did you see the cowboy on the palomino with a ten-gallon hat? *(Was the cowboy or the horse wearing the hat?)*

After

Did you see the cowboy with a ten-gallon hat on the palomino? *(Better, but readers still might think that the palomino is wearing a hat.)*

Better

Did you see the cowboy with a ten-gallon hat who was riding the palomino?

Before

The dancer leaped across the stage with scarves and ribbons flying. *(Is "with scarves and ribbons flying" describing the stage's decorations or the dancer's?)*

After

With scarves and ribbons flying from her hands, the dancer leaped across the stage.

Misplaced modifiers

The placement of a modifier, whether it's a word or a phrase, affects the meaning or emphasis of a sentence. **Always place a modifier as close as possible to the word it modifies.** A misplaced modifier inadvertently modifies the wrong word and hampers understanding.

Be especially careful with the adverbs *only* and *just*—they can modify nouns, verbs, and other parts of speech.

Examples

We will only notify you when there is a change. *(We won't do anything else.)*
We will notify you only when there is a change. *(We won't notify you for any other reason.)*

Mary only poked him in the eye. *(That's all she did; no punching, no biting.)*
Only Mary poked him in the eye. *(Nobody else poked him.)*
Mary poked only him in the eye. *(She didn't poke anybody else.)*
Mary poked him in the only eye. *(And now he has none.)*

T I P   Generally, place *only* only where it belongs: right before the word or phrase it applies to.

If you include a **modifier before a series**, make sure that it's clear whether that modifier belongs with the first word in the series or with them all. You may need to reorder the series or to rewrite the sentence.

Example

Before

The cafeteria's menu includes peanut-free granola, salads, and cookies. *(Are all the items peanut-free?)*

After

The cafeteria's menu includes salads, cookies, and peanut-free granola. *(Reorder the series to clarify.)*
or
The cafeteria's menu lists several peanut-free foods, including granola, salads, and cookies. *(Rewrite the sentence to make it clear that all the items are peanut-free.)*

4. Parallelism: Matching, balancing, making sense

Parallelism, broadly speaking, refers to matching the parts of speech (all verbs, for instance) in certain related parts of a sentence—for example, in a series or list.

Example

Not parallel

Sun-min likes traveling, reading, and wants to climb more mountains. *("Traveling" and "reading" are both gerunds, but "wants to climb" doesn't fit.)*

Parallel

Sun-min likes traveling, reading, and mountain climbing.
or
Sun-min, who likes traveling and reading, wants to climb more mountains.

A sentence that is parallel is easy to read. A sentence that is not parallel may make the reader stumble or even backtrack to figure out what you were trying to say.

Parallel structure around *and, or,* and other conjunctions

And—like the other coordinating conjunctions *but, or, nor,* and *yet*—signals a need for parallel treatment. For example, a romance novelist might give the hero of her story:

- A verb followed by two prepositional phrases: Jake swept *through the plains* and *into her heart.*
- A verb and two objects: He excited *her mind* and *her dog.*
- Two verbs: He *rode* hard and *drank* infrequently.
- Two adjectives: He was *dark* and *tidy.*

Any elements joined by conjunctions should take the same grammatical form.

Examples

Before

She is a team player, well-organized, and represents our company well.
(What's wrong with that sentence? It says "She is a well-organized" and "She is a represents our company well.")

After

She is a team player, she is well-organized, and she represents our company well.

Better

A team player and a well-organized executive, she represents our company well.

Before

BuggleBox allows you to upload video, create playlists, and makes it easy to share playlists with friends.

After

BuggleBox allows you to upload video, create playlists, and share playlists with friends.

Better

With BuggleBox you can upload video, create playlists, and share playlists with friends.

Correlative conjunctions such as ***not only–but also, either–or, neither–nor, both–and,* and *as–so* also signal a need for parallel treatment.**

Quick grammar glossary

conjunction: A word that joins two parts of a sentence. *And, but, or,* and *nor* are common conjunctions. Many other words can also serve as conjunctions, including *how, when, once, since,* and *because.*

correlative conjunction: A pair of conjunctions that are not adjacent to each other but that connect a pair of nouns, verbs, prepositional phrases, or clauses in a sentence. *Either-or, neither-nor, both-and, as-so,* and *not only–but also* are common correlatives.

prepositional phrase: A phrase beginning with a preposition (such as *to, from, on, for, about,* or *with*) that is followed by a noun or noun phrase (its object).

object: A noun, pronoun, or clause that receives the action of a verb or that follows a preposition.

Sentences with correlatives are like seesaws: To stay in balance, the word or phrase following the first part of the correlative conjunction (for example, following *neither*) must be the same part of speech as the word or phrase following the second part (for example, following *nor*). Constructions like "That's neither *here* nor *there*" and "We aim to win not only *their hearts* but also *their minds*" illustrate this principle.

Try reading the sentence as two separate sentences, each with a joined element. For the first sentence, take the beginning of the original sentence (up until the first word of the correlative, such as *either*) plus the bit in between the two correlatives (for example, in between *either* and *or*). For the second sentence, take the same beginning of the sentence, but now add the bit following the second part of the correlative (for example, following *or*). If the two resulting sentences are grammatically and syntactically correct, you've placed the correlatives correctly.

Example

Try this technique with the sentence "Flower arrangements are either delivered to home addresses or to office addresses." If you split this sentence, you'd get:

→ Flower arrangements are delivered to home addresses.
→ Flower arrangements are to office addresses.

Before

	delivered to home addresses
Flower arrangements are (either)	(or)
	to office addresses

(Not good. The second sentence is missing a verb, "delivered," and it doesn't make sense—so the correlative is not parallel.)

To make the sentence structure parallel, move *delivered* before *either* so that it can apply to both halves of the correlative. The phrase after *either* is now parallel to the phrase after *or*: "Flower arrangements are delivered either *to home addresses* or *to office addresses*." If you split this sentence, you'd get:

→ Flower arrangements are delivered to home addresses.
→ Flower arrangements are delivered to office addresses.

After

	to home addresses
Flower arrangements are delivered (either)	(or)
	to office addresses

(Now the sentence structure is parallel.)

Example

Before
The funds will either be debited from your account when the check is issued or when the payee cashes the check.

After
The funds will be debited from your account either when the check is issued or when the payee cashes the check.

Take special care with the correlative conjunction *not only–but also*. One of the two elements (the *not only* or the *but also*) is frequently misplaced or used incompletely. But using this correlative correctly can sometimes produce a sentence that sounds stilted. If that is the case, consider rewriting the sentence.

Example

Before
You can change not only your password but your email address.

After
You can change not only your password but also your email address.

Better
You can change your password and your email address.

TIP Occasionally, *but* by itself rather than *but also* is appropriate. This occurs when the first part of the conjunction is a member, or an example, of the second part. In the declaration "I sampled not only the Brie but *also* all the cheeses," Brie does not seem to be a cheese. "I sampled not only the Brie but all the cheeses" makes sense, and so does "I sampled not only the Brie but also the grapes." (Note that the idea of *also* can be worded as *too* or *as well*. You could say, "I sampled not only the Brie but the grapes as well.")

Nonparallel lists

Mistakes in parallelism appear frequently in vertical lists, where they are even more obvious than in running text. When you create a bulleted or numbered list, make sure not only that each item in the list follows smoothly from the phrase that introduces the list, but also that all the items in the list take the same grammatical form (noun, verb, and so on).

Examples

Before

On yesterday's show I learned:

- How to cook a turkey *(a conjunction with an infinitive "to" phrase)*
- The essentials of flower arrangement *(a noun phrase)*
- To save bread-wrapper twists *(an infinitive phrase)*

After (using all conjunctions with infinitive phrases)

On yesterday's show I learned:

- How to cook a turkey
- How to arrange flowers
- What to do with bread-wrapper twists

After (using all noun phrases)

On yesterday's show I learned:

- The best way to cook a turkey
- The essentials of flower arrangement
- Great uses for bread-wrapper twists

5. Change of person: Sliding from second to third

Writing in the first person means using *I* or *we;* in the second person, *you;* in the third person, *he, she,* or *it*—as well as *customer, subscriber, member, user*.

If you're referring to your reader as *you,* whether explicitly or implicitly, **don't switch** to the third person. It's disorienting. For instance, don't use *you* and *the customer* interchangeably in the same text.

Example

Before

Sign up for our mailing list and be notified of the latest releases and deals. In addition, subscribers are eligible to enter our weekly drawing. *(The subject of the first sentence—an implied "you"—is in the second person; the subject in the next sentence—"subscribers"—is in the third person.)*

After

Sign up for our mailing list and be notified of the latest releases and deals. You'll also be eligible to enter our weekly drawing. *(The subject throughout—"you"—is in the second person.)*

Avoid using the imperative (which has an implied subject of "you") with the first person. This type of construction leads to unclear text that can prevent the reader from immediately understanding your message.

Example

Before

Check the box to hide my contact information from other users. *(Uses both the second person "you," implied by the imperative, and the first person, implied by "my")*

After

Check the box to hide your contact information from others. *(Uses the second person consistently)*

I want to hide my contact information from others. *(Uses the first person consistently)*

---

6. Change of tense: Back to the future

Past, present, future—which tense is appropriate for your copy? The present tense works best for most business communications, but each tense has its place. In an essay about *Jane Eyre* or a blog entry about the book you just read, you'd refer to characters and action in the present tense, because those works exist in the present. But in a newspaper report, you'd refer to last week's political convention in the past tense.

Regardless of the tense you choose, **don't change it midsentence (or midparagraph)—** you'll give your reader temporal whiplash.

Example

Before (present, future)
Visitors to the outdoor museum enjoy beautiful weather most days and quick access from the train station. On display will be artifacts from the archaeological dig, centuries-old frescoes, and a partially unearthed coliseum.

After (present)
Visitors to the outdoor museum enjoy beautiful weather most days and quick access from the train station. On display are artifacts from the archaeological dig, centuries-old frescoes, and a partially unearthed coliseum.

7. The superfluous *as*: Much as we like it, it has to go

It's true that comparisons such as "She was as silly as a goose" require the use of *as* twice: once before the first element (*silly*), and once before the second (*a goose*). But in constructions like *As silly as she was,* the first *as* is incorrect, because no comparison is being made. The second *as* means "though": *Silly though she was,* or *Silly as she was,* is correct. So, difficult as it may be, **leave out that first *as*.**

Example

Before
As much as I liked her performance, I felt the play itself lacked energy.

After
Much as I liked her performance, I felt the play itself lacked energy.

8. False comparisons: Mismatched pairs

Sometimes a word or phrase is missing from a comparison, which results in constructions like *Unlike last week, box-office receipts this week were higher than expected.* The writer intends to compare *this week's receipts* with *last week's receipts,* but that sentence compares *receipts* with *last week.*

Make sure that comparisons are between two comparable subjects—in this case, a week and another week: *Unlike last week, this week saw higher-than-expected box-office receipts.*

Example

Before
Unlike Mr. Straw's performance in the film, the play featured an actor less skilled in physical comedy.

After
Unlike the film, which showcased Mr. Straw's gift for physical comedy, the play featured an actor less skilled in that arena.
or
Unlike Mr. Straw, who starred in the film, the play's lead doesn't have a gift for physical comedy.

Old "rules" that no longer apply

Quick! Name three important grammar rules:

1. Never split an infinitive.
2. Never end a sentence with a preposition.
3. Never start a sentence with a conjunction.

Wrong. Following these old saws can lead to unnatural or unnecessarily formal language.

1. Splitting infinitives

An infinitive is the *to* form of a verb; for example, *to go, to download,* and *to subscribe* are all infinitives. A split infinitive places an adverb between *to* and the principal verb, as in the *Star Trek* line "to *boldly* go where no one has gone before."

People object to splitting infinitives for various reasons. One common argument is that *to* is an essential part of the verb—the infinitive is two words functioning as one and therefore should not be divided. However, the objection to split infinitives is at best a preference, not a rule; there's no linguistic reason why inserting an adverb is incorrect. In fact, it is sometimes necessary to split an infinitive to add emphasis in the right place, to produce a more natural rhythm, or to reduce ambiguity by placing the adverb next to the verb it modifies. Your best course of action is to say a phrase out loud both ways—*to faithfully execute* and *to execute faithfully,* for example—and decide which construction sounds better, clearer, and more appropriate.

Examples

To quickly go to the homepage, click the icon.
You can expect to more than double your sales.

TIP   Many people who object to split infinitives also get worked up when writers separate helper verbs from main verbs. But again, you should let your ear guide you: *In the finals, Spain will easily defeat Brazil* sounds more natural than *Spain easily will defeat Brazil.* And *Spain will defeat Brazil easily* falls somewhere in between—it sounds natural enough, but *easily* loses some of its emphasis when moved farther from the verb.

2. Ending with a preposition

At one time, writers took great care to avoid ending a sentence with a preposition (a word such as *at, about, of, in, with, by, for,* or *from*). It was something at which they worked hard. Unfortunately, they created sentences like the previous one, which doesn't reflect common speech.

Examples

Before
This is the service for which you've been waiting.

After
This is the service you've been waiting for.

Before
That's exactly the subject about which we're talking!

After
That's exactly what we're talking about!

Ending a sentence with a preposition is fine in casual and informal writing. For more formal writing, you may want to avoid ending a sentence with a preposition. But instead of using stilted language that doesn't reflect common speech, try rewriting the sentence.

Example

Before
Contact the seller if you don't receive the item for which you have paid.
("For which" is a slightly unnatural-sounding construction used to avoid ending the sentence with "for")

After
Contact the seller if you don't receive the item you bought.
or
Contact the seller if you don't receive the item.
or
If you don't receive the item you paid for, contact the seller.

3. Starting with a conjunction

Most authorities now accept a coordinating conjunction (like *and, but,* and *or*) as the opening to a sentence in informal writing—but not all. And those who don't have their reasons: Words like *and* and *but* are technically meant to join two clauses of a complete sentence. Some people feel that beginning a sentence with one of these words creates a sentence fragment, or only half a thought. But you'll have to consider your site's voice and decide for yourself.

If your website's voice is highly professional and formal, you may want to use language and grammar more conservatively—especially if your readers are self-proclaimed sticklers who might think that you're making mistakes rather than purposely ignoring outdated rules. In that case, rewrite sentences to avoid unnatural language.

Ideas in Practice

Exercise: Dig into the details

Each of the following sentences has one or more grammar, spelling, or usage mistakes. See if you can dig up all 20.

 To see our solution, turn to page 483.

1. Since Carla got her urban garden allotment, she has been able to grow alot of tomatoes and okra.

2. Your embarassing everyone with your sloppy typing, bad grammar, and with stubbornly refusing to use a spell-checker.

3. Both of the twins are taking driving lessons, but neither Anya nor Alexei have driven further than the airport yet.

4. The person which first wrote a computer program was Ada Lovelace, who beside being Lord Byron's daughter created an algorithm for calculating Bernoulli numbers with Charles Babbage's analytical engine.

5. Looking at the length of Darnell's beard, his wife has been out of town for two weeks, I'd guess.

6. If Sean wants to join a sports team, his mom will let him play anything that doesn't require padding, so he could think about either playing tennis or rugby.

7. If you don't pack each of those collectable teacups in bubble wrap, you will definately end up with a box of worthless shards.

8. He'd rather take vitamins then eat fruit and vegetables everyday.

9. Kendra is obsessed with that film and wants to see everything: the sneak peaks at the principle photography, Cannes premier, and DVD extras.

10. Eric says he's buying a pass to the "Star Trek" convention—the ticket price doesn't phase him.

Chapter 15

Proofread and Test Before You Publish

In this chapter

- **Ensure a good user experience.** Content errors diminish your credibility, and bad links and navigation cause visitors to leave.
- **Inspect your copy at least twice.** Check it before it's posted, and check it onscreen before it goes live.
- **Know what to check on webpages and in emails.** See what the most common errors are and where to watch for them.
- **Pick up some proofreading tricks.** Give yourself the best chance to spot errors by using these proven techniques.

You've put a lot of effort into writing your content and creating a site that your audience will enjoy. Next step: Proofread everything before you put it online.

Why? Can't you just fix errors later, after readers notice them?

Sure, but that's hardly an ideal solution. For one thing, as soon as you publish your story online, you no longer have complete control over it. Someone may copy text from your site—mistakes and all—or take a screenshot of it, or the flawed story may immediately appear in a news feed, which is content that sites export to people who have signed up for it. So, even if you fix an error, your original story could still be out there. And email presents an obvious problem: If you send a faulty email newsletter to thousands or millions of subscribers, you probably can't recover it.

But the potential permanence of errors isn't the only reason to ensure that your copy is posted right the first time. The biggest reason is this: You want to provide a superior user experience that attracts a loyal audience to your website. People notice mistakes, and seemingly small **errors like typos and bad links can make a site look unprofessional or unreliable** and can drive visitors away. Testing your content is an essential part of the online publishing process.

Ensure a good user experience

It's almost impossible to create error-free content on your first try. Everyone needs an editor, even if it means acting as your own. The last step in the editing process—proofreading—is your last chance to make your content error-free.

In the print-publishing world, proofreaders look for problems that may have slipped through previous editing stages, such as typos, misspellings, misused words, misstatements of fact, and potential legal issues. As an online proofreader, you do that and more: You must also test links, photos and slideshows, videos, site features, and so on. In short, online proofreading means making sure your story or your webpage *works*.

Proofreading is a simple—but vital—step because:

- **Error-free content keeps readers focused on your message and delivers a smooth user experience.** When the content says exactly what you intend and everything on the site works as it should, everyone's happy. On the other hand, even the tiniest inconsistency can distract certain readers. And a whopper will derail the thought train of anybody who notices it. An error can even negate your message, making it say the opposite of what you mean.

Examples

If you have never taken a mule ride down Bright Angel Trail or joined a whitewater farting excursion on the Colorado's rapids, you can take the trips in your mind's eye through these spectacular full-colour and mostly full-page images. *(From an eBay description about a book on the Grand Canyon)*

Together we can work to relive your pain and discomfort. *(From the website of an orthopedic practice)*

- **Error-free content underscores your site's credibility.** The Web Credibility Project at the Stanford University Persuasive Technology Lab found that typographical errors are one of the top 10 factors reducing a site's credibility.[30] In the 2002 "Stanford-Makovsky Web Credibility Study" (a research report by the Stanford lab and Makovsky & Company), researchers noted that "Web users do not overlook simple cosmetic mistakes, such as spelling or grammatical errors. In fact, the findings suggested that typographical errors have roughly the same negative impact on a website's credibility as a company's legal or financial troubles."[31] Once credibility is diminished or lost, it can be hard to rebuild.

! **Address Not Found**
Firefox can't find the server at www.bootleg-baby.com.

When people click a broken link on your website and land on a page like this, their next step may be to leave your website for one that works correctly.

Using a spell-checker is not enough

You can't rely on a spell-checker alone to find errors. A spell-checker will catch many misspelled words, but it can't tell:

- Whether words are used correctly in their context. For example, it can't tell which of the following pairs is appropriate in a given sentence.

desert/dessert	loose/lose	their/they're/there
hole/whole	our/out	your/you're
form/from	passed/past	

- Whether proper names are correct (*Osama* or *Obama, windows* or *Windows*).
- Whether a word or a part of a word is missing.

Example

A spell-checker wouldn't have helped the so-called Wicked Bible of 1631. That infamous edition omitted the word *not* from the seventh commandment, so it read: "Thou shalt commit adultery."

- Whether a word should be hyphenated, open, or closed up: *any more* or *anymore, well known* or *well-known.*
- Whether certain words should be capitalized: *President Palmer* or *the U.S. president, earth* or *Earth.*
- Whether a variant spelling is acceptable: *adviser* or *advisor, judgment* or *judgement.*

A spell-checker will allow *uninformed* when you want *uniformed, faulty* when you want *faculty,* even *pubic* when you want *public.* Our advice: **Use a spell-checker, but make sure that human eyes review your copy, too.**

Inspect your copy at least twice

Writers often compose webpage text in a word-processing program and then paste it into a Web publishing tool or send it to someone who will format it for online posting. It's crucial to check copy at both stages:

1. **Before you put it into the publishing tool or submit it for publishing.** In some organizations, this is the copyediting stage. Once you've edited your content, read through it again and proof it. It's usually easier to change copy in a word-processing document than in a content-publishing tool.

2. **After the page has been built and you can preview the content as it will appear online.** Onscreen, copy may seem quite different. Make sure that it still reads well (you may need to cut more words), that the words and images are all there and all correct, and that links and other interactive elements work.

   Always check the copy in its final format—Web, email, or print—before it goes out to the public. You may have missed errors, or the designer, the producer, or the content-publishing tool may have accidentally introduced some.

T I P Don't allow your word-processing application to automatically format special characters or typography styles in copy that you're publishing online or sending in an email. These characters and styles can turn into garbage text, marring your otherwise clean copy. Be sure to disable the software's tendency to format apostrophes and single quotation marks, double quotation marks, em dashes, en dashes, ellipsis points, ordinal numbers with superscripts, and fractions. If you do want to use special characters in your Web copy, use the appropriate code instead—see "Special characters" on page 386.

Know what to check on webpages and in emails

You can proofread more efficiently when you know what types of errors to look for. It also helps to prioritize what page areas and what types of errors deserve your attention first. Be sure to look at the following potential trouble areas:

1. The most visible elements

On a webpage, these are the **hot spots** that people are most likely to read:

- **The webpage title** (from the **<title>** tag). Make sure that the page has an error-free title that accurately describes the page. See "Page titles" on page 119 for more details.
- **Headlines and headings.** Check that they're correct and fit the page or story. See "Headings" on page 50.
- **Buttons and other user-interface copy.** Is the text short and clear? Does it orient the person to the page and state clearly how to get to the next point? Are there any typos, bad links, or other errors? See Chapter 7, "Write Clear User-Interface Text."
- **Link text.** Make sure that it's free of mistakes and that it gives site visitors the right idea about where they'll go if they click the link.

- **Brand, site, and product names.** Get these right, whether they're your own or another organization's. Protect your own or your company's trademarks by using them correctly. And remember that using someone else's trademarked name incorrectly can earn you a "cease and desist" letter or worse. For more on trademarks, see Chapter 18, "Understand the Basics of U.S. Law for Online Content."

T I P Headings and links, the pieces of page copy that are most likely to be read, can also boost your search rankings. Use the most relevant words in these areas, and make sure that they are correct in spelling and in fact. For tips on choosing keywords that can help with search engine optimization, see Chapter 17, "Optimize Your Site for Search Engines."

In an **email**, check these eye-catching points:

- The subject line
- Headings and subheadings
- Link text
- Brand, site, and product names
- The **From** field
- The **To** field
- The **Cc** and **Bcc** fields

Create and use a checklist

Make a list of specific areas or elements that you need to check before you publish a page or send an email newsletter. A checklist can prevent you from overlooking something. (Don't worry about putting together a comprehensive checklist the first time. Even an incomplete checklist is better than none.)

Some checklist guidelines:

- List the elements that you need to scrutinize, problems that tend to recur, terms that are often misspelled or misused.

- Include rules on your checklist. For example, list the elements that every story must include (title, byline, photo, minimum and maximum number of links), set rules for headlines (character count, capitalization style, punctuation style), or establish guidelines for email subject lines (character count, format, word order).

- Share the list with everyone on your team.

2. Formatting

Hasty cutting and pasting, coding problems, or trouble with a content feed can cause cutoff sentences and paragraphs.

In particular, watch for these types of **missing text or punctuation**:

- Missing periods or quotation marks at the end of a paragraph
- Missing sentences at the end of the page
- Footnote markers (such as asterisks) in the body of the text without corresponding footnotes; footnotes without corresponding markers in the body of the text

Common **coding mistakes** include:

- Mismatched fonts (for example, part of a story appearing in Arial, part in Courier).
- Missing HTML "close tags," which can cause errors such as an entire page or paragraph incorrectly appearing in boldface or italics or as an underlined link. To learn more about coding boldface or italics or about close tags, see Chapter 16, "Get Familiar With Basic Webpage Coding."

Example

Before
Coded text: The series began with <em>Outlander, first published in 1991.
Displayed text: The series began with *Outlander, first published in 1991.*

After
Coded text: The series began with <em>Outlander, </em> first published in 1991.
Displayed text: The series began with *Outlander,* first published in 1991.

- Dead or missing links or navigational elements.
- Incorrectly rendered characters (for example, *Guantánamo* displaying as *Guant□namo*). If you use **special characters** on your site, you will need to code them (see "Special characters" on page 386) and also **make sure that they will render correctly for every format and platform**: in a PDF file, an email, a Web browser, a cell phone browser, an RSS feed, and so on.

Design or layout problems include bad line breaks and spacing issues. One common example is text wrapping that causes a single word to appear by itself under an image while the rest of the paragraph sits above the image or to the side.

3. Potential legal issues

Be on the lookout for:

- Incorrect usage of brand names and trademarks. Be careful with other companies' trademarks.
- Copyright infringement. Assume that other people's photos, videos, artwork, and text are protected by copyright.
- Defamation and libel (basically, publishing false information about someone).

For more information on these topics, see Chapter 18.

TIP If you find factual errors or problems with legal issues in the proofreading stage, that's great—but it's also a little late. Potential legal problems and incorrect "facts" should ideally be caught earlier by the writer or an editor. Avoid this situation by ensuring that your organization's editorial process involves more than a single proofreading pass performed moments before content is scheduled to go live.

4. Consistency and accuracy

Check for errors in **proper names and titles**:

- Are names and titles spelled correctly? For example, is it *Elizabeth* or *Elisabeth*? *Jon* or *John*?
- Are they spelled and capitalized consistently throughout your page or piece? For instance, are you using *Kazakhstan* or the equally acceptable *Kazakstan*? Choose one and stick with it.
- Are they introduced and used in a clear way? For example, have you used the full name or title on first mention (*Water Resources Control Board President Josh Hartley* instead of just *Hartley; The Associated Press Stylebook* instead of *AP*)? Will the name and title be immediately understood by a reader who's skimming paragraphs and skipping from page to page?

Ensure consistency and accuracy in the **names of site elements** (such as buttons, links, site features, and processes) so that the site visitor understands and knows what to do. For example:

- Does an instruction say "Click the Submit button" but the button label is "Enter"?
- Do you refer to a feature as "Streaming Quotes" in one place and "Stock Ticker" in another?
- Do you refer to a process as "registration" in one place and "creating an account" in another?

Scrutinize **bulleted and numbered lists**:

- Do all bulleted or numbered items in a list begin and end the same way? For example, does each start with a capital or a lowercase letter? Does each end with punctuation, or without it?

■ Do bulleted points have parallel construction? For example, does each begin with the same part of speech—a noun, an imperative verb, or another part of speech? Are all bulleted points full sentences, or fragments? For more on parallel structure, see "Lists" on page 65 and "Parallelism: Matching, balancing, making sense" on page 341.

■ Does a top 10 list have 10 items?

■ Are the numbers in a numbered list in the correct sequence? (Someone reordering the list may have forgotten to update the numbers.)

■ Is an alphabetized list still in alphabetical order? (Someone editing the list may not have paid attention to the order.)

Look out for **inconsistent capitalization**. Make sure that all same-level headings have the same capitalization style: sentence case or title case. For a description of styles, see "Capitalization" on page 239.

Sniff out **bad math and wrong numbers**. These include:

■ Percentages that don't add up

■ Measurement units that don't make sense

Examples

Our study found that 37 percent of people were very bothered by people talking on a cell phone in a restaurant; 47 percent were mildly bothered; and 20 percent were not bothered. *(37 + 47 + 20 = 104 percent; percentages should add up to 100.)*

Butterfly bar soap: $8 (6 fl. oz.) *(Bar soap isn't fluid and shouldn't be measured in fluid ounces.)*

T I P   Several Web-based resources offer help on statistics, percentages, and other number-related topics that can give the average person trouble. See our online Resources page at http://styleguide.yahoo.com for links.

Find **instructions that don't work** by trying your own instructions (or at least by imagining yourself trying them). Doing so can help you notice common errors like:

■ Missing steps or information (for example, ingredients missing from a recipe).

■ Instructions that tell readers to do something they can't possibly do (for example, an instruction to click the **Save** button on a page that has no **Save** button).

Finally, look for any **errors of fact**. Don't assume the text is correct—if it seems doubtful, look into it.

Example

Before

In 2002 former President George W. Bush was honored at his 60th reunion at Phillips Academy.

After

In 2002 former President George H.W. Bush was honored at his 60th reunion at Phillips Academy.

5. Spelling, grammar, punctuation

Potential areas for mistakes in this category include **commonly misspelled words** (see "Frequently misspelled words" on page 331) and **words that people tend to use incorrectly** (see "Commonly confused words" on page 317). Pay attention also to these **common grammar traps**:

- **Subject-verb agreement.** If you're using a singular subject, match it with a singular verb and singular pronouns.

Example

Before

The company is announcing their fourth-quarter results.

After

The company is announcing its fourth-quarter results.

- **Parallel structure.** One example of parallel structure is starting each item in a list or series with the same part of speech—for instance, all imperative verbs: *I want you to **take** your feet off the cushions, **sit** up straight, and **quit** looking at me like that.* (To learn more about parallelism, see "Parallelism: Matching, balancing, making sense" on page 341.)

Example

Before

The candidate is rested, refreshed, and looks ready to lead. *(In this structure, "is" precedes each element set off by commas—two adjectives and one verb. The result: The sentence says that the candidate "is looks ready to lead.")*

After

The candidate is rested, refreshed, and ready to lead. *(Now all three items in the series are adjectives that can follow "is.")*

The candidate, rested and refreshed, looks ready to lead. *("Looks ready to lead" is no longer forced into the same series with the adjectives "rested" and "refreshed.")*

Common punctuation mistakes include:

- **Missing serial commas**; for more on the serial comma, see page 204.
- Incorrect or inconsistent **hyphenation**; for guidelines on hyphenating compounds, see "Hyphens" on page 216.
- **Unnecessary apostrophes** in plurals (like *the 1980's*), and in possessive adjectives like *its* and *your*.

Example

Before

Sadly, the product's warranty is it's most reliable feature. *(The word "it's" is a contraction of "it is.")*

After

Sadly, the product's warranty is its most reliable feature.

T I P When proofing copy, read contractions as if they were the words they stand for. For instance, read the previous example to yourself (silently or out loud): "The product's warranty is it is most reliable feature." You'll notice the error right away.

For other common errors, see Chapter 14, "Avoid Common Pitfalls in Word Choice, Grammar, and Spelling."

6. Images and video

Be sure to check **image alt text** for the following:

- Is alt text included and error-free? (Alt text, the image description you type into an image's **alt** attribute in the page's HTML code, helps people who can't see the image understand what it depicts. See "Alt text and image captions" on page 132.)
- Does the alt text accurately describe the image, using search keywords if possible?
- Does it describe the image in a way that will be helpful to visually impaired people using a screen reader to access your site?
- Do you need to include an attribution, or credit line, for the image (for example, if you got permission to use someone else's photo)?

With **image captions**, consider:

- Do they make sense with the image?
- Do you need to include an attribution for the image?

For **text accompanying video**, check for the following:

- Are video titles and closed captions accurate and error-free?
- Does your transcript or other video-related page copy accurately describe the video's content?
- Does your copy use keywords, which may help with search engine optimization?

For more on using keywords to aid search engine optimization, see Chapter 17.

7. Readability

Look for ways you can tighten text and increase clarity, particularly in the following areas. (For information on creating easy-to-scan text, see Chapter 1, "Write for the Web," and Chapter 4, "Construct Clear, Compelling Copy.")

- **Titles and headings.** Will a reader skimming *only* the headline and subheadings know what the story or page is about?
- **The top of the page.** Does the first paragraph contain the most important information? If the page is long, would it help the reader to insert a summary of its content or a brief list of its topics at the top?
- **Paragraphs and sentences.** Shorten anything you can. For tips on streamlining text, see Chapter 13, "Shorten and Strengthen Sentences."

Triage tips for online editors in a hurry

Web publishing tends to run at high speed, sometimes allotting mere minutes to proofread, test, and fact-check a story. Online editors must balance two important and sometimes contradictory goals: quality and speed. The following guidelines will help you prioritize.

1. Give priority to copy that:

- Has the **largest audience** (such as homepage copy).
- **Can't be corrected** later (such as email newsletters).
- Is otherwise important to **get exactly right** (such as legal documents, product fact sheets, or contracts).

2. Focus first on:

- The **most visible areas** of the page: browser **<title>** tags, headings and subheadings, link text, and areas the reader is most likely to scan. (See "Shape your text for online reading" on page 3.)
- **Formatting** errors: missing text or punctuation, coding mistakes (like incorrectly rendered characters), dead or missing links or navigation elements.
- Any potential **legal issues**: particularly trademark, copyright, or defamation issues (ideally, these should be caught earlier by the writer or editor). For information on these topics, see Chapter 18.

3. Read it through: If you ran through the first two steps quickly and have more time, go back and read the content for any remaining errors.

Pick up some proofreading tricks

Even professional proofreaders can't catch everything simply by reading straight through a piece of copy—so they've come up with a few tricks. These techniques force you to slow down and concentrate on every word, sentence, and punctuation mark. They help you see what's actually on the screen or the page, not what you expect to see there.

Use at least one of these techniques, or combine a few:

- **Print your page.** Reading a printout is a great tactic for spotting errors. You'll see the page and the words differently.
- **Wait.** When you've been staring at a piece for too long, you start to see what it's *supposed* to say, not what it *actually* says. Take a time-out. Get a cup of coffee or work on something else for a while to clear your head. It's ideal to let a longer piece sit overnight, but even 10 minutes can help you see your text with new eyes.

■ **Ask someone else to read your copy.** Having a second reader is one of the best ways to clarify and correct your copy. A new reader will be more likely to see mistakes and discrepancies and to point out anything confusing.

T I P Try the buddy system: Swap edits with a colleague.

■ **Read backward.** This technique is too time-consuming for most content. But it's great for proofreading numbers, and it's useful when you absolutely need to make sure that a piece of text is perfect: Your company name and slogan being immortalized in a logo, for instance, or the top headline on your homepage, or the subject line of an email newsletter being sent to thousands of subscribers.

■ **Read out loud.** Reading out loud—or using screen-reading software—will make you take in the words differently. This technique can be especially helpful for editing text with lots of numbers or unusual words. It's also a good way to check the "voice" of your piece and whether the text flows smoothly.

T I P Most operating systems include screen-reading software. For example, to see various accessibility tools in the Windows operating system (including a screen reader called Narrator), go to the **Start** menu and choose **All Programs** > **Accessories** > **Accessibility** (or **Ease of Access**, in Windows Vista). On the Mac, go to the Apple menu, then choose **System Preferences** > **Speech** > **Text-to-Speech**. For Ubuntu, you can run Orca, which gives you access to a screen reader: Press Alt+F2, type **orca**, and press Return.

■ **Read line by line, word by word.** This method forces you to look at each word, which can be helpful for complex or technical text. Some ideas:
  ◆ Print out your page and cover part of it so that only one line is revealed at a time.
  ◆ Touch each word with your pen (if you're using a printout) or, onscreen, point to each word with your cursor.

■ **Use a spell-checker.** Spell-checkers miss a lot of mistakes (see "Using a spell-checker is not enough" on page 355) and may not use the dictionary you prefer. But they're a sound first or last step, particularly if you're in a hurry or can't find a second reader. Some spell-checker tips:
  ◆ If your email program doesn't include a spell-checker, copy and paste email text into a word-processing document to check it.

◆   If you always misspell certain words, set up an automatic correction:

1.   In Microsoft Office Word 2007 for Windows, click the **Microsoft Office** button, **Word Options**, then **Proofing**. Click the **AutoCorrect Options** button.
2.   Check "Replace as you type."
3.   Enter the word as you typically misspell it, and then enter its properly spelled replacement.

(The process is similar in other versions of Microsoft Word.)

■   **Change the look.** In your browser, change the font size: In Microsoft Internet Explorer or Mozilla Firefox, go to the **View** menu to find text zoom options—or press Ctrl (or Command, on the Mac) and the plus sign (+) to increase the type, Ctrl (or Command) and the minus sign (the hyphen: -) to decrease it. When you're proofing text in a word processor, you can change the background color, the font size, or the text color:

◆   In Microsoft Office Word 2007 for Windows, go to the **Home** menu and locate the **Font** group (to change the font size or color) or the **Paragraph** group (to change the background color).

◆   In Microsoft Word for the Mac, go to the **Format** menu and choose **Font** (to change the font size or color) or choose **Borders and Shading** and the **Shading** tab (to change the background color).

Timesavers

Templates and boilerplates are great timesavers. Edit them once, and you'll save time fixing numerous errors over and over. But proof them anyway: Mistakes in templates and boilerplate copy can show up anytime you use them.

■   Create boilerplate text for frequently used copy, such as customer-service messages, help text, or contract clauses.

■   Create templates for email, newsletters, blogs, or story types.

Ideas in Practice

Exercise: Perfect your text before you publish

Proofread the following copy from fictional MemeTeam, looking for typos, missing or misused words, inconsistencies, and other errors. Read the copy at least twice, applying one or more of the proofreading techniques described on pages 364–366, and follow Yahoo! style. Try using a different color pen or pencil each time you go through so that you can see how much you missed in the previous rounds.

 To see our solution, turn to page 485.

10 tips for Bitter Blogging

By MemeTeam staff

The great thing about blogging is that anyone can do it. The lousey thing about blogging is that plenty of people *do* blog☐and many of them could write much more engaging posts only if they observed a few guidelines. Here are Meme Team's ten tips to creating a more frisky and focused blog.

1. Blog your passions. Write about topics that matter to you—and that matter to your audience, too. Nobody wants to here about your new electric toothbrush (unless it spontaneously combusted after an especially-vigorous scrubbing). When you write about subjects that you love (or hate), your more confident, your more likely to commit to blogging regularly, and readers will find your enthusiasm infectious.

2. Have an opinion; add value. Online infomation reproduces like rabbits, and readers have a lot of sites to choose. So, make *your* distinct voice and perspective a selling point: A fresh point of view inspires readers to share links to your site and to come back for more. And if you☐re blogging about some thing that lots of other writers are covering, then don't just regurgitate the facts-add something unique and valuable to teh post, whether it's extra information, a photo, your informed opinion, a sense of humor, or something else.

3. Converse.   Although a blog very much needs your point of view, it's not a monologue or your boring personal journal—it's a dialog with your readers. Let them in to the conversation by blogging about subjects they can relate to, by encouraging Comments, and buy cultivating a sense of community. (Tell us what you think of this blog by clicking the Feedback button at the end.

4. Set a Schedule. Establish an ambitious but reasonable frequency for posting stories, and stick to the time table. A number of factors will effect the frequency: how time sensitive your stories are, how often readers accept new material, how much content you can crank out, and so forth. Remember, though: quantity is not a substitute for quality.

6. Keep it short, sweet and neat. Readers come to blogs for a quick hit, not for War and Peace or 3000 words about how your cat spat a hairball onto your DVD's. Write about one solid topic per blog, try to keep your posts in the 200 to 300-word range, and organize information so that its easily skimmed.

5. Make your headline count. A good headline is short, full of keywords, and gives readers a sneak peak at the story. Write a brief, proper noun-loaded headline that will play nicely with engines, mobile browsers and news feeds. A catchy, clever headline will get clicks, but above all it should be clear—a person may not click if they see a stand-alone headline and can't tell what the story's about.

7. Link, link, link Blogging is about building community and sharing the love. A blogroll and related links give readers valueable context and shows that you have some expertise. Make sure that links exclude keywords for SEO.

8. Visuals. Add photos and videos to your posts. As the clich☐ says, a picture is worth a thousand words, and visual elements are a big benefit of Web features. Get permission to use material that's not your's, make sure that embedded videos form other sources will disappear, and don't forget alt text and captions.

9. An ounce of prevention. Readers will call you out—loudly if you post copy with typo's, bad links, or factual errors. Proofread your text, test your user interface and quickly correct any mistakes that slip though.

10. Be blog savvy. Learn from your peers: Check our blogs written by your readers and your competitors, as well as popular blogs (see <u>our picks) on subjects other than your own. You'll discover new widgets and writing strategies, and you might even find coverage gaps that your blog can fill.</u>

Comment

Resources

Chapter 16

Get Familiar With Basic Webpage Coding

In this chapter

- **HTML and XHTML.** How markup code makes the text and images on a webpage appear the way you want them to.
- **Boldface and italics.** When and how to use bold and italic type to enhance your content.
- **Special characters.** How to format ©, §, and other symbols you won't find on your keyboard.

As a content creator, you are primarily concerned with communicating. But you also need to consider how your words will appear onscreen: Errors in coding, formatting, or character rendering can make your message difficult to read or even obliterate it.

It's true that certain content-publishing applications, such as many blogging tools, require minimal—or no—knowledge of HTML. And depending on the technical setup of your site, you may not need to insert HTML into your text. Many sites also use Cascading Style Sheets (CSS), which may reduce the amount of HTML required.

But it's hard to escape coding completely. Online editors sometimes need to make edits to an already built webpage, or to write alt-text descriptions (see page 132) on the fly for images. Fortunately, you don't need to be a programmer to understand some basics about tags and coding.

HTML and XHTML

HTML is a series of instructions (code) that tell webpage-viewing tools like browsers how to render your page. HTML tells Web browsers where to place graphics, which typeface and color the text should be, how to lay out columns, which page a link should take the user to when the link is clicked, and so on.

Most webpages are built using HTML, which stands for *Hypertext Markup Language*. The HTML "marks up" the textual and graphical content of a page, using devices such as "tags" to tell a browser how to display the content.

Example

Text marked up with HTML
Do <strong>not</strong> use the Housekeeper 3000 robot for this purpose.

Text as the browser displays it
Do **not** use the Housekeeper 3000 robot for this purpose.
*(The **<strong>** tag instructs the browser to place emphasis on the word "not"; usually the word will appear in boldface type. A "voice browser," or screen reader, may use a different tone when reading "not.")*

Anatomy of a webpage

You can see the HTML "instructions" for any webpage by looking at the page's source code. For example, in Mozilla Firefox 3.0, go to the webpage you want to examine, click the **View** menu, and choose **Page Source**. You will see a daunting pageful of code. But once you know what to look for, you may be surprised at how easy it is to understand.

Tags tell the browser what to do. The page probably has at or near the top an "open tag" that looks like this: **<html>**. That tag tells the browser, "Start interpreting HTML now, and don't stop until you get a command to stop interpreting HTML."

Now scroll to the bottom of all that code. At or near the end of the page you'll see a "close tag" that looks like this: **</html>**. It tells the browser, "Stop interpreting HTML now." A close tag has a forward slash (/) after the opening angle bracket (<) but otherwise matches its corresponding open tag.

Examples of common tags include:

Open tag	Close tag	Effect
<h1>	</h1>	Text between these tags appears as a top-level headline.
<em>	</em>	Text between these tags is emphasized and usually appears in italics.
<strong>	</strong>	Text between these tags is strongly emphasized and usually appears in boldface.

Although much of HTML works on the "open tag, close tag" principle, a few open tags don't have corresponding close tags. For example, the line-break tag **
** has none. However, XHTML does require a close tag for every open tag—even for tags such as **\
**. So, for tags that in HTML have no close tag, a person using XHTML must add a space and a slash so that the tag will "self-close."

Example

In HTML
Ring around the rosy,\
A pocket full of posies;\

In XHTML
Ring around the rosy,\
A pocket full of posies;\

The following example shows some simple HTML in action.

Example

```
<html>
<head>
<title>This Is the Text That Appears in a Browser's Title Bar</title>
<meta name="description" content="This page illustrates some basic HTML
markup in action. (This description may appear, along with the title
above, in search results listings.)">
</head>

<body>
<h1>This is a top-level heading, or headline</h1>
<p>This is the first paragraph appearing under the headline.</p>
<p>This is another paragraph, with <strong>this part of it in boldface
type.</strong></p>
<p>This is another paragraph, with <em>this part in italic.</em></p>

<h2>This is a secondary heading</h2>
<p>This is a paragraph that includes a link to
<a href="http://www.yahoo.com/">the Yahoo! homepage</a>. (When this
page is displayed, "the Yahoo! homepage" will be clickable and will
link to Yahoo!.)</p>
<p>This is a paragraph introducing a block quotation that has forced
line breaks at the end of each line:</p>

<blockquote>Let's say your block quote is a poem<br>
One with short lines, so short<br>
```

You need line-break tags to break them.</blockquote>

This code is creating a bulleted (unnumbered) list:
<ul>
<li>First bullet point</li>
<li>Second bullet point</li>
<li>Third bullet point</li>
</ul>

This code is creating a numbered list:
<ol>
<li>First item in the list</li>
<li>Second item in the list</li>
<li>Third item in the list</li>
</ol>

<h3>This is a tertiary heading</h3>
<p>Here is a paragraph to tell you that the code below is for an image. The image source tag (img src) tells the browser where on your computer or on the Web to find the image in order to display it; the width and height numbers tell the browser how big a space the picture will require on the page, and the alt text is there to fill the space in case the image doesn't appear (the alt text will also be read by screen-reading software used by people who can't see images).</p>

<img src="picture.jpg" width="534" height="800" alt="This is the alt text that appears if the image doesn't load.">

<p>This is the last paragraph on the page. So, following the end paragraph tag are a close tag to tell the browser that this is the end of the "body" of the page and then a close tag to tell the browser that this is the end of this HTML page altogether.</p>
</body>
</html>

———————

A screenshot showing how the sample HTML page appears in a Firefox browser

How to mark up copy

Following is a quick primer on how to format some basic elements in HTML. But before you incorporate any tags into your copy, check with your site administrator or producer to find out which tags your content-publishing system requires.

What are Cascading Style Sheets?

Cascading Style Sheets (CSS) specifications simplify webpage design. With CSS, site designers can specify the layout, fonts, background color, and other visual aspects of a webpage by embedding blocks of style information in the webpage's source code or by linking the webpage to a *style sheet,* which is a separate document containing instructions about the webpage's appearance. When designers embed style information in a webpage's code or when they link that webpage to a style sheet, they are essentially telling browsers such as Mozilla Firefox and Microsoft Internet Explorer to refer to that style information or style sheet when they display the webpage. Style sheets are especially handy if you have multiple pages that look alike—they can all link to the same style sheet. Then, if you want to change the appearance of those pages (change the background color from blue to pink, for instance), all you need to do is adjust the one style sheet that they are all linked to.

T I P To comply with XHTML rules, lowercase the tags: Use **<strong>**, not **<STRONG>**. In addition, if multiple tags apply to one piece of text, the tags must be properly "nested" inside each other: If an open tag begins inside another set of tags, that tag must also end inside that other set of tags. For example, here an **<em>** tag begins inside a set of **<p>** tags, so it must also end inside the set of **<p>** tags: *<p>This sentence with one word <em>emphasized</em></p> is correctly nested. <p>This sentence with one word <em>emphasized</p></em> is not correctly nested.*

Paragraphs and line breaks

Insert a **<p>** tag when you want to begin a new paragraph. The closing **</p>** tag is required in XHTML, and it doesn't hurt to use it in HTML—so you might as well use it.

Example

<p>Tuscany, schmuscany. If you're looking for simple yet flavorful, rustic yet sophisticated Italian cuisine with a focus on fresh ingredients, try a taste of Sicily.</p>

<p>Invaded time and again by a procession of settlers and conquerors, the island of Sicily has been fought over and occupied by Phoenicians, Greeks, Romans, Arabs, Berbers, Spanish Muslims, and Normans, not to mention Barbarians and Vandals. The legacy of this tortuous history is a cuisine rich in delicious diversity.</p>

To force a line to break at a particular point, insert a **
** tag. But use a self-closing **
** tag if your website uses XHTML.

Example

HTML
Shall I compare thee to a summer's day?
Thou art more lovely and more temperate.

XHTML
Shall I compare thee to a summer's day?
Thou art more lovely and more temperate.

Links

To create a link to another page on your site or to a page on another site, use the "hyperlink reference" or "href" anchor tag (the *a* at the beginning and end of the code stands for *anchor*): *<a href="URL goes here">Text to be linked goes here</a>*.

T I P Notice the quotation marks around the URL: It's important to put the name of the URL in quotes, but make sure they're straight quotes (" "), not smart ones (" "). Never use smart (also called curly) quotes in code.

Example

Marked-up text
Learn how to make Sicilian specialties in your own kitchen, including savory
<a href="siteURL/street-snacks">street snacks</a>, <a href="siteURL
/palermoseafood">Palermo-style seafood</a>, and irresistible <a href="siteURL
/siciliandesserts">desserts</a> such as cannoli.

Displayed text
Learn how to make Sicilian specialties in your own kitchen, including savory
<u>street snacks</u>, <u>Palermo-style seafood</u>, and irresistible <u>desserts</u> such as cannoli.

Bulleted and numbered lists

To create a **bulleted list** (or unnumbered list, which is what the *ul* in the code stands for), use the following code:

```
<ul>
<li>First bullet point</li>
<li>Second bullet point</li>
<li>Third bullet point</li>
</ul>
```

TIP It may help to remember that *li* stands for *list item.*

• First bullet point
• Second bullet point
• Third bullet point

A screenshot showing how the bulleted list example appears in a browser

To create a **numbered list** (or ordered list, which is what the *ol* stands for), use this code:

```
<ol>
<li>First item in the list</li>
<li>Second item in the list</li>
<li>Third item in the list</li>
</ol>
```

1. First item in the list
2. Second item in the list
3. Third item in the list

A screenshot showing how the numbered list example appears in a browser

Block quotation

Sometimes you may want to display text—a long quote, for example—as an indented "extract," or "block text." Use the **<blockquote>** tag around the text you want indented.

Example

```
<p>In this passage from what is perhaps her best-known book, Jane Austen's
writing shines:</p>
```

<blockquote>More than once did Elizabeth, in her ramble within the park, unexpectedly meet Mr. Darcy. She felt all the perverseness of the mischance that should bring him where no one else was brought, and, to prevent its ever happening again, took care to inform him at first that it was a favourite haunt of hers. How it could occur a second time, therefore, was very odd!</blockquote>

In this passage from what is perhaps her best-known book, Jane Austen's writing shines:

More than once did Elizabeth, in her ramble within the park, unexpectedly meet Mr. Darcy. She felt all the perverseness of the mischance that should bring him where no one else was brought, and, to prevent its ever happening again, took care to inform him at first that it was a favourite haunt of hers. How it could occur a second time, therefore, was very odd!

A screenshot showing how the block quotation example appears in a browser

HTML and XHTML quick-reference guide

To add	Use
strongly emphasized text (usually appears as boldface)	Text goes here
emphasized text (usually appears as italic text)	Text goes here
top-level heading	<h1>Heading goes here</h1>
second-level heading	<h2>Heading goes here</h2>
third-level heading	<h3>Heading goes here</h3>
paragraph break	<p>Paragraph goes here</p>
line break (HTML)	Text goes here
line break (XHTML)	Text goes here
indented text	<blockquote>Text goes here</blockquote>
linked text	<a href="URL goes here">Text goes here</a>
image with alt text (HTML)	<img src="Location of image file goes here" width="Number of pixels wide" height="Number of pixels high" alt="Alt text goes here">
image with alt text (XHTML)	<img src="Location of image file goes here" width="Number of pixels wide" height="Number of pixels high" alt="Alt text goes here" />

To add	Use
bulleted list	<ul> <li>First list item goes here</li> <li>Second list item goes here</li> <li>Third list item goes here</li> </ul>
numbered list	<ol> <li>First list item goes here</li> <li>Second list item goes here</li> <li>Third list item goes here</li> </ol>

Some online-publishing tools are so simple that you can post a blog without ever encountering an angle bracket. Still, learning even a smidgeon of basic HTML will give you a lot of control over your content. You can ensure that the text follows your style rules (for italics or quotation marks, for instance), and you can find formatting bugs when you view a page's source code.

When things go wrong on a webpage

If computer software does not receive specific instructions delivered in a specific way, it may not work. A mistake in a webpage's source code can cause problems in how the page is displayed.

Example

Before

Text marked up with HTML:

View our <a href="http://careers.yahoo.com/">job openings/a> to find your perfect job.

Text displayed in browser:

View our job openings/a> to find your perfect job. *(Because the close tag is not complete, the browser doesn't get the message to stop turning text into a link. It also displays the erroneous tag, not understanding that **/a>** was meant to be invisible code, not text to display.)*

After

Text marked up with HTML:

View our <a href="http://careers.yahoo.com/">job openings</a> to find your perfect job.

Text displayed in browser:

View our <u>job openings</u> to find your perfect job. *(The properly constructed close tag **</a>** effectively tells the browser to stop displaying text as a link.)*

Display problems can also occur if the browser or other Web-viewing tool doesn't have the capability or the information it needs to interpret your webpage's characters.

The XYZs of HTML, XML, and other webpage-building technologies

The World Wide Web Consortium (W3C) sets standards for the use of HTML and other webpage-building technologies. Ideally, all pages on the Internet use the same types of instructions, and all browsers, email clients, content management systems, and other tools are programmed to interpret those instructions correctly. In practice, of course, standards are not always followed, resulting in display problems. What's more, standards are continually being updated, and website builders need to use the latest technologies to ensure that future tools can display their pages.

HTML, XHTML, and XML: Some websites today go beyond HTML and use XHTML, a reformulation of HTML that is designed to work with XML. XML is a markup language that some developers expect to eventually replace HTML because of its flexibility and other technical advantages for developers. By using XHTML instead of HTML, developers can prepare for the future: A step between HTML and XML, XHTML was developed to ensure that webpages using it would still work on browsers designed to read HTML and would also work with XML tools.

But wait: At this writing, some organizations that shifted to XHTML have grown disillusioned and moved back to HTML again . . . as we said, standards are continually being updated. Luckily, the differences between HTML and XHTML are not that numerous—nor are they hard to grasp. This chapter focuses on HTML but also offers some tips for understanding XHTML.

Typography and special characters: Setting standards for the World Wide Web and implementing them is a monumental work in progress. Some elements of webpage design and typography are still unsettled—and are therefore not guaranteed to show up correctly in all situations. In particular, Web writers and editors should carefully consider whether to use typographical styles such as boldface and italics, and special characters such as em dashes (—), smart quotes (" "), case fractions ($\frac{1}{2}$), and accented letters (á, é, ç). See Chapter 10, "Punctuate Proficiently," to learn more about using em dashes, en dashes, and other special characters, and see "Special characters" on page 386 for the right way to insert them in your copy.

Text you want to display
"Look at my smart quotes!" she said proudly.

Text that appears instead
â€œLook at my smart quotes!â€☐ she said proudly.

The rest of this chapter contains information that will help you avoid or fix these kinds of display problems.

Boldface and italics

Boldface, **italics**, and **underlining** all change the appearance of text, but not all are suitable for online reading. Too much italic type, for example, is hard to read. And the overuse of boldface for emphasis creates the opposite effect—the reader can't tell what's important.

Consider the following guidelines when deciding when (or whether) to use typographical styles such as boldface and italics to enhance online text:

- If you decide to use boldface and italics, **use them sparingly**. The test should always be whether or not they enhance understanding.
- Always **test whether typographical styles will be displayed correctly** in their intended destination: in a PDF file, in an email, in a cell phone browser, in a feed, and so on. One place they may not show up correctly is in a plain-text (non-HTML) email.
- **Don't combine bold and italic** fonts to increase emphasis—the result is akin to shouting.

Before
Sign up *now* for a free account!

After
Sign up *now* for a free account!
Sign up **now** for a free account!

- To ensure consistency, **record your decisions about where you will and won't use boldface and italics.** (For information on creating a style guide that will include such decisions, see Chapter 19, "Keep a Word List.")

Boldface

Boldfaced text can be effective when used:

- **To visually emphasize a word or concept.**
- **For headlines and subheads**, to make the page easy to scan.
- **To distinguish button names and other user-interface elements from the surrounding text**, such as the name of a webpage button from instructions on how to sign up for a newsletter. (For more information on the visual treatment of such elements—including help with deciding whether to use boldface, quotation marks, or no special visual treatment at all—see "User-instruction mechanics" on page 144.)
- **For a warning message** or other text that's crucial for the reader to see. (Judicious use of ALL UPPERCASE is an acceptable alternative to bold type for this purpose in plain-text emails and newsletters.)

T I P Boldfaced text also plays an important role in search engine optimization (SEO), so if you use it, use it wisely. To learn more about SEO, see Chapter 17, "Optimize Your Site for Search Engines."

Italics

Italic text can be effective when used:

- **To emphasize** a single word or phrase. (An alternative for plain-text emails and cases where italic text may not appear correctly: *asterisks* flanking the word.)

Example

If you can use italics
It was supposed to say "Thou shalt *not* commit adultery," not "Thou *shalt* commit adultery"!

If you cannot use italics
It was supposed to say "Thou shalt *not* commit adultery," not "Thou *shalt* commit adultery"!

- **For titles of works** such as artwork, books, films, TV shows, and CDs. However, we generally recommend using quotation marks for these online, because such titles occasionally appear in headlines, which show up in RSS feeds. (Italic text may not appear correctly in an RSS feed.) For more information, see "Titles of works" on page 251.

- **For letters referred to as letters, and words referred to as words:** the letter *B*, the word *robot*. However, we generally recommend quotation marks for these in online copy; a single italicized letter can be hard to read onscreen. See "Quotation marks" on page 224.
- **For foreign words** that are not in your dictionary. Quotation marks are an acceptable alternative.

Examples

Dinner, if you can call it that, consisted of hors d'oeuvres—light hors d'oeuvres, at that. *(The French term "hors d'oeuvre" needs no special visual treatment; it is common enough to appear in English dictionaries.)*

On September 16, Mexicans celebrate the overthrow of the *gachupines,* Mexican-born Spanish rulers who exploited the people for generations. *(Use italic type if you know it will be displayed correctly.)*

On September 16, Mexicans celebrate the overthrow of the "gachupines," Mexican-born Spanish rulers who exploited the people for generations. *(Use quotation marks if you aren't sure that italic type will be displayed correctly everywhere the content may appear.)*

TIP Italic text **may not appear properly in RSS feeds**, email, and other areas. If your content might end up there, it's safer to use quotation marks in place of italics. But watch out: Placing quotation marks around a word can cause the reader to think that you are using the word in an ironic way: *You can order a bottle of "air putih" (clean water) from any restaurant in Bali.*

How to make text appear bold or italic

The **<strong>** tag usually makes text appear in **boldface**.

Example

Text marked up in HTML
Be sure to <strong>read the installation instructions</strong> before clicking the <strong>Download Now</strong> button and installing the software on your computer.

Don't underline online

The rule for when to underline is simple: **Don't underline**. Online readers automatically think that underlined words are links, so using this typographical device for other purposes may cause confusion.

Example

My book report on <u>Johnny Got His Gun</u> made a lot of people want to read that book. *(Online readers will expect "Johnny Got His Gun" to be a clickable link leading them to a page about this book; if it isn't, they'll be confused and irritated.)*

Text as a browser displays it

Be sure to **read the installation instructions** before clicking the **Download Now** button and installing the software on your computer.

The **\<em>** tag usually makes text appear in **italics**.

Example

Text marked up in HTML

Students were asked to create a Facebook page for the \<em>Catcher in the Rye \</em> character Holden Caulfield. Interest in the assignment was unprecedented, with \<em>all 30 students\</em> participating.

Text as a browser displays it

Students were asked to create a Facebook page for the *Catcher in the Rye* character Holden Caulfield. Interest in the assignment was unprecedented, with *all 30 students* participating.

Check with your website designer or site producer to learn your site's preferred method for applying boldface or italics to online text. Many websites use Cascading Style Sheets (CSS) instead of HTML to apply these typographical styles. (For more on CSS, see "What are Cascading Style Sheets?" on page 376.)

Special characters

Special characters are the ones that weren't included on the original QWERTY keyboard back when typewriters were the way people generated copy. They include everything from punctuation like the formatted em dash (—) and smart quotes ("") to symbols like © and ® and accented letters like ñ and ó. They also include dingbat symbols like hearts (♥) and arrows (→). **Not all software renders special characters correctly**, so you may be wise to avoid using them in online or email documents.

If you do use special characters online, **follow these guidelines**:

- **Don't copy and paste into your webpage special characters that your word processor has created.** This method of inserting special characters is the most likely to result in display problems.
- **Ask your website's designer or technical staff** whether your content management system supports special characters. If it does, then ask the right way to code characters for *that* system, since there are various markup options. For instance, you can code a copyright symbol (©) by using its character entity reference (which is *©*) or by using one of two types of numeric character references (the decimal form *©* or the hexadecimal form *©*).
- **Run a test before you publish.** Make sure that any special characters you use will be displayed correctly in a browser, in an RSS feed, in a text message, or anywhere else your copy might appear. Special characters have been known to appear incorrectly in RSS feeds, text messages, and email messages in particular.

T I P   Disable your word processor's tendency to format smart quotes, em dashes, en dashes, ellipsis points, ordinal numbers with superscript, and fractions. For example, in Microsoft Office Word 2007 for Windows, click the **Microsoft Office** button, then **Word Options > Proofing**. Click **AutoCorrect Options**. On the **AutoFormat** and **AutoFormat As You Type** tabs, uncheck the appropriate boxes. The process is similar in other versions of Word.

How to include special characters in your online content

To insert special characters, **type the code for each character into the text where you want the character to appear**.

Examples

Coded text: Text © Jo March. All rights reserved. *(Character entity reference used for the copyright symbol)*

Displayed text: Text © Jo March. All rights reserved.

Coded text: Text © Jo March. All rights reserved. *(Hexadecimal numeric reference used for the copyright symbol)*

Displayed text: Text © Jo March. All rights reserved.

Coded text: “You don’t mean…” Her voice trailed off. *(Character entity references used for smart quotes, an apostrophe, and an ellipsis character)*

Displayed text: "You don't mean…" Her voice trailed off.

Coded text: “You don’t mean…” Her voice trailed off. *(Decimal numeric references used for smart quotes, an apostrophe, and an ellipsis character)*

Displayed text: "You don't mean…" Her voice trailed off.

The following table shows three different **ways to code the common special characters and symbols** listed in the left column.

T I P   Although all these coding styles (and more!) are in use, decimal numeric character references may be more commonly used and tend to be well-supported—that is, browsers and other software tend to be able to read them if they can read special characters at all. But check with your site administrator or technical staff to find out which is the best option for your site.

Character	Entity	Decimal numeric	Hexadecimal numeric
em dash (—)	&mdash;	&#8212;	&#x2014;
en dash (–)	&ndash;	&#8211;	&#x2013;
single opening quote (')	&lsquo;	&#8216;	&#x2018;
single closing quote (')	&rsquo;	&#8217;	&#x2019;
double opening quote (")	&ldquo;	&#8220;	&#x201C;
double closing quote (")	&rdquo;	&#8221;	&#x201D;

Character	Entity	Decimal numeric	Hexadecimal numeric
ellipsis character (…)	&hellip;	&#8230;	&#x2026;
nonbreaking space			
inverted question mark (¿)	&iquest;	&#191;	&#xBF;
case fraction: one quarter (¼)	&frac14;	&#188;	&#xBC;
case fraction: one half (½)	&frac12;	&#189;	&#xBD;
case fraction: three quarters (¾)	&frac34;	&#190;	&#xBE;
superscript: two (²)	&sup2;	&#178;	&#xB2;
superscript: three (³)	&sup3;	&#179;	&#xB3;
copyright symbol (©)	&copy;	&#169;	&#xA9;
registered trademark symbol (®)	&reg;	&#174;	&#xAE;
unregistered trademark symbol (™)	&trade;	&#8482;	&#x2122;
degree symbol (°)	&deg;	&#176;	&#xB0;
currency symbol: euro (€)	&euro;	&#8364;	&#x20AC;
currency symbol: pound (£)	&pound;	&#163;	&#xA3;
currency symbol: yen (¥)	&yen;	&#165;	&#xA5;
section sign (§)	&sect;	&#167;	&#xA7;
small a with accent grave (à)	&agrave;	&#224;	&#xE0;
small a with accent acute (á)	&aacute;	&#225;	&#xE1;
small a with umlaut (ä)	&auml;	&#228;	&#xE4;
small c with cedilla (ç)	&ccedil;	&#231;	&#xE7;
small e with accent grave (è)	&egrave;	&#232;	&#xE8;
small e with accent acute (é)	&eacute;	&#233;	&#xE9;
small e with umlaut (ë)	&euml;	&#235;	&#xEB;
small i with accent grave (ì)	&igrave;	&#236;	&#xEC;
small i with accent acute (í)	&iacute;	&#237;	&#xED;
small i with circumflex (î)	&icirc;	&#238;	&#xEE;
small i with umlaut (ï)	&iuml;	&#239;	&#xEF;
small n with tilde (ñ)	&ntilde;	&#241;	&#xF1;
small o with accent grave (ò)	&ograve;	&#242;	&#xF2;
small o with accent acute (ó)	&oacute;	&#243;	&#xF3;
small o with umlaut (ö)	&ouml;	&#246;	&#xF6;
small u with accent grave (ù)	&ugrave;	&#249;	&#xF9;
small u with accent acute (ú)	&uacute;	&#250;	&#xFA;
small u with umlaut (ü)	&uuml;	&#252;	&#xFC;

TIP   To find codes for characters not listed here, search for "character reference" at www.w3.org.

Ideas in Practice

Exercise: Crack the code

The sample copy below should appear exactly the same on a webpage. Insert the HTML codes that would create this look: headings, lists, boldface, special characters, and so forth. But don't worry about the **<html>**, **<title>**, **<head>**, and **<body>** tags—assume you are working on content within the body of the page.

How much code do you need to plug in? In real life, your webmaster can tell you. For instance, you may not need to enter paragraph breaks, and it may be better to make an em dash with two hyphens (--) rather than with code (—). For our purposes, however, assume you'll need to do just about everything.

To see our solution, turn to page 488.

How to invent a stupid band name

You've been racking your brains for a band name that will express your singular musical genius, and you've come up with ... zilch. Never fear, we can help you come up with something stupid in five minutes or less. And let's face it: You probably won't invent anything sillier than the average boy-band moniker.

Step 1: Make a list of words

Pop-culture references are good, and so are unusual words, but don't spend more than a minute or two on this step—just jot down whatever pops into your head. These categories often yield fruitful results:

Animals and mythical creatures
Natural disasters

Children's book title or character
Interjections (*oh, wow, shh, hooray*)
Colors
Song lyrics
Name or nickname of a person you like
Character in a cult movie
Hairstyles
Fruit
Moods
Auto parts

Step 2: Mix and match

Now combine two or more of your words. Puns can work (we are aiming for stupid, after all), and so can counterintuitive pairings. Those two things don't belong together? All the better. We coughed up these 10 dorky concoctions in about 60 seconds:

Centaur Mullets
Goodnight Loon
Night of the Living Jed
The Recalcitrant Kiwis
Spicoli and the Custom Vans
Cyclone Clutch
Sid Capricious
Helen and the Heck Yeahs
Napoleon Pillow Fight
Ice-T Phone Home

Step 3: Search and deploy

Consult your bandmates—if you really care what the drummer thinks—to narrow down the list. Go to a search engine and search on each name, in quotes ("Centaur Mullets"). If you're serious about using the name, then also search a trademark database (in the U.S.: www.uspto.gov) and consider registering your name to protect it. Don't see any other bands using the name? Then congratulations, you can now set up a homepage, start printing T-shirts, and maybe think about actually recording some songs.

Related links:

How to write stupid lyrics

How to record your stupid demo

Sponsored link:

Buy rock 'n' roll baby clothes at Bootleg Bäby

Chapter 17

Optimize Your Site for Search Engines

In this chapter

- **SEO basics.** Techniques that help search engines find your site.
- **Copywriting for SEO.** Four steps for adding search terms to website copy.
- **Images and video.** SEO can help people find all kinds of files.

Is your copy playing hard to get? Coyness can seem charming, but it can also prevent readers from discovering your pages via search engines.

Newsletters, advertising, and other marketing efforts are all good avenues for promoting your website. But chances are that most people who discover your site will do so through a search engine. To make sure that search engines will find your site—and rank it high on their lists—your site's copy should be appealing, relevant, and understandable not only to your audience but also to search engines. The time that you invest in optimizing your pages for search can have a big payoff in the number of readers attracted to your site.

SEO, short for *search engine optimization,* refers to numerous **techniques you can use to raise your website's ranking in search engine results**. *Ranking* refers to a website's position in a list of search results—the goal is to appear in the first 10 results. Applied with some thought, SEO can help your site compete more effectively.

 ### What does *optimize* mean in SEO?

To optimize a *website* means to design it, code it, and write for it in a way that makes search engines rank it high. To optimize a *webpage* for a particular keyword means to strategically weave that keyword into the text. To optimize an *image* for search engines means to describe it with keyword-rich alt text (see "Images and video" on page 412) and to use other SEO techniques.

SEO basics

Search engines help connect Internet users with the information they're seeking. **Here's how search engines work:**

Search engines analyze the words on webpages, especially words that are repeated or otherwise called out: in boldface, in a headline, in a link, and so on. The engine records those important words and phrases—the page's *keywords*—on its servers.

When you type the words you're looking for into a search box, the engine tries to match your words with the words from webpages it has analyzed, and it then delivers a list of matches. **The engine organizes that list from best to worst**, ranking the results according to a variety of criteria (such as how many other sites find a page valuable and link to it).

People usually click the links on the first page of results, so **sites at the top of the list are more likely to get visitors**. And more visitors can mean more page views, more leads, more sales, more ad revenue, and other business benefits.

A search result showing the top two sites returned when we searched on "yahoo finance"

A number of SEO techniques exist to give sites an advantage in this ranking, and many of these apply to Web design. But as a content creator, your best SEO techniques are (1) to write information-rich copy that people will want to read and link to and (2) to figure out which words people are likely to use in searches, and then embed those keywords throughout your copy. This chapter explains how to do just that.

SEO copywriting is about using the exact terms that people are searching on so that it's completely obvious what your page or article is about. SEO copywriting is not about trying to trick search engines by stuffing content with unrelated keywords or with so many keywords that the copy sounds silly. **Good**

SEO copywriting makes your page more readable for both search engines *and* humans. It helps your website attract visitors, but it also helps your visitors find substantial, relevant content.

Best practices in brief

SEO is competitive: There's no guarantee that you'll be able to get your site on a first page of search results. But as a content creator, **you can help bump up your site's ranking just by optimizing the text and links**.

Here are the **basic principles of good SEO for writers and editors**:

- Offer original content with genuine value and relevance to your readers.
- Strategically seed your copy with keywords that describe your content and that correspond with the phrases people are using to perform their searches.
- Embed keywords where they matter most: in the title, headings, links, metadata (part of your page's source code—see page 410), and image and video tags.
- Make every page of your site unique: In addition to original content, each page should have its own topic, title, and page-specific keywords (though you can use the highest-volume keywords throughout your site—see "Keyword selection strategies" on page 401 for more information).
- Deliver on the promise of your keywords: Don't lure people to your site with words that don't accurately represent your content.
- Link to other relevant sites, and encourage those sites to link to yours. (See "Step 3: Incorporate links" on page 407 for ideas.)
- Optimize your site for people first—through clear, concise writing—and for search engines second. Implement SEO without turning your text into nonsense.

TIP All the SEO copywriting skill in the world won't help your site if a search engine can't read it. This is the case with text saved as an image: The image looks like a blank portion of the page to a search engine. Avoid saving text as an image.

How search engines read a webpage

Even though people and search engines scan webpages differently, there are some similarities:

- **Page title.** Both people and search engines need to know at a glance what a page is about. The page title, sometimes called the **<title>** tag, is inserted in the code of a webpage. You'll see it in the top bar of a Web browser, as in the following example.

Example

*The **<title>** tag for this page is "The top news headlines on current events from Yahoo! News."*

See "Anatomy of a webpage" on page 372 for examples of other HTML tags, both in page code and as they will appear in a browser.

- **Headlines, emphasized words, and lists.** Both people and search engines know that anything called out in headlines or subheadings, in boldface or italics, or in bulleted lists is likely to be important. Make sure headings, links, and lists in your Web copy are called out with HTML tags (see "Code your text to attract search engines" on page 406).
- **Introduction and conclusion.** Readers will scan your opening paragraph or your summary for quick information. And search engines, to understand what the subject of a page is, look for keywords throughout that page, including at the top (the introduction) and the bottom (the conclusion). But don't just shove keywords into the top or the bottom of your page—distribute them evenly throughout.
- **Related links.** Humans appreciate options for more information. Search engines, too, like to see that you've linked to other websites and that other websites have linked to yours.

Search engines and people both like:

- **Verbosity.** In the search engine world, *verbosity* means substantial, relevant, original content. Do fill your page with words, but write succinctly: Make sure that every word you write is relevant to your audience and to the topic you're addressing.
- **Good writing.** To a search engine, good writing means using variations of your keywords, including those with different endings. For example, if you are targeting the phrase *job interview,* use the singular, plural, *-ing,* and *-ed* forms, such as *job interviews* and *job interviewing.*

Search engines and people both dislike:

- **Bad writing.** Search engines are more likely to penalize your website when you stuff your copy with unrelated keywords, strand a list of keywords at the bottom of your page, and rely *too* much on headlines and links. Your entire page should be relevant: Like a muffin with the right amount of blueberries, it should have juicy keywords distributed evenly throughout, but not so many that they overwhelm the whole.

■ **Broken links.** Search engines want to provide a great experience for their customers by directing them to a useful and informative website that works properly. Broken links tell people *and* search engines that a site is poorly maintained and will give people a bad experience.

Copywriting for SEO

To optimize webpages for search, follow these basic steps, drawn from "The Four Steps for Copywriting for SEO," part of the In-house SEO Implementation Program provided by SEOinhouse.com:

1. Select the best keywords.
2. Add keywords to your page copy.
3. Incorporate links.
4. Use keywords in page titles and metatags.

Step 1: Select the best keywords

The best keywords for your site are the ones most relevant to and popular with your target audience— the words and phrases they are most likely to type into search boxes.

Selecting the right keywords is vital to your site's success. The competition is fierce: Using the same keyword phrase, thousands of pages are competing for a high rank, yet only 10 or so will appear on the first page of the search results.

Figuring out which words are *your* keywords takes time and care, but it's a crucial first step—it's so important that some sites hire SEO specialists to determine the best keywords. If you have the budget, hiring a specialist can be a good investment for your site. If you don't have that luxury, you will be responsible for selecting the keywords for each page that you create.

Keep in mind that:

■ **Small variations in words can make a big difference in search rankings.** For instance, if you write for a technology site, you might use *notebook* and *laptop* interchangeably. But keyword research will quickly show you that far more people search on *laptop,* making it a superior keyword.

■ **Search engines are literal.** They look for *exact matches* of keywords. If your site is optimized for the keyword *mahogany desk* but people are searching on *wood desk,* search engines probably won't recognize your page as relevant to those searches and will give it a lower rank. The only exact match for *wood desk* is *wood desk*.

■ **The best key*words* are actually multiword *phrases.*** In fact, an increasing number of keywords entered in search engines in the U.S. comprise three words, four words, even five or more

---

Search engine secrets: Looking for No. 1

What do search engines consider when picking which site ranks No. 1? Too many things to list here!

A search engine may evaluate more than 200 elements in determining page rank, including what content is on the page, how many links it has, which other sites are linking to it, what the sites linking to it are about and what their quality is, and how old the site is. This complex, constantly fluctuating process involves formulas on top of formulas, as well as hundreds of people working to continually improve the quality and relevance of search results.

For information on how Yahoo! Search works, visit http://help.yahoo.com/l/us/yahoo/search/index.html.

---

words.[32] You won't garner a high ranking with single words, because just about any single word appears so frequently on the Web that the competition to rank high for it is too tough.

What you'll be looking for

Before you can settle on three to five keywords for each webpage you optimize, you'll need to research a number of possible words and phrases. Get ready to collect and analyze these types of data for each word or phrase:

- **Search volume.** This is a representative sample of the number of times a keyword was searched on in search engines. A high-volume keyword is a good thing: It means lots of people use that keyword in searches.
- **Keyword difficulty.** This refers to the competitiveness of a term—how hard it would be for your site to rank high in results for that keyword. A keyword with a high difficulty score is a bad thing: The keyword is so common that the competition to rank high for it is fierce.
- **Your site's current ranking.** Your current ranking is the position (if any) that your website holds in the list of search results for a given keyword. The lower your page's current rank, the higher your page has to climb—and the less likely you are to achieve success with that keyword.

Ideally, **you want to find terms that are high in volume and low in difficulty**, and that give your site a decent chance of improving its ranking.

TIP Before you begin your keyword research, prepare a spreadsheet to organize your findings. Record your data under the following column headings (see our partially completed example on page 400):

Keyword
Search volume
Keyword difficulty
Current ranking

Charting keywords with a keyword research tool

Begin your keyword research with the aid of a keyword research tool, such as Trellian's Keyword Discovery (free), Google AdWords (free), or the Wordtracker Keyword Research Tool (free trial). For information about these and other keyword research options, see our online Resources page at http://styleguide.yahoo.com.

These tools and others like them are useful for brainstorming: For every keyword you enter, the tool suggests a list of related keywords and the search volume for each. (Note: The search volume in these tools is a data sample, so don't be surprised if the number seems low.)

To get started:

1. In the tool, enter a word or phrase that people looking for your type of content might use in their search. Remember to consider your audience: Instead of using only internal marketing terms, choose vocabulary that your potential site visitor or customer might use. For example, to find keywords for a travel site, you might start with *low fares* as a keyword—but also try *cheap flights,* which someone who doesn't work in the travel industry may be more likely to use.

2. Scan the tool's list of suggestions for other promising words and phrases that apply to your webpage, and make a note of those, too.

T I P It's fine to begin your research with single-word keywords—they can lead you to better, multiword terms, or you can find ways to incorporate them into multiword phrases. But you won't choose single-word keywords for your ultimate list—too many other sites are using them, too.

3. Continue entering different words and phrases into the tool, noting the resulting suggestions and search volume data each time. Test at least 10 terms so that you'll have a long list of potential keywords when you have finished testing.

Chart each possible keyword in a spreadsheet so that you can easily see which terms have the highest search volume, lowest difficulty, and so on. In your initial chart, include any keywords that make sense for your site. (Later you will pare down the list to three to five keywords.)

4. Test the difficulty of your potential keywords. A common word like *cat,* for instance, carries a sky-high difficulty score; the word appears on so many sites, that only big-name, long-established sites will rank anywhere near the first page of search results when a person types *cat* into a search box. By contrast, a phrase like *silver tabby* would have a lower difficulty score, so a site optimized for *silver tabby* would have a better chance of getting a high page ranking in search results. (Note: You may want to skip testing the difficulty of those keywords that seem barely related to your site—those you wouldn't be able to reasonably work into your page copy several times.)

Example

Keyword	Search volume (Wordtracker)	Keyword difficulty (SEOmoz)	Current ranking
mangosteen	614	60%	
mangosteen fruit benefits	126	41%	
mangosteen for sinus problems	108	skipped (keyword is barely relevant)	
mangosteen juice for health benefits	72	skipped (keyword is barely relevant)	
mangosteen facts	64	36%	
mangosteen juice	60	skipped (keyword is barely relevant)	
mangosteen fruit as anti-inflammatory	59	skipped (keyword is barely relevant)	
health benefits of mangosteen	51	39%	
mangosteen fruit	45	51%	
mangosteen and health	41	33%	
mangosteen pigment test	24	skipped (keyword is barely relevant)	
mangosteen scam	22	skipped (keyword is barely relevant)	
mangosteen side effects	20	skipped (keyword is barely relevant)	
mangosteen fruit safe	13	skipped (keyword is barely relevant)	
where can I purchase mangosteen fruit	13	37%	

Part of a partially completed sample keyword chart for the homepage of a fictional mangosteen farm and tropical-fruit tree nursery. (Search volume information gathered in April 2009 using the Wordtracker Keyword Research Tool. Keyword difficulty information gathered in April 2009 using the SEOmoz keyword difficulty tool. Ranking information would be gathered at a later stage.)

The SEOmoz keyword difficulty tool (http://www.seomoz.org/keyword-difficulty), a paid service, gives you useful information on how tough it would be to rank high for a particular keyword. Google's Search-based Keyword Tool (http://www.google.com/sktool) can provide "competition" information that is somewhat comparable to keyword difficulty data—see our online Resources page at http://styleguide.yahoo.com to find out more and to see if any free keyword difficulty tools have been developed since this book went to press.

T I P SEO specialists consider many other factors when assessing keyword quality. For instance, they also perform in-depth evaluations of the sites that *are* ranking in the top 10 for a given keyword—how frequently they are using the keyword, the quality of the links pointing to those sites, and so on—to find out whether it's feasible for you to compete with those top sites and, if so, what you need to do to compete.

Keyword selection strategies

When selecting keywords for your chart, follow these guidelines:

- Put together longer, more specific phrases. For example, instead of *pet clothes,* consider *designer pet clothes*. The smaller your website and the fewer the links pointing to it, the more likely you are to need longer keyword phrases for optimal success.

- Scan your entire list of keyword results for words that may be lower in volume but that repeat throughout the list. Integrate these words into your keyword phrases. For instance, if phrases with *clothes* are popular, you might use *dog clothes, cat clothes,* and so on.

- Combine high- and low-volume keywords in a single phrase. For example, *buy mangosteen fruit* contains both *buy mangosteen* (a low-volume keyword) and *mangosteen fruit* (a higher-volume keyword).

- Consider page type when selecting your most important keywords and other, optional keywords. Plan to:

  - Optimize your homepage for the highest-volume keywords. You want your most valuable page optimized for the most competitive keywords.

  - Optimize section- or category-level pages for phrases specific to the section or category they represent. For example, for a site that sells clothes for dogs, cats, and other pets, you might optimize the entire site for *designer pet clothes* but also optimize a dog-specific section for *dog clothes, terrier clothes,* and so on.

Narrowing your choice of keywords

Next, clear your list of the less effective keywords to reveal those that are best for your copy. Here's how:

1. Sort the keyword list by search volume, highest to lowest.

2. Beginning at the top of the list, delete any single-word keywords.

3. Delete terms that are barely relevant to your website. For example, a site that sells designer pet clothes is not likely to rank high for the keyword phrase *dog fashion show* because the site is mainly about clothes—not about the fashion shows where the clothes are displayed. But if one page on that site focuses on dog fashion shows, and if it seems natural to repeat that exact phrase several times throughout the page copy, then *dog fashion show* could be a good keyword for that particular page.

4. Delete terms that you cannot reasonably repeat in your page copy at least four or five times. (Plan to use each of your three to five top keywords to optimize at least three or four pages—overlapping keywords is good.)

5. Now you'll have a much smaller list of keywords, each consisting of two or more individual words. With this small list, go to the top search engines (at this writing, Google, Yahoo!, and Bing) and enter each phrase into the search box to test it. For each phrase, focus on the 10 sites listed on the first page of the search results. These are your online competitors, even if in the offline world you do not perceive them as such. (Sometimes they aren't even in your field, depending on the keyword.) Ask the following questions:

◆ **Does the list contain sites that are in a totally different category from yours?** If a keyword brings up sites that are completely unrelated to your business, your target audience searching on that keyword is going to see the same thing: that the keyword isn't effective for finding the information category you are in. Someone potentially interested in a site like yours who is faced with results like these will probably start over with a different keyword—and so should you.

◆ **Do these sites *deserve* to rank above yours?** In other words, are the sites in the top 10 more relevant to that keyword than yours is?

◆ **Does the list include major brand names that you couldn't compete with offline?** Sites such as these are typically huge and boast lots of links to and from other big-name, authoritative sites, such as CNN, MSN, and the like, making them highly attractive to search engines and very hard to compete with.

◆ **Do any of the domain names of these sites end in *.gov, .org,* or *.edu*?** Sites such as these may also have many links to and from authoritative sites, and thus have more clout with search engines.

If the answer to any of these questions is yes for most of the listings on that first page of search results, you'll probably struggle to rank above those sites. Delete any keyword that brings up extremely competitive results like these, and move on to the next keyword.

T I P See if locale or other factors can differentiate your site from big-name competitors. For example, a small-town doctor in the U.S. who chooses *health care* or *internal medicine* or other general terms for her webpage, then realizes she's competing with Aetna and Kaiser Permanente in search results, might consider incorporating her locale: *internal medicine, Stanardsville, Virginia*. If your site serves a local audience, including the locale can be useful.

6. Now gather your rankings for the remaining keywords and record them in your chart. To do this, conduct searches using each remaining keyword, counting each listing in the search results until you find your own listing. (Tools exist to help you do this—but they go against search engine guidelines. See related Tip below.) If your ranking is 50 or higher for any keywords, focus on those. They will likely be the easiest for you to pursue.

T I P The Firefox Rank Checker plug-in is a tool that can help you determine your page's current ranking for a given keyword—but if you're going to use it, don't use it at the office or at a café. A tool such as this "pings" a search engine so quickly and so frequently as it gathers data for you that the search engine may block the computer (or the entire network!) that all the activity is originating from. An alternative is the SEOmoz Rank Tracker tool, which checks SEOmoz servers rather than the search engines.

7. After you have completed this research and have discovered a short list of keywords, choose the three to five that are most important for the page that you are optimizing. To make your selections, balance search volume, keyword difficulty score, and your current rankings.

Step 2: Add keywords to your page copy

After you've selected your keywords, incorporate them into your page copy. **Think about SEO at two points:**

- As you prepare your topic and begin writing
- When your draft is about 80 percent complete

T I P Consider SEO for your existing webpages. Check your site traffic and optimize the pages getting the most traffic—say, the top 10 percent of pages—or at least the pages that *should* be getting the most traffic. Your homepage, for example, should be in that top 10 percent.

Focus on the top three to five keywords you selected in step 1 as you begin to incorporate keywords into your first draft.

Develop a plan

Plan your page copy, layout, and so forth so that you can **incorporate your keyword phrases several times without sounding repetitive**. As you begin to write, anticipate how you can weave them in.

As a guideline, you'll want to **include two to four repetitions for every 200 words**. If your keyword has a high difficulty score, you'll need more repetitions (and more links to that page) to help boost your ranking.

Plan to **include keywords in**:

- The story headline (marked with HTML tag **<h1>**).
- Subheadings (**<h2>**, **<h3>**, etc.).
- The beginning, middle, and end of the body copy. Make sure to put your keywords at least once "above the fold," or in the top part of the webpage that people see when they first land on the page, before scrolling down, so that site visitors can spot them quickly.
- Bulleted and numbered lists (marked with **<ul>**, **<ol>**, etc.).

Incorporate keywords as you write

Write concisely—but don't be too much of a minimalist. Search engines like pages with a healthy word count better than pages that are terse and sparse. To please site visitors *and* search engines, **strive for at least 250–300 words to a page**, excluding header and footer text, and repeat the keyword phrases throughout.

Make certain that each keyword you add is an exact match of your chosen phrase. If the keyword is singular or present tense, keep it singular or present tense. For example, if *designer pet fashions* is your keyword, use the exact match *designer pet fashions*—not *designer pets fashions,* not *designer pet fashion,* not *designer's pet fashions*. (Note: You will have a chance to add keywords that are similar but not exact at a later stage—see "Refine your draft" on page 406.)

Example

Before
Keyword: designer pet fashions
Find designer pet fashions for dogs and cats.
Here are today's designer clothes for pets.
Even your pets look good in designer apparel.

After

Keyword: designer pet fashions

Find designer pet fashions for dogs and cats.

Your animals will be the talk of the park wearing designer pet fashions.

Get recommendations for designer pet fashions.

Dress your pet in today's designer pet fashions.

If your copy starts to sound odd because of the keyword repetition, or if you're working with a quirky keyword phrase, you can **break up a keyword phrase with punctuation** and it will still be considered an exact match. (But don't break up keyword phrases with additional words.) Use these characters to break up keywords:

; : - — , & / ? ! ( ) .

Example

Keyword: designer pet fashions

Now available from your favorite designer: pet fashions!

What's the latest to come from this famous designer? Pet fashions.

For those who own a designer pet: Fashions for Fido and Fluffy are now on sale!

Some collections include children's wear, too (it depends on the designer). Pet fashions are also showing up on some runways this season.

Be creative

Write content that people will want to link to. To be ranked high by search engines, you need incoming links as much as you need good keywords. Some ideas:

- Use lists, humor, unusual directions.
- Select an angle and a story title that will make people want to tell others about the article and that make the page attractive to other websites. Examples of headline types that tend to attract links:
  - ◆ Why ____ Hates _____
  - ◆ 10 Reasons to _____
  - ◆ How to Make the Perfect _____

T I P If you're struggling for title ideas, scour popular magazines to see how they use short, snappy headlines to attract readers. Or look at Digg.com for examples of popular titles that attract links.

If you're a retailer, you may find it easiest and most efficient to rely on manufacturer details to describe the products on your site. However, if you copy the manufacturer's text, your search engine ranking will probably drop. Search engines want to list only one version of a given piece of content, so they will demote duplicate content. **Help your site stand out with personal takes on your products** that qualify as 100 percent original content.

Code your text to attract search engines

Search engines give extra weight to certain formatted elements within a page. Words set off by HTML—header tags, for example—are among the most valuable words on the page for SEO. Apply these standard HTML tags to your page, and make sure these elements include exact-match keywords:

- Top-level headline (one per page): **<h1>**
- Subheadings: **<h2>**, **<h3>**, and **<h4>**
- Bold text: **<strong>**
- Italicized text: **<em>**
- Links: **<a href>**
- Bulleted or numbered lists: **<ul>** or **<ol>**

Specify these elements with standard HTML tags; otherwise, search engines will see the elements as regular body copy and your site will see no benefit. If you are passing the content on to your webmaster or someone else who will publish it online, specify where to apply these standard HTML tags: which line is **<h1>**, which line is **<h2>**, and so on. To learn more about applying HTML tags such as these to text, and how they make text appear on a webpage, see Chapter 16, "Get Familiar With Basic Webpage Coding."

Refine your draft

By the time your draft is 80 percent complete, you should have been able to repeat your exact keywords several times throughout the page (two to four repetitions for every 200 words is a general guideline). **At this stage you can go beyond exact repetitions of your keywords.** Add other variations—different verb tenses, singular or plural forms of the keyword, and so on—so that the text sounds natural.

Example

Before

Keyword: designer pet fashions

Dress your pet in today's designer pet fashions. Your sweetie will be the talk of the park! We feature clothes for cats, dogs, and other furry friends. Visit the Catwalk to see pets in their outfits, and browse our Couture Closet to buy hats, coats, capes, and more, from the elegant to the adorable.

After

Keyword: designer pet fashions

Dress your pet in today's designer pet fashions. Your sweetie will be the talk of the park! We feature clothes for cats, dogs, and other furry friends. Visit the Catwalk to see photos of fashionable pets modeling the latest designs, and browse our Couture Closet to buy hats, coats, capes, and more, from the elegant to the adorable.

When you have finished your draft, review your copy. Make sure that you have repeated your keywords, and that the text is fluid and readable. Above all, **remember to write for people first, search engines second**.

T I P   Print a draft and highlight the keywords. Check that they are numerous, distributed throughout, and formatted correctly (using HTML tags such as **<h1>**, and so forth).

Step 3: Incorporate links

Links to your page are like votes for your content. Search engines count these "votes" when they evaluate a webpage's importance. When one of your webpages links to another of your pages, or to another site, it passes a "vote" to that target page and can influence its relevancy. The **link text tells the search engine what the page being linked to is about**.

For example, let's say your story "How to Get Dates This Summer" is on a webpage named page_one.html, and embedded in the story's text is a link to an online-dating article deeper in your website, on a page named page_two.html. You choose the text *online personals* for the embedded link to the second story. The fact that page_one.html is about "How to Get Dates This Summer" passes on some relevancy to page_two.html. However, the greatest value comes from the embedded link text, *online personals,* which tells search engines that page_two.html is about online personals.

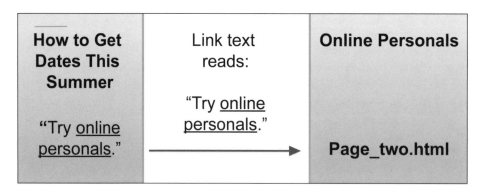

Embedded link text: Try <u>online personals</u>. HTML text: Try <a href ="http://www.site _name.com/page_two.html">online personals</a>.

TIP Link text that reads "click here" is a missed opportunity: It is meaningless to users and doesn't tell search engines what the page being linked to is about. See for yourself: Search the Web for *click here* and see if you find anything relevant. For more information on writing effective link text, see "Text links" on page 123.

Follow these **guidelines for creating effective links**:

- Link to pages with **similar topics**.
- **Place the links within body copy.** Search engines consider integrated links more valuable than links in headlines, lists, or navigation. Links within the body copy indicate more clearly to search engines that the page you are linking to is relevant to the topic covered on your page.
- For **internal links** (links to other pages on your website), identify the top keywords for the page that you are linking to, and use those keywords in your link text. For example, if you have determined that *dog clothing* is a top keyword for a page you are linking to, use *dog clothing* in the link text.
- For **external links** (links to pages on other websites): It's fine to link to two or three outside web-pages from a given page on your site. More is OK if it makes sense for your audience, but don't go overboard. Too many links on a page devalue the page, especially if you have more links than text.

And remember to **encourage other sites to link to your webpage**:

- Ask online peers for links.

- Submit your site for inclusion in a directory, such as the Yahoo! Directory (http://search.yahoo.com/info/submit.html).
- Create content that people will want to link to. See "Be creative" on page 405.

Step 4: Use keywords in page titles and metatags

Descriptive page titles and meta description tags are essential to SEO success.

Page titles

The page title (marked with the HTML tag **<title>**) is **the single most important piece of SEO copy you will write** for a given webpage. The page title does not appear in the body copy, but it is visible at the top of the Internet browser window. (To see how a page title is coded in HTML and subsequently appears in a browser, see "Anatomy of a webpage" on page 372.)

Example

The page title for this webpage is "News, Blogs, and Tools for Living Green | Yahoo! Green."

One reason that page titles are so important to SEO: They become the link shown in a list of search engine results. Moreover, the title may be the only text in that list that you can control.

Example

> News, Blogs, and Tools for Living **Green I Yahoo! Green**
> News, blogs, and tools for living **green**. Environmental tips to save money, stop pollution, and help fight global warming.
> green.yahoo.com - 166k - Cached

When someone searches for "Yahoo! Green," this is how the page title appears in the list of search results.

Follow these **guidelines for creating page titles**:

- Limit yourself to 65 characters, including spaces. A search engine may index only the first 65 characters of your page title.
- Fill the title with keywords:
  - ◆ Use as many exact matches of your top keywords as possible.
  - ◆ Use at least one exact match plus individual words of other top keywords.

Example

Bill's Autos has determined that its top site keywords are *used-car financing, used cars,* and *used-car warranty*—with *used-car financing* being the best keyword of the three. A good page title for the company's homepage would be:

Quality used cars: Used-car financing & warranty - Bill's Autos

---

- Write titles that accurately represent the content that people will find on the page.
- Create a unique page title for each page. Don't use the same title for every page on your site.
- Use words that will tempt someone to click the link when it appears in a list of search results.
- Keep your company's name at the end of the title, unless you are an industry leader with strong brand recognition.

Example

Before
Bill's Autos - Quality used cars, used-car financing, warranty

After
Quality used cars: Used-car financing & warranty - Bill's Autos

---

For more tips on writing effective page titles, see "Page titles" on page 119.

Metatags: Descriptions and keywords

Metatags are elements in a page's HTML code that contain *metadata,* or data that describes data—essentially, information about the page. The metadata that is inserted in these **<meta>** tags helps to classify the page and therefore helps search engines, but it is not usually visible to readers. (To see an example of metadata in the code of a page, see "Anatomy of a webpage" on page 372.) Though metatags are less important to SEO than they used to be, you should still include them. For one thing, the meta description text can appear in search results and can play a very important role in coaxing people to click.

There are two **<meta>** tag attributes to write: keywords and description. The **meta keywords** should include the same three to five keywords you selected at the end of step 1. The **meta description** is a 250-character text block that describes your webpage's content.

Meta keywords formerly helped search engines match pages to search queries, but most search engines don't pay attention to this element anymore. However, it is still considered a best practice to include meta keywords. They can at least serve as a reminder months from now when you're trying to remember which keywords you optimized a particular page for. One caveat: If you include keywords in the metadata for your page, your competitors will be able to see them and thus find out which words you optimized your page for.

The meta description—if it contains the keyword that the person searched on—may become part of the blurb that appears on a page of search results.

Example

> News, Blogs, and Tools for Living **Green I Yahoo! Green**
> News, blogs, and tools for living **green**. Environmental tips to save money, stop pollution, and help fight global warming.
> **green.yahoo.com** - 166k - Cached

The words below the title (highlighted here in gray) are the meta description as it might appear on a search results page. (Meta keywords remain invisible; they don't appear in a search results list or on the page itself.)

Follow these **guidelines for writing meta descriptions**:

- Write an enticing, keyword-rich 250-character (including spaces) page description in one, two, or three sentences.
- Create a unique description for every single page.
- Include in the description the top three to five keywords you chose for the page.
- Search on your competitors' names in a search engine and look at their meta descriptions. Make yours more keyword-rich and appealing.

Example

Before

Keywords: used cars for sale, used-car dealers, used-car prices, used-car reviews
Find new-car pictures, used-car prices, and new-car reviews on new cars. Get a

free price quote for new cars, compare new- and used-car prices, and find new- and used-car dealers near you.

After

Keywords: used cars for sale, used-car dealers, used-car prices, used-car reviews
Search used cars for sale nationwide at Yahoo! Autos. Find used-car prices for economy to luxury vehicles at used-car dealers nationwide. Find used-car reviews, pictures, and tips for getting the best price on used cars for sale at a dealer near you.

T I P   Keywords are useful for marketing campaigns, too. Visit the Yahoo! Search Marketing blog (www.ysmblog.com), a community forum for sharing news, tips, and strategies. You can connect to people and products that can help you make sense of the ever-changing world of online marketing.

Images and video

Don't optimize just your text for SEO. Images and videos are additional places to work in keywords.

Optimizing images

Search engines cannot see graphics and photos, and neither can visually impaired people using screen readers to browse a webpage. For these reasons, **use alt text to describe images on your site**. *Alt text,* or alternative text, refers to the image description you type into an image tag's **alt** attribute in the HTML code. The description will appear if the image doesn't.

Example

When the image appears

When the image doesn't appear

What the "green collar" economy means for you
By Lori Bongiorno Posted Thu Jan 29, 2009 6:21pm PST for greenpicks   138 Comments

Construction workers, iStockPhoto

Learn which industries will benefit from the new economic stimulus plan and what old skills can be repurposed into eco-friendly jobs. Read full post »

Alt text can also help search engines find images when people limit their search to images.

Example

Web | Images | Video | Local | Shopping | more ▾
cat clothes   **Search**   Options ▾   YAHOO!

*Clicking **Images** above the Yahoo! Search box enables you to search only for image files. The search demonstrated here would bring up image results related to "cat clothes."*

For more information about alt text, see "Alt text and image captions" on page 132. To read about how alt text can contribute to accessibility, see Chapter 6, "Make Your Site Accessible to Everyone."

Follow these **guidelines for writing alt text**:

- Write alt text for **every single image**.
  Exception: You may not need alt text for an image that is purely decorative, text-free, and not informational, such as dividing lines or tiny graphics used as bullet points.
- Make the alt text **unique** for each image.
- Write a **short one-sentence or one-phrase description that includes keywords** and describes the image or how the image fits into the page.

Example

Before
Dog wearing coat

After
A poodle wearing the latest in designer pet fashions *(Uses the target keyword "designer pet fashions")*

In addition to using alt text, you can **optimize images with these methods**:

- Name image files using keywords (for example, *poodle-designer-pet-fashions.jpg*).
- Include a keyword-rich caption under the image.
- Save photos in JPEG format (with the extension *jpg*) and save other images, such as illustrations or graphics, as GIFs (with the extension *gif*).
- If you use the same image on multiple pages, save the file to one place and use the same URL for that image each time you use it. Don't upload the same image several times.
- Place all images in a specific directory folder rather than in many directories.
- Optimize the page that the image appears on.

Optimizing video

To a large extent, search engines discover what your video is about through all the SEO on the page, not just tags associated with your video. But here are some **guidelines for helping your video rank higher** in search engine results:

- Optimize the entire page: the page title (text in the **<title>** tag), headlines (**<h1>**), body copy, and so on.
- Play video on the page rather than force browsers to open a pop-up player window. On-page video is usually better for SEO.
- Add a video transcript or a keyword-rich summary of the video.
- Fill in as many metadata fields as you can.

If you are the video's creator, take steps to **optimize the video itself**:

- Include keywords in the video title.
- Use keywords for any speaking parts in a video (for example, in the voice-over or script). It's only a matter of time before video search tools will be able to use speech recognition.

Ideas in Practice

Example: Seed copy with keywords for SEO

Writing that's direct *and* strategically suffused with keywords improves the odds that searchers will find your site in search results, consider your page relevant to their needs, click through, and engage with the content they see.

In this example—a webpage from a fictional site that sells baby clothes—see how a shy piece of prose can be made over to sell itself. Here are the steps we followed to optimize it:

1. Select a variety of possible keywords.
2. Check keyword search volume.
3. Check keyword difficulty.
4. Choose three to five keywords.
5. Integrate the three to five keywords into the copy.

Before

Bootleg Bäby

We sell rockin' togs for newborns and toddlers. You don't want your baby to look like every other kid on the block in pink and blue, bunnies and teddy bears. Dress your mini Ozzy and Siouxsie like the rock stars they already are—screaming, staying up all night, drinking till they spit up.

We sell rock-and-roll tops, onesies, bottoms, and accessories for every head-banging babe. For the future metal master, we have snap-on faux leather trousers, studded cuffs (no sharp or swallowable parts, of course), and black tops with a variety of designs, including a flame-detailed stroller and a skull with a pacifier (our best-seller). For the punk princess, we have tees with tattoo designs, tartan skirts, mesh tights, lace-up booties, and the ever-popular baby Mohawk hat.

Shopping for a band T-shirt? Bootleg Bäby has the largest online selection of band tees for babies, including rock, metal, hip-hop, punk, goth, and indie band logos and images. Can't find your favorite group? We customize: Send us your vintage concert tees, and we'll cut them down to baby-sized T-shirts or onesies.

All of our baby clothes are 100% organic cotton, ultrasoft, and machine-washable. We think you'll find them longer-lasting than the overpriced baby clothes you find in stores—and a lot cooler, too. Start shopping now!

Keyword selection notes

Bootleg Bäby is a website that sells baby clothes, so *baby clothes* was our first search in the Wordtracker Keyword Research Tool (for information on other keyword research tools, see our online Resources page at http://styleguide.yahoo.com). Of course, using that keyword would be a bad SEO strategy—Bootleg Bäby would compete with big national and international retailers and wouldn't improve its search rankings. However, the search revealed some related terms, such as *punk baby clothes,* that could be fruitful.

We eliminated some other keywords: *Baby rocker* was too generic, referring to rocking baby seats as well as to clothes for the rocker baby. And *rock star baby* was too specific, with most results referring to an established site that would compete directly with Bootleg Bäby.

We had better luck with various phrases that combine *baby, clothes,* and *rock* or other music terms. But as you can see in the chart, spelling matters: *Rock and roll baby clothes* got more searches than *rock n roll baby clothes,* and terms varied in whether they performed better with *T-shirts, tee shirts,* or *T.*

Here's our keyword chart, from highest search volume to lowest (all numbers as of May 2009):

Keyword	Search volume (Wordtracker)	Keyword difficulty (SEOmoz)
punk baby clothes	43	45%
rock baby clothes	44	44%
rock and roll baby clothes	20	38%
baby rock and roll clothes	20	40%
baby clothes rock and roll	20	37%
punk rock baby clothes	12	43%
baby punk rock clothes	12	41%
rocker baby clothes	4	41%
baby rocker clothes	4	39%
rock n roll baby clothes	3	36%
baby rock T-shirts	1	26%
goth baby clothes	1	24%
baby rock apparel	0	22%
rock clothes for baby	0	20%
rock and roll baby T-shirts	0	16%
baby concert T	0	16%

Keyword	Search volume (Wordtracker)	Keyword difficulty (SEOmoz)
cheap rocker baby clothes	0	15%
baby band T-shirt	0	15%
baby mohawk hat	0	14%
rock band baby clothes	0	12%
mohawk hat for kids	0	11%
baby rock tee shirts	0	11%
skull pacifier T-shirt	0	6%

For our main keywords, we chose:

- *punk baby clothes*
- *rock baby clothes*
- *rock-and-roll baby clothes* (Note: Despite the hyphens, this term is a match for *rock and roll baby clothes*.)

We made a second list of terms that would be good to use if we could incorporate them without making the copy sound strange. These secondary keywords are:

- *cheap rocker baby clothes* (which includes another keyword, *rocker baby clothes*)
- *rock and roll baby T-shirts* (despite a low search volume, it worked well as a heading when it was punctuated)
- *skull pacifier T-shirt* (because that's the site's best-selling item, people might search on that term, and the phrase has the lowest keyword difficulty on our list)
- *Mohawk hat for kids* (likewise, a top product for the site with relatively low keyword difficulty)

Keyword integration notes

In revising the copy, we focused on placing keywords throughout the copy, especially in high-profile areas such as the headline, subheadings, and links. For links, we assumed that the site has—or could create—subpages for punk, goth, and rock apparel, as well as for individual products. We rewrote a few sentences to squeeze in more keywords. You could go a step further and rewrite some of the copy as lists, with keywords in the bulleted points.

We repeated primary keywords only twice each, except for *punk baby clothes,* which appears three times. Though we could have shoehorned in more keywords, the copy is so brief and the phrases are so similar—all contain *baby clothes*—that we decided more repetitions would sound odd.

After

Punk baby clothes for your little screamer

Bootleg Bäby sells rock-and-roll baby clothes for newborns and toddlers. You don't want your baby to look like every other kid on the block in pink and blue, bunnies and teddy bears. Dress your mini Ozzy and Siouxsie like the rock stars they already are—screaming, staying up all night, drinking till they spit up.

Rock-and-roll baby clothes for girls and boys

We sell rockin' tops, onesies, bottoms, and accessories for every head-banging babe. For the future metal master or lord of darkness, we have **rock baby clothes** like snap-on faux leather trousers, studded cuffs (no sharp or swallowable parts, of course), and a variety of black tops, including a flame-detailed stroller tee and the skull pacifier T-shirt (our best-seller). For the punk princess, we have **punk baby clothes** like tees with tattoo designs, tartan skirts, mesh tights, lace-up booties, and the ever-popular Mohawk hat for kids.

Rock and roll, baby: T-shirts from all your favorite bands

Bootleg Bäby has the largest online selection of band T-shirts for babies, with images and logos from the finest bands in punk, metal, hip-hop, goth, indie, and rock—baby clothes you and your kid will love to go out in. Can't find your favorite group? We customize: Send us your vintage concert tees, and we'll cut them down to baby-sized T-shirts or onesies.

Cool, comfy, and cheap rocker baby clothes

All of our baby clothes are 100% organic cotton, ultrasoft, and machine-washable. We think you'll find them longer-lasting than the overpriced baby duds you find in stores—and a lot cooler, too. Start shopping now for the best selection of rock-and-roll, goth, and punk baby clothes!

Chapter 18

Understand the Basics of U.S. Law for Online Content

In this chapter

- **Online content creators and the law.** The rules that affect you.
- **Defamation.** Libel and slander defined.
- **Copyright.** Think you can use that photo? Better make sure.
- **Trademarks.** Be careful how you use them—yours and others'.
- **Publicity rights.** For celebrities and average joes alike.
- **Trade secrets.** They're supposed to stay secret.

Internet law, like the Internet itself, is still in its infancy. Online law is groundbreaking, fascinating, and complex: groundbreaking because it must respect existing law while it calls for fresh applications, fascinating because publishing information online can pose unprecedented issues, and complex because it can be affected by the laws of every country on earth. Online or off, laws vary from state to state and from country to country.

Because of these umpteen variables, this chapter will familiarize you with just the **basics of U.S. law affecting Internet activity**. Still, the basics are enough to give any Web content creator a clearer understanding of certain common legal terms and an awareness of potential legal pitfalls.

Keep in mind that the laws of other countries and regions may apply to your Web operations. For example, the European Union has strict privacy laws, including those that limit the transfer of personal data outside the EU.

A lawyer will be able to counsel you on the specifics of your situation and locale.

Online content creators and the law

Whether you publish original content, import content created by others, or allow site visitors to post content on your webpages, it's smart to know about the laws that affect you. This chapter's guidelines can help you spot possible legal issues in advance, help minimize legal problems that might arise, and help ensure a higher degree of accuracy and quality on your site.

Learn to recognize risks

Two of the main legal areas pertaining to Internet content creators are **defamation** (libel and slander) and **intellectual property** (copyrights, trademarks, and trade secrets).

Defamation and intellectual property laws could come into play in numerous ways on the Web—for example, when you:

- Create a webpage.
- Post a blog entry.
- Send a newsletter.
- Post an image on your site.
- Host a message board on your site.
- Allow the public to post content on your site.
- Display content provided by third parties.
- Publish business information that might be a trade secret.

Use your best judgment—and seek help when in doubt

The guidelines in this chapter are intended to help content creators avoid a variety of **pitfalls that relate to U.S. law**. These guidelines should serve as a reference—but by no means are they an ultimate authority.

When legal questions arise for your site, think about the potential consequences before taking action. If you are ever unsure about how to proceed with a situation, contact a lawyer or an appropriate legal resource, such as an individual who is an expert in the area of law you are dealing with.

Defamation

Defamation is generally understood to be **a false written or oral statement about someone that damages that person's reputation**. Defamatory statements can include those that wrongfully attribute negative characteristics—such as professional incompetence or criminal behavior—to people or organizations.

In general, written defamation is called **libel** and could include headlines and photographs. Spoken defamation is generally called **slander** and typically includes oral conversations. Defamation can also include video content.

Defamation laws don't protect individuals only; they can also protect companies. The laws regarding defamation are complex and are influenced by federal and state laws, so consult a lawyer for any specific issues you may have.

Copyright

Anyone creating or posting content on the Web needs to be aware of laws that protect intellectual property rights, such as copyright.

Copyright law protects original works, whether published or unpublished, that have been fixed in a tangible medium of expression. These include, for example, literary, dramatic, musical, choreographic, and artistic works such as poetry, novels, movies, songs, computer programs, photographs, and architecture.[33] Digital media can be considered "tangible," so even if a work exists only online, it may still be protected by copyright.

Copyright does not protect facts, ideas, systems, or methods of operation, although it may protect the way these things are expressed.[34] For instance, you cannot copyright a method of cooking, such as braising, but you could probably copyright an original recipe for boeuf bourguignon.

The **owner of the copyright in a work has the exclusive right to**:

- Reproduce the copyrighted work.
- Prepare derivative works based on the copyrighted work.
- Distribute copies of the work to the public.
- Publicly perform the copyrighted work (a play or a song, for example).
- Publicly display the copyrighted work (a painting or a sculpture, for example).[35]

Protect your own works

You may find it worthwhile to **register your own copyrighted works**. Registering your work is not necessary (you own the copyright in your work whether you register it or not), but in the United States there are certain benefits to registration. For example, in the U.S., you must register your work before you can sue someone for infringing your rights in that work. And people who have registered their work within a certain timeframe after it was created may be eligible, if they sue and then win their case, to receive statutory damages and to seek payment of their attorneys' fees. (Statutory damages are penalties based on what a statute, or law, calls for—not on the consequences of the infringement.)

To register your work in the U.S. and to find out more about the benefits of doing so, visit www .copyright.gov (you can even register online). In the U.K., find out more about copyright protection at the Intellectual Property Office website (www.ipo.gov.uk). For links to intellectual property offices in other countries, visit the World Intellectual Property Organization's directory at http://www.wipo .int/directory/en.

Respect others' rights in their work

You must get permission to use a work that someone else holds the copyright in.

Using a copyrighted work without permission from the copyright owner is called *infringement*—and the consequences can be serious. Depending on the circumstances, you may have to pay the copyright owner's actual damages and lost profits, or you may have to pay statutory damages. Statutory damages generally range from $750 to $30,000 per violation, but they can be as high as $150,000 for "willful" infringement or as low as $200 for "innocent" infringement. Criminal penalties can also apply.

Obtaining permission to use someone else's work

First, consider whether you really need to use someone else's work: Are you sure you can't create your own content instead? Seeking permission to use a copyrighted work may be a long process.

Seeking permission can involve:

- Determining who owns the rights to the work in question. (This is not always obvious; for example, a newspaper photo might belong not to the newspaper but to a wire service or a freelance photographer.)
- Contacting the rights holder or that person's agent—if you can find either. For corporate websites, you can look for a permissions link or check the company information pages for contacts.
- Getting permission in writing so that you have documentation.

But be warned: Even after taking the trouble to find and contact the copyright owner, you may not get the permission you ask for.

Common misunderstandings about copyright

Copyright law is frequently misunderstood. And online it's often deceptively simple to copy someone else's text and graphics—a situation that may add to the public's confusion or at least lead to wishful thinking that copyright law doesn't apply to content on the Internet.

It does apply. Common misconceptions can lead people to think, for example, that:

- The work is public, so they can copy and reuse it freely.
- They can make a copy as long as they provide attribution to the author.
- If there is no copyright symbol (©), the work is in the public domain.

None of that is true. Copyright law applies no matter how easy it is to copy something.

Fair use

Certain uses of copyrighted material—in particular for purposes such as criticism, commentary, news reporting, research, and education—may be considered "fair use" rather than copyright infringement. The Copyright Act of 1976 lists four criteria for determining whether a particular use is "fair":

- The purpose and character of the use, including whether such use is of a commercial nature or for nonprofit educational purposes
- The nature of the copyrighted work
- The amount and substantiality of the portion used in relation to the copyrighted work as a whole
- The effect of the use on the potential market for the copyrighted work or on the value of the copyrighted work[36]

Fair use is a gray area. Questions of copyright must be assessed on a case-by-case basis. A valid use in one circumstance may be infringement in another. Always consult legal counsel before making your own determination that a particular use is fair use.

T I P To learn more about copyright, to register a copyrighted work, or to find out about ownership of works registered in the United States, try the U.S. Copyright Office website at www.copyright.gov. And for more resources on copyright, check our online Resources page at http://styleguide.yahoo.com.

Trademarks

Companies and individuals establish trademarks to protect the identity of their brand, products, or services and to keep consumers from being confused about the source of those products and services. A trademark can be a word, phrase, symbol, or design or a combination of words, phrases, symbols, or designs (or even, in rare cases, sounds or smells) used to identify and distinguish the goods or services of one party from those of others.[37]

The Digital Millennium Copyright Act: How it affects content creators

Have you ever tried to play a Web video of a major sports or entertainment event and gotten a message that said something like "This video has been removed"? The content may have been removed because it infringed someone else's copyright.

If you post content on your site that someone else holds the copyright in, the copyright holder can take action against you, starting with demanding that you remove the content. One of the ways the copyright holder might make this demand is to involve the company hosting your website, blog, or other content.

Perhaps you post your content on a video-sharing site or a blogging service, or you maintain your website on space provided by your ISP. Be aware that these types of hosting services or service providers **may remove content from your site if they receive a notice that your use of the content is infringing someone else's copyright**. This is because the Digital Millennium Copyright Act (DMCA) protects these service providers from copyright liability as long as they comply with certain requirements—such as promptly taking down any content that may violate copyright laws when they receive a notice from the true rights holder.

If your service provider removes content from your site, the removal will not protect you: The copyright holder could still decide to sue you for copyright infringement.

Of course, if you feel that a mistake has been made—that you are *not* infringing anyone's copyright and the DMCA notice was sent in error—you have recourse under the DMCA. For more information, consult a lawyer.

To learn more about the DMCA, download the U.S. Copyright Office summary: http://www.copyright.gov/legislation/dmca.pdf.

Examples

A word: Yahoo!

A phrase: Apple's "Think different."

A symbol: $\mathbf{YAHOO!}$

Proper use of trademarks

If you want to use a trademark, especially in logo or design form, you almost always need **proper prior permission from the trademark owner**. Steps for seeking permission are similar to those for seeking copyright permission:

- Determine who owns the trademark.
- Contact the owner (ideally in writing) and ask for permission. Look on the trademark owner's website for a permissions link or check the company information pages for contacts.
- Get permission in writing so that you have a record of it.

    In general, follow these **guidelines for trademarks**:

- When using any trademark, try to use the appropriate marking. For registered marks, use ®. For marks that are not registered but are still protectable, use ™ or ℠, whichever is applicable. Different trademark owners may have different views as to whether you should use the relevant trademark symbol every time the trademark appears. At a minimum, it's a good idea to use the symbol in the first or most prominent place a trademark appears on each page (often, but not always, in logos or in a header).

- Do not insert punctuation (like hyphens) or otherwise change trademarked words.
- Do not change the appearance of design marks such as logos.
- Use marks as adjectives, not as nouns or verbs.

Examples

Before

In the doll category, Toy Captain's Tamsie™ is suddenly at the top of every little girl's list. Parents may have trouble finding Tamsies after the Christmas season arrives. Order your Tamsie today!

After

In the doll category, Toy Captain's Tamsie™ doll is suddenly at the top of every little girl's list. Parents may have trouble finding Tamsie™ dolls after the Christmas season arrives. Order yours today!

Before

The Portage-ease™ from Azore Sports makes portage of rafts large and small easier than you can imagine. On our test run down the Merced River, it took only two of us to Portage-ease™ the raft around North Fork Falls.

After

The Portage-ease™ carrying system from Azore Sports makes portage of rafts large and small easier than you can imagine. On our test run down the Merced River, it took only two of us to portage the raft around North Fork Falls.

- Provide an attribution/ownership tagline. The appropriate tagline may be dictated by the trademark owner's policy or contract. For example: "_____ and the _____ logo are the trademarks and/or registered trademarks of [trademark owner company name]; all other marks are the marks of their respective owners."

Example

Tamsie and the Tamsie logo are the trademarks and/or registered trademarks of Toy Captain; all other marks are the marks of their respective owners.

Noncommercial contexts

In some circumstances, it may be possible to use a third party's trademarked word without first obtaining that party's permission. One example is **in news reporting** (and by that we mean traditional journalism, not the News page of your company website where you post press releases). In news reporting, if it's necessary to identify a brand name or product in a story, it's OK to use those trademarked words without getting permission or using the ® or ™ symbols. But even in this type of situation, try to respect a trademarked word's punctuation and capitalization, and use the word as an adjective, not as a noun or a verb.

> **Example**
>
> Apple today unveiled a new, smaller version of its iPod shuffle music player. *(News story: Company spelling and capitalization of "iPod" and "shuffle" have been retained, and the trademarked name has been used as an adjective.)*

You may have similar leeway with using brand names **in a noncommercial blog** entry such as the following example—but it's best to use generic terms if you can: *tissue* instead of *Kleenex tissue*, *hot tub* instead of *Jacuzzi hot tub*, *digital music player* instead of *iPod music player*. And watch for any use of trademarked words alongside the sale of goods or services. **Using trademarked words without permission or marks is far less risky in noncommercial contexts**; if you are selling goods or services, your situation may not qualify as noncommercial.

Consult a lawyer to find out how trademark law applies to your particular situation.

> **Example**
>
> **Raising Blaine: Adventures in Parenting**
>
> Well, we survived the birthday party despite the rain (eight 4-year-old boys in our living room! for four hours!), and I have just one question: How many Hot Wheels cars does a kid need? Blaine already has a whole fleet, and by far the Gift of the Day was the package from Jamal with the four Hot Wheels in it. Blaine very nearly forgot about all the other presents to open, he was so excited! But I just don't get it, myself. He already had some.
>
> Update: Hubby says I don't get it because I'm female. He's in there playing with the cars right now. And no, not with Blaine, either: Blaine's outside in the hot tub with my sister!
>
> *(When possible even in noncommercial contexts, use trademarked words such as Mattel's "Hot Wheels" as adjectives, not as nouns or verbs—though as in this case, you may have more freedom in a casual blog entry where the writing reflects how the blogger speaks. But favor generic terms whenever possible, such as "hot tub" in the last sentence instead of a popular brand name for that product.)*

T I P Two reliable resources for more information about trademarks are the International Trademark Association (INTA), at www.inta.org, and the U.S. Patent and Trademark Office (USPTO), at www.uspto.gov.

Publicity rights

Every person has **the right to control the commercial use of his or her name, image, likeness, voice, or other identifiable aspects**. This right, typically called a right of publicity, is protected in certain circumstances. For instance, more than one business has gotten into trouble for using an image of a celebrity in such a way that it looked as though the celebrity endorsed the company's product—when in fact the celebrity did not.

Rights of publicity are largely based on state laws, so they differ widely from one state to the next. Consult a lawyer for more information about rights of publicity.

Trade secrets

In general, a trade secret is information that is not generally known to the public and that, because it is unknown, provides some sort of economic benefit to its owner. Examples include a secret recipe for a sauce, a formula for a lotion, and blueprints for a building. But for information to be considered a trade secret, its owner must make reasonable efforts to maintain its secrecy.

As a general rule, **never publish information that is known to be (or should be known to be) a trade secret—yours or anyone else's**. If something is marked "confidential" or "trade secret," you should presume that it is information that should not be published—not in a news story, not in a blog, not anywhere. Publishing trade secrets can expose you to individual liability.

For more information, consult a lawyer.

Ideas in Practice

Checklist: Are you at risk?

Before you publish your content on the Web, think about possible legal ramifications. Run one last check and ask yourself whether the content is OK or whether it's exposing you to potential trouble.

The following list poses some basic questions you should ask about your content. **A "yes" answer means you may be at risk** in a particular area, so do some research to learn more. You may need to contact a lawyer before publishing your material.

Question	Yes	No
Defamation (libel or slander)		
Does your website contain any potentially false statements about people or companies that could damage their reputation?		
Could any of the photos you plan to publish damage someone's reputation by suggesting something false about the person?		
Does any video you want to publish contain any potentially false statements about people or companies that could damage their reputation?		
Copyright		
Are you publishing, without written permission, any text on your website that belongs to someone else?		
Are you posting, without written permission, any photos or images that belong to someone else?		
Are you using, without written permission, any music or other audio that belongs to someone else?		
Trademarks		
Are you posting any company or organization logos on your site without the owner's permission?		
Trademarks should be used only as adjectives. Are you using a trademark as a noun or a verb?		
Publicity rights		
Are you posting a picture of a celebrity on your site so that it looks as though the celebrity is endorsing your product when in fact that person is not?		
Trade secrets		
Are you publishing information that is a known trade secret?		
Are you publishing information that is sensitive or confidential and that might be considered a trade secret?		

Chapter 19
Keep a Word List

In this chapter

- **Why compile a word list.** Make your work easier, maintain editorial standards, and give your site a consistent voice.
- **What to put in your list.** Entries that supplement, and occasionally override, the dictionary.
- **How to maintain your list.** Update, edit, and document your ever-evolving word decisions.
- **The Yahoo! word list.** How Yahoo! treats certain terms.

Spelling is easy, right? You just consult the latest edition of your favorite dictionary, and—*voilà!*—problem solved. But wait: Is it *smartphone* or *smart phone*? *Slideshow presentation, slide-show presentation,* or *slide show presentation*? **Handy as dictionaries are, they don't have all the answers**, particularly when it comes to the ever-shifting vocabulary of technology and communication, and to the best choice of words and spellings for your site.

Enter your word list. **A word list is an important part of a site's style guide.** It tracks your decisions, helps you enforce them to maintain your site's voice and editorial standards, and keeps editors from having to make the same kinds of decisions over and over again—possibly coming to contradictory conclusions each time.

 ## What's an editorial style guide?

It's a document of your site's editorial policies and guidelines that is created for and available to everyone who writes or edits copy on your site. It may include your voice template (see Chapter 3, "Define Your Voice"), rules on capitalization and other formatting issues, conventions for your user-interface text (see Chapter 7, "Write Clear User-Interface Text"), policies regarding trademarks (see Chapter 18, "Understand the Basics of U.S. Law for Online Content"), and the rest of the many small decisions about consistency that shape your website. This book, of course, is itself a style guide. But you'll need to create a guide specific to your site to document decisions that are right for your content and your organization.

Why compile a word list

Consistency reinforces your site's voice and helps make your site one that visitors feel they can trust. A big part of that consistency is how you handle the spelling, capitalization, punctuation, and usage of the basic building blocks of your copy: words.

Among the best reasons for compiling a word list:

- **It makes your life easier.** Deciding how to handle certain words and phrases can require research, discussion, and debate. The process isn't always easy, and you won't want to repeat it each time you want to use a certain word or category of words.

- **It helps you express and reinforce your site's voice.** Readers form an impression of your site based in part on how you use words. Even the way you spell can affect your image. Compare the following paragraphs on two hypothetical blogs:

Example

Blog 1
Sergeant York sent an e-mail last night inviting the squad to a hard-core session of "Warcraft," a.k.a. the biggest time sink on Earth. For an old Baby Boomer, he can still rock and roll!

Blog 2
Sgt. York sent an email last night inviting the squad to a hardcore session of Warcraft, aka the biggest time-sink on earth. For an old baby boomer, he can still rock 'n' roll!

Even with the evidence of only two sentences, you might get the impression that blogger 1 is older (he left the hyphen in *e-mail,* capitalized *Earth,* and spelled out *rock and roll*) and perhaps more fastidious than blogger 2 (who thought it was fine to leave the periods out of *aka*).

Both versions are essentially correct, but each expresses a slightly different personality. Writers should express ideas in their own voice, but your site's voice needs to stay consistent. One way to maintain that consistency is by adhering to a word list.

- **It helps visitors trust your site.** Approaching words differently every time you use them— *rock and roll, rock-and-roll, rock-n-roll, rock 'n' roll*—leaves visitors with the impression that you don't know what you're doing, don't care, or both. Being consistent in how you treat even the simplest word gives people confidence in your site and makes it easier for them to read and understand your content.

T I P If you encounter a word you're not sure how to spell, follow this path to the answer: Look first in your own word list—someone else may already have solved this problem for you. If it's not there, look in your chosen dictionary. If it's not there, refer to whatever other resources you and your co-workers have agreed to use. If you still can't find the answer, do your own research and formulate a decision. You may have to discuss the decision with others for approval, but then the decision should be added to your word list. (See "Word list resources" on page 434 for research strategies.)

What to put in your list

Err on the side of including too much rather than too little—your staff is more likely to refer to the company word list than to an external resource like a dictionary. Plus, your own word list will reflect your company's specific needs and determinations.

Include words on your list that you and your staff use frequently, especially if those words are:

- **Exceptions to the dictionary.** Dictionaries generally reflect rather than dictate spelling and usage. For instance, your dictionary may spell *dis* (a slang abbreviation for *disrespect*) with only one *s*, but you have always seen it as *diss,* with two *s*'s. Your company's editors agree that *dis* looks like a mistake, and so *diss* enters your word list. (You may find that if *diss* becomes more common than *dis,* the next edition of your dictionary will show *diss* as the preferred spelling. The same principle holds for *email, online, website,* and other Web-related words.)

T I P Avoid contradicting your dictionary unless you have an excellent reason to do so. The more often you make exceptions to your dictionary, the longer your word list will be and the more cumbersome it will be to use and maintain.

- **Exceptions to your own general rules.** Suppose you follow the generally accepted rule that the prefix *post-* and a root word are usually closed up, as in *postwar*. If you decide that *postwinnings* should have a hyphen, then that decision should be documented in the word list.
- **Commonly misspelled or misused words.** *Acknowledgements* or *acknowledgments*? *A historical* or *an historical*? *Jive, jibe,* or *gibe*? Homophones—words that sound alike but have different meanings—are particularly prone to being confused with each other. So, your word list might note, for example, that *recession-racked* is correct, not *recession-wracked*.
- **New words and usages.** If your site deals with technology, you're sure to encounter new words that aren't in the dictionary yet. Once you decide how to treat them, record your decisions in your word list. (For help with decisions on new words, see "Word list resources" on page 434.)

Word list resources: Get help with decisions about how to treat words

Plenty of guidance is available for editors deciding how to treat everyday words, terms from a particular industry or discipline, or words that are so new they haven't yet made anyone's list. Call on established resources first.

- **The dictionary.** Dictionaries don't always agree with each other. The solution is to pick the most recent edition of an accepted standard dictionary—such as the *American Heritage Dictionary of the English Language* or *Merriam-Webster's Collegiate Dictionary*—and to make sure that everyone on your team is using that version. If you disagree with a term's spelling in the dictionary, note your reasons on your word list.

- **Other standard professional references.** For example, the style guide of the American Medical Association (AMA) can provide guidance on editing medical copy; APA (American Psychological Association) style covers issues related to psychology and other social sciences.

- **Technical or industry standards.** The websites of the World Wide Web Consortium (W3C) and the Institute of Electrical and Electronics Engineers (IEEE) are smart first stops when you're trying to determine how to spell technical and computer-related terms that are not typically found in reference books. See www.w3.org and www.ieee.org.

- **Search results and keyword research.** If you come across a word that's too new or specialized to be in a dictionary or reference, test variations of it in a search engine to see which treatment is most popular. Enter the variations one at a time (with quotation marks around any open or hyphenated terms so that the search engine looks only for that exact phrase), and look at the top right of the search page to see how many results each variation brings up. Case in point: If you've never seen the shortened form for *keystroke logger,* you might think that *key logger* is the best way to treat this term. But in fact, *keylogger* brings up many, many more search results than *key logger,* so it's likely the wiser treatment for search engine optimization. (For more on search engine optimization, see Chapter 17, "Optimize Your Site for Search Engines.")

- **Company and manufacturer websites.** For the correct spelling of a product name, go to the source. These sites should be consistent in how they treat the names of their own products or technologies. If a company is inconsistent in how it treats its own name (a surprisingly common situation), you can follow the name on the company's copyright notice or the name filed with the SEC. Note that a company name is often styled differently in a logo: It may be rendered in all lowercase letters, with no spaces, for example, and does not necessarily represent how the name should be treated in text. For example, if you looked only at the Frito-Lay logo, you'd think that the correct spelling of the company name was *FritoLay*. (For more on how to treat company and product names, see "Company and product names" on page 242.)

■ **Your company's PR and marketing departments.** For terms pertinent to your own company, these departments may already have compiled guidelines about the treatment of company titles, departments, product names, and so on.

■ **Your company's legal department.** Ask for advice on how to handle trademarks, copyrights, and other legal issues—your own and those of other organizations (see Chapter 18).

For more specific ideas, see our online Resources page at http://styleguide.yahoo.com.

■ **Company-specific terms.** Record brand-specific guidelines, such as how to spell and capitalize your company name and product names.

■ **Words specific to your site.** Examples include the nicknames *Rotties* and *Yorkies* for dog breeds on a pet site.

■ **Foreign words.** Do you italicize *à la*? Do you spell the holy book *Koran* or *Quran*? Are *weltschmerz* and *schadenfreude* capitalized? If your site uses such words frequently, you may want to include them on the word list.

■ **Names that may be written more than one way.** Will you write *Osama Bin Laden* or *Osama bin Laden*? *Qaddafi, Kaddafi,* or *Gaddafi*? Choose one spelling and record your decision.

■ **Frequent search terms.** The way you spell a word can make a difference in how well search engines can find your site. Let's say that your SEO specialist informs you that people search on *video conferencing* more frequently than *videoconferencing,* both on your site and on search engines. So, even though your dictionary spells *videoconferencing* as one word, you might decide to make it two words to help your customers and to improve your ranking with search engines. Along with the entry, a brief explanation of why your decision was made could prevent future questions, confusion, and inconsistency. (For more details on SEO, see Chapter 17.)

How to maintain your list

A word list should be ever-expanding, but it should also be amended, edited, and pared down from time to time. Follow these guidelines to prevent your list from getting out of date and out of hand.

■ **Update it frequently.** The Web is fertile ground for growing new words. Determine which of these new words are useful and how your site will treat them. Make sure that the word list document or webpage shows the date of its most recent update.

■ **Appoint one person to be in charge of the list.** If you are running a small site yourself and hiring writers as needed, maintain your own list and make sure that new writers get a copy.

If you have an editorial department, the managing editor or the copy chief will probably be in charge of the word list. The list owner will likely consult with others—such as copy editors and perhaps section editors and other company employees who use a word or term frequently—before ruling on a word list term. Still, access to the original document should be limited. You don't want dueling entries or entries that have not been thoroughly thought out.

- **Document why the decision was made.** Particularly do so if an entry goes against what your dictionary or another basic reference source says. If the word list doesn't note why your company treats *video conferencing* as two words, for example, editors who were not involved in the original decision might think the term needs to be changed to what the dictionary calls for: *videoconferencing*.

- **Make it available to everyone.** Ideally, every employee should have access to the style guide and word list on an intranet. The document should be locked so that only certain people can make changes to it. But make sure that everyone who needs it can download and print it, and that everyone knows when the document has been updated.

 ## How much detail do I need to include?

A word list entry should make the following clear at a glance:

- How to **capitalize** (Do you refer to *baby boomers* or *Baby Boomers*?)
- How to **punctuate** (Will you write *9 pm* or *9 p.m.*?)
- How to **format** (italics, bold, superscript, and so on)
- Whether words should be **hyphenated, open, or closed** (Will it be *cell phone, cell-phone,* or *cellphone*? *Voicemail box, voice mailbox,* or *voicemailbox*?)
- How to treat different **parts of speech** (for example, you might hyphenate *decision-making* as an adjective, but leave out the hyphen when it's used as a noun)
- Whether any **alternative spellings** and treatments are (or are not) acceptable, and when (for example, *dialog* and *dialogue*)
- How to form **plurals** when it isn't obvious (If you abbreviate *operating system* as *OS,* will you write *two OSs, two OS's,* or *two OSes?*)
- What **acronyms and other abbreviations** stand for, how to treat them, and when they're OK to use
- **What a term means**, if a definition seems needed (for example, if a term is new or specialized and does not appear in your dictionary)

Practicing consistency

Consistency is relatively easy to achieve in print or on a website where you're the lone writer. But the degree of difficulty multiplies when many people contribute content and when the site grows continually. No matter how disciplined you are, your site may have pages and elements that seem to be beyond your control: old content in an outdated format; third-party stories in a news feed with a different headline style; user-generated content with misspellings; sister sites or microsites with varying voices, styles, or layouts; error and help messages, forms, page headers and footers, and navigational elements written by a producer or a programmer who doesn't know your house style; and so on.

Keeping a large, ever-changing site consistent can seem as tricky as controlling tribbles. So how do you contain the chaos? Try these tactics:

1. If your site is complex, create a full style guide in addition to a word list. Document not only your decisions, but also your reasons for making them.

2. Make friends. Talk to your fellow content creators about problems they've encountered, solutions they've found, and any tips they've recorded. If your company is large enough to have marketing, public relations, design, production, or related departments, they may be excellent resources for things like brand guidelines; lists of the company's products, services, and features to ensure correct spelling; and rules about the treatment and placement of webpage elements.

3. Choose your battles. Be prepared to defend your editorial choices: Know how a point of consistency or style affects the site's credibility, readability, navigability, searchability, and so forth. But while you defend, don't be defensive; be positive, helpful, and open to changing the decision. Consider which points are deal breakers—you wouldn't compromise on the spelling of the company name, for example—and which points have a lower priority or are hard to fix, such as news-feed headlines that automatically appear in title case on a page that otherwise uses sentence case.

4. Communicate consistency. When your style guide, word list, or other guidelines have received a sign-off from interested parties, be sure to communicate them to everyone who creates content for your site.

5. Audit your pages and workflow. Just as you may need to choose your battles on style decisions, so you may need to prioritize which pages get your editorial scrutiny. Obviously your homepage should be a priority, as should any heavily visited pages—comb through these periodically. For new content, establish a clear process: Must all content be edited before it can be published? For pages that change less often, such as standing features or category pages, how frequently should an editor check them? And for older stories, think about whether they should be removed, archived, or updated—and when.

The Yahoo! word list

Following is a healthy sampling of the Yahoo! word list. It is part of a list developed over time for use by Yahoo! U.S., reflecting not only technology and communications terminology, but also terms related to other topics Yahoo! editors come across frequently on the Yahoo! network in the United States. The list also identifies words that are trademarks and notes the right way to treat them (see "Trademarks" on page 424).

Your own list may naturally have very different entries, but you may find ours useful as a springboard or as an additional reference.

Key to abbreviations and symbols

adj. = adjective

adv. = adverb

n. = noun

obj. = object

v. = verb

❶ = attention

Numerics

24/7 — Note slash. Example: *The phones are staffed 24/7.*

3D — No space. Not *3-D.*

3G, 4G — Types of cell phone networks.

50-50 — Note hyphen and use of numerals. Example: *They figure their candidate has a 50-50 chance.*

8x, 16x — Format for values that denote the speed of drives such as CD and DVD drives. Example: *The DVD-RW drive boasts write, rewrite, and read speeds of 16x, 8x, and 16x, respectively.*

9/11 — Acceptable abbreviation for *September 11, 2001,* when space is tight; however, *Sept. 11* is the preferred abbreviation.

A

a lot — Two words. Not *alot*.

A.D. — Note capital letters and periods, no space after the first period. Place before the year. Example: *The city of Hippos was destroyed by an earthquake in A.D. 749.* For more information, see "Years" on page 267.

a.m. — Lowercase, no space after first period. Include a space between the number and *a.m.* (*9 a.m.*). See "Time" on page 269.

ActiveX — Note capitalization of this Microsoft trademark. Term should be used as an adjective only. Example: *ActiveX control, ActiveX technologies.* For more about proper use of trademarks, see "Trademarks" on page 424.

actor — Use *actor* for everyone, not *actress* for female actors. See "Write gender-neutral copy" on page 77.

add-on (n., adj.), **add on** (v.) — Note hyphen when used as a noun or adjective. Two words when used as a verb.

address book

adware

African American (n., adj.) — Two words, no hyphen. This term may be used interchangeably with *black*. But note: The term *black* applies to any person of African descent; *African American* applies only when you know for certain that the person is American and not Canadian, Haitian, or another nationality.

afterparty (n.) — One word. A party that takes place after a big event or larger party. Example: *She wore one designer's creation on the red carpet, another's to the afterparty.*

aka — Abbreviation for *also known as.* Lowercase, no periods, no spaces.

all right — Two words. Not *alright*. Hyphenate when it precedes the word it modifies. Examples: *Do you feel all right? It was an all-right day—not great, but not bad, either.*

all-star (n., adj.) — Note hyphen. Capitalize when referring to sports events and teams with *all-star* as part of the official name: *This is his third time being picked as an MLB All-Star. The All-Star Game will air next week.* Lowercase when using it generically: *The movie features an all-star cast.*

alright — ❗ Don't use. See "all right."

alt text — Short for *alternative text,* which is text entered into the HTML **alt** attribute associated with an image on a webpage. See "Alt text and image captions" on page 132.

American Indian (n., adj.) — Two words, no hyphen. Can be used interchangeably with *Native American* where appropriate, but follow the subject's preference and use a more specific name (such as *Lakota Sioux* or *Navajo*) where possible.

amid, amidst — The preferred U.S. word is *amid. Amidst* is chiefly British and is considered a variant of *amid* in the United States.

among, amongst — The preferred U.S. word is *among. Amongst* is chiefly British and is considered a variant of *among* in the United States.

anti- — Generally, close up this prefix with root words unless the root word starts with an *i* or a capital letter—if it does, hyphenate. Examples: *anti-intelligence, anti-American, antispyware.*

antivirus — Lowercase when used generically. When referring to the name of a specific antivirus product, use the manufacturer's spelling, hyphenation, and capitalization. Example: *Our review of antivirus software starts with Symantec's Norton AntiVirus.*

app — Short form of *application.* Plural: *apps.* ❗ Do not use if there's any room for confusion.

ASCII — Acronym for *American Standard Code for Information Interchange.* Acronym is always OK.

Asian American (n., adj.) — Two words, no hyphen.

Asian Pacific American (n., adj.) — Three words, no hyphen. Refers to Americans of Asian and Pacific Islander descent.

audio conference

auto-renew (adj., v.) — Note hyphen. Example: *The software includes an auto-renew feature.* For the verb, it's preferable to use *automatically renew,* unless space is very tight and the meaning of *auto-renew* will be clear from the context. Examples: *Your subscription will automatically renew. Check this box to auto-renew.*

autumn — Lowercase the season name. See also "seasons."

avatar — Lowercase when used generically.

B

B2B — Abbreviation for *business-to-business*.

baby boomer (n.), **baby-boomer** (adj.)

back-to-school (adj.), **back to school** (adv.) — Note hyphens when it precedes the word it modifies. Three words in all other cases. Examples: *Back-to-school shopping can be a painful experience. The kids are headed back to school in the fall.*

backup (n., adj.), **back up** (v.) — One word when used as a noun or an adjective. Two words when used as a verb. Examples: *When the backup is complete, you'll see a list of all backup files. We automatically back up your website.*

backward, backwards (adv.) — Use *backward* in American English; *backwards* is more prevalent in British English.

bar code (n., adj.) — Two words, no hyphen.

BA — Abbreviation for *bachelor of arts*. No periods.

backdoor (n., adj.) — One word. A method or tool for surreptitiously gaining access to a computer system.

B.C. — Note capitals and periods. No space after the first period. Place *B.C.* after the year. Example: *The ruins of the city date back to around 900 B.C.* For more information, see "Years" on page 267.

Bcc (adj., v.) — Abbreviation for *blind carbon copy*. Abbreviation is always OK. Example: *Put email addresses in the **Bcc** field if you don't want anyone else to see them. If you send that email, be sure to Bcc me.*

best-seller (n.), **best-selling** (adj.) — Note hyphen.

beta — Capitalize *beta* if it is part of an official product name. Otherwise, lowercase it. Examples: *Sign up for the new Yahoo! Messenger beta. Try the beta version of Yahoo! Messenger.*

biannual(ly), bimonthly, biweekly — ❶ Don't use any of these words. They can mean either every other year, month, or week, or twice a year, month, or week. Instead, use the longer but unambiguous *every two years, months,* or *weeks,* or *twice a year, month,* or *week.*

bil — Acceptable as an abbreviation for *billion* when space is tight. Include a space between the number and *bil*. Example: *Senate passes $20 bil financial aid plan.* See also "billion."

billion — Use numerals with *billion*. Don't hyphenate the numeral and *billion* even before a noun. As part of a hyphenated compound, use a hyphen between the numeral and *billion*. Examples: *4 billion people, a $2 billion contract, 5-billion-year history*. In general, spell out *billion*. If space is tight, *bil* is an acceptable abbreviation. See also "bil."

biodiesel (n., adj.)

birth date — Two words. Not *birthdate*.

bitstream (n.) — One word. A stream of data.

black (n., adj.) — Lowercase when referring to race. *African American* may also be used when it is certain that the person is American. Plural: *black people* or some other phrase using *black* as an adjective is preferable to *blacks* (see "Banish bias" on page 75).

black-and-white, black and white — Note hyphens when it precedes the word it modifies. Three words in all other cases. Examples: *You can print the map in black and white. You can print a black-and-white map.*

BlackBerry (adj.) — One word. Note capitalization of this Research In Motion (RIM) trademark. Plural: *BlackBerry devices* (because the word is a trademark, don't use *BlackBerrys* unless it's part of a direct quotation). For more about proper use of trademarks, see "Trademarks" on page 424.

blog (n., adj., v.) — Preferred to *weblog*.

blogroll (n.) — One word. A blogger's list of other recommended blogs.

Bluetooth — One word. Note capitalization of this Bluetooth SIG trademark. Use the term as an adjective, and do not add an *s* to make it a plural noun. For more about proper use of trademarks, see "Trademarks" on page 424.

Blu-ray — No *e* in *Blu*. Note capitalization and hyphen of this Blu-ray Disc Association (BDA) trademark. Use the term as an adjective, and do not add an *s* to make it a plural noun. For more about proper use of trademarks, see "Trademarks" on page 424.

BMP — Abbreviation for *bitmap*. Generally used to refer to a graphic file (the file extension is *.bmp*). Abbreviation is always OK.

bowl — Capitalize when used in a proper noun: *Rose Bowl Stadium, Fiesta Bowl*. Lowercase when used generically: *college bowl games, bowl schedule*.

bps — Abbreviation for *bits per second*. Lowercase. Do not include a space between the number and *bps*. Abbreviation is always OK.

breadcrumb — One word. A navigational term for the path you've taken to get to a certain webpage. (*Breadcrumb* is short for *breadcrumb trail;* it can also refer to the individual links in the trail.) To see an example of a breadcrumb trail, see "User-interface text basics" on page 118 and "Example: Give visitors good directions" on page 150.

brick-and-mortar (adj.) — Note hyphens.

browsable — Not *browseable.*

businessperson — Use this gender-neutral term instead of *businessman* or *businesswoman.* See "Write gender-neutral copy" on page 77.

C

°C — Acceptable abbreviation for *degrees Celsius.* (To create the degree symbol, see "Special characters" on page 386.) Example: *The average summer temperature is 23°C in the valley.* (No space between the numeral and *°C,* no period after *°C.*)

café — OK to use accented character in webpage copy and HTML emails, but use *cafe* (with no accent) in plain-text emails or copy that may appear in an RSS feed.

camera phone

cancellation (n.), **canceled, canceling** (v.) — The preferred U.S. spelling has two *l*'s in noun form and one *l* in verb forms. The preferred British spelling has two *l*'s in all forms.

CAPTCHA — Acronym for *Completely Automated Public Turing Test to Tell Computers and Humans Apart.* Acronym is always OK. Plural: *CAPTCHAs.*

Cascading Style Sheets — A Web-building technology (see Chapter 16, "Get Familiar With Basic Webpage Coding"). OK to abbreviate as *CSS* after initial explanation. Use lowercase *style sheets* to refer to CSS documents. Example: *Cascading Style Sheets (CSS) specifications allow a site designer to use style sheets to specify layout and other visual aspects of a webpage.*

Celsius — An acceptable abbreviation for *degree(s) Celsius* is *°C.* See also "*°C.*"

Cc (adj., v.) — Abbreviation for *carbon copy.* Abbreviation is always OK. Example: *When sending email to colleagues, Cc those people who need to know about your message but who don't necessarily need to act on it.*

CD — Abbreviation for *compact disc.* Abbreviation is always OK. Plural: *CDs.*

CDMA — Abbreviation for *code division multiple access,* a digital communication method used by some mobile devices. Abbreviation is always OK.

CD-R — Abbreviation for *CD-recordable.* Note hyphen. Plural: *CD-Rs.*

CD-ROM — Abbreviation for *CD-read-only memory.* Note hyphen. Abbreviation is always OK. Plural: *CD-ROMs.*

CD-RW — Abbreviation for *CD-rewritable.* Note hyphen. Plural: *CD-RWs.*

cell phone (n., adj.) — Two words, no hyphen. Examples: *He left the message on my cell phone. Type in your cell phone number.* Note: *Cell phone* is interchangeable with *mobile phone* in the U.S.; in the U.K., *mobile phone* is the more common term. In parts of Asia, *handphone* is common.

centigram — An acceptable abbreviation for *centigram(s)* is *cg* (no period).

centiliter — An acceptable abbreviation for *centiliter(s)* is *cl* (no period).

centimeter — An acceptable abbreviation for *centimeter(s)* is *cm* (no period).

cg — Acceptable abbreviation for *centigram(s).* Include a space between the number and *cg.* For information about when it's OK to use the abbreviation, see "Units of measure" on page 273.

chair, chairperson — Use these gender-neutral terms rather than *chairman* or *chairwoman.* See "Write gender-neutral copy" on page 77.

chat room

checkbox

checkout (n., adj.), **check out** (v.) — One word when used as a noun or an adjective. Two words when used as a verb. Examples: *The checkout process is very short. You enter this information during checkout. You'll find that you can check out very quickly.*

cl — Acceptable abbreviation for *centiliter(s).* Include a space between the number and *cl.* For information about when it's OK to use the abbreviation, see "Units of measure" on page 273.

click (v.) — Depending on the object, use *click* (for a button, link, or other interface element) or *click on* (for a file, photograph, icon, etc.). For details, see "Mouse actions" on page 149.

clickable

clickthrough (n., adj.), **click through** (v.) — One word when used as a noun or an adjective. Two words when used as a verb. Examples: *The company's online ads consistently earn a high clickthrough rate. Click through to the last page to see your score.*

client/server (adj.) — A type of network (*a client/server network*).

clip art

closed caption (n.), **closed-caption** (adj.) — Two words when used as a noun, hyphenated when used as an adjective. Example: *Provide closed captions with your videos. Search engines may be able to crawl your closed-caption files to search for keywords.*

cm — Acceptable abbreviation for *centimeter(s)*. Include a space between the number and *cm*. For information about when it's OK to use the abbreviation, see "Units of measure" on page 273.

CO2 — Abbreviation for *carbon dioxide*. (Subscript 2 is not recommended for online content.)

co- — Generally, use a hyphen between this prefix and a root word unless the word is one that your dictionary closes up (for example, *cooperation, coordinate*). But always use a hyphen when the resulting word denotes a shared occupation or status. Examples: *co-creator, co-host, co-parent, co-star, co-worker*.

codec — Short for *coder/decoder*. Short form is always OK.

commercial-free — Hyphenate in all instances.

Congress — Use when referring to both the U.S. Senate and the House of Representatives. Note capitalization.

congressman, congresswoman — ❗ Don't use. Before a name, use *Rep.* or *Sen.*: *Sen. John McCain*. In references without a name, use *senator, representative,* or *congressperson*: *The congressperson from Ohio spoke first.* See "Write gender-neutral copy" on page 77.

congressperson — Use this term (or *representative* or *senator*) rather than *congressman* or *congresswoman*. See "Write gender-neutral copy" on page 77.

corrupted — Use *corrupted,* not *corrupt,* to describe a file or data. Example: *The file was corrupted—I couldn't open it. Delete the corrupted file.*

crowdsource, crowdsourcing

craftsperson — Use this term instead of *craftsman* to refer to a person. See "Write gender-neutral copy" on page 77.

crawl (v.) — OK to use as transitive verb meaning "to sift through." Example: *Search engines crawl websites to assess the sites' relevance for a particular search term.*

CSS — Abbreviation for *Cascading Style Sheets*. Abbreviation OK after first explanation.

CSV — Abbreviation for *comma-separated values,* a file type. Generally used to refer to a file containing values separated by commas. OK to abbreviate after first explanation.

CTR — Abbreviation for *clickthrough rate*. Abbreviation OK after first explanation.

cubic feet, cubic foot — An acceptable abbreviation for *cubic feet* and *cubic foot* is *cu. ft.* (note the periods).

cubic inch — An acceptable abbreviation for *cubic inch(es)* is *cu. in.* (note periods).

cubic kilometer — An acceptable abbreviation for *cubic kilometer(s)* is *cu km* (no periods).

cubic meter — An acceptable abbreviation for *cubic meter(s)* is *cu m* (no periods).

cubic yard — An acceptable abbreviation for *cubic yard(s)* is *cu. yd.* (note periods).

cu. ft. — Acceptable abbreviation for *cubic foot* and *cubic feet*. Note the periods. Include a space between the number and this abbreviation. For information about when it's OK to use the abbreviation, see "Units of measure" on page 273.

cu. in. — Acceptable abbreviation for *cubic inch(es)*. Note the periods. Include a space between the number and this abbreviation. For information about when it's OK to use the abbreviation, see "Units of measure" on page 273.

customizable — Note spelling. Not *customizeable*.

cu km — Acceptable abbreviation for *cubic kilometer(s)*. Include a space between the number and this abbreviation. For information about when it's OK to use the abbreviation, see "Units of measure" on page 273.

cu m — Acceptable abbreviation for *cubic meter(s)*. Include a space between the number and this abbreviation. For information about when it's OK to use the abbreviation, see "Units of measure" on page 273.

cu. yd. — Acceptable abbreviation for *cubic yard(s)*. Note the periods. Include a space between the number and this abbreviation. For information about when it's OK to use the abbreviation, see "Units of measure" on page 273.

cyber- — Generally, close up this prefix with root words unless the root word starts with a capital letter—if it does, hyphenate. (But note that the prefix *cyber-* is dated.) Examples: *cyberattack, cybercrime, cybergang, cyberterrorism, cyberracket, cyber-CIA.*

D

data — Treat *data* as a mass noun like *information,* taking a singular verb. Example: *The data is lost.*

daylight saving time — Lowercase in all uses. Note singular *saving,* not *savings.* Example: *During daylight saving time, clocks are turned forward one hour.*

debut — In general, use *debut* when referring to people and *premiere* when referring to events. See also "premiere."

decision maker (n.) — Two words, no hyphen.

decision making (n.), **decision-making** (adj.) — Two words when used as a noun, hyphenated when used as an adjective.

Democrat, democrat (n.) — Capitalize when referring to a specific member of the Democratic Party: *Barack Obama and other Democrats convened. The Illinois Democrat spoke.* The plural form may be abbreviated as *Dems* if it will be understood in context: *The Dems have reason to celebrate.* Lowercase only when referring to someone who's an advocate for democracy but not necessarily a member of the party: *Many experts believe the ancient Greeks were the first democrats.*

Democratic, democratic (adj.) — Capitalize when referring to the party, a member of the party, or the committee: *Democratic Party, Democratic National Committee, Democratic Sen. Hubert Humphrey.* Lowercase only when referring to something or someone characterized by democracy in a general sense, but not necessarily affiliated with the Democratic Party: *The class came up with a democratic solution: Put it to a vote.*

denial-of-service (adj.) — A type of hacker attack (*denial-of-service attack*). Abbreviation *DoS* OK after initial explanation.

DHTML — Abbreviation for *Dynamic Hypertext Markup Language*. Depending on audience, may require explanation on first reference.

dialog, dialogue — Use *dialog* in the term *dialog box*. Otherwise use *dialogue*.

dial-up (n., adj.), **dial up** (v.) — Note hyphen when used as a noun or adjective. Two words when used as a verb. Examples: *Many people in remote areas are still relying on a dial-up connection. Get high-speed access for the price of dial-up. My computer takes forever to dial up and connect.*

digicam — One word. Acceptable abbreviation for *digital camera* when writing for a tech-savvy audience.

digital age

digital divide

dingbat (n., adj.) — A typographical ornament such as ♥ or ☑.

disabled (adj.) — OK to use as an adjective when referring to people with disabilities. Example: *Can disabled people access your site?* ❶ Do not use *disabled* as a noun, as in *the disabled*.

disc, disk — Use *disk* when referring to a computer hard disk or floppy disk. Use *disc* when referring to optical disks such as compact discs (CDs), digital video/versatile discs (DVDs), and laser discs. Also: *disc brake, disc jockey, videodisc.*

doc — Abbreviation of *document*. ❶ Do not use if there's any room for confusion.

DoS — Abbreviation for *denial of service*. See also "denial-of-service."

do's and don'ts — Note apostrophes.

dot-com (n., adj.) — Note hyphen, lowercase. Examples: *dot-com bubble, dot-com crash, dot-com era.*

double check (n.), **double-check** (v.) — Two words when used as a noun, hyphenated when used as a verb. Examples: *A thorough double check of the data revealed some problems. Please double-check your information for accuracy.*

double-click (n., adj., v.) — Note hyphen.

dpi — Acceptable abbreviation for *dots per inch*. No periods. Insert a space between the numeral and this abbreviation: *300 dpi.*

drag-and-drop (adj.), **drag and drop** (v.) — Note hyphens when used as an adjective. Not *drag-n-drop* or *drag 'n' drop*. Three words when used as a verb. Examples: *Add photos quickly with the drag-and-drop feature. Just drag and drop photos onto the album.* Or: *Just drag photos to the album.*

dreamed, dreamt — The preferred U.S. spelling is *dreamed*. *Dreamt* is chiefly British and is considered a variant of *dreamed* in the United States.

drop-down box — ❶ Avoid. Use *pull-down menu, menu,* or *list* instead.

drop-down menu — ❶ Avoid. Use *pull-down menu, menu,* or *list* instead.

DTV — Abbreviation for *digital television*. Abbreviation is always OK. Plural: *DTVs.*

DVD — Abbreviation for *digital video disc* or *digital versatile disc*. Abbreviation is always OK. Plural: *DVDs.*

DVR — Abbreviations for *digital video recorder*. Abbreviation is always OK. Plural: *DVRs.*

E

e.g. — Abbreviation meaning *for example*. Note periods. Don't include a space after the first period. OK to use when space is a consideration; otherwise, use *for example, for instance, such as*. If used, include a comma after the last period. See also "i.e." and "ex." Example: *Enter a search term (e.g., recipes, horoscopes, gifts) into the box.*

Earth, earth — Capitalize when used as the proper name of the planet. Lowercase in all other uses. Examples: *The third planet from the sun is Earth. The earth was ready for planting.*

eBay — Note capitalization of this company name. See "Capitalization" on page 239 for information on how to treat names such as this in a title or a sentence.

e- — In general, insert a hyphen between this prefix and root words, especially if they are new. Exception: *email,* which is now widely accepted as one word. Examples: *e-book, e-business, e-card, e-commerce, e-reader, e-tail.*

email (n., adj., v.) — One word, no hyphen. Plural: *email messages* and *emails* are both acceptable.

ESP — Abbreviation for *email service provider.* Abbreviation OK to use after initial explanation. Plural: *ESPs.*

Ethernet — Note capitalization.

EULA — Abbreviation for *end user license agreement;* pronounced "you-la." Abbreviation OK to use after initial explanation or when context makes the meaning clear. Example: *You must sign the EULA before installing the program.*

EV — Abbreviation for *electric vehicle*. Abbreviation OK to use after initial explanation.

ex. — Note period. Acceptable abbreviation for *example* when space is tight or in contexts where many examples are used (such as in help documents) and *e.g.* is insufficient or likely to be misunderstood. Example: *Some user-interface elements (for ex., buttons) should always use title-case capitalization. Ex.: A button with the text "See more info" should read "See More Info".*

ExpressCard (adj.) — Trademarked name for a PCMCIA hardware standard and for related hardware devices, such as a card that you can plug into a computer to provide memory storage, wireless connectivity, or other features. Plural: *ExpressCard modules*. Example: *The computer comes with an ExpressCard/34 card slot. Insert the ExpressCard module into the ExpressCard slot.* For more about proper use of trademarks, see "Trademarks" on page 424.

eye tracking (n.), **eye-tracking** (adj.) — Two words when used as a noun, hyphenated when used as an adjective. Example: *Eye-tracking studies give us a clue about how people scan webpages.*

F

°F — Acceptable abbreviation for degree(s) Fahrenheit. (To create the degree symbol, see "Special characters" on page 386.) Example: *The average summer temperature is 75°F in the valley.* No space between the numeral and *°F*, no period after the abbreviation.

Fahrenheit — An acceptable abbreviation for *degree(s) Fahrenheit* is *°F.* See "*°F.*"

fall (n., adj.) — Lowercase the season name. See also "seasons."

fansite (n.)

FAQ — Stands for *frequently asked question* but generally refers to a list of such questions. Can be pronounced two ways: (1) "fak" (in this case the singular form takes the article *a*: *a FAQ*) or (2) "eff-ay-cue" (in this case the singular form takes the article *an*: *an FAQ*). Either treatment may be used as long as it is used consistently. Plural *FAQs* (pronounced "faks" or "eff-ay-cues"). Example: *Many sites include a FAQ to avoid answering the same customer questions repeatedly.*

Fast Ethernet — Note capitalization.

fax

feed reader — Two words. Another name for *newsreader*.

feet, foot — An acceptable abbreviation for *feet* and *foot* is *ft.* (note the period).

fifty-fifty — ❶ Using numerals ("50-50") is preferable.

file name — Two words. Not *filename*.

firefighter — Use this term instead of *fireman*. See "Write gender-neutral copy" on page 77.

flak — Not *flack*, when referring to heavy criticism: *Palin took flak for her $150,000 shopping spree.*

flash (adj.) — Lowercase when referring to flash memory or a flash drive.

Flash — Capitalize when referring to Adobe Flash multimedia technologies. Use this Adobe Systems trademark as an adjective. For more about proper use of trademarks, see "Trademarks" on page 424.

flight attendant — Use this term instead of *steward* or *stewardess*. See "Write gender-neutral copy" on page 77.

flow chart (n.), **flow-chart** (adj., v.) — Two words when used as a noun, hyphenated when used as an adjective or a verb.

fl. oz. — Acceptable abbreviation for *fluid ounce(s)*. Note periods. Include a space between the number and this abbreviation. For information about when it's OK to use the abbreviation, see "Units of measure" on page 273.

fluid ounces — An acceptable abbreviation for *fluid ounce(s)* is *fl. oz.* (note periods).

foreign (adj.) — ❶ In some contexts, using the term *foreign* is appropriate: *Rice plans to write a book about American foreign policy.* In other contexts, using *foreign* can seem exclusionary: It assumes that the reader has the same home country as you, which may not be true—in fact, your reader may be a part of whatever you describe as "foreign."

former Pres. — Acceptable abbreviation for *former President*: *The guest speaker was former Pres. George W. Bush.* See also "former president."

former president — Do not use *president* or *ex-president* when referring to past presidents. Capitalize as *former President* only when used before a name: *former President George W. Bush* (it may also be abbreviated as *former Pres. George W. Bush*). Lowercase when used without a name: *The former president offered his congratulations.*

forward (adv.) — Use *forward* to refer to direction in American English; *forwards* is more prevalent in British English.

friend (n., v.) — OK to use as a verb when referring to inviting someone to be your friend on a social-networking site. Example: *Would you friend your boss? You'll never believe who just friended me.*

ft. — Acceptable abbreviation for *feet* and *foot*. Note the period. Include a space between the number and *ft*. For information about when it's OK to use the abbreviation, see "Units of measure" on page 273.

FTP — Abbreviation for *File Transfer Protocol*. Abbreviation is always OK. Verb usage is also OK: *Please FTP that file if it's larger than 3MB.*

function keys — Lowercase. Refers to the F1 through F12 keys on a keyboard.

G

g — Acceptable abbreviation for *gram(s)*. Include a space between the number and *g*. For information about when it's OK to use the abbreviation, see "Units of measure" on page 273.

G — ❶ Don't use as an abbreviation for thousand, gigabyte, or gigahertz. Instead, use *K*, *GB*, and *GHz*, respectively. See also "K," "GB," and "GHz."

gal. — Acceptable abbreviation for *gallon(s)*. Note period. Include a space between the number and *gal.* For information about when it's OK to use the abbreviation, see "Units of measure" on page 273.

gallon — An acceptable abbreviation for *gallon(s)* is *gal.* (note period). Note: A gallon is a different measurement in the U.S. and the U.K.

Game Boy — Two words. Do not add *s* to form the plural of this Nintendo trademark. For more about proper use of trademarks, see "Trademarks" on page 424.

GameCube — One word. Note capitalization of this Nintendo trademark. Do not add *s* to form the plural. For more about proper use of trademarks, see "Trademarks" on page 424.

GB — Abbreviation for *gigabyte*. Don't include a space between the number and *GB*.

Gbps — Abbreviation for *gigabits per second*. Note capitalization—especially the lowercase *b*, which distinguishes this from *GBps,* a different measurement. Don't include a space between the number and the abbreviation. See also "GBps."

GBps — Abbreviation for *gigabytes per second*. Note capitalization—especially uppercase *B,* which distinguishes this from *Gbps,* a different measurement. Don't include a space between the number and the abbreviation. See also "Gbps."

Generation X, Generation Xer, Gen Xer — All are acceptable.

Generation Y, Gen Y — Both are acceptable.

geolocation — One word. The geographic location of an Internet-connected computer, or the process of determining that location.

geotagging (n.), **geotag** (v.) — One word. The verb means to add geographic data (such as longitude and latitude coordinates) to a photo or other media file.

GHz — Abbreviation for *gigahertz*. Note capitalization. Don't include a space between the number and *GHz*.

GIF — Acronym for *Graphic Interchange Format.* Generally used to refer to an image file with the file name extension *gif*. Acronym is always OK. Plural: *GIFs*.

gigabyte — OK to abbreviate as *GB*. See "GB."

Google — ❶ According to Google guidelines, it is not OK to use this trademark as a verb.[38] Use *search, search for,* or *search on* instead. For more about proper use of trademarks, see "Trademarks" on page 424.

GOP — Abbreviation for *Grand Old Party,* referring to the Republican Party in the United States.

governor — Use *Gov.* or *Govs.* before a name: *Gov. Sarah Palin; Govs. Palin and Schwarzenegger.* Otherwise lowercase and don't abbreviate: *The governor declared a state of emergency.*

govt. — Acceptable abbreviation for *government*. Use only when space is tight. Note period.

GPS — Abbreviation for *global positioning system*. Abbreviation is always OK.

gram — An acceptable abbreviation for *gram(s)* is *g* (no period).

gray, grey — The preferred U.S. spelling is *gray*. *Grey* is chiefly British and is considered a variant of *gray* in the United States.

grayware — One word. Software that is not quite malware but is still undesirable.

Ground Zero, ground zero — Capitalize when referring to the site of the September 11, 2001, attacks in the United States. Lowercase when used generically.

GSM — Abbreviation for *Groupe Speciale Mobile* or *Global System for Mobile Communications,* a digital communication standard used by some mobile devices. Abbreviation is always OK.

guestbook

GUI — Abbreviation for *graphical user interface*. Abbreviation OK to use after initial explanation. Plural: *GUIs*.

H

handheld (n.), **hand-held** (adj.) — The noun refers to a personal digital assistant, or PDA.

handphone — One word. Term used for cell phone or mobile phone in parts of Asia.

hang on to — Not *hang onto.* The phrasal verb is *hang on*, and *to* is the preposition. Example: *He tried to hang on to his sense of pride while unemployed.*

hard core (n.), **hard-core** (adj.) — Hyphenated when used as an adjective.

HD DVD — Two words, no hyphen. Abbreviation for *high-definition digital video disc* or *high-definition versatile disc*. Abbreviation is always OK. Plural: *HD DVDs*.

HDTV — One word. Abbreviation for *high-definition television*. Abbreviation is always OK. Plural: *HDTVs*.

help pages

high speed (n.), **high-speed** (adj.) — Two words when used as a noun, hyphenated when used as an adjective. Examples: *Sign up now and soar through the Internet at a truly high speed. Get high-speed Internet access.*

hip-hop (n., adj.)

Hispanic — see "Latino, Latina."

hit — ❶ Avoid as a substitute for *press* or *click*. When referring to a key on the keyboard, use *press*. Use *click* (for a button, link, or other interface element) or *click on* (for a file, photograph, icon, etc.) for the mouse action. See "Mouse actions" on page 149 for details.

hold on to — Not *hold onto*. The phrasal verb is *hold on,* and *to* is the preposition. Example: *She held on to her smile during the interrogation.*

homepage

Hon. — Abbreviation for *Honorable*. When used before a person's name, precede with *the*. See "Honorable."

Honorable — An honorary title. The abbreviation *Hon.* is always OK. When used before a person's name, *Honorable* and *Hon.* are preceded by *the*. Example: *The record shows that the Honorable Donald Brown presided over the case.*

horsepower — May be abbreviated as *hp* (no period).

host name

hotspot (n.), **hot spot** (n.) — One word when referring to a Wi-Fi access point: *Connect to the nearest hotspot to access the Internet.* Otherwise, use two words: *Paparazzi lurked outside Hollywood's latest hot spot.*

hot swap (n.), **hot swapping** (n.); **hot-swappable** (adj.), **hot-swap** (v.) — Two words when used as a noun, hyphenated as an adjective or a verb. The noun means adding or removing computer peripherals or components without having to reboot the computer. Example: *A USB flash drive is hot-swappable: Just plug it in and start using it—no need to restart the computer.*

hour — An acceptable abbreviation for *hour(s)* is *hr.* Note the period.

House of Representatives — Always capitalize the singular form: *U.S. House of Representatives, California House of Representatives*. May also be shortened: *the House, the U.S. House, the California House*. Lowercase the plural form: *the Virginia and North Carolina houses*.

hover — ❶ Don't use to describe the action of holding the mouse pointer over an area of the page. Use a simpler, clearer phrase such as *pass* (or *roll* or *move* or *hold) your mouse cursor over,* or an equivalent phrase.

how-to (n., adj.) — Note hyphen when used as a noun or an adjective. Plural noun: *how-tos*. Examples: *Your How-to Guide to Home Buying* (headline set in title case), *Home-Buying How-To* (another headline in title case), *How-tos include insider tips as well as basics you'll need to understand the process* (sentence).

hp — Acceptable abbreviation for *horsepower*. No period.

hr. — Acceptable abbreviation for *hour(s)*. Note the period. Include a space between the number and *hr*. For information about when it's OK to use the abbreviation, see "Units of measure" on page 273.

HTML — Abbreviation for *Hypertext Markup Language*. Abbreviation is always OK.

hyperlink (n., adj., v.) — ❶ One word, but the term is dated. Use *link* instead.

I

ID (n., v.) — All capitals, no periods, no space. Not *Id, id*. Other acceptable forms: *IDs, ID'ed*.

i.e. — Abbreviation meaning *that is*. Note periods. Don't include a space after the first period. OK to use when space is a consideration; otherwise, use *that is, in other words,* or equivalent. If used, include a comma after the last period. See also "e.g."

IM (n., adj., v.) — Acronym for *instant message*. All capitals, no periods, no space. Other acceptable forms: *IMs, IM'ed, IM'ing*. See also "instant message."

image editing (n.), **image-editing** (adj.) — Two words when used as a noun, hyphenated when used as an adjective.

in. — Acceptable abbreviation for *inch(es)*. Note the period. Include a space between the number and *in*. For information about when it's OK to use the abbreviation, see "Units of measure" on page 273.

inbox

inch — An acceptable abbreviation for *inch(es)* is *in.* (note period).

info — In general, use *information* rather than *info*. In some circumstances, such as if space is tight, *info* is acceptable.

inkjet

instant message (n.), **instant-message** (adj., v.) — Two words when used as a noun. Note hyphen when used as an adjective or a verb. See also "IM." Examples: *She got an instant message from her boss. I'll instant-message you when I arrive. The instant-message conversation proved informative.*

instant messenger — Lowercase except in brand names such as *AOL Instant Messenger*.

Internet — Note capitalization. OK to abbreviate as *Net*. See also "Net."

Internet service provider — Note capitalization. OK to abbreviate as *ISP*. See also "ISP."

intranet — Note lowercase. A private internal network typically accessible only to a select group of individuals.

IP — Abbreviation that can stand for *Internet Protocol* or *intellectual property*.

iPhone — Note capitalization of this Apple trademark. See "Capitalization" on page 239 for information on how to treat names such as this in a title or at the beginning of a sentence. ❶ Do not add an *s* to make the term plural. For more about proper use of trademarks, see "Trademarks" on page 424.

iPod — Note capitalization of this Apple trademark. See "Capitalization" on page 239 for information on how to treat names such as this in a title or at the beginning of a sentence. ❶ Do not use this brand name generically to refer to all MP3 players, and don't add an *s* to make the term plural. For more about proper use of trademarks, see "Trademarks" on page 424.

IR — Acceptable abbreviation for *infrared*.

ISP — Abbreviation for Internet service provider. Plural: *ISPs*.

IT — Abbreviation for *information technology*. Abbreviation is always OK.

iTunes — Note capitalization of this Apple trademark. See "Capitalization" on page 239 for information on how to treat names such as this in a title or at the beginning of a sentence. For information on the proper use of trademarks, see "Trademarks" on page 424.

J

Java — Capitalize when referring to the programming language and related technologies. The term is a Sun Microsystems trademark. For information on the proper use of trademarks, see "Trademarks" on page 424.

JavaScript — One word. Note capitalization of this Sun Microsystems trademark. For information on the proper use of trademarks, see "Trademarks" on page 424.

JD — Abbreviation for *juris doctor* (doctor of law). No periods.

JPEG — Abbreviation for *Joint Photographic Experts Group*. Generally used to refer to any graphic image file produced by using the JPEG standard. Abbreviation is always OK. Plural: *JPEGs*.

Jr., Junior — Abbreviate as *Jr.* only in the full name of a person. Do not precede with a comma. Example: *Sammy Davis Jr. was born on December 8, 1925.*

junk mail

K

K — Acceptable as an abbreviation for *thousand* when space is tight—but only if the meaning is clear, since it can also stand for *kilobytes, kilobits,* and *kilograms*. Don't include a space between the number and *K*. Example: *Toddler Finds $100K in Trash Bin.* See also "thousand."

KB — Abbreviation for *kilobyte*. All capitals. Don't include a space between the number and *KB*.

Kbps — Abbreviation for *kilobits per second*. Note capitalization—especially the lowercase *b,* which distinguishes this from *KBps,* a different measurement. Don't include a space between the number and the abbreviation. Example: *Imagine connecting to the Internet with a dial-up connection as slow as 14.4Kbps.* See also "KBps."

KBps — Abbreviation for *kilobytes per second*. Note capitalization—especially uppercase *B,* which distinguishes this from *Kbps,* a different measurement. Don't include a space between the number and the abbreviation. See also "Kbps."

keylogger, keylogging (n.) — Short for *keystroke logger, keystroke logging*. A *keylogger* is a tool that can log (record) people's keystrokes as they type; for example, to steal sensitive information such as user names and passwords.

keyword, key word (n.) — One word when referring to terms that are used on a webpage to optimize it for search engines. (See Chapter 17.) Use two words in other cases—for example, when *key* is a synonym for *primary* or *most important*. Examples: *An SEO specialist can help you determine the best keywords to use on your webpage so that your page will appear in search results when people search on those words. She heard little else that he said; the key word in the sentence was "love."*

kg — Acceptable abbreviation for *kilogram(s)*. Include a space between the number and *kg*. For information about when it's OK to use the abbreviation, see "Units of measure" on page 273.

kHz — Abbreviation for *kilohertz*. Note capitalization. Don't include a space between the number and *kHz*.

kilobyte — OK to abbreviate as *KB*.

kilogram — An acceptable abbreviation for *kilogram(s)* is *kg* (no period).

kiloliter — An acceptable abbreviation for *kiloliter(s)* is *kl* (no period).

kilometers per hour — An acceptable abbreviation is *km/h* (no periods).

kl — Acceptable abbreviation for *kiloliter(s)*. Include a space between the number and *kl*. For information about when it's OK to use the abbreviation, see "Units of measure" on page 273.

km — Acceptable abbreviation for *kilometer(s)*. Include a space between the number and *km*. For information about when it's OK to use the abbreviation, see "Units of measure" on page 273.

km/h — Acceptable abbreviation for *kilometers per hour*. Include a space between the number and *km/h*.

L

l — Acceptable abbreviation for *liter(s)*. Include a space between the number and *l*. For information about when it's OK to use the abbreviation, see "Units of measure" on page 273.

L.A. — Abbreviation for *Los Angeles*. Note periods (to avoid confusion with the postal abbreviation for Louisiana). Use only when space is tight.

LAN — Acronym for *local area network*. Acronym OK to use after initial explanation.

Latino, Latina (n., adj.) — Generally preferred to *Hispanic*. *Latino* refers to men; *Latina* refers to women. Plural: *Latinos, Latinas*. When possible, be more specific: *Colombian, Mexican American, Puerto Rican*.

layperson — Use this term instead of *layman*.

layup (n.)

lb. — Acceptable abbreviation for *pound(s)*. Note period. Include a space between the number and *lb*. For information about when it's OK to use the abbreviation, see "Units of measure" on page 273.

LCD — Acronym for *liquid-crystal display*. Acronym is always OK. Plural: *LCDs*.

learned, learnt — The preferred U.S. spelling is *learned*. *Learnt* is chiefly British and is considered a variant of *learned* in the United States.

LED — Acronym for *light-emitting diode*. Acronym is always OK. Plural: *LEDs*.

left-hand side — ❶ Don't use. Use *left side* instead.

LGBT — Acronym for *lesbian, gay, bisexual, transgendered*. Acronym OK to use after an explanation.

Li-ion — Acceptable abbreviation for *lithium-ion*, a type of battery. Note capital *L*. See also "lithium-ion."

lineup (n.), **line up** (v.) — One word when used as a noun. Two words when used as a verb.

Linux — Note capitalization of this trademark owned by Linus Torvalds. Not *LINUX*.

liter — An acceptable abbreviation for *liter(s)* is *l* (no period).

lithium-ion (n., adj.) — Lowercase the written-out form of this type of battery. See also "Li-ion."

login (n., adj.); **log in, log in to** (v.) — One word when used as a noun or an adjective. Two words when used as a verb, which may be followed by the preposition *to*. Note that *sign in* is preferred because it sounds less technical. See "sign-in."

logoff (n., adj.), **log off** (v.) — One word when used as a noun or adjective. Two words when used as a verb. Note that *sign out* is preferred because it sounds less technical. See "sign-out."

logon (n., adj.); **log on, log on to** (v.) — One word when used as a noun or adjective. Two words when used as a verb, which may be followed by the preposition *to*. Note that *sign in* is preferred because it sounds less technical. Don't use *log on* to mean simply visiting a website. See "sign-in."

logout (n., adj.), **log out** (v.) — One word when used as a noun or adjective. Two words when used as a verb. Note that *sign out* is preferred because it sounds less technical. See "sign-out." Example: *If you forget to log out, you'll get a logout reminder.*

lookup (n., adj.), **look up** (v.) — One word when used as a noun or adjective: *Have you tried a reverse phone number lookup?* Two words when used as a verb: *I tried to look up her phone number.*

low-fat (adj.) — Note hyphen.

M

m — Acceptable abbreviation for *meter(s)*. Include a space between the number and *m*. For information about when it's OK to use the abbreviation, see "Units of measure" on page 273.

M — ❶ Don't use as an abbreviation for *million* or *thousand*. See "million" and "thousand."

MA — Abbreviation for *master of arts*. No periods.

Mac — Abbreviation for *Macintosh,* an Apple trademark. Abbreviation is always OK.

machine — ❶ Don't use when referring to a computer. Use *computer*. Example: *After 10 seconds, restart the computer.*

mailbox

mail carrier — Use this term instead of *mailman*. See "Write gender-neutral copy" on page 77.

malware

man (n., v.) — ❶ Don't use to refer to both men and women. Use *person* or *people* instead for the noun; *to staff* or *to operate* for the verb. See "Write gender-neutral copy" on page 77.

mankind — ❶ Don't use to refer to all people. Use *humanity* or *humankind* instead. See "Write gender-neutral copy" on page 77.

manmade — ❶ Don't use. Use *handmade, machine-made, synthetic, artificial*, or other words instead. See "Write gender-neutral copy" on page 77.

manpower — ❶ Don't use. Use *staff, workforce,* or other words instead. See "Write gender-neutral copy" on page 77.

mashup (n., adj.), **mash up** (v.) — One word when used as a noun or an adjective. Two words when used as a verb. Examples: *Anyone can create a mashup with the right technology. Use our technology to mash up RSS feeds into a single stream.*

MB — Abbreviation for *megabyte*. All capitals. Don't include a space between the number and *MB*. See also "megabyte."

MBA — Abbreviation for *master of business administration*. No periods.

Mbps — Abbreviation for *megabits per second*. Note capitalization—especially the lowercase *b*, which distinguishes this from *MBps*, a different measurement. Don't include a space between the number and the abbreviation. See also "MBps."

MBps — Abbreviation for *megabytes per second*. Note capitalization—especially uppercase *B*, which distinguishes this from *Mbps*, a different measurement. Don't include a space between the number and the abbreviation. See also "Mbps."

Mbyte — ❶ Don't use as an abbreviation for *megabyte*. See "MB."

mcg — Acceptable abbreviation for *microgram(s)*. Include a space between the number and *mcg*. For information about when it's OK to use the abbreviation, see "Units of measure" on page 273.

media — Treat *media* as a mass noun with a singular verb, unless you can distinguish the individual "mediums" (modes of communication) making up a use of *media*. Examples: *The media is ignoring the story completely* (singular verb when "the media" is a mass noun like "the press"). *Various media are covering the story differently: Print newspapers seem to be burying it, but TV stations and online sites are highlighting it* (plural verb when "media" comprises distinguishable "mediums").

megabyte — OK to abbreviate as *MB*. Don't use *Mbyte*. See "MB."

menu — Lowercase. Also OK: *pull-down menu, list*. Not *drop-down menu*.

message boards — Lowercase when used generically.

metadata (n.)

metatag (n.)

meter — An acceptable abbreviation for *meter(s)* is *m* (no period).

mg — Acceptable abbreviation for *milligram(s)*. Include a space between the number and *mg*. For information about when it's OK to use the abbreviation, see "Units of measure" on page 273.

MHz — Abbreviation for *megahertz*. Note capitalization. Don't include a space between the number and *MHz*.

mi. — Acceptable abbreviation for *mile(s)*. Note the period. Include a space between the number and *mi*. For information about when it's OK to use the abbreviation, see "Units of measure" on page 273.

mice — Plural of *mouse* even when referring to a computer mouse.

microblog (v.), **microblogging** (n., adj.) — No hyphen. *To microblog* is to post short status updates about yourself or about an event using a microblogging service such as Twitter.

microgram — An acceptable abbreviation for *microgram(s)* is *mcg* (no period).

mid- — When forming words with the prefix *mid-,* don't use a hyphen unless a capitalized word follows: *midcentury, mid-Victorian*.

MIDI — Acronym for *Musical Instrument Digital Interface*. All capitals. Acronym is always OK.

mil — Acceptable as an abbreviation for *million* only when space is tight. Include a space between the numeral and *mil*. See also "million." Example: *Rare card sells for $2.3 mil* (headline).

mile — An acceptable abbreviation for *mile(s)* is *mi.* (note period).

milligram — An acceptable abbreviation for *milligram(s)* is *mg* (no period).

milliliters — An acceptable abbreviation for *milliliter(s)* is *ml* (no period).

millimeter — An acceptable abbreviation for *millimeter(s)* is *mm* (no period).

million — Use numerals with *million*. Don't hyphenate the numeral and *million,* even before a noun. As part of a hyphenated compound, use a hyphen between the numeral and *million*. Examples: *2.8 million, a $3 million budget, a 7-million-year-old fossil*. In general, spell out *million*, but if space is tight, *mil* is an acceptable abbreviation. Don't abbreviate as *M*. See also "mil."

min. — Acceptable abbreviation for *minute(s)*. Note the period. Include a space between the number and *min.* For information about when it's OK to use the abbreviation, see "Units of measure" on page 273.

MiniDisc — One word. Note capitalization of this Sony product name. Plural: *MiniDisc devices* or *MiniDisc cartridges*.

minute — An acceptable abbreviation for *minute(s)* is *min.* Note the period.

ml — Acceptable abbreviation for *milliliter(s)*. Include a space between the number and *ml*. For information about when it's OK to use the abbreviation, see "Units of measure" on page 273.

mm — Acceptable abbreviation for *millimeter(s)*. Include a space between the number and *mm*. For information about when it's OK to use the abbreviation, see "Units of measure" on page 273.

mobile (n., adj.) — Acceptable as a noun when it's a shortened form of *mobile phone*. *Mobile phone* is interchangeable with *cell phone* in the U.S.; in the U.K., *mobile phone* is the more common term. In parts of Asia, *handphone* is common.

moblog (n., v.), **moblogging** (n.) — Lowercase. Abbreviated form of *mobile blogging*.

moon — Lowercase. Examples: *On July 20, 1969, Neil Armstrong became the first man to walk on the moon. Mercury does not have a moon.*

mouseover (n.), **mouse over** (v.) — ❶ Don't use to describe the action of holding the mouse pointer over an area of the page. Use *roll, move,* or *pass your mouse cursor over,* or an equivalent phrase.

MP3 — Abbreviation for *MPEG-1 Audio Layer 3*. All capitals, no spaces, no periods. Abbreviation is always OK. Plural: *MP3s.*

mpg — Abbreviation for *miles per gallon*. All lowercase, no spaces, no periods. Include a space between the number and *mpg*.

mph — Abbreviation for *miles per hour*. All lowercase, no spaces, no periods. Include a space between the number and *mph*.

multi- — Generally, close up this prefix with root words unless the root word starts with an *i* or a capital letter—if it does, insert a hyphen. Examples: *multiplayer, multiuser, multi-industry.*

music fest — Two words. Plural: *music fests.*

N

NASCAR — Note capitalization of this National Association for Stock Car Auto Racing trademark.

Nasdaq — Note capitalization of this Nasdaq Stock Market trademark.

nanogram — An acceptable abbreviation for *nanogram(s)* is *ng* (no period).

nanometer — An acceptable abbreviation for *nanometer(s)* is *nm* (no period).

Native American (n., adj.) — Two words, no hyphen. Can be used interchangeably with *American Indian* where appropriate, but follow the subject's preference and use a more specific name (such as *Lakota Sioux* or *Navajo*) where possible.

Net — Capitalize when referring to the Internet. Abbreviation is always OK.

news feed (n.)

newsreader

ng — Acceptable abbreviation for *nanogram(s)*. Include a space between the number and *ng*. For information about when it's OK to use the abbreviation, see "Units of measure" on page 273.

NIC — Acronym for *network interface card,* pronounced "nick" (*a NIC*). Acronym OK to use after initial explanation. Plural: *NICs*.

nickel-metal hydride (n., adj.) — Lowercase the written-out form of this battery type. See also "Ni-MH."

Ni-MH — Acceptable abbreviation for *nickel-metal hydride,* a type of battery. Note capitalization, hyphen.

nm — Acceptable abbreviation for *nanometer(s)*. Include a space between the number and *nm*. For information about when it's OK to use the abbreviation, see "Units of measure" on page 273.

non- — Generally, close up this prefix with root words unless the root word starts with a capital letter—if it does, insert a hyphen. Examples: *noncommercial, nonfiction, nonprofit, non-Darwinian*.

no-no (n.) — Note hyphen. Plural: *no-no's* (note apostrophe).

NYC — Abbreviation for *New York City*. All capitals, no periods, no spaces. Use only when space is tight.

O

OEM — Abbreviation for *original equipment manufacturer*. Abbreviation OK to use after initial explanation. Plural: *OEMs*.

offline

offscreen

OK — All capitals. Not *okay, Ok,* or *ok*.

online

onscreen

open source (n.), **open-source** (adj.) — Two words when used as a noun, hyphenated when used as an adjective. Example: *With open-source software, individuals can study the software's source code and try to improve the product.*

opt-in (n., adj.), **opt in** (v.) — Hyphenated as a noun or an adjective. Two words as a verb. Examples: *The opt-in has been disabled. Read our opt-in policy. To receive electronic statements, you must opt in.*

OS — Abbreviation for *operating system*. Abbreviation OK to use after initial explanation. Plural: *OSes*.

ounce — An acceptable abbreviation for *ounce(s)* is *oz.* (note period).

outbox

overclocking (n.), **overclock** (v.) — One word. Refers to practice of adjusting a computer's CPU to make it run faster than the manufacturer intended it to.

oz. — Acceptable abbreviation for *ounce(s)*. Note period. Include a space between the number and *oz.* For information about when it's OK to use the abbreviation, see "Units of measure" on page 273.

P

Pacific Islander (n., adj.) — Two words, no hyphen. Refers to the native peoples of Polynesia (including Hawaii, Samoa, Tahiti, and Tonga), Micronesia (including Guam, the Northern Marianas, and Palau), and Melanesia (including Fiji and Papua New Guinea).

page view — Two words. The viewing of a webpage by one visitor. (Advertisers consider how many page views a site receives when deciding where and how to advertise.)

passcode

passphrase

password

password-protect (v.) — Note hyphen. Example: *Be sure to password-protect sensitive files on the intranet.*

PayPal — One word. Note capitalization of this eBay trademark.

PC — Abbreviation for *personal computer.* Abbreviation is OK as long as context is clear (abbreviation can also mean *politically correct*). Plural: *PCs.*

PC call — OK to use for a PC-to-PC phone call. Use as a noun only. For a verb form, use *place a PC call, make a PC call, use your PC to call, make calls from your PC,* or similar.

PDA — Abbreviation for *personal digital assistant.* Abbreviation is OK as long as context is clear (abbreviation can also mean *public display of affection*). Plural: *PDAs.*

PDF — Abbreviation for *Portable Document Format.* Generally used to refer to files created by using Adobe Acrobat. Abbreviation is always OK. Plural: *PDFs.*

peer-to-peer (adj.) — Note hyphens.

percent — See "Percentages" on page 282.

pharming — Redirecting traffic from a legitimate website to a hacker's spoof website that appears legitimate.

PhD — Abbreviation for *doctor of philosophy.* No periods.

phishing — Sending email that is supposedly from a legitimate business (such as a trusted financial institution) in an attempt to trick the recipient into responding and submitting sensitive information. Other forms: *phish, phisher.*

PIN — Abbreviation for *personal identification number.* All capitals. Not *PIN number.*

pint — An acceptable abbreviation for *pint(s)* is *pt.* (note period). Note: A pint is a different measurement in the U.S. and the U.K.

pixel — Short for *picture element,* a unit of measurement.

playlist

PlayStation — One word. Note capitalization of this Sony trademark. Do not add an *s* to make the term plural. For more about proper use of trademarks, see "Trademarks" on page 424.

plug-in (n., adj.), **plug in** (v.) — Note hyphen when used as a noun or adjective. Not *plugin*. Two words when used as a verb.

p.m. — Lowercase, no space. Include a space between the number and *p.m.* See also "Time" on page 269.

podcast

police officer — Use this term instead of *policeman* or *policewoman*. See "Write gender-neutral copy" on page 77.

pope — Lowercase unless used as a formal title before a name. Examples: *The pope pushed for social and health care reforms. The president met with Pope Benedict XVI.*

pop-up (n., adj.), **pop up** (v.) — Note hyphen when used as a noun or adjective. Not *popup*. Two words when used as a verb. Examples: *Get rid of pop-ups before they pop up. Stop pop-up ads from ever annoying you again.*

post- — Generally, close up this prefix with root words unless the root word starts with a capital letter—if it does, insert a hyphen. Examples: *postgame, posttrial, postproduction, post-Victorian.*

postal worker — Use this term instead of *postman*. See "Write gender-neutral copy" on page 77.

pound — An acceptable abbreviation for the unit of English measure *pound(s)* is *lb.* (note period).

pre- — Generally, close up this prefix with root words unless the root word starts with an *e* or a capital letter—if it does, insert a hyphen. Examples: *pre-enrollment, preproduction, pre-MP3.*

premiere (n.) — In general, people have debuts, while movies and other events have premieres. A *premier* is a prime minister. See also "debut," and see "Commonly confused words" on page 317.

Pres. — Acceptable abbreviation for *President*: *Pres. Obama.* See "president, President."

president, President — Lowercase unless used as a formal title before a name: *President Barack Obama.* In this case, it may also be abbreviated as *Pres.* (note period): *Pres. Obama.* Do not use *president* or *President* to refer to former presidents. See "former president."

president-elect (n.) — Note hyphen. Refers to a candidate who has been elected but not yet inaugurated. Use *President-elect* before a name: *President-elect Barack Obama.* Otherwise use *president-elect*: *He was the first African American president-elect.*

press — When referring to a key on a keyboard, use *press.* Use *click* (for a button, link, or other interface element) or *click on* (for a file, photograph, icon, etc.) for the mouse action. See "Mouse actions" on page 149 for details.

print (v.) — When instructing readers to create a hard copy of a document, use *print*. In the U.S., *print out* can also be used; in the U.K., *print off*.

printout (n.), **print out** (v.) — One word when used as a noun. Two words when used as a verb. Example: *I'll print out a copy of the article and mark my edits on the printout.*

promo — Short form of *promotional message, promotional announcement,* or something similar. OK to use when space is tight as a heading for a promotion or promotional box.

PS2, PS3 — OK to use as abbreviations for Sony products *PlayStation 2* and *PlayStation 3* as long as their meaning has been made clear. All capitals, no spaces.

pt. — Acceptable abbreviation for *pint(s)*. Note period. Include a space between the number and *pt*. For information about when it's OK to use the abbreviation, see "Units of measure" on page 273.

pull-down menu — Note hyphen. Not *drop-down menu* or *drop-down box*. Also OK: *menu, list*.

push-to-talk (n., adj.) — Lowercase, hyphenated. Example: *They used push-to-talk to keep in touch during the night.*

Q

Q&A — Abbreviation for *question and answer*. All capitals, no spaces. Note ampersand.

quart — An acceptable abbreviation for *quart(s)* is *qt.* (note period). Note: A quart is a different measurement in the U.S. and the U.K.

QuickTime — One word. Note capitalization of this Apple trademark. For information on the proper use of trademarks, see "Trademarks" on page 424.

qt. — Acceptable abbreviation for *quart(s)*. Note period. Include a space between the number and *qt*. For information about when it's OK to use the abbreviation, see "Units of measure" on page 273.

R

RAM — Abbreviation for *random access memory*. Abbreviation is always OK.

readme file — Informational text file that is often included with software.

real time (n.), **real-time** (adj.) — Two words when used as a noun, hyphenated when used as an adjective. Examples: *Watch the file stream in real time. Get real-time updates delivered to your phone.*

re- — Generally, close up this prefix with root words unless the root word starts with an *e* or a capital letter—if it does, insert a hyphen. Exceptions: *re-create, re-cover,* and *re-sent* (to avoid confusion with *recreate, recover,* and *resent*). Examples: *re-elect, reunify, resubscribe, re-FTP.*

representative — For members of Congress, use *Rep.* or *Reps.* before a name: *Rep. John Smith*; *Reps. Smith and Jones*. Otherwise lowercase and don't abbreviate: *The representative from Illinois. Representative* is also a good gender-neutral alternative to *salesman* or *saleswoman*: *Call your sales representative.* See "sales representative."

Republican (n., adj.) — Capitalize when referring to the party, a member of the party, or the committee: *Republican Party, Republican National Committee, Republican John McCain.* Lowercase only when referring to something or someone characterized by republicanism in a general sense, but not necessarily affiliated with the Republican Party.

resubscribe (v.)

resumé — Accent on the last *e* only. OK to use accented character in webpage copy and HTML emails, but use *resume* (with no accent) in plain-text emails or copy that may appear in an RSS feed.

Rev. — Abbreviation for *Reverend*. When used before a person's name, precede with *the*. See "Reverend."

Reverend — An honorific. The abbreviation *Rev.* is always OK. When used before a person's name, *Reverend* and *Rev.* are preceded by *the*. Examples: *The Reverend Ralph David Abernathy was an associate of Martin Luther King Jr. Last week the Rev. Miller presided over the service.*

right-click (n., v.) — Note hyphen.

right-hand side — ❶ Don't use. Use *right side* instead.

ringtone

rock 'n' roll — Note apostrophes. The variant *rock-and-roll* (hyphenated) is also acceptable, although *rock 'n' roll* is preferred.

roundup (n.)

RSS — Acronym for *Really Simple Syndication*. All capitals. Abbreviation is always OK—but avoid using *RSS* on its own, since few people know what it means. Use *news feed, RSS news feed,* or *RSS newsreader* as appropriate.

S

sales representative — Use this term instead of *salesman* or *saleswoman*. See "Write gender-neutral copy" on page 77.

schwag — ❶ Do not use. See "swag."

screen — Use only to refer to the computer screen, not to a page on a website. When referring to a website, use *page*.

screen capture

screencast

screen name

screen reader — An assistive technology (typically software) that vision-impaired people can use to hear the words on a webpage. See "Accessibility tools" on page 106.

screensaver

screenshot

scroll bar

scroll wheel

seasons — Lowercase the names of seasons and derivatives (for example, springtime, wintertime). Don't include a comma between a season name and a year. Example: *Yahoo! Mail launched in fall 1997.*

sec. — Acceptable abbreviation for *second(s)*. Note the period. Include a space between the number and *sec.* For information about when it's OK to use the abbreviation, see "Units of measure" on page 273.

second — When referring to time, an acceptable abbreviation for *second(s)* is *sec.* Note the period.

security key

Senate — Always capitalize the singular form: *U.S. Senate, state Senate, the Senate.* Lowercase the plural form: *the Virginia and North Carolina senates.*

senator — Use *Sen.* or *Sens.* before a name: *Sen. Olympia J. Snowe*; *Sens. Snowe and McCain.* Otherwise lowercase and don't abbreviate: *The senator from Maine.*

Senior, Sr. — Abbreviate as *Sr.* only in the full name of a person. Do not precede *Senior* or *Sr.* with a comma. Example: *Frank M. Hines Sr. retired from his post as CEO of Dodd Inc.*

SEO — Abbreviation for *search engine optimization*. OK to abbreviate after initial explanation.

Sept. 11 — Preferred abbreviation for *September 11, 2001*. When space is very tight, *9/11* may also be used.

setup (n., adj.), **set up** (v.) — One word when used as a noun or an adjective. Two words when used as a verb. Examples: *Set up your Yahoo! store. Check your Yahoo! store setup. Your setup fee has been waived.*

s/he — ❶ Avoid this usage. See "Write gender-neutral copy" on page 77.

showtime — Lowercase unless referring to the cable network.

shwag — ❶ Do not use. See "swag."

sign-in (n., adj.); **sign in, sign in to** (v.) — As a noun or an adjective, it's hyphenated. As a verb, it's two words, which may be followed by the preposition *to*. Because it sounds less technical, Yahoo! prefers *sign in* to *log in* or *log on*. Examples: *All visitors must sign in on the sign-in page. Visitors can sign in to Yahoo! Mail automatically. Choose your preferences for sign-in and security.*

sign-in seal — Lowercase. Note hyphen. A secret message or image created to help protect against phishing. Examples: *Create a sign-in seal for this computer. My sign-in seal is not displaying.*

sign-out (n., adj.); **sign out, sign out of** (v.) — As a noun or an adjective, it's hyphenated. As a verb, it's two words, which may be followed by the preposition *of*. Because it sounds less technical, Yahoo! prefers *sign out* to *log out* or *log off*.

sign-up (n., adj.), **sign up** (v.) — Hyphenate when used as a noun or an adjective. Two words when used as a verb. Examples: *Sign up for the service. Fill in the sign-up form. Sign-up is free.*

SIM card — SIM stands for *subscriber identity module,* a card used in cell phones. Abbreviation is always OK.

site map

slideshow (n., adj.)

smart card

smartphone

SMS — Abbreviation for *short message service,* used for text messaging. Abbreviation OK to use after initial explanation.

snail mail

sneak peek — Not *peak*.

Social Security number — Note capitalization. See also "SSN."

social network (n.), **social-network** (adj.) — Two words when used as a noun. Note hyphen when used as an adjective. Examples: *Social-network analysis is a key technique in modern sociology. Add contacts to expand your social network.*

social networking (n.), **social-networking** (adj.) — Note hyphen when used as an adjective. Two words when used as a noun. Examples: *The social-networking phenomenon has really taken off. To attract users, the site added social networking.*

spacebar

spam (n., adj., v.) — Lowercase when referring to unsolicited email or the act of sending such email.

spammer

spell-checker (n.), **spell-check** (v.) — Note hyphen.

spokesperson — Use this term instead of *spokesman* or *spokeswoman*. See "Write gender-neutral copy" on page 77.

spring, springtime — Lowercase the season name. See also "seasons."

spyware

square foot — An acceptable abbreviation for *square foot* and *square feet* is *sq. ft.* (note the periods).

square inch — An acceptable abbreviation for *square inch(es)* is *sq. in.* (note periods).

square kilometer — An acceptable abbreviation for *square kilometer(s)* is *sq km* (no periods).

square meter — An acceptable abbreviation for *square meter(s)* is *sq m* (no periods).

square mile — An acceptable abbreviation for *square mile(s)* is *sq. mi.* (note periods).

square yard — An acceptable abbreviation for *square yard(s)* is *sq. yd.* (note periods).

sq. ft. — Acceptable abbreviation for *square foot* and *square feet*. Note the periods. Include a space between the number and this abbreviation. For information about when it's OK to use the abbreviation, see "Units of measure" on page 273.

sq. in. — Acceptable abbreviation for *square inch(es)*. Note the periods. Include a space between the number and this abbreviation. For information about when it's OK to use the abbreviation, see "Units of measure" on page 273.

sq km — Acceptable abbreviation for *square kilometer(s)*. Include a space between the number and this abbreviation. For information about when it's OK to use the abbreviation, see "Units of measure" on page 273.

sq m — Acceptable abbreviation for *square meter(s)*. Include a space between the number and this abbreviation. For information about when it's OK to use the abbreviation, see "Units of measure" on page 273.

sq. mi. — Acceptable abbreviation for *square mile(s)*. Note the periods. Include a space between the number and this abbreviation. For information about when it's OK to use the abbreviation, see "Units of measure" on page 273.

sq. yd. — Acceptable abbreviation for *square yard(s)*. Note the periods. Include a space between the number and this abbreviation. For information about when it's OK to use the abbreviation, see "Units of measure" on page 273.

SSN — Abbreviation for *Social Security number*. Do not use *SSN number*. See also "Social Security number."

standalone (adj.)

startup (n., adj.), **start up** (v.) — One word when used as a noun or an adjective. Two words when used as a verb.

style sheet (n.) — Two words; lowercase even when referring to style sheets created with CSS language.

sub- — Generally, close up this prefix with root words unless the root word starts with a capital letter—if it does, insert a hyphen. Example: *subdomain*.

SULEV — Acronym for *super-ultra-low-emission vehicle*. Acronym OK to use after initial explanation. Pronounced "soo-lev" (*a SULEV*). Plural: *SULEVs*.

summer, summertime — Lowercase the season name. See also "seasons."

super- — Generally, close up this prefix with root words unless the root word starts with a capital letter; if it does, insert a hyphen. Examples: *superdelegate, superfood, super-PC*. (Note: If you can substitute *fabulous* or *excellent* for *super,* it's an adjective, not a prefix.)

SUV — Acronym for *sport-utility vehicle*. Acronym is always OK.

swag — Free goods. Not *schwag* or *shwag*.

sync, synched, synching (v.) — No *h* in *sync*. The other verb forms have an *h* to make them easier to read correctly at first glance. (Without the *h*, people may initially read *syncing* as "since-ing.")

T

techno- — Generally, close up this prefix with root words unless the root word starts with an *o* or a capital letter—if it does, insert a hyphen. Examples: *technobabble, technoelitist, technophobia.*

text (n., v.) — Short form of *text message*. Plural: *texts*. Other forms: *texted, texting*. Examples: *Did you get my text? Don't text while driving. She was texting during the lecture.* See also "text message."

text box

text message (n.), **text-message** (adj., v.) — Two words when used as a noun. Note hyphen when used as an adjective or a verb. Examples: *She had a heated text-message argument with her boyfriend. Did you get my text message? I'll text-message you with the details.*

thank-you (n., adj.), **thank you** (v. + obj.) — Note hyphen when used as a noun or an adjective. Two words when used as a verb and object. Plural: *thank-yous*. Examples: *As a thank-you for your participation, you'll receive a $10 gift card. Please accept this thank-you gift for your participation. We would like to thank you for participating.*

theater, theatre — The preferred U.S. spelling is *theater*. *Theatre* is chiefly British.

thousand — In general, spell out *thousand*, but if space is tight, *K* is an acceptable abbreviation. Don't abbreviate as *M* or *G*. See "K." Example: *Contestant wins $5K on game show* (headline).

thumb drive — Two words, lowercase. Another name for *flash drive*. See also "flash."

timeshift, timeshifting — One word. Refers to recording and storing a program to watch or to listen to later.

TiVo — Note capitalization. ❶ Do not use this trademark generically or as a verb, and don't add an *s* to form a plural. For more about proper use of trademarks, see "Trademarks" on page 424.

toolbar — Lowercase when used generically.

tooltip — One word, lowercase. A small box containing informational text that appears onscreen when the mouse cursor or pointer rolls over an item on a webpage. Also called a help tag.

TOS — Abbreviation for *terms of service*. Abbreviation OK on second reference.

touchpad (n., adj.)

touchscreen (n., adj.)

toward, towards — The preferred U.S. spelling is *toward*. *Towards* is chiefly British and is considered a variant of *toward* in the United States.

trackball (n., adj.)

trainwreck (n.)

trans fat (n.)

traveler (n.); **traveled, traveling** (v.) — The preferred U.S. spelling has one *l*. The preferred British spelling has two *l*'s.

Trojan horse — Note capitalization.

troubleshoot

T-shirt — Note capitalization and hyphen.

turnout (n.), **turn out** (v.) — One word when used as a noun: *We expect a huge voter turnout.* Two words when used as a verb: *Let's see how many voters turn out for this election.*

TV — Abbreviation is always OK. Plural: *TVs*.

U

UI — Abbreviation for user interface. Abbreviation OK to use after initial explanation.

U.K. (n., adj.) — Abbreviation for *United Kingdom*. Note periods, no space. Use *UK* (with no periods) only in postal addresses.

U.N. (n., adj.) — Abbreviation for *United Nations*. Note periods, no space.

UNIX

upper-left corner — Note hyphen. Not *upper-left-hand corner*.

upper-right corner — Note hyphen. Not *upper-right-hand corner*.

up-to-date — Note hyphens. Examples: *Keep your calendar up-to-date. Keep an up-to-date calendar.*

URL — All capitals. Stands for *Uniform Resource Locator*. Abbreviation is always OK. Plural: *URLs*. Pronunciation "yoo-ar-el" is most common (*a URL*); however, pronouncing *URL* as "earl" is also acceptable (*an URL*) as long as it is done consistently.

U.S. (n., adj.) — Abbreviation for *United States*. Note periods, no space. Not *US* or *U. S.* The single exception is specifying currency in prices; in this case, do not include the periods. Example: *US$299*.

USA — Abbreviation for *United States of America*. Abbreviation is always OK.

USB — Abbreviation for *Universal Serial Bus*. Abbreviation is always OK.

user — Because of the techie, impersonal nature of the term *user*, consider using *member, subscriber, customer, reader, visitor,* or similar. For more details, see "User–instruction mechanics" on page 144.

user name — Lowercase, two words. Not *username*.

V

VGA — Abbreviation for *video graphics array*. Abbreviation is always OK.

vice president (n.) — Two words, no hyphen. Capitalize before a name: *Vice President Joe Biden*. Otherwise lowercase: *She would have been the first female vice president*. In both cases, it may be abbreviated as *VP: VP Joe Biden; the first female VP*.

vice-presidential (adj.) — Always hyphenated.

vidcast — One word, lowercase. Short for *video podcast*.

video camera

videoconference

video game

video gamer

videophone

vlog — One word, lowercase. Short for *video blog*.

voicemail — One word, lowercase. Not *voice mail*.

voicemail box

VoIP — Abbreviation for *voice over Internet Protocol*. Abbreviation OK to use after initial explanation.

VPN — Abbreviation for *virtual private network*. Abbreviation OK to use after initial explanation.

W

WAN — Acronym for *wide area network*. Acronym OK to use after initial explanation.

WAP — Abbreviation for *Wireless Application Protocol*. Abbreviation OK after initial explanation.

Washington, D.C. — Note the comma and periods. The abbreviation stands for *District of Columbia*. When space is tight, *Wash. DC* is an acceptable abbreviation. *Washington* may also be used if there is no chance it will be confused for the state of Washington.

Web (n., adj.) — Note capitalization. Examples: *Yahoo! Search helps you find information on the Web. Cut and paste the address into your Web browser.*

webcam

webcast

Web conference

Web feed

Web hosting

webinar — A seminar conducted online.

webisode

weblog — Use only when describing the origin of the word *blog,* which is the preferred usage. See also "blog."

webmaster

webpage

website

white — Lowercase when referring to race.

Wi-Fi — Short for *wireless fidelity*. Note capitalization and hyphen. Shortened form always OK.

Wii — Note capitalization and spelling of this Nintendo trademark. Do not add an *s* to form the plural. For more about proper use of trademarks, see "Trademarks" on page 424.

wiki — Lowercase. Plural: *wikis*.

winter, wintertime — Lowercase the season name. See also "seasons."

word-of-mouth (n., adj.) — Note hyphens when used as a noun or adjective.

word processing (n.), **word-processing** (adj.) — Two words when used as a noun, hyphenated when used as an adjective.

workflow

world phone — Two words, lowercase. A cell phone that works on networks around the world.

World Wide Web — Note capitalization.

worldwide (adj., adv.)

WWW — All capitals. OK to use as an abbreviation for World Wide Web.

WYSIWYG — Acronym for *what you see is what you get.* Abbreviation is always OK.

X

Xbox — One word. Note capitalization of this Microsoft trademark. Do not add *es* to form the plural. For more about proper use of trademarks, see "Trademarks" on page 424.

XHTML — Abbreviation for *Extensible Hypertext Markup Language.* Depending on audience, may require explanation on first reference.

XML — Abbreviation for *Extensible Markup Language.* Depending on audience, may require explanation on first reference.

X-ray — Note capitalization and hyphen.

Y

Yahoo (n.) — When referring to an employee or user of Yahoo!, use uppercase *Y* and no exclamation point. Plural: *Yahoos.* Example: *Yahoo! employs many Yahoos.*

yahoo (v.) — When using *yahoo* as a verb, use lowercase *y* and no exclamation point. Don't use *yahoo* (the verb) as an exclamation. Example: *Yahoo! employees are a dedicated group, often found yahooing on their own time.*

Yahoo! — When referring to the company, its brands, products, or services, use uppercase *Y.* Note that the exclamation point is considered a character, not a punctuation mark. Possessive: *Yahoo!'s.*

yard — An acceptable abbreviation for *yard(s)* is *yd.* (note period).

yd. — Acceptable abbreviation for *yard(s).* Note the period. Include a space between the number and *yd.* For information about when it's OK to use the abbreviation, see "Units of measure" on page 273.

YouTube — One word. Note capitalization of this Google trademark.

Z

zero-emission (adj.) — Hyphenated when used as an adjective: *zero-emission car*. Note that there is no *s* at the end of *emission*.

ZIP code — Note capitalization. Not *Zip code*.

Exercise Answer Keys

Chapter 10 exercise

Did you find all 37 errors? While some of the punctuation mistakes are subtle, many of them make the sentences more difficult to read, forcing you to insert your own mental pauses to break up the phrases, or causing you to slow down or backtrack to understand the meaning. Proper punctuation clarifies and simplifies.

1. Yes, Bill's CDs are alphabetically organized; so are his vintage '80s concert T-shirts, his canned vegetables, and his not-so-effective self-help books.
   Better: Create two sentences instead: Yes, Bill's CDs are alphabetically organized. *So are his vintage '80s concert T-shirts, his canned vegetables, and his not-so-effective self-help books.*

2. Why don't you explore the diverse landscapes of New Zealand, where you can see beaches, tropical forests, alpine mountains, fjords, volcanoes, and caves.
   Better: Delete the first three words and start with Explore.

3. Archimedes' study of levers led him to boast, "Give me a place to stand on, and I can move the earth."

4. A typical member of Generation Y, Emily learned her ABCs from "Sesame Street" but learned numbers by playing with her dad's defunct cell phone.

5. To have a happy, healthy spring break:
   - Choose a room above the hotel's first floor, which may be easy to break into.
   - Travel with a buddy, especially at night.
   - Drink alcohol responsibly: Know your limits.

6. Students enrolling in the MBA program will see their tuition rise by $5,000 per year.

7. Jewelers recommend spending two months' salary on a diamond engagement ring. However, you might save a little by buying just after Valentine's Day or Christmas, because sales peak before those two most popular days to propose.

8. Paris's abduction of Helen started the Greeks' 10-year siege of Troy; Odysseus's Trojan-horse ruse finally ended the war.

9. The tuberculosis strain that killed the St. Paul, Minnesota, man is drug-resistant, unresponsive to either first- or second-line medications.

10. Europe discovered the Bahamas when Christopher Columbus landed on one of the islands in October 1492. Before Sidney Poitier, the most famous—or infamous—resident of the Bahamas was the pirate Blackbeard.

Chapter 11 exercise

Capitalization, abbreviation, and punctuation are small style matters, but handling them inconsistently can give visitors a rocky reading experience and may lead to confusion. Plus, the more eagle-eyed members of your audience may question your expertise. Read on to see how we smoothed out the sentences according to the guidelines in this book.

1. "Alternative text" is text that you enter as an HTML attribute for an image.
2. Gadfly Games has had a surprise hit with its Sandcastle phone game, thanks to Senior Designer Luke Jackson's inventive sand structures and hilarious castle-stomping monsters.
3. Inspired by the Web video "An Engineer's Guide to Cats," Demetri is recording his kittens, Petaflop and Nanobot, for a piece called "A Physicist's Guide to Feline Mechanics."
4. The "Zoo News" podcast has just released an episode called "All About Alligators."
5. To upload a photo:
    1. Go to the Upload Photos and Videos page: http://www.flickr.com/photos/upload
    2. Click the **Choose photos and videos** link to browse your hard drive.
    3. Select the file you want and click **Open**. You can upload JPEGs, nonanimated GIFs, TIFFs, and BMPs.
    4. Click the **Upload Photos and Videos** button.
6. EFreebird is a new mobile-phone download for concertgoers. When you load the app, it displays a flickering lighter; requests "Freebird"; and shouts, "More cowbell!" and five other annoying concert clichés.
7. The recommended daily allowance (RDA) for calcium is 1,000 mg for adults 19 to 50 years old, the amount in 30 oz. (a little less than 1 qt.) of fortified orange juice, which will also provide more than the RDAs for vitamins C and D.
8. Ms. Cha is managing editor of the Southeast Asia bureau of Global News Inc.
9. Jade is catching up on some of the novels she never read in college: "The Heart Is a Lonely Hunter," "Far From the Madding Crowd," "Slaughterhouse-Five," "Winesburg, Ohio," "Things Fall Apart," and "Play It as It Lays."
10. The candidate has a great resumé, but Human Resources questioned her judgment when she listed her email address, BoozeHound@yahoo.com, and her party-girl blog, Too Much Information (www.TooMuchInformation.net).
    (Many people will understand the acronym "HR," but it's not in all major dictionaries, so you might want to spell it out—or, if your audience will understand the acronym, add "HR" to your word list [see page 433] as an acronym that's always OK to use.)

Chapter 12 exercise

Numerals are compact and exact, and that makes them a friend to online readers. Our eyes are drawn to dollar signs and digits, and often numbers offer the most relevant information in a headline, an opening paragraph, or anywhere else on the page. But poorly formatted, inconsistently treated numbers can make copy *less* readable. Edits such as the following can help an audience navigate the numbers.

1. The World Wide Web was born on December 25, 1990, when Tim Berners-Lee sent the first communication between Web client and server.
2. Off-season rates apply, except during spring break, March 7–21.
3. With wild mushrooms priced at $25 per pound in some markets, it might be cheaper to rent a truffle pig for an hour.
4. The state's "first dog" is used to crowds—she was the 9th puppy in a litter of 10.
5. More than 6,000 languages are spoken worldwide, though some linguists estimate that 7.5% are nearly extinct, and many more—about 50% total—are endangered because no children speak them. *(Using the word "percent" after both numerals would also be correct if that is your style choice: "7.5 percent are nearly extinct, and many more—about 50 percent total—are endangered." See "Percentages" on page 282.)*
6. Bouquets often feature an odd number of stems, such as 5 or 15, but be aware that in the language of flowers, 3 red roses can mean "I love you."
7. State troopers attacked 600 peaceful protesters for civil rights in the March 7, 1965, march to Montgomery, Alabama.
8. Brazil led Venezuela 1–0 at the half but ended up losing by 2 points.
9. In 1996 a notebook with a 133MHz processor, a 1.3GB hard drive, and a 28.8Kbps modem cost about $3,000; in 2009 the same money will buy a loaded laptop with a 2.5GHz processor, a 320GB hard drive, and built-in wireless.
10. Hadrian's Wall was begun in A.D. 122 and was staffed by Roman soldiers until the legions pulled out of Britain in the early 5th century.
11. The help desk is open from 9 a.m. to 5 p.m. When it's closed, call 800-XXX-XXXX for assistance.
12. The 6-foot-2-inch (1.88-meter) George Washington was grander in stature than the average male colonist in the 1700s, who was 5 feet 9 inches tall. Still, the colonists were 2 inches taller than the English.

Chapter 13 exercise

Each of the original sentences contained lots of fat and little muscle—and many opportunities for trimming. For instance, in the first example, the original sentence contained 19 words and 102 characters (with spaces), whereas our solution contains just 9 words and 48 characters—half its former self. Here are some possible answers:

1. To reset your password, go to My Preferences.
2. For the best deals on personal jetpacks, visit www.flyastroboy.com.
3. Before you decide who'll get your vote for mayor, look at all the candidates and their policies.
4. Sign up for our community-supported agriculture program to get fresh fruits and vegetables delivered to your home each week.
5. To buy tickets, click the shopping cart icon.
6. Avoid bear raids: Hang your food sacks between trees.
7. With Phone-E, you can call your email contacts from your PC or other Web-enabled device.
8. Search for local restaurants and make a reservation, too.
9. To upload photos from your phone to your website, download our free photo widget.
10. To make our site your homepage in Firefox for Windows:
    1. Go to the **Tools** menu.
    2. Choose **Options**.
    3. Click the **Main** button.
    4. In the **Home Page** box, enter **http://www.yahoo.com**.
    5. Click **OK**.

Chapter 14 exercise

Did you find all 20 spelling and grammar pitfalls? Read on for our explanations of the errors, and give yourself a gold star if you edited sentences (1) and (4) more rigorously.

1. **Now** that Carla has an urban garden allotment, she grows **a lot** of tomatoes and okra.
   (2 mistakes: "a lot" is two words, and "since" has multiple meanings, so you should avoid it when you can. Bonus: You can trim "has been able to grow" to just "grows.")

2. **You're embarrassing** everyone with your sloppy typing, bad grammar, and stubborn **refusal** to use a spell-checker.
   (3 mistakes: "Your" should be "You're" or "You are"; "embarrassing" has two r's; and the list should have a parallel structure following "your"—noun, noun, noun rather than noun, noun, verb.)

3. Both of the twins are taking driving lessons, but neither Anya nor Alexei **has** driven **farther** than the airport yet.
   (2 mistakes: First, the twins are driving a distance, so you should use "farther" rather than "further." Second, "both" takes a plural verb, but in "neither-nor" constructions, the verb should match the latter subject, in this case a singular.)

4. The person **who** first wrote a computer program was Ada Lovelace, who **besides** being Lord Byron's daughter created an algorithm for calculating Bernoulli numbers with Charles Babbage's analytical engine.
   (2 mistakes: "person" should be followed by "who," not "which," and "beside" should be "besides." Bonus: Improve the sentence further with a rewrite: "Ada Lovelace, Lord Byron's daughter, wrote the first computer program, an algorithm for calculating Bernoulli numbers with Charles Babbage's analytical engine.")

5. Looking at the length of Darnell's beard, **I'd guess that** his wife has been out of town for two weeks.
   (1 mistake: a dangling modifier. In the original sentence, the "Looking" phrase modifies "his wife"—and she can't be looking; she's presumably out of town. The person who's looking is the same one who's guessing: "I.")

6. If Sean wants to join a sports team, his mom will let him play anything that doesn't require padding, so he could think about **playing either** tennis or rugby.
   (1 mistake: The elements on both sides of "or" should be parallel: "either playing tennis or playing rugby" or—the shorter solution—"playing either tennis or rugby.")

7. If you don't pack each of those **collectible** teacups in bubble wrap, you will **definitely** end up with a box of worthless shards.
   (2 mistakes: The preferred spelling of "collectible" is with "-ible" rather than "-able," and "definitely" isn't spelled with an "a.")

8. He'd rather take vitamins **than** eat fruit and vegetables **every day**.
(2 mistakes: "then" should be "than," and "everyday" should be "every day.")

9. Kendra is obsessed with that film and wants to see everything: the sneak **peeks** at the **principal** photography, **the** Cannes **premiere**, and **the** DVD extras.
(4 mistakes: "peaks" should be "peeks," "principle" should be "principal," "premier" should be "premiere," and the list should be parallel, with "the" preceding each element.)

10. Eric says he's buying a pass to the *Star Trek* convention—the ticket price doesn't **faze** him.
(1 mistake: "phase" should be "faze.")

Chapter 15 exercise

Our sample blog may not look too bad at first glance, but that copy contains more than 65 small problems—either errors or inconsistencies with Yahoo! style. For starters, you may have noticed that the headline and the subheadings had conflicting capitalization styles, that the bold headings were not in numerical order and were not parallel in structure (two began with nouns rather than verbs), and that one heading (number 9) did not describe the text that followed. Remember the heading test: Can you understand what the story is about by reading only the headline and subheadings?

In the solution below, brackets mark each correction. How many errors did you find?

10 tips for [b][e]tter [b]logging

(You may wish to use title case for your headings; we chose sentence case. See "Establish heading styles" on page 57. Whichever style you choose, be consistent.)

By MemeTeam staff

The great thing about blogging is that anyone can do it. The [lousy] thing about blogging is that plenty of people *do* blog[—]and many of them could write much more engaging posts [if only] they observed a few guidelines. Here are Meme[ ]Team's [10] tips [for] creating a more frisky and focused blog.

(Remember to code any special characters so that they don't show up as garbage text, as the dash between "blog" and "and" did. See "Special characters" on page 386. And we changed "ten tips" to "10 tips" because Yahoo! style for numbers is to spell out one through nine and to use numerals after that. See "The basics" on page 261.)

1. Blog your passions. Write about topics that matter to you—and that matter to your audience, too. Nobody wants to [hear] about your new electric toothbrush (unless it spontaneously combusted after an especially[ ]vigorous scrubbing). When you write about subjects that you love (or hate), you['re] more confident, you['re] more likely to commit to blogging regularly, and readers will find your enthusiasm infectious.

2. Have an opinion; add value. Online info[r]mation reproduces like rabbits, and readers have a lot of sites to choose [from]. So, make *your* distinct voice and perspective a selling point: A fresh point of view inspires readers to share links to your site and to come back for more. And if you[']re blogging about [something] that lots of other writers are covering, then don't just regurgitate the facts[—]add something unique and valuable to [the] post, whether it's extra information, a photo, your informed opinion, a sense of humor, or something else.

(When curly quotes are formatted by word-processing software, they may display incorrectly on your webpage—as you may have noticed with the apostrophe in "you're." Be sure to do one of two things: (1) Use straight quotation marks, whether single or double, or (2) use code to create these special characters. See "Special characters" on page 386.)

3. Converse.[ ] Although a blog very much needs your point of view, it's not a monologue or your boring personal journal—it's a dialog[ue] with your readers. Let them in to the conversation by blogging about subjects they can relate to, by encouraging [c]omments, and [by] cultivating a sense of community. (Tell us what you think of this blog by clicking the [Comment] button at the end.[)]

4. Set a [s]chedule. Establish an ambitious but reasonable frequency for posting stories, and stick to the [timetable]. A number of factors will [a]ffect the frequency: how time[-]sensitive your stories are, how often readers [expect] new material, how much content you can crank out, and so forth. Remember, though: [Q]uantity is not a substitute for quality.

[5]. Keep it short, sweet[,] and neat. Readers come to blogs for a quick hit, not for ["]War and Peace["]or 3[,]000 words about how your cat spat a hairball onto your [DVDs]. Write about one solid topic per blog, try to keep your posts in the 200[-] to 300-word range, and organize information so that [it's] easily skimmed.

(Depending on your organization's style, you might put a book title in italics instead of double quotation marks. We recommend quotation marks for the Web. See "Titles of works" on page 251 and "Quotation marks" on page 223.)

[6]. Make your headline count. A good headline is short [and] full of keywords, and [it] gives readers a sneak pe[e]k at the story. Write a brief, proper[-]noun-loaded headline that will play nicely with [search] engines, mobile browsers[,] and news feeds. A catchy, clever headline will get clicks, but above all it should be clear—[people] may not click if they see a [standalone] headline and can't tell what the story's about.

(In the original sentence beginning "A good headline . . . ," the series was not parallel: It had the linking verb "is" preceding not only the adjectives "short" and "full" (which is fine) but also the verb "gives." So, not only was it saying that a good headline "is short" and "is full," but it was also saying that a good headline "is gives" readers a sneak peek.

We chose to insert "and," which puts the first two adjectives into a parallel series by themselves; then, the verb "gives" gets a new subject: "it." You may have found a different way to fix the problem.)

7. Link, link, link[.] Blogging is about building community and sharing the love. A blogroll [(a list of blogs that you recommend)] and related links give readers [valuable] context and [show] that you have some expertise. Make sure that links [in]clude keywords for [search engine optimization] [(]SEO[)].

(A short explanation of potentially unfamiliar terms like "blogroll" will make your site more reader friendly. See "Junk the jargon" on page 308.)

8. [Add] [v]isuals. Add photos and videos to your posts. As the clich[é] says, a picture is worth a thousand words, and visual elements are a big benefit of Web features. Get permission to use material that's not [yours], make sure that embedded videos [from] other sources will [not] disappear, and don't forget alt[ernative] text [(an image description that appears when the image doesn't)] and captions.

(Accented characters, such as the one in "cliché," must be coded to ensure that they appear properly. See "Special characters" on page 386.)

9. [Test your page]. Readers will call you out—loudly[—]if you post copy with [typos], bad links, or factual errors. Proofread your text, test your user interface[,] and quickly correct any mistakes that slip th[r]ough.

10. Be blog savvy. Learn from your peers: Check [out] blogs written by your readers and your competitors, as well as popular blogs (see [MemeTeam's favorite blogs][) on subjects other than your own. You'll discover new widgets and writing strategies, and you might even find coverage gaps that your blog can fill.]

Chapter 16 exercise

If you were to view the page source for our sample text, it might look like this:

```
<h1>How to invent a stupid band name</h1>

<p>You've been racking your brains for a band name that will express
your singular musical genius, and you've come up with &#8230; zilch.
Never fear, we can help you come up with something stupid in five
minutes or less. And let's face it, you probably won't invent anything
sillier than the average boy-band moniker.</p>

<h2>Step 1: Make a list of words</h2>
<p>Pop-culture references are good, and so are unusual words, but don't
spend more than a minute or two on this step&#8212;just jot down
whatever pops into your head. These categories often yield fruitful
results:</p>
<ul>
<li>Animals and mythical creatures</li>
<li>Natural disasters</li>
<li>Children's book title or character</li>
<li>Interjections (<em>oh, wow, shh, hooray</em>)</li>
<li>Colors</li>
<li>Song lyrics</li>
<li>Name or nickname of a person you like</li>
<li>Character in a cult movie</li>
<li>Hairstyles</li>
<li>Fruit</li>
<li>Moods</li>
<li>Auto parts</li>
</ul>

<h2>Step 2: Mix and match</h2>
<p>Now combine two or more of your words. Puns can work (we are aiming
for stupid, after all), and so can counterintuitive pairings. Those two
things don't belong together? All the better. We coughed up these 10
dorky concoctions in about 60 seconds:</p>
```

```
<ol>
<li>Centaur Mullets</li>
<li>Goodnight Loon</li>
<li>Night of the Living Jed</li>
<li>The Recalcitrant Kiwis</li>
<li>Spicoli and the Custom Vans</li>
<li>Cyclone Clutch</li>
<li>Sid Capricious</li>
<li>Helen and the Heck Yeahs</li>
<li>Napoleon Pillow Fight</li>
<li>Ice-T Phone Home</li>
</ol>

<h2>Step 3: Search and deploy</h2>
<p>Consult your bandmates&#8212;if you really care what the drummer
thinks&#8212;to narrow down the list. Go to a search engine and search
on each name, in quotes ("Centaur Mullets"). If you're serious about
using the name, then also search a trademark database (in the U.S.: <a
href="http://www.uspto.gov/">www.uspto.gov</a>) and consider registering your
name to protect it. Don't see any other bands using the name? Then
congratulations, you can now set up a homepage, start printing
T-shirts, and maybe think about actually recording some songs.</p>

<p><strong>Related links:</strong><br>
<a href="[domain name]/stupidlyrics.html">How to write stupid lyrics
</a><br>
<a href="[domain name]/stupiddemo.html">How to record your stupid
demo</a><br></p>

<p><strong>Sponsored link:</strong><br>
<a href="http://www.bootlegbaby.com/">Buy rock 'n' roll baby clothes at
Bootleg B&#228;by</a><br></p>
```

Acknowledgments

Many experts contributed to this book and made it possible.

A core team of Yahoo! editors reconceived the company's in-house style guide, addressing new concepts and re-examining the old to produce a guide that's both road-tested and up-to-date. The members of this small but mighty team included:

- Heather Hutson, who managed the project, edits, and revisions with utmost skill and grace. In addition to writing the chapter on basic webpage coding as well as other pieces, she kept us on the right track while always striving for clarity. Heather has worked for more than a decade as an editor and writer in both print and online media.

- Julie Wildhaber, who helped edit the whole shebang and wrote the chapters on audience, voice, and writing for the world, as well as pieces of several other chapters and most of this guide's "Ideas in Practice" exercises and examples. Julie trains writers and editors for Yahoo! and has been editing on the Web since 1996.

- Maria Cianci, who asked lots of important questions throughout the editing process and sought to cut, combine, and clarify information. Maria is a Yahoo! editor and an expert on user-interaction writing.

- Karen Seriguchi, who compiled much of the punctuation chapter, including some very fun examples. Karen also contributed her thorough knowledge of grammar, usage, and style as well as her familiarity with numerous other style guides and with styles in use at other publications to help us make well-informed decisions that took into account traditional principles and actual practice.

- Naomi Lucks, who bravely agreed to plunge into this complex project in progress. Naomi lent her outsider's eye and years of eclectic writing, development, and editing experience to the tasks of shaping the chapters in line with the book's own principles (helping us *get to the point already!*) and helping to harmonize the varied voices of our numerous contributors.

- Trystan L. Bass, who concentrated particularly on reviewing the guide's recommendations for writing user-interface text, always considering the website user's experience. A Yahoo! editor since 2001, Trystan is an adamant defender of the serial comma.

- Michele Meyer, who lent her skills to editing several chapters and who contributed many terms to the word list. With Yahoo! since 2004, Michele copyedits content across the Yahoo! network.

- Amy Weaver Dorning, who provided solid ideas for shortening and simplifying longer passages of text and for streamlining steps in a process. Amy also copyedits content across the Yahoo! network.

- Laura Barcella, who was able to approach the text from a general reader's perspective, focusing on whether it would be comprehensible to a broad audience. Laura is also a Yahoo! copy editor.

- Tony Herr, our extraordinary technical editor, who pored over the intricacies of Web coding and alerted us to the many ways it can trip up writers.
- Marla Miyashiro, the amazing copy editor and proofreader whose skill, thoughtfulness, and stamina improved the entire book as we brought the project to a hectic close.

Special thanks to Alan Brightman, PhD, and Victor Tsaran for their leadership on the issue of Web accessibility. Thanks to the legal team led by Andrew Savage—David Brightman, Laura Covington, J. Scott Evans, Jeremy Kessel, and Abigail Phillips—for the content in "Understand the Basics of U.S. Law for Online Content" and for their endless reviews.

Other current and former Yahoos who must be thanked include Diana Cernobori, Adam Chaput, Dennis Chu, Evelyn Chua, Sue Coakley, Gabriel Coan, Bill Gannon, Denise Garlick, Meg Garlinghouse, Havi Hoffman, Nancy Hubbard, Gordon Hurd, Prasad Kantamneni, Mike Krumboltz, Christine Lee, Molly McCall, Patrick McLoughlin, Chris Moeller, Jen Moyse, Margot Neebe, Allen Olivo, Miranda Pinckert, Jill Robinson, Keith Saft, Laura Varteressian, and Cathryn Weems.

Our gratitude to SEO strategist and former Yahoo Jessica Bowman of SEOinhouse.com, who contributed the chapter "Optimize Your Site for Search Engines" and answered countless questions on search engine optimization. Thanks, too, to Andrea Behr, features copy chief of the *San Francisco Chronicle,* for teaching us the poetry of writing strong headlines.

Thanks to Srinija Srinivasan for her avid support and her historical perspective on Yahoo!, and to Leanne and Gerry Sindell of Thought Leaders Intl./IPM for helping to bring this book to market.

Special thanks to Carol Bartz for being a champion of content, and to Elisa Steele, Penny Baldwin, and Eric Channing Brown for their immediate backing of this project.

Finally, thanks to Kathy Huck, Lisa Senz, and all our new friends at St. Martin's Press.

Chris Barr
Senior Editorial Director
Yahoo!

Notes

1. Jakob Nielsen, "How Users Read on the Web," *Alertbox,* October 1, 1997, http://www.useit.com /alertbox/9710a.html.

2. Jakob Nielsen, "Fancy Formatting, Fancy Words = Looks Like a Promotion = Ignored," *Alertbox,* September 4, 2007, http://www.useit.com/alertbox/fancy-formatting.html.

3. Trystan L. Bass, "Go Meatless Just One Day a Week," Green Picks, April 21, 2009, http://green .yahoo.com/blog/greenpicks/240/go-meatless-just-one-day-a-week.html (accessed June 1, 2009).

4. Lyndsey Parker, "Reality Flashback: Lady Gaga on SYTYCD," Reality Rocks, March 15, 2009, http://new.music.yahoo.com/blogs/realityrocks/150394/reality-flashback-lady-gaga-on-sytycd/ (accessed June 1, 2009).

5. Jay Busbee, "Morning Drive: Golf's Youth Movement Gets Even Younger," Devil Ball, June 29, 2009, http://sports.yahoo.com/golf/blog/devil_ball_golf/post/Morning-Drive-Golf-s-youth-movement -gets-even-y?urn=golf,173447 (accessed July 17, 2009).

6. Jennifer Romolini, "Live Blogging Michelle Obama's Inaugural Style: The Gown Is by Jason Wu!" Fashion + Beauty on Shine, January 19, 2009, http://shine.yahoo.com/channel/beauty/live -blogging-michelle-obamas-inaugural-style-the-gown-is-by-jason-wu-354416/ (accessed February 27, 2009).

7. Lili Ladaga, "Obama Inauguration: Hits and Misses," The Yahoo! Newsroom, January 20, 2009, http://news.yahoo.com/s/ynews/20090120/pl_ynews/ynews_pl220;_ylt=AjcdCgwlY2XuYPRc4n 4ucTsDq594 (accessed February 27, 2009).

8. Vera H-C Chan, "Addressing the Inaugural Dresses," The Buzz Log, January 20, 2009, http://buzz .yahoo.com/buzzlog/92186 (accessed February 27, 2009).

9. Many of these strategies are based on ideas from Casey Miller and Kate Swift, *The Handbook of Nonsexist Writing,* 2nd ed. (Lincoln, NE: iUniverse, 2001), and from Jean Hollis Weber, "Gender-Neutral Technical Writing," http://jeanweber.com/newsite/?page_id=55 (accessed July 16, 2009).

10. For more suggestions, see Miller and Swift, *Handbook of Nonsexist Writing,* 155–161.

11. ComScore, "Global Internet Audience Surpasses 1 Billion Visitors, According to comScore," press release, January 23, 2009, http://www.comscore.com/press/release.asp?press=2698.

12. U.S. Department of Education, Institute of Education Sciences, National Center for Education

Statistics, 2003 *National Assessment of Adult Literacy,* http://nces.ed.gov/naal/kf_demographics.asp (accessed July 6, 2009).

13. Hyon B. Shin with Rosalind Bruno, *Language Use and English-Speaking Ability: 2000,* U.S. Census Bureau, Census 2000 Brief, October 2003, 2, http://www.census.gov/prod/2003pubs/c2kbr-29 .pdf.

14. U.S. Census Bureau, American Community Survey, *United States: Selected Social Characteristics in the United States: 2005–2007,* http://factfinder.census.gov/servlet/ADPTable?_bm=y&-geo _id=01000US&-qr_name=ACS_2007_3YR_G00_DP3YR2&-ds_name=ACS_2007_3YR_G00_& -_lang=en&-_caller=geoselect&-redoLog=false&-format=.

15. U.S. Census Bureau, American Community Survey, *Texas: Selected Social Characteristics in the United States: 2005–2007,* http://factfinder.census.gov/servlet/ADPTable?_bm=y&-context=adp& -qr_name=ACS_2007_3YR_G00_DP3YR2&-ds_name=ACS_2007_3YR_G00_&-tree_id=3307& -redoLog=true&-_caller=geoselect&-geo_id=04000US48&-format=&-_lang=en.

16. U.S. Census Bureau, American Community Survey, *California: Selected Social Characteristics in the United States: 2005–2007,* http://factfinder.census.gov/servlet/ADPTable?_bm=y&-context=adp& -qr_name=ACS_2007_3YR_G00_DP3YR2&-ds_name=ACS_2007_3YR_G00_&-tree_id=3307& -redoLog=true&-_caller=geoselect&-geo_id=04000US06&-format=&-_lang=en.

17. David Crystal, *The Cambridge Encyclopedia of Language,* 2nd ed. (Cambridge: Cambridge University Press, 1997), 98.

18. John R. Kohl, *The Global English Style Guide: Writing Clear, Translatable Documentation for a Global Market* (Cary, NC: SAS Institute Inc., 2008), 115.

19. Ibid., 65–68.

20. Matthew W. Brault, *Americans With Disabilities: 2005,* U.S. Census Bureau, Household Economic Studies, Current Population Reports, December 2008, 3, http://www.census.gov/prod/2008pubs/ p70-117.pdf.

21. World Health Organization, *Disability, Including Prevention, Management and Rehabilitation,* http://www.who.int/nmh/a5817/en/index.html (accessed April 1, 2009).

22. U.S. Department of Labor, Office of Disability Employment Policy, "Business Ownership: Cornerstone of the American Dream," in *Getting Down to Business: A Blueprint for Creating and Supporting Entrepreneurial Opportunities for Individuals With Disabilities,* 2000, http://www.dol .gov/odep/pubs/business/business.htm (accessed March 29, 2009).

23. *The Compact Edition of the Oxford English Dictionary* (Oxford: Oxford University Press, 1971).

24. Marketing Sherpa's 2006 study shows a 60 percent abandonment rate; PayPal and comScore's 2008 research found a 66 percent rate. Sources: Graham Charlton, Econsultancy, "Why Do Customers Abandon the Checkout Process?" http://econsultancy.com/blog/1459-why-do-customers-abandon -the-checkout-process (accessed July 5, 2009); PayPal, "PayPal Survey Reveals Consumers' Top Reasons for Abandoning Online Purchases," https://www.paypal-media.com/releasedetail.cfm ?ReleaseID=312548 (accessed July 5, 2009).

25. Nielsen Norman Group, executive summary of "Email Newsletter Usability: 165 Design Guidelines for Newsletter Subscription, Content, Account Maintenance, and RSS News Feeds Based on Usability Studies," 3rd ed., http://www.nngroup.com/reports/newsletters/summary.html (accessed July 5, 2009).

26. Ibid.

27. U.S. Department of Education, Institute of Education Sciences, National Center for Education Statistics, 2003, *National Assessment of Adult Literacy,* http://nces.ed.gov/naal/kf_demographics.asp (accessed July 6, 2009).

28. Most dates from Christine Ammer, *The American Heritage Dictionary of Idioms* (Boston: Houghton Mifflin Company, 1997). "Think outside the box" date from David Wilton, Wordorigins.org, http:// www.wordorigins.org/index.php/site/comments/think_outside_the_box/ (accessed July 9, 2009); "low-hanging fruit" from *Dictionary.com's 21st Century Lexicon,* Dictionary.com, http://dictionary .reference.com/browse/low-hanging%20fruit (accessed July 9, 2009).

29. H. W. Fowler, *A Dictionary of Modern English Usage,* 2nd ed., rev. Ernest Gowers (New York: Oxford University Press, 1965), 701–702.

30. B. J. Fogg, "Stanford Guidelines for Web Credibility." A research summary from the Stanford Persuasive Technology Lab, Stanford University, May 2002, http://credibility.stanford.edu/ guidelines/ (accessed December 29, 2008).

31. B. J. Fogg et al., "Stanford-Makovsky Web Credibility Study 2002: Investigating What Makes Web Sites Credible Today." A research report by the Stanford Persuasive Technology Lab and Makovsky & Company, Stanford University, http://captology.stanford.edu/pdf/Stanford-Makovsky WebCredStudy2002-prelim.pdf (accessed December 29, 2008).

32. Hitwise, "Google Received 72 Percent of U.S. Searches in January 2009," press release, February 24, 2009, http://hitwise.com/hk/press-centre/press-releases/google-searches-jan-09/ (accessed July 14, 2009).

33. *The Copyright Act of 1976,* Title 17, *U.S. Code,* sec. 102(a).

34. Ibid., sec. 102(b).

35. Ibid., sec. 106.

36. Ibid., sec. 107.

37. U.S. Patent and Trademark Office, "Trademark, Copyright or Patent?" http://www.uspto.gov /web/offices/tac/doc/basic/trade_defin.htm (accessed July 20, 2009).

38. Google Permissions, "Guidelines for Third Party Use of Google Brand Features," http://www .google.com/permissions/guidelines.html (accessed July 20, 2009).

Selected Bibliography

The following resources are those that the *Yahoo! Style Guide* editors have relied on most frequently, or that contain additional information related to topics covered in this book. Many of these sources have played a role in building our knowledge of style that works and have thus played a role in shaping this book.

For more reference works, see our online Resources page at http://styleguide.yahoo.com.

Dictionaries

The American Heritage Dictionary of the English Language. 4th ed. Boston: Houghton Mifflin Company, 2000.

Ammer, Christine. *The American Heritage Dictionary of Idioms.* Boston: Houghton Mifflin Company, 1997.

Dictionary.com. Available online at http://dictionary.reference.com.

Merriam-Webster's Collegiate Dictionary. 11th ed. Springfield, MA: Merriam-Webster Inc., 2003.

Merriam-Webster's Dictionary of English Usage. Springfield, MA: Merriam-Webster Inc., 1994.

OneLook Dictionary Search. Available online at http://www.onelook.com.

Webster's New World College Dictionary. 4th ed. Foster City, CA: IDG Books Worldwide, 2004.

Webster's Third New International Dictionary of the English Language, Unabridged. Springfield, MA: Merriam-Webster Inc., 1993.

Grammar and usage

Garner, Bryan A. *Garner's Modern American Usage.* New York: Oxford University Press, 2003.

Spears, Richard A. *NTC's Dictionary of Grammar Terminology.* Lincolnwood, IL: National Textbook Company, 1991.

Specific topics

Brightman, Alan. *DisabilityLand.* New York: Select Books, 2008.

Kohl, John R. *The Global English Style Guide: Writing Clear, Translatable Documentation for a Global Market.* Cary, NC: SAS Institute Inc., 2008.

Nielsen, Jakob. "Alertbox: Current Issues in Web Usability." Online column published every other week and available at http://www.useit.com/alertbox.

SEOinhouse.com. Videos on keyword research available online at http://www.seoinhouse.com.

World Wide Web Consortium (W3C). Information on webpage-building standards and technologies (including accessibility recommendations) available online at http://www.w3.org.

Style

Goldstein, Norm, ed. *The Associated Press Stylebook and Briefing on Media Law.* New York: Basic Books, 2007.

Microsoft Corporation Editorial Style Board. *Microsoft Manual of Style for Technical Publications.* 3rd ed. Redmond, WA: Microsoft Press, 2004.

The Oxford Style Manual. Edited and compiled by R.M. Ritter. New York: Oxford University Press, 2003.

Sabin, William A. *The Gregg Reference Manual: A Manual of Style, Grammar, Usage, and Formatting.* 10th ed. New York: McGraw-Hill/Irwin, 2005.

University of Chicago Press. *The Chicago Manual of Style.* 15th ed. Chicago: University of Chicago Press, 2003.

Walsh, Bill. *The Elephants of Style: A Trunkload of Tips on the Big Issues and Gray Areas of Contemporary American English.* New York: McGraw-Hill, 2004.

Writing and editing

Butcher, Judith, Caroline Drake, and Maureen Leach. *Butcher's Copy-Editing: The Cambridge Handbook for Editors, Copy-editors and Proofreaders.* 4th ed. Cambridge: Cambridge University Press, 2006.

Copyediting: Because Language Matters. Bimonthly newsletter published by McMurray Newsletters. Also available online at http://www.copyediting.com.

Index